"An encyclopedic look at the myriad of ways that female anger has been repressed, silenced, and omitted to preserve and perpetuate the status quo. . . . Chemaly's case for female rage is inarguably prescient. This book will make you angry—in a really, really good way."

—Liz Plank, executive producer, Vox.com

"This explosive, vital, and unapologetic book lifts the lid on a hugely important but little-discussed aspect of gender inequality. With skill, wit, and sharp insight, Chemaly peels back layers of cultural norms and repression to lay bare the reality of women's rage. She joins the dots to trace the connections between misogyny, violence, and the repression of female anger. She weaves a path that takes us from pornography to the playground, media to medicine. This book should make you furious. It is a battle cry for women's right to rage—teaching us that we have every right to be angry and demanding that the world pays attention to that anger."

—Laura Bates, author of *Girl Up* and *Everyday Sexism*

"By taking us through her own journey as a daughter, mother, and writer, Chemaly forces us to examine why gender matters in anger, how we can un-gender our emotions, encouraging her reader to be angry, be loud, and embrace the rage that burns inside of you."

—Anushay Hossein, writer and political commentator

RAGE BECOMES HER

THE POWER OF WOMEN'S ANGER

Soraya Chemaly

ATRIA BOOKS

NEW YORK   LONDON   TORONTO   SYDNEY   NEW DELHI

ATRIA
BOOKS

An Imprint of Simon & Schuster, Inc.
1230 Avenue of the Americas
New York, NY 10020

First Atria Books hardcover edition September 2018

ATRIA BOOKS and colophon are trademarks of Simon & Schuster, Inc.

For information about special discounts for bulk purchases, please contact Simon & Schuster Special Sales at 1-866-506-1949 or business@simonandschuster.com.

The Simon & Schuster Speakers Bureau can bring authors to your live event. For more information or to book an event, contact the Simon & Schuster Speakers Bureau at 1-866-248-3049 or visit our website at www.simonspeakers.com.

Interior design by Suet Yee Chong

Manufactured in the United States of America

10 9 8 7 6 5 4 3 2 1

Library of Congress Cataloging-in-Publication Data

Names: Chemaly, Soraya L., author.
Title: Rage becomes her / by Soraya L. Chemaly.
Description: First Atria Books hardcover edition. | New York : Atria Books, 2018.
Identifiers: LCCN 2018010867| ISBN 9781501189555 (hardcover) | ISBN 9781501189562 (trade pbk.) | ISBN 9781501189579 (ebook)
Subjects: LCSH: Women—Psychology. | Anger. | Women—Social conditions.
Classification: LCC HQ1206 .C455 2018 | DDC 155.3/33—dc23 LC record available at https://lccn.loc.gov/2018010867

ISBN 978-1-5011-8955-5
ISBN 978-1-5011-8957-9 (ebook)

To angry women,
shameless girls,
and the men who trust us,
especially,
for their love and encouragement,
my mother, Norma;
my daughters, Isabelle, Caroline, and Noel;
and my husband, Thomas

Our feelings are our most genuine paths to knowledge.

—AUDRE LORDE

Every act of becoming conscious
(it says here in this book)
is an unnatural act.

—ADRIENNE RICH, *THE PHENOMENOLOGY*
  OF ANGER

CONTENTS

NICE TO MEET YOU, RAGE

My parents' 1965 wedding was a lavish affair that went on for more than twenty hours, with over five hundred guests in attendance. Photos show glamorous women in long evening gowns and smiling men in carefully tailored black tie standing, in glittering groups, around a cake that covered the expanse of a five-foot square table.

Among the most prized gifts my parents received that day was their wedding china. These white-and-gold plates were more than an expensive gesture: they were an important symbol of adulthood and their community's and family's approval of marriage in general and of this marriage in particular. For my mother, they represented a core aspect of her identity: that of being a woman, soon to be mother, the nurturer of her family. Growing up, these look-but-don't-touch dishes were at the top of a hierarchy of plates that my mother established. When my siblings and I were small, we used them only on the rarest and most special occasions and always with great care.

That's why, one day when I was fifteen, I was dumbfounded to see my mother standing on the long veranda outside our kitchen, chucking one china plate after another as far and as hard as she could into the hot, humid air. Our kitchen was on the second floor of a house that sat perched at the top of a long, rolling hill. I watched each dish soar through the atmosphere, its weight generating a sharp, steady trajectory before shattering into pieces on the terrace far below.

While the image is vivid in my mind, I have no memory of any sound. What I remember most was that there was no noise at all as my mother methodically threw one, then another, then another, over and over until her hands were finally free. She didn't utter a sound the entire time. I have no idea if she even knew anyone was watching. When she was done, she walked back into the kitchen and asked me how my school day had gone, as though nothing out of the ordinary had happened. I desperately wanted to know what I had witnessed, but it didn't feel like a good time to ask questions, so I sat and worked on my homework as my mother prepared dinner and the day morphed into night. We never talked about anger.

———

Why do we so rarely learn how to be angry?

Like most of us, I learned about anger in a vacuum of information, by watching the people around me: what they did with their anger, how they responded to other people when they were mad. I don't remember my parents or other adults ever talking to me about anger directly. Sadness, yes. Envy, anxiety, guilt, check, check, check. But not anger. It turns out that, for girls, this is par for the course. While parents talk to girls about emotions more than they do to boys, anger is excluded. Reflect with me for a moment: How did you first learn to think about emotions, and anger in particular? Can you remember having any conversations with authority figures or role models about how to think about your anger or what to do with it? If you are a woman, chances are the answer is no.

As far as my own early understanding of anger, the plate-throwing incident said it all. My mother may have been livid, but she gave every appearance of being cheerful and happy. By staying silent and choosing this particular outlet for her feelings, she communicated a trove of information: for example, that anger was experienced in isolation and was not worth sharing verbally with others. That furious feelings are best kept to oneself. That when they do inevitably come out, the results can be scary, shocking, and destructive.

My mother was acting in a way that remains typical for many women: she was getting her anger "out," but in a way that explicitly separated it from her relationships. Most women report feeling the angriest in private and interpersonal settings. They also prioritize their relationships—at home, work, and even in political contexts—in determining, consciously or not, if and how to express negative emotions.

Throwing plates is an example of a coping mechanism, but it is not an effective or healthy way to express anger. Coping often involves self-silencing and feelings of powerlessness. Getting anger out in this way is not the same as envisioning anger as a transitional tool that helps you to change the world around you. Plate throwing did, however, allow my mother to be angry without seeming angry. In this way, it allowed her to be a "good" woman, which, significantly, meant not being demanding, loud, or expressing her own needs. Even though this episode happened more than thirty-five years ago, it remains true that social norms continue to dictate how we think and feel about emotions, especially when it comes to women and anger.

But first, what happens when we experience anger? Feeling anger involves a constellation of factors, including physiology, genetics, and cognitive processing. These make up the character of anger. For example, you might be a person who tends to get angry quickly, known as "trait anger"; or you might be slower to anger and experience it mainly when provoked. That is called "state anger." Context is equally critical, however. Our responses to provocation, our assessments, and our judgments always involve a back-and-forth between character and context. Where you are and who you may be angry with, as well as the broader social construction of anger (part of what's called an "emotional culture") matter.

While we experience anger internally, it is mediated culturally and externally by other people's expectations and social prohibitions. Roles and responsibilities, power and privilege are the framers of our anger. Relationships, culture, social status, exposure to discrimination, poverty, and access to power all factor into how we think about, experience, and utilize anger. Different countries, regions—even neighboring communities in the same state—have been shown to have anger profiles, exhibiting different patterns of behavior and social dynamics. So, for example, in some cultures anger is a way to vent frustration, but in others it is more for exerting authority. In the United States, anger in white men is often portrayed as justifiable and patriotic, but in black men, as criminality; and in black women, as threat. In the Western world, which this book focuses on, anger in women has been widely associated with "madness."

Anger is also not unidirectional but part of endless mental, physical, and intellectual feedback loops that operate below our conscious understanding. It is sometimes called a "secondary" emotion—resulting from other, often hidden, feelings of shame or fear. You might not always identify anger as part of what may be causing you discomfort, pain, or distress, but chances are that if you look closely, unexpressed or inadequately expressed anger plays a part in what you are experiencing. For some of us, being angry causes anxiety, which, in turn, makes us angrier. For others, anger becomes part of our bodies, causing physical discomfort, which then makes us short tempered, unhappy, and impairs our health. These anger feedback loops often directly implicate unacknowledged social injustice. One of the most common feedback loops that women live with involves anger caused by discrimination that, if denied, intensifies, increasing stress and its effects.

Of course, everyone feels anger. Studies show that differences between men's and women's experiences of feeling angry are virtually nonexistent. Where there is a difference, they defy stereotypes about men being the so-called angry sex. For a variety of reasons, which we will explore, women report feeling anger more frequently, more intensely, and for longer periods of time than men do. Most episodes involving anger do not involve physical interactions but verbal ones, and women are more likely than men to use angry and aggressive language. Additionally, men more frequently associate feeling powerful with experiencing anger, but women, notably, associate powerlessness with their anger.

If everyone feels anger, why focus on women? Why does gender matter?

Because while women and men feel anger similarly, there are stark differences in how we respond to those feelings and how they are received by the people around us. Men and women also tend to have different physiological responses to anger-stimulating provocation. Gender-role expectations, often overlapping with racial-role expectations, dictate the degree to which we can use anger effectively in personal contexts and to participate in civic and political life. Despite differences, women's responses are routinely ignored in public discussion, in analyses of anger dynamics, and in many proposed "anger management" solutions.

Binary gender schemas are being challenged and dismantled every day, but they still profoundly govern our lives. Gender schemas—organizing generalizations that we learn early in life—simplify the world around us, but they also reproduce problematic discrimination. Male and female categories assigned at birth immediately form the basis, in our families, for how we assign roles, attributes, responsibilities, and status. They determine just as powerfully how we experience our feelings, as well as how they are perceived and responded to by others.

At home, children still learn quickly that for boys and men, anger reinforces traditional gender expectations, but that for girls and women, anger confounds them. It's as children that most of us learn to regard anger as unfeminine, unattractive, and selfish. Many of us are taught that our anger will be an imposition on others, making us irksome and unlikeable. That it will alienate our loved ones or put off people we want to attract. That it will twist our faces, make us ugly. This is true even for those of us who have to use anger to defend ourselves in charged and dangerous situations. As girls, we are not taught to acknowledge or manage our anger so much as fear, ignore, hide, and transform it.

On the other hand, anger and masculinity are powerfully enmeshed and reinforce one another. In boys and men, anger has to be controlled, but it is often seen as a virtue, especially when it is used to protect, defend, or lead. Anger is thought of in terms of disruption, loudness, authority, vulgarity, and physical aggression and domination, and couched in terms of violence and clichés of masculinity. Boys learn early on about anger, but far less about other feelings, which handicaps them—and society—in different ways. Socially discouraged from seeming feminine (in other words, being empathetic, vulnerable, and compassionate), their emotional alternatives often come down to withdrawal or aggressive expressions of anger.

As we move from our families to our communities, we become engaged in systems that distribute not only resources and cultural capital but also emotional expression. Gender combines with race, class, age, and other aspects of our identities and social status to alter how we behave and are treated.

There is not a woman alive who does not understand that women's anger is openly reviled. We don't need books, studies, theories, or specialists to tell us this. During the past several years, I've spoken to thousands of girls and women at schools, conferences, and corporations. Without fail, afterward they come up to me to say the same two things: they want to know how to stand up for themselves "without sounding angry or bitter," and they want to share stories about how, when they do express anger about issues specifically relevant to their lives as women, people respond with doubt and often aggression.

Women experience discrimination differently, but we share the experience—in anger or merely when simply speaking assertively—of being told we are "crazy," "irrational," even "demonic." If we are worried, and, as studies show, compelled to repackage, ignore, divert, or trivialize our anger, it is because we well understand the costs of displaying it. Our society is infinitely creative in finding ways to dismiss and pathologize women's rage. I have always understood that being seen as an "angry woman"—sometimes simply for sharing my thoughts out loud—would cast me as overemotional, irrational, "passionate," maybe hysterical, and certainly a "not-objective" and fuzzy thinker.

When a woman shows anger in institutional, political, and professional settings, she *automatically* violates gender norms. She is met with aversion, perceived as more hostile, irritable, less competent, and unlikeable—the kiss of death for a class of people expected to maintain social connections. The same people who might opt to work for an angry-sounding, aggressive man are likely to be *less tolerant* of the same behavior if the boss were a woman. When a man becomes angry in an argument or debate, people are more likely to abandon their own positions and defer to his. But when a woman acts the same way, she's likely to elicit the opposite response. For some of us, considered angry by nature and default, the risks of asserting ourselves, defending ourselves, or speaking out in support of issues that are important to us can be significant. Black girls and women, for example, routinely silenced by "Angry Black Woman" stereotypes have to contend with abiding dangers of institutionalized violence that might result from their expressing justifiable rage. The fact that men, as studies find, consider anger power enhancing in a way that women don't, makes sense because for men, anger is far more likely to *be* power enhancing.

The lessons are subtle and consistent. We go from being "cute princesses," to "drama queens," to "high-maintenance bitches." Girls who object to unfairness or injustice are often teased and taunted. Adult women are described as oversensitive or exaggerating. Representations and responses like these, whether in families or in popular culture, teach us that our anger is not something we or anyone else should take seriously. Women come to expect and dread mockery and ridicule as likely responses to their anger. This persistent denial of subjectivity, knowledge, and reasonable concerns—commonly known as gaslighting—is deeply harmful and often abusive. Women's anticipation of negative responses is why so many women remain silent about what they need, want, and feel, and why so many men can easily choose ignorance and dominance over intimacy.

Women's anger is usually disparaged in virtually all arenas, except those in which anger *confirms* gender-role stereotypes about women as nurturers and reproductive agents. This means we are allowed to be angry but not on our own behalves. If a woman is angry in her "place," as a mother or a teacher, for example, she is respected, and her anger is generally understood and acceptable. If, however, she transgresses and is angry in what is thought of as a men's arena—such as traditional politics or the workplace—she is almost always penalized in some way.

Women aren't somehow magically protected from these ideas and social norms. We frequently internalize them, seeing our anger as incompatible with our primary designated roles as caretakers. Even the incipient suggestion of anger—in themselves or in other women—makes some women profoundly uncomfortable. In an effort not to seem angry, we ruminate. We go out of our way to look "rational" and "calm." We minimize our anger, calling it frustration, impatience, exasperation, or irritation, words that don't convey the intrinsic social and public demand that *anger* does. We learn to contain our selves: our voices, hair, clothes, and, most importantly, speech. Anger is usually about saying "no" in a world where women are conditioned to say almost anything but "no." Even our technology incorporates these ideas, in deferential female-voiced virtual assistants (Siri, Alexa, and Cortana come to mind) for whom the responses "yes" and "what can I do for you?" are prime directives and raisons d'être.

A cultivated feminine habit of prioritizing the needs of others and putting people at ease frequently puts us at a disadvantage. In particular, girls and women learn to put aside anger in order to de-escalate tension or conflict, lowering the temperature of encounters or situations that put us or others at risk. We understand that abandoning our anger is a necessary adaptation to a perpetual undercurrent of possible male violence. In a society where male violence toward women is a reality for many of us, we simply cannot know how a man—whether someone familiar or a stranger—will respond and if he will be violent. We can only trust, hope, and minimize risk.

Layered on top of these habits is pervasive silence around the fact that we are constantly making these assessments. And so, as we will see, the men around us at home, school, and work often actively deny our experiences or can be ignorant of the constant calculus we make when it comes to expressing ourselves. If men knew how truly angry the women around them often are—and understood the structures enforcing women's silence—they would be staggered.

It's important to note, up front, how much these behaviors are learned and tied to gender specifically. There are plenty of men who exhibit stereotypically "female" anger behaviors, just as many women display "male" habits. People who score higher for masculine traits are more likely to express their anger openly and to feel comfortable doing so, whereas those who are more feminine exhibit more control over their anger, often masking it in other expressions. Androgynous, nonbinary/gender-fluid people, freer from gender-based displays and roles, tend to be able to express anger more productively and, in general, to develop a robust ability to control and use their emotions more effectively.

Anger is like water. No matter how hard a person tries to dam, divert, or deny it, it will find a way, usually along the path of least resistance. As I will discuss in this book, women often "feel" their anger in their bodies. Unprocessed, anger threads itself through our appearances, bodies, eating habits, and relationships, fueling low self-esteem, anxiety, depression, self-harm, and actual physical illness. The harms are more than physical, however. Gendered ideas about anger make us question ourselves, doubt our feelings, set aside our needs, and renounce our own capacity for moral conviction. Ignoring anger makes us careless with ourselves and allows society to be careless with us. It is notable, however, that treating women's anger and pain in these ways makes it easier to exploit us—for reproduction, labor, sex, and ideology.

Ask yourself, why would a society deny girls and women, from cradle to grave, the right to feel, express, and leverage anger and be respected when we do? Anger has a bad rap, but it is actually one of the most hopeful and forward thinking of all our emotions. It begets transformation, manifesting our passion *and* keeping us invested in the world. It is a rational *and* emotional response to trespass, violation, and moral disorder. It bridges the divide between what "is" and what "ought" to be, between a difficult past and an improved possibility. Anger warns us viscerally of violation, threat, and insult.

Like many women, I am still constantly being reminded that it's "better" if women didn't "seem so angry." What does "better" mean, exactly? And why does it fall so disproportionately on the shoulders of women to be "better" by putting aside anger in order to "understand" and to forgive and forget? Does it make us "good" people? Is it healthy? Does it enable us to protect our interests, bring change to struggling communities, or upend failing systems?

An unqualified no.

Mainly, it props up a profoundly corrupt status quo.

When we are angry and expect a reasonable response, we are walking, talking refutations of this status quo. In expressing anger and demanding to be heard, we reveal the deeper belief that we can engage with and shape the world around us—a right that, until now, has almost always been reserved for men. Saying "I am angry" is a necessary first step to "Listen." "Believe me." "Trust me." "I know." "Time to do something." When a girl or woman is angry, she is saying "What I am feeling, thinking, and saying matters." As the treatment of our anger and the state of our politics vividly confirm, this is not an assurance that we can take for granted.

This is the real danger of our anger: it makes it clear that we take ourselves seriously. This is true in our homes and in our public lives. By effectively severing anger from "good womanhood," we chose to sever girls and women from the emotion that best protects us against danger and injustice.

———

That anger metaphors are filled with kitchen imagery—anger simmers and smolders before reaching a boiling point; a person has to "mull things over" and "cool off"; we are supposed to "contain" or "put a lid" on our anger, or it will leave a bad "taste in the mouth"—strikes me as more than an interesting coincidence. As women, we often have to bite our tongues, eat our words, and swallow our pride. It's almost, as one of my daughters put it, as if we are supposed to keep our anger in the kitchen. Where we might, for example, throw plates.

I don't throw plates, but I do throw words. It took me years to acknowledge my own anger, and when I did, I didn't know what to do with it. I had the distinct sensation of being alien to myself—which was ironic, since the real inauthenticity was in my denying anger, not my recognizing it. Now I write and write and write. I write my rage onto paper and into bits and bytes. I write anger out of my head and my body and put it out in the world where, frankly, it belongs. This can cause deep discomfort in the people around me, and, at times, it has brought personal or professional costs. But it also leads to richer and more productive experiences, relationships, and life outcomes. It took me too long to realize that the people most inclined to say "You sound angry" are the same people who uniformly don't care to ask "Why?" They're interested in silence, not dialogue. This response to women expressing anger happens on larger and larger scales: in schools, places of worship, the workplace, and politics. A society that does not respect women's anger is one that does not respect women—not as human beings, thinkers, knowers, active participants, or citizens.

Women around the world are clearly angry and acting on that emotion. That means, inevitably, a backlash often among "moderates" who are fond of disparaging angry women as dangerous and unhinged. It is easier to criticize the angry women than to ask the questions "What is making you so angry?" and "What can we do about it?"—the answers to which have disruptive and revolutionary implications.

There is real urgency behind these questions. We are living in what feels like an age of pronounced rage and near-constant outrage. There is a lot to be angry about, and everywhere you turn, people seem furious, indignant, and impatient. Every time I see a bold, outspoken, and unapologetically angry woman, I applaud her because of what her expression represents culturally.

This book is about shifting our public understanding of anger. It is about why girls and women saying the words "I am angry" matters to us as individuals and to our society. It is *not* an endorsement of unbridled rage, or permission to deliver a swift roundhouse kick to the face of anyone who upsets you, or to regularly fill the spaces you live and work in with hostility and discomfort. It's also distinctly not a self-help or anger management book. Self-help, different from self-efficacy, is frequently what you do when you aren't getting the help you need from your society. We cannot "self-help" our way to being heard, taken seriously, paid fairly, cared for adequately, or treated with dignity. We cannot "self-help" our way to peace or to justice.

This book is, rather, an interrogation of questions that demand our attention, such as: *What would it mean to ungender our emotions?* What would the world look like if all of us were allowed to experience and productively express the full range of our emotions without penalty? What if girls and women were not so often and effectively cut off from this particular emotion as a function of being feminine? What do we lose, personally and as a society, by not listening to women's anger or respecting it when it does have a voice? And, importantly, how does our treatment of women's "anger-free emotionality" relate to democracy and put us at risk of authoritarianism?

My hope is that *Rage Becomes Her* will change our thinking about anger, gender, emotional life, and their political impacts. I hope that it will arm you with tools to see yourself and your environment more clearly, ultimately improving both your life and the lives of those in your orbit. Because the truth is that anger isn't what gets in our way—it *is* our way. All we have to do is own it.

MAD GIRLS

[My mother] had handed down respect for the possibilities—and the will to grasp them.

—Alice Walker

Each morning in preschool, my daughter constructed a tall and elaborate castle out of blocks, ribbons, and paper, only to have the same classmate, a little boy, gleefully destroy it. Over a period of several weeks, one or the other of the boy's parents, both invariably pleasant, would step forward after the fact and repeat any number of well-worn platitudes as my daughter fumed: "He's just going through a phase!" "He's such a boy! He loves destroying things," and, my personal favorite, "He. Just. Can't. Help. Himself!" Over time, my daughter grew increasingly frustrated and angry.

But my daughter didn't yell, kick, throw a tantrum, or strike out at him. First, she asked him politely to stop. Then she stood in his way, body blocking him, but gently. She built a stronger foundation, so that her castles would be less likely to topple. She moved to another part of the classroom. She behaved exactly how you would want someone to behave if she was following all the rules about how to be a nice person. It didn't work.

For weeks, his parents never swooped in before he took apart her building, they only commented afterward. Like many parents, I followed an unspoken rule about not disciplining other people's children. In the meantime, I imagined his mother and father thinking, because they often did their thinking out loud, "What red-blooded boy *wouldn't* knock it down?"

It was so tempting. She was building a glittery tower in a public space. He was a boy who couldn't control himself and, being a boy, had violent inclinations. Besides, ultimately, wasn't she responsible for keeping her building safe? It's not like she made a big fuss when he knocked it down, so she mustn't have cared that much. As a matter of fact, she did what studies show is common among girls this age. Angry school-age girls tend not to vent but, instead, to dig in and find ways to protect their interests quietly.

Meanwhile, what example did I set for my angry daughter? It depends on your perspective. Many people would say it was good for her to learn to be patient and kind, polite and understanding. Looking back, I think I set an awful example. My attempts to teach her how to avoid damage, live cooperatively with others, and be a good citizen were gendered in unhelpful ways. I tried to help her to accomplish her goal—an intact building—but I didn't give her anger the uptake, meaning validation and support, that it deserved. Neither did any of the other adults. She had every right to be angry, but I didn't encourage her to express herself in a way that was public, disruptive, or demanding.

In the interest of classroom relations, I politely talked to the boy's parents. They sympathized with my daughter's frustration but only to the extent that they sincerely hoped she found a way to feel better. They didn't seem to "see" that she was angry, nor did they understand that her anger was a demand on their son in direct relation to their own inaction. They were perfectly content to rely on *her* cooperation in *his* working through what he wanted to work through, yet they felt no obligation to ask him to do the same. Even in this early, and relatively innocent setting, he was already mislearning the meaning of "no." He was running roughshod, with no sense of consequences, over the people around him. By default, his feelings were prioritized, and he was not only allowed but also encouraged to control the environment.

Scenarios like this one play out over and over again throughout childhood. In my experience, it is difficult for many adults to accept that boys can and should control themselves and meet the same behavioral standards that we expect from girls. It is even harder to accept that girls feel angry and have legitimate rights not to make themselves cheerfully available as resources for boys' development. In 2014, researchers from multiple universities conducted a large-scale, four-country study into preschool preparedness and gender. Children in the United States showed the largest gender gaps in self-regulation. Researchers found that parental and teacher expectations of gender informed the way that children acted and were evaluated, and, ultimately, whether or not they were held accountable for controlling themselves. Sex differences in self-control, other research indicates, are almost certainly what we call epigenetic, reflecting the interaction of genetic predisposition and social and cultural expectations.

Had my daughter responded with a disruptive, loud display of anger, the focus of the discussion probably would have concerned *her* behavior, not the boy's. It would have been falsely equated with, or even prioritized over, the boy's lack of control or empathy, instead of being seen as a justifiable response to his bad behavior.

———

In 1976, in one of the earliest attempts to understand how parental biases influence behavior, researchers deliberately masked babies' gender and asked adults to describe what they saw when they observed them. Adults "saw" different emotional states depending on whether they thought the baby was a boy or a girl. A fussy boy, for example, was considered irritable and angry, whereas a fussy girl was more likely to be described as fearful or sad. Adults even attribute gendered emotions to simple line drawings. A series of 1986 experiments revealed that when adults studying a particular drawing thought that the artist was a boy, they were inclined to describe the images as angrier, or more violent and hostile.

The finding that adults have emotion gender biases holds true decades later. Harriet Tenenbaum, a developmental psychologist at England's University of Surrey, has studied the ways that parents talk to children. "Most parents say they want boys to be more expressive," she explains, "but don't know [they] are speaking differently to them." Parents speak to daughters more about emotions, using a wider range of words. The one exception to what researchers call "emotion talk"? Anger and negative feelings. Parents talk to boys about being mad but don't do the same with girls. Mothers in particular tend to use words related to anger when talking to boys or telling them stories.

Assumptions about emotionality and gender extend well into adulthood.

In 2011 Dr. Kerri Johnson, an assistant professor of communication studies and psychology at UCLA, released the findings of an innovative study on perceptions of gender and emotion. "It's okay—even expected—for men to express anger," she said. "But when women have a negative emotion, they're expected to express their displeasure with sadness."

Sex bias leads us to see happiness and fear on women's faces more easily, categorizing women's neutral faces as less angry than men's faces. In studies, women's neutral faces are described as "submissive," "innocent," "scared," and "happy." In one, women's faces were labelled by participants as "cooperative" and "babyish." Multiple experiments reveal that an angry woman's face is one of the most difficult for people to parse, and an androgynous face with an angry expression is overwhelmingly categorized as male.

A "sad" woman and an "angry" man might be experiencing similar negative emotions, but these words, and the stereotypes they elicit, produce radically different outcomes. The difference is not trivial.

Power, considered by some theorists to be the "entrance requirement" for anger, is not necessary for sadness. Anger is an "approach" emotion, while sadness is a "retreat" emotion. Thinking of a person as sad makes us see them as weaker and more submissive. Anger, not sadness, is associated with controlling one's circumstances, such as competition, independence, and leadership. Anger, not sadness, is linked to assertiveness, persistence, and aggressiveness. Anger, not sadness, is a way to actively make change and confront challenges. Anger, not sadness, leads to perceptions of higher status and respect. Like happy people, angry people are more optimistic, feeling that change is possible and that they can influence outcomes. Sad and fearful people tend toward pessimism, feeling powerless to make change.

Social science researchers Matthijs Baas, Carsten De Dreu, and Bernard Nijstad have shown that anger, unlike sadness, encourages "unstructured thinking" when a person is engaged in creative tasks, and that people who are angry are better at generating more ideas. Even more interesting, one study found that the ideas they came up with were highly original.

There are cognitive benefits to sadness, however. For example, sadness often means that a person is thinking more deeply and methodically about what is upsetting her; sad people tend to consider social ills instead of assigning individual blame. Sad people are also more generous. On the downside, sadness can easily turn into paralyzing rumination, lowered expectations, and costly impatience. Sad people expect and are satisfied with less.

What does separating anger from femininity mean for us as women? For one thing, it means that we render women's anger ineffective as a personal or collective public resource. This treatment of women's anger is a powerful regulation; an ideal way to reduce women's pushback against their own inequality.

In 2012 an in-depth analysis of research into gender, childhood, and emotional regulation canvased three decades of studies into how children display emotions. The studies included more than twenty-one thousand subjects and looked not only at how children express themselves, but also at how adults responded and how children, in turn, adapted to expectations. Researchers found "significant, but very small gender differences" in boys' and girls' expression and experience of emotions, but significant differences in how their emotions were treated by others.

At home or in child care, babies learn about their emotions as subjects of gender bias, meaning few interactions with adults do not involve their being treated differently depending on assigned sex. Girls are expected by most adults to display a pleasant affect and to be more affiliative, helpful, and cooperative. When a baby girl shows positive emotions or is compliant, she is far more likely to be rewarded with smiles, warmth, and food, whereas a boy tends to be similarly rewarded for being stoic and tough. As they leave toddlerhood, girls express negative emotions and aggression—both verbal and physical—less and less openly.

By the time they are preschoolers, children already associate anger with masculine faces and report believing that it is normal for boys to be angry, but not for girls. As they move from the intimacy of their homes into schools, sports clubs, and places of worship, children come under more intense social pressure to behave in stereotypical ways. Observed gaps in how boys and girls display anger grow largest outside of their families as children try to reduce friction by conforming to dominant norms.

By the time they enter school, most children already think of disruptive behaviors and assertiveness—for example, using loud voices, interrupting, burping, joking, and cursing—as linguistic markers of masculinity, acceptable for boys but not for girls. Children fine-tune their response to adult expectations, and adults consistently demonstrate discomfort with the idea of a righteously angry girl making demands. Girls, admonished to use "nicer" voices three times more often than boys are, learn to prioritize the needs and feelings of people around them; often this means ignoring their own discomfort, resentment, or anger.

Ask most parents, and they will swear that they teach children to be polite in the same way, regardless of gender. But as it turns out, boys and girls are not learning this lesson in equal measure. In one study, researchers deliberately disappointed children in a series of gift-giving scenarios. Regardless of how they felt, girls were more likely, on average, to smile, say thank you, and appear to be happy, despite feeling disappointed. Studies show that girls who begin to exhibit behavioral problems at these ages score high in measures of feeling that they are unable to openly express displeasure or anger, even in private, after a disappointment. These tendencies—self-silencing and acting out—are bidirectional, with each one acting on the likelihood of the other.

Girls learn to smile early, and many cultures teach girls explicitly to "put on a pretty face." It is a way of soothing the people around us, a facial adaptation to the expectation that we put others first, preserve social connections, and hide our disappointment, frustration, anger, or fear. We are expected to be more accommodating and less assertive or dominant. As girls' smiles become less authentic, so, too, does their understanding of themselves.

For black girls, being expected to smile is additionally infused with racism and historic demands that black people set white people at ease by showing they are not actually unhappy with circumstances of inequality. Yet few people are interested in thinking about the ways that encouraging girls to be "nice," maybe admonishing, "You're prettier when you smile," is also related to social status.

We are so busy teaching girls to be likeable that we often forget to teach them, as we do boys, that they should be respected.

CULTURAL RELEVANCE MATTERS TO HOW WE FEEL AND THINK ABOUT OURSELVES

After a period that psychologists call latency, girls enter puberty and begin to express emotions, including anger, more openly and frequently again. When they become more assertive, especially about things that make them unhappy, adults are sometimes taken aback. "What happened to my sweet little girl?" is a common question. Girls, however, often express negative emotions without being able to say why they have them.

Every girl learns, in varying degrees, to filter herself through messages of women's relative cultural irrelevance, powerlessness, and comparative worthlessness. Images and words conveying disdain for girls, women, and femininity come at children fast and furiously, whereas most boys' passage to adulthood—even for boys disadvantaged by class or ethnicity—remains cloaked in the cultural centrality of maleness and masculinity.

When girls consume media or participate in cultural events such as watching popular films or attending exciting sporting events, they frequently have to make a simple choice: either put themselves in men's and boys' shoes or consider what the relative invisibility, silence, and misrepresentation of girls and women who look like them means. Women aren't acknowledged on most national currencies or as public statues. Books, movies, games, and popular entertainment feature men and boys two to three times more often as protagonists—more often white than not. As children get older, similar metrics become even more true.

Every year, media analyses come to the stubbornly unchanging conclusion that men, again overwhelmingly white, hold roughly 70 percent to 73 percent of the roles in top US films, as well as the majority of speaking parts and creative and executive positions on-screen and off. The gender breakdown in films globally is equally skewed. According to a report studying gender, race, and LGBTQ film portrayals in 2014, no women over forty-five years of age performed a lead or colead role. Only three lead or colead women were from minority backgrounds. Not one woman protagonist played a lesbian or bisexual character.

Similar patterns are evident in media ranging from video games to school materials. Many adults worry about video games because of violence, but most don't consider the erasure and common sexualization of girls and women serious enough to prohibit certain games. For example, EA Sports's phenomenally popular FIFA soccer video game franchise didn't include any women's teams until a 2015 release. Does it matter that players of this video game rarely or never see women as players, managers, coaches, or even audience members within the game?

Even in school, children get subtle messages about whose stories matter. Literature classes routinely feature literature written by women and men of color as exceptional (one among many white male writers) or available for study in some schools as elective classes only. A recent global review found that gender bias is also "rife in textbooks." The result of pedagogical choices like these shape self-esteem, empathy, and understanding. They also shape resentment, confusion, and anger.

A few years ago, I asked a roomful of more than a hundred students ages fourteen to eighteen if they had learned about slavery and the civil rights movement. All had. That day, we were talking about sexual assault on campus, so I asked how many had knowledge of the rapes of black women in slavery, during Jim Crow, and the civil rights movement. Virtually none. How many students, I asked, had heard and laughed at rape jokes in popular movies, for example? More than 90 percent. I asked for a show of hands of who'd been taught about centuries of women's fight for liberation in the United States or its indivisibility from fights for racial equality and LGBTQ rights. Maybe six. Sojourner Truth, I felt like explaining, is not the name of an indie band.

Because of the prevalence of boys' and men's perspectives, girls learn early to put themselves in boys' and men's shoes. A girl's imagination would be a barren place if she didn't. Boys, however, are far less likely to do this and are, in some cases, shamed for doing this. Boys generally don't look up to women as role models, and they don't have to cross-gender empathize when they consume media. The centrality and visibility that exist, particularly, in the United States, for young, white boys is a source of confidence, invisible capital that becomes evident in self-esteem.

But the problem for girls is more than erasure, bias, and stereotypes. It's the quiet and largely unremarked-upon degradation of femininity that fills the air. Phrases such as "cry like a girl," "throw like a girl," and "scream like a girl," are still socially acceptable staples of childhood in many circles. Everyday language is peppered with slurs that swing from positive to pejorative, reflecting the structural inequality between *masculine* and *good*, versus *feminine* and *bad*. We are all sluts and hos in waiting. "Reappropriated" words, like *slut* or *bitch*, are casually connected to the threat of violence. "Happy birthday, Bitch!" escalates into "Suck my dick, bitch," in the blink of an eye. Most everyone knows that making someone your bitch might not mean that person is female, just as they also know it means that being dominated and powerless are feminine states of being.

Social media comes under harsh criticism for the role it plays in bullying and abuse, but it's important to consider the deeply traditional roots of online abuse. Bullying, which is what we have always called sexism, racism, and homophobia, now has network power, but the root problem is not technology as much as it is cultural mores. The upside, however, is that people online are freer to represent themselves in ways that they could not before, to find communities, and to counter denigration.

This is an important cultural force. Much of girls' social media output—photographs, Snapchats, memes, commentary—powerfully challenges stereotypes that portray women in negative or impossibly idealistic ways. The creation of memes and the use of selfies, for example, allow girls to confront, undermine, and critique unhelpful and damaging media portrayals with creativity, humor, and anger. Girls can frame, narrate, define, make, and own this media. Those with "unruly" bodies can refute shaming.

However, even as we use tech to generate our new norms, we remain subjected to dominant ones that are cheaply and easily proliferated. Selfie culture has virtues, but it also has a focus on thinness, whiteness, and idealized beauty, highlighting ways that girls and women are "supposed" to look. In all forms of media, for example, girls and women are at least four times more likely to be portrayed as underweight and physically diminished, conveying fragility, weakness, and helplessness. The more physically winnowed a girl is, the more socially popular she might become. Studies of children around the world show that by age ten, girls already believe that they are, indeed, weak, vulnerable, not as brave as boys, and in need of "protection." Girls are turning this information around and around in their heads just as they are made to feel the limiting and worrisome effects of their physical vulnerability. Studies show that even parents, many of whom would say they support equality, tacitly treat girls as more fragile and less capable. They impose real physical restrictions on girls that convey threat, for example, limiting their movement at night or teaching girls to go to the bathroom using the buddy system. The learned sense of vulnerability and helplessness that we impose on many girls makes developing resilience to harms, whether personal or cultural, more difficult.

As girls work their way intellectually through these demands, they are also considering what it means that a woman's words, ideas, interests, abilities, and hard work seem to take a back seat to her appearance. Women are most visible as sexualized entertainment. On the day I was writing this, for example, I wondered what a girl would see if she searched for "women athletes." The number one result was "The Top 50 Hottest Female Athletes of 2017." In 2015 a search for "women CEOs" turned up, as the first image, not an actual woman but a picture of a Barbie doll. That's right. A *Barbie doll* whose name, by the way, is CEO Barbie.

These motifs are accompanied by a pronounced lack of sorority in representation of women. Women, isolated from other women, are frequently portrayed as existing in a sea of men. If a woman is brilliant or powerful, it is because she is unique. Even fabulously successful films featuring iconographic "empowered" girls and women—*Wonder Woman* being among the most recent and popular—struggle to cultivate camaraderie with other women. For example, once Wonder Woman leaves her Amazonian paradise her primary fighting comrades and archnemeses are men. There are admirable female role models, positive depictions of women's friendships, and programming that reflects the diversity of the world, but as studies show, year after year, women remain on the margins and often, still, on their own.

I have focused on binary gender descriptions because there is very little research about childhood, emotional regulation, and gender fluidity, and because we do not, as a culture, have social "scripts"—the unconscious guidelines we follow to organize thoughts and behavior—for nonbinary people. Almost all studies use traditional binary frameworks for analysis. There are few positive dominant stereotypes about bi, trans, and queer people that shape childhood. Children who defy binaries are caught in the crosshairs, leaving parents to either create safe environments and force social change, or else contribute, wittingly or not, to damaging demands that their children conform.

It is important to note how deeply female denigration can shape the lives and emotions of children and adults who do not conform to traditional gender expectations. The vast majority of childhood bullying stems from variations of gender policing, in the form of homophobia, transphobia, and sexist harassment. Disciplining children who don't conform to binaries—gender or sexual—is harshest, for example, for boys who willingly choose femininity or for girls who renounce it to claim male prerogatives.

"I find that those who wish to ridicule or dismiss me," trans activist Julia Serano has explained, "do not simply take me to task for the fact that I fail to conform to gender norms. Instead, more often than not, they mock my femininity. From my perspective, most of the anti-trans sentiment that I have had to deal with is probably better described as misogyny."

It's a cruel trick we play on girls, exposing them to these realities at the same time that we exert the most social pressure on them to ignore and hide the anger they provoke. We look away from girls' anger and collude in the systems that erode their sense of worth; then we turn around and wonder what it is about their "nature" that makes them so lacking in confidence as women.

Undermining girls' confidence goes hand in hand with the denial, disparagement, and diversion of their anger. The first response to a girl's being angry might be someone taking a picture or filming a video of her expressing her anger. An angry little girl is "cute" and "sassy," two of the most highly ranked adjacent terms to the words "angry girl" on Google. Teenage girls who express anger or frustration are less cute. If they are dusky and dark, they are less cute and become "uppity."

Ageism, homophobia, and racism all play a part in how our anger is perceived. There is no time of life when our anger is acceptable. Teenage girls are spoiled, silly, or moody for standing up for themselves. Older women, fed up and saying so, are bitter castrators. Angry women are butches, lesbians, and man haters. We are called Sad Asian Girls, Hot-tempered Latinas, Crazy White Women, and Angry Black Women. It goes without saying that "angry women" are "ugly women," *the* cardinal sin in a world where women's worth, safety, and glory are reliant on their sexual and reproductive value to men around them. None of this leads us to think of anger as the moral or political property of women.

In spite of my awareness of all of this, I was unprepared for my own biases or how stubbornly impactful these ideas could be. My response to what was happening in my daughter's classroom evoked familiar habits. I considered the costs and decided that, coming from me, overt anger in a conversation with the boy's parents would not do my daughter any favors. This is called "preemptive self-condemnation," and it's common in women when they are angry. I was sensitive to how poorly my anger might be received, so I set about using some well-developed alternatives. I made polite suggestions. I asked the teacher if she could intervene. I listened patiently to his parents. I wanted to preserve the peace and cultivate relationships. Anger and an angry expression of frustration, I thought, were futile and potentially damaging.

WHEN ANGER IS SEEN AS A RISK NOT WORTH TAKING, WHAT HAPPENS TO SELF-ESTEEM?

Anger rarely makes an appearance in popular debates of gender confidence gaps. Up until the age of roughly five, girls and boys essentially enjoy similar levels of self-esteem, feelings of competence and ambition. Most girls regard themselves as highly as boys do, they feel pride in themselves and in their own gender, they have lofty aspirations, and they are no more likely to report feelings of shame than boys are.

After the age of five, however, girls' faith in their own abilities falters and trips in ways that boys' do not. One 2017 study of American children found that, at five years old, girls and boys are equally likely to associate genius with their own gender. One year later, boys still make that association, but girls don't. At six and seven, 65 percent of boys believe that boys and men are "really, really smart," while only 48 percent of girls think girls and women are. It may be that boys are overconfident and that girls are actually more realistic, but the gap is notable in any case. Even the framing of a confidence-gap issue often assumes that a standard of male confidence is what girls and women should seek to achieve.

Throughout adolescence, boys retain the sense that they are exceptional and competent, despite the fact that girls outpace them in grade point average and college ambitions. Boys' high estimation of themselves and, in particular, their leadership abilities have no age limit, whereas the opposite is true of girls, whose relative lack of confidence follows them into adulthood. In the United States, from age six or seven on, despite superior performance in school, most girls are less likely to feel capable or act like leaders in mixed company, and they are less likely to run for student government or to support other girls, particularly white girls, who do. Our daughters leave school with *less*, not more, confidence than they go in with.

Lyn Mikel Brown, Carol Gilligan, and Rachel Simmons are experienced and notable psychologists and educators who have studied and written extensively about the emotional lives of girls during this period of transition. Throughout their work, they've turned increasingly to the importance of understanding anger and aggression, demonstrating how girls—operating in a vacuum of information about their negative emotions—channel their anger and aggression covertly, resorting to gossiping and spreading untruths about others, for example. Girls also police themselves to avoid the negative judgment of other girls.

In their decades' worth of investigation, the three researchers have observed differences in how girls' social location, meaning their status in a pecking order, affects the way they express anger. Most studies about gender, emotions, and self-esteem, they've explained, reflect dominant norms of white middle-class femininity. Marginalized and minority girls express anger more freely and demonstrate a more developed sense of how and when to use anger consciously. "Where economic struggle and disenfranchisement prevail, self-assertion and aggression become as much a part of the social landscape as playgrounds and ice cream trucks," writes Simmons in her book, *Odd Girl Out: The Hidden Culture of Aggression in Girls.* "In this world, silence can mean invisibility and danger."

Anger is particularly treacherous. Any displays of emotions, vulnerability, and passivity—"traditional feminine" characteristics—signal weakness. But implicit-bias studies show that girls who are assertive, don't hedge their speech, actively claim verbal space, and, yes, maybe say they are mad, are considered rude, confrontational, uncooperative, and transgressive by adults.

By adolescence, most girls know that overt displays of anger threaten their safety and success. They understand their anger puts status, likeability, and relationships at risk. Worse, unlike most boys they encounter, girls are far more likely to associate anger with shame. For working-class and black girls, who also feel that anger is shameful and know that the expression of anger is frowned on, anger is particularly complicated and risky, because it is also often a valuable and necessary self-defense.

Before accusations of "angry black women" are used to stereotype, silence, and police women, they are used to penalize girls for "talking back," "being belligerent," and "having too much attitude." These girls, labelled "angry" and "disruptive," are often acting in ways that are indistinguishable from behaviors seen in young white boys as "rambunctiousness" and signs of "leadership potential." Starting in early childhood, adults see black girls as less innocent or less in need of nurturing or protection. Starting in kindergarten, black girls are significantly more likely to be disciplined, suspended, or expelled at between, depending on where they live, five to seven times the rate of their peers. Biases such as these are pushing black girls into a well-documented school-to-prison pipeline. In school environments like these, many girls go out of their way to be "good" and to avoid expressing anger under any circumstances, even in self-defense.

Latina girls are more likely to face dismissal when they "act out." "Mainstream people often do not hear what we are saying," writes Edén E. Torres in *Chicana Without Apology*, "because they are listening to us through stereotypes that paint us as hot-blooded and explosive." Mental health advocate Dior Vargas distinctly remembers gendered expectations, which are often passed on by mothers and grandmothers, themselves grappling with anger. "Women were more subdued about negative emotions. I was expected to not talk about them. It feels like a weight on your chest," she explained to me. "We are socialized to understand that we can't express anger, but that it's okay to cry. When I saw emotion in women, it meant tears. I thought men could not biologically cry. Even crying, however, can be discouraged, leaving us with few ways to express what we feel."

Girls of Asian descent on the other hand are more often to encounter the expectation that they will "naturally" be quiet and agreeable. "While growing up, I would see my brother's tantrums explained away or not disciplined well. Meanwhile, my parents and all the adults around me came down hard on any expression of anger from me," explained Regina Yau, a writer and women's rights activist, when we spoke. Her words will resonate with many women. "The stereotype of the dutiful, obedient, tractable daughter meant that the adults around me were perplexed. I had a temper and was made to feel like it was a grave shortcoming. I was told repeatedly that I am not allowed and 'do not have the right' to be angry at anything. What I eventually taught myself to do is to channel my anger into empowering my feminist activism—to do something about the conventions and cultures that tell women that emotions and feelings are weaknesses and that they cannot handle female anger while giving men a pass for maiming/injuring/killing women just because they can't handle their own anger at rejection."

In 1994, Lela Lee, at the time a college student, drew and produced an animated short she called *Angry Little Asian Girl*. The main character of the series, Kim Lee, went on to be featured in a popular book series.

Lee explains that as she explored the theme of anger over time in her art, she "began to understand that women of all ages and backgrounds felt that they were not allowed to be angry." (The title text of her current website is now simply, "Anger Is a Gift.")

Middle-class white girls appear to be the most likely to suppress negative feelings and the least likely to be openly angry. A distancing from emotions like this is necessary to maintain standards of femininity built around relative helplessness, vulnerability, sadness, thinness, and passivity as dominant norms. This is also an ideal of femininity that can be easily weaponized. The need to protect white women, portrayed as frail, innocent, and defenseless, is a centuries-old justification for terroristic racist violence. For example, in news media, the exaggerated vulnerability of white girls and women is called "missing white woman syndrome," an almost fetishistic fascination with violent stranger dangers to white girls and women at the expense of missing and murdered dark ones. Young white girls are seen as and portrayed in American culture as the apex of innocence, in need of masculine protection. It is no accident that these are the girls and women who are seen as least capable to lead or to feel as though they can.

"When girls make a choice to value their emotions," explains Simmons, "they value themselves."

IN GIRLS AND WOMEN, ANGER, AGGRESSION, AND ASSERTIVENESS ARE SEEN AS ONE BEHAVIOR

One of the most persistent problems girls and women encounter when it comes to managing strong negative emotions is passive aggression, an expression of anger that has generated an entire "mean-girl" entertainment genre. By adolescence, most girls understand what relational and indirect aggression *between* girls and women looks like. Gossip, quiet exclusion, slights, and innuendo, for example, are familiar to us all. They are also passive-aggressive behaviors associated mainly with girls and women.

Being indirectly aggressive is one way that many women navigate strong negative emotions and competition in the face of social prohibitions on displaying them more openly. It is also a way to regulate group behavior. A girl or a woman who is brazenly ambitious, "too popular," or "winning"—gender transgressions—can find herself on the receiving end of gossip, exclusion, and bullying both online and offline.

In women in particular, assertiveness, aggression, and anger are often considered one and the same. Anger is an emotion, but assertiveness and aggression are behaviors. For example, I have a blunt speaking style. This does not mean I'm angry, but it can be unsettling to some people. Sometimes I joke that all I have to do to be considered aggressive is walk into a room. But it's not actually a joke at all because perceptions matter.

It is possible to be both assertive and aggressive without anger. You can also be filled with anger yet have a peaceful demeanor. Aggression is more hostile than assertion: the former suggesting less care for another's needs or perspectives, the latter being a clear display of need expressed within understood constraints and norms of behavior.

In adolescence girls experience the daily conflict of having feelings of anger and aggression but knowing that those feelings and behaviors are out of sync with femininity. Many girls conform to gender norms because it's easier and more comfortable for everyone involved, and they are conditioned to put others at ease.

This does not mean that we are "naturally" less aggressive or that boys and men are not passively aggressive. Girls and women are capable of aggression and are also increasingly physically aggressive.

However, physical aggression is still not the preferred expression of anger or response to anger for women, who, as a result, become expert at controlling such impulses. The ability to assess and adapt in this way, meaning, basically, having to control oneself in situations that often generate a sense of risk or threat, is a skill that sometimes results in women being described as "manipulative" and "deceptive."

Despite the fact that passive aggression is *a form of* aggression, aggressiveness is still conflated with physicality, associated with men and masculinity. For many people, that equation is reduced to one simple word: testosterone. How many times have you heard, or perhaps even asserted, that women are not as angry or aggressive as men are because men's anger and aggressiveness—and their inability to regulate them—are governed by their biology? I have lost track.

The popular understanding of this relationship is that testosterone causes aggression and anger, and that because boys and men produce far more testosterone than women do—indeed, it *is* the male sex hormone—they are more prone to aggressive, angry behavior. More interestingly, however, is that while testosterone results in more aggression (not anger), acting aggressively, in turn, spurs the body to release *more testosterone* into the bloodstream.

This effect was discovered in an ingenious experiment conducted by psychologist Sari van Anders, who, along with others at the University of Michigan, researches how social norms affect hormones. Hormones, the body's chemical "messengers," stimulate certain physical responses and regulate mood and behavior. In 2015 van Anders and her team worked with a theater troupe, producing a script in which some of the actors would "fire" other cast members in particularly hostile, humiliating, and cruel ways. Before and after each performance, saliva swabs were taken from participants and tested, revealing that the people who acted aggressively not only had higher testosterone levels afterward but also that they *felt* aggressive—and for a prolonged period of time—due to the hormonal shift. This was true in both men and women. Another study that measured the effects of behavior on hormonal production found similar dynamics. Men who physically care for infant children, for example, experience steep declines in testosterone.

In the theater troupe experiment simply acting "manly" did not alter hormone production, the researchers found. Exerting power did. The actors in this study, both men and women, were instructed by researchers to conform to gender stereotypes while playing their parts. These performances resulted in negligible differences in testosterone production. The most influential quality affecting testosterone production was what van Anders and her associates labelled "wielding power." Firing a person increased testosterone in men by 3 to 4 percent. In women it generated a 10 percent increase.

Traditional childhood gender socialization encourages boys, in virtually any way you can consider, to wield power with their bodies, words, voices, and space. Part of this is learning to associate anger and aggression with being "real" men, behaviors that, as we will see later, actually make relationships more enraging for women. The research asks us to consider how teaching boys to act in physically expansive, aggressive, and prototypically understood "masculine ways" might be altering their hormones. The same is true for girls.

Attributing certain displays of emotion and behavior to hormonal activity is a common, simple, and comforting way to evade challenging complexity. When teenage girls begin to articulate frustration or exhibit anger and strong negative emotions, adults are prone to falling back on this explanation. With a roll of the eye, many adults wave off frustration, anxiety, anger, and more with a "She's in the raging hormone stage and out of control!" There is no doubt that hormones affect us all, but to dismiss girls in this way is counterproductive. "In fact," explains psychologist Lisa Damour, author of *Untangled: Guiding Teenage Girls Through the Seven Transitions into Adulthood*, studies show that "hormones respond to, or may even be trumped by, other factors that influence your daughter's mood, such as stressful events or the quality of her relationship[s]."

In truth, anger in girls is highly rational. We live in a culture that grinds their pride and confidence in being girls into a fine pulp and then blows it back in their faces. They acutely feel the very real disparate impact of limitations on their physical freedom and behavior. Feelings of anger become enmeshed in ideas about being "good," and about beauty, bodies, food, relationships, and power. Experiences like these provoke frustration, depression, anxiety, and sometimes violence in even the most rational men. When it does, we don't talk about *their* hormones. Among the most striking examples of this double standard I found while researching this book were professional websites dedicated to helping boys and men with anger management during frustrating experiences. Most described anger and frustration as a function of legitimate concerns that are often related to life stage changes, such as new school transition difficulties, joblessness, the birth of children, or retirement. I could not find one example of hormones being referenced as a cause.

COMING TO TERMS WITH INEQUALITY

It is during our girlhoods that what we are taught about anger begins to manifest in our feelings of self-worth, deservedness, and legitimacy, preconditions to high self-confidence, self-esteem, and a sense of our own rights.

When asked what triggers their feelings of anger and aggression, most girls cite some form of social inequality, experienced in varying degrees, as a significant factor. They are also aware, even when very young, that their feelings of anger will face adult resistance and peer sanction. A feedback loop exists between self-esteem, anger, and how a community responds to a person's needs.

In 2017 Erin B. Godfrey, Carlos E. Santos, and Esther Burson studied self-esteem in low-income and ethnic minority children to see how a sixth grader's belief in the essential fairness of the world would affect later trajectories of behavior. They observed that children with strong beliefs in fairness and meritocracy were, in sixth grade, "good" students. They were conscientious, worked hard, and generally reported high levels of self-esteem. Two years later, however, those who had the most faith in our system's basic fairness, and with it the power of the individual to overcome any and all obstacles, showed the greatest shifts toward damaged self-esteem, and destructive and delinquent behaviors. The more that youngsters believed in meritocracy, the more they grappled to come to terms with their own experiences of inequality, and the more they began to lose faith in themselves.

The three researchers' findings shed light on the wider experiences of girls, even those privileged by race and class. As girls approach puberty and silence their anger, many exhibit the troubling and risky behaviors found in the study, such as displaying signs of mental distress, self-harm, and hypervigilance, a state of anxious alertness to possible risk. In middle school, lying, skipping school, and social awkwardness become issues for girls who were previously "good." Bullying spikes during this period, as girls increasingly turn to aggression, sarcasm, apathy, and meanness. Early signs of emotional distress or forms of self-harm become evident.

According to clinicians, anger as a significant component of anxiety and depression is a *specific type* of anger, the kind of anger caused by a perceived or actual loss or rejection. Faced with these feelings, young girls find ways to cope; sometimes they compartmentalize; sometimes they agitate for change; sometimes they bury their heads in the sand; sometimes they conform and self-objectify. Sometimes, though, they get very, very angry. When they do, that anger is, more often than not, turned into a form of illness instead of given free expression, because the adults around them would rather call what they are feeling anything but anger.

When media focus on gaps in confidence and lower self-esteem, they tend to homogenize a diversity of experiences. Hispanic girls report slightly higher self-esteem than white girls do, but both groups of girls record lower self-esteem than their male peers. Girls of Asian descent have the lowest recorded self-esteem and one of the largest gaps between the sexes, a gap that may be tied to cultural orientation toward communalism and not individualism.

Black children in the United States exhibit a different pattern. They are much more likely to report high self-esteem and have the smallest gender gap. By twelfth grade, African American students are the only subgroup in which girls have higher self-esteem than boys do. The difference extends to adulthood, where fewer than 50 percent of white women strongly agree with the statement, "I see myself as someone who has high self-esteem," compared with 66 percent of black women.

What matters appears to be parental support for a girl's staying true, first and foremost, to herself, and community honesty about discrimination and building resilience to that discrimination. Furthermore, black children are able to look up to black women, as mothers, valued members of extended families, and leaders of their communities in ways that many of their peers in other ethnic groups might not. Additionally, African American parents understand the risks their children will face and the impossibility of preserving their innocence in a society hell-bent on denying it. Because of racial alienation and the need to take active steps to combat discrimination, black mothers, studies show, are less likely to socialize their daughters to be subservient to the powers that be.

It is hard to overstate how problematic the transfer of anger, as a resource, from girls to boys and women to men is—not only to us as individuals but also to our society. This transfer is critical to maintaining white supremacy and patriarchy. Anger remains the emotion that is least acceptable for girls and women because it is the first line of defense against injustice. Believing that you have the *right* to use your anger with power reflects multiple, overlapping social entitlements.

In the end, faced with yet another morning of Destructo Boy and his parents, I broke my own rule about not interfering with disciplining of other people's children. I knelt down and looked the boy in the eye. I asked him to stay at least an arm's length away from my daughter and her castle forever. I explained that it was important to respect her work and listen to her words. If he felt like gleefully destroying a tower, I said, he could always build his own. He confirmed that he understood, and he didn't do it again. It worked, but using my status as an adult did nothing to contribute to my daughter's sense of her control over her environment or her knowledge that her feelings and rights deserved to be socially respected and validated. In the traditional way, I was perpetuating a sort of ignorance around anger.

When we are taught that our anger is undesirable, selfish, powerless, and ugly, we learn that *we* are undesirable, selfish, powerless, and ugly. When we forgo talking about anger, because it represents risk or challenge, or because it disrupts a comfortable status quo, we forgo valuable lessons about risk and challenge and the discomforts of the status quo. By naturalizing the idea that girls and women aren't angry but are sad, by insisting that they keep their anger to themselves, we render women's feelings and demands mute and with little social value. When we call our anger sadness instead of anger, we often fail to acknowledge what is wrong, specifically in a way that discourages us from imagining and pursuing change. Sadness, as an emotion, is paired with acceptance. Anger, on the other hand, invokes the possibility of change and of fighting back.

What I wish I had taught my daughter in that moment was that she had every right to be angry, and subsequently demand that the adults around her pay attention to that anger. Only then can she feel she has the right to make demands on the world.

WOMEN ≠ TOASTERS

Why can't you see me? Everyone else can.
—Warsan Shire, "Anger" (included
in the film *Lemonade* by Beyoncé)

Several years ago, I was invited to talk to students at a midsize New England college about feminism, gender, and violence. It was a lively conversation in which the students' doubts about gender inequality quickly became clear. For an hour, we went back and forth, establishing mutual understandings about differences between bias, prejudice, and discrimination. We considered how the framing of narratives influences how information is understood. Eventually we turned to social media, homing in on a phenomenon that everyone in the room had personal experience with: sexting.

Roughly 20 percent of teenagers share sexualized photographs of themselves. By age twenty-four, that number is 33 percent. Almost all have seen sexts, even if they haven't sent or received them. Sexting feels "equal" but is, in fact, not. Even boys as young as eleven and twelve years old are two to three times more likely than girls to share pictures, usually *of* girls, without consent. Boys are also significantly more likely to share and receive images of girls from other boys. Girls report feeling immense pressure to share naked images. In the same way that magazine covers featuring half-clothed women outsell those featuring men, cell phone photos of girls are more valuable currency. Boys use them for cred. Teens are aware of the double standards that expose girls to greater social and reputational risks under these circumstances. They don't, however, associate that double standard with inequality, sexism, violence, or dominance—despite the fact that even when girls send photos, headless shots (an attempt to preserve privacy and safety) aren't sufficient. "Girls in middle school and high school often feel pressured to comply with requests to send naked photos of themselves to boys who demand them. They do it because they feel they have to, not because they want to," explains Leora Tanenbaum, author of *I Am Not a Slut: Slut-Shaming in the Age of the Internet.* "This exchange tends to uplift boys' popularity at the expense of girls' reputations. Some boys collect photos of girls like playing cards, assigning value to each image. Essentially, girls are treated as sex objects and punished for doing what is expected of them."

Put out by the suggestion that the sexism implied by these patterns was real or potentially constituted a form of violence, a nineteen-year-old man at the back of the classroom asked, "What's the difference between sharing a picture of my toaster and sharing a picture of my naked girlfriend? Either way, the picture is mine."

The student may have been trying to be amusing, but he asked the question with a straight face. He was sitting in a scrum of men who were also eager for an explanation. "I mean, if she gives it to

him," another asked, "what does she expect?" I waited to see if anyone in the class was going to disagree.

The young man's choice of a toaster was fascinating. He equated
the woman in the photograph with an actual tool, perceiving both in
terms of their instrumentality. They were inert, possessions to be used,
and lacking in self-determination. A toaster, coincidentally, contains
warm slits and produces consumable pleasures. If the woman, unlike
a toaster, had any boundaries that should be respected, they were easily done away with in the subtle shift from subject to object. Stymied
and laughing to myself, I couldn't figure out how to answer his question in the scant few minutes left. Women and toasters are different.
Did I really have to explain this? Out loud?

The other students were cavalier about the question. It was clear
that they could comfortably overlook the fact that the issue didn't
hinge on the man's possession of the woman's picture or his use of a
particular technology, but, instead, on his disregard for the woman
as a person. No one brought up the woman's potential emotional
response, consent, privacy, or agency. The entire conversation centered around the man's property rights and, as one student insisted,
his "freedom of expression."

No one seemed outraged by his carelessness and what it represented. Perhaps the women in the room did feel personally insulted
and angry, but no one said anything. The slight represented by the
man's question was irrelevant to them. It certainly didn't strike them
as gendered, despite the overwhelmingly gendered nature of what
he was describing. His assertion was, in a deep way, an assertion of
relative status. In it, I saw threats to safety, health, physical integrity,
and a whole host of other practical outcomes. Maybe, I thought, the
women simply saw an asshole and felt no insult or threat. The issue
of dignity didn't come up at all. I perceived insult; others did not.

Insults are the most common provocation for anger because,
whether we think about this or not, they generate social imbalances.
Why weren't the women students insulted? His question hinged on

an imaginary scenario but not an uncommon one. The overwhelming majority of people harassed and abused by nonconsensual sharing of sexualized images are women or girls; in fact, the problem is
so common that it goes by the popular misnomer "revenge porn."
Where, I wondered, was the indignation?

Toaster Boy, to provoke indignation, would have had to violate
norms, but he didn't; he confirmed them. The relationship between
"woman" and "dignity" and "rights" is far weaker than that between
"man" and "property" and "free speech." In fact, if anyone was indignant, it was Toaster Boy, and his anger held purchase among his peers.

Being indignant is a powerful emotional response to insults and
to threats against dignity. It is a specific kind of anger rooted in believing that you are being treated unfairly. A precondition for indignation
is a secure sense of your worth and an equally strong sense that some
valuable standard or norm has been violated. Subjecting someone to
indignity involves making a person feel shame or a loss of self-respect.
It's the core of humiliation, embarrassment, and loss of face as well as
pride. It is the bleeding edge of dehumanization and violence.

When your ability to gauge insult is worn away by learning to see
yourself mainly in terms of usefulness to others, there *is* no expectation. No expectation means no violation, and no violation means
no anger in response. The cycle goes round and round.

The kind of objectification the man was describing causes feelings of shame and anger in women *every day*, but we frequently
ignore both the objectification and the feelings because even the
idea of being insulted or demanding dignified treatment is difficult
to reconcile with certain types of femininity. Indeed, indignity can
often feel immanent in femininity.

If you ask the average person, "Are women human?" a predictable
response is ridicule, followed by the accusation that you are stupid
because *obviously* women are human. But it's a legitimate question,

because many of us perceive women as existing in a liminal state of humanity. It is a legitimate question because women's bodies are treated in ways that belie our equality. It's virtually impossible to go through a day without images of girls' and women's shellacked, shaved, tied-up, emaciated, and often, if you pause to seriously look, mutilated bodies invading your imagination. Our bodies are used to market everything from toys and clothing, to food and games. Women pose as tables for people to eat off of, chairs for people to sit on, and bicycles for people to ride. And that's all before the mindlessly sexist and racist fetishizing of mainstream pornography, which in its most popular forms frequently eroticizes violence. Often women's bodies appear with no heads. No head, no brain. No head, no mouth. No brain, no mouth, no objections.

There is practically no period of life that doesn't involve people talking about how we, and the women around us, look, often strictly and punitively enforcing appearance-based rules.

By age six, most American girls already think of their bodies as sex objects, expressing the desire to dress in revealing and sexualizing ways in order to be liked. Almost 35 percent of five-year-old girls restrict their food intake, 28 percent because they want to achieve the idealized bodies they see in the media. In one study, less than 20 percent of young girls rejected the idea that they were failing to meet the thinness ideals. More than half of young girls think they are too fat, a finding that holds true across the globe. One study revealed that most of the girls surveyed believed, in a meaningful connection, that showing anger actually made them ugly; therefore, when they felt angry, they responded, unconsciously, by doing things like not eating dinner and throwing out snacks and school lunches. The association between being angry and ugly becomes tesselated into wanting to be liked and therefore more attractive, or, the opposite of ugly, "pretty."

Pressure to conform to feminine beauty ideals is virtually unavoidable. The first thing a girl hears when she meets or greets a person, in almost any context, more often than not concerns her appearance. "What a pretty dress!" "You have beautiful eyes!" "Where's that smile?" Film and television programming studies show that girls and women are up to five times more likely to have their appearances remarked upon.

Girls are rarely asked about their feelings regarding these pressures and the impact of stereotypical expectations that what matters is not their thoughts, words, character, or ambitions, but how they look to others.

A 2015 survey of nearly 2,000 people, aged seven to twenty-one, in the United Kingdom revealed that 55 percent of girls reported that because of their gender they could not speak freely. Fifty-seven percent said gender expectations determined how they acted in school and how they chose to dress. In life, the commentary is likely to come with the additional imposition of shame.

The summer my daughters were six and four, we were at the beach one day and went for a long walk. It was astonishingly hot, and the sun, bouncing off a clear sea and blinding sand, was relentless. Wearing bikini bottoms but no tops, my children alternated between making sandpiles and running into the sea to cool off. The beach was empty. Eventually a woman and her son appeared in the distance, moving lazily in our direction. The boy seemed to be around the same age. Eventually the children came together, playing in the water with one another but not talking. His mother and I, farther back in each direction, waved and smiled.

I thought we would just keep walking, but when we got close to the children, she said loudly, "You really should put tops on them." At first, I didn't understand her.

"Thanks," I replied. "They're covered in sunscreen."

"They're girls," she said. It wasn't until she was near my daughters that she'd realized this.

I was dumbfounded. She might have been equally dumbfounded if I had taken the time to explain that her statement was an overtly sexist sexualization. The four children were physically indistinguishable, physically active on a hot beach. When I made no move toward shielding her son from the girls' scary, tempting, and corrupting bodies, she pulled him out of the water by the arm. They rushed down the beach before it crossed my mind to whip off my own top. Aggression takes many forms.

It pays to remember that the root of the word *shame* comes from the West Germanic meaning "to cover."

During the past two decades, "Strong is the new pretty" girl-power campaigns and social movements have sprung up to counter-act the barrage of identity-shaping imagery and words that we are exposed to. Major brands tout women's power, athletic prowess, and ambition, but the current of sexism and racism remains powerful.

Incidents like these were common as my daughters grew up, including in school, where a focus on how girls look turns into early and inappropriate sexualization. Dress codes, often posited as an attempt to stem a fire hose of girls' sexualization, unfortunately, tend to unintentionally contribute to it instead. Adults genuinely want to make sure that girls know they are more than just sex on legs, but dress codes that disproportionately target girls with developing bodies or for showing skin do exactly that by centering the gazes of the heterosexual boys and men around them. Before my children's seventh-grade administrators pulled them and their friends aside to talk to them about skirt lengths and how to sit properly—using words such as *appropriate*, *professional*, and *distracting*—few of them were waking up worried about male sexual entitlement. Which is, at its heart, what schools are justifying by prioritizing the perspectives of straight boys. What might be distracting to straight girls and LGBTQ kids is rarely a topic of conversation.

Dress coding exists on a spectrum of daily sexual objectification that affects all students. Nearly half (48 percent) of girls in grades seven through twelve say they experience some form of sexual harassment regularly in school, with 56 percent of girls who had had these experiences describing their harassment as "physical and intrusive." Girls and women with any number of concurrent marginal identities are harassed more frequently. Black girls and women in the United States, for example, consistently report higher incidences of in-person sexual objectification, as do Latinas. LGBTQ students are the most frequent targets of sexual harassment that is also institutionalized, masked, for example, in dress codes.

There are some who believe that women's humanity is actually not in question, but rather that it is women's humanity, taken seriously, that is the problem because it reminds us of birth, death, and decay. Our physicality—the leaking, bleeding, lactating bodies that we manage—provoke terror, and the response, a defensive one, is to figuratively turn us into objects.

The form that objectification takes, in the end, is irrelevant. What matters is its multifaceted impact, the most consequential of which is the elimination of voice in a situation where the right to a voice is essential. Because girls are primed by the expectation that we put others first, it often becomes second nature to make other people's perspectives, and the demands that come with them, our own. This socialization makes the internalization of objectification second nature in processes known as self-objectification and self-surveillance. Women and girls vary in the degree to which they turn the culture's hyperexamined and dissected understandings of bodies into hyperexamined and dissected understandings of themselves, but we all do it.

Self-objectification and -surveillance become mechanisms of vigilance as we think about how we appear to others, how we compare to other women, and how we compare to images of idealized beauty. Both are linked to higher rates of suppressed anger, self-silencing, and their negative spillover effects. Because it is impossible to achieve an idealized, perfect state, as well as avoid a grossly degraded one, women habitually find fault with themselves. In one survey of teens, 94 percent of girls regarded their bodies as unattractive, inadequate, and *wrong*, compared with 64 percent of boys. Women's unhappiness, disgust, anger, and shame about their own bodies is so universal that researchers refer to these feelings collectively as "normative discontent."

An influential 2012 study found that, regardless of their sex or gender identity, participants viewing images of women saw them in terms of their parts, but recognized men best as whole. For many men, just seeing a woman in a sexually objectifying pose, such as in a bikini, *deactivates* the part of the brain's prefrontal cortex, the part of the brain where thinking about people and their intentions, feelings, and actions happens. Instead, the region of the brain that lights up on imaging scans, for example positron emission tomography (PET), is the one that reacts to looking at inanimate objects, such as a pen or a ball. In what researcher Susan Fiske described as a "shocking finding," in some of the men studied the part of the brain that is activated when thinking of another person's intentions did not light up at all. It should come as no surprise that the more prone a man is to seeing women in these ways, the higher his measures of hostile sexism. On implicit-bias tests, after viewing sexually objectified women, men are more inclined to use gendered slurs such as *ho*, *bitch*, *slut*, and *cunt* to describe women.

When Toaster Boy posited his question, his words almost certainly had an immediate effect on everyone in the room. Each woman had to, in that moment, make a choice: think of the woman in the photo as an object or think of ourselves as the woman in the picture—naked, shared, silent. Willingly or not, we self-surveilled.

Girls' and women's thinking is impaired by self-objectification. Sexualized pictures, for example, lead women to spend mental resources managing their body surveillance, shame, and self-esteem. Additionally, when a person is aware that she is part of a stigmatized group—a category that sexualized women fall into despite protests to the contrary—she grows anxious about confirming negative images about that group but ends up doing *exactly* that! This process is known as stereotype threat. It actively disrupts cognitive processing and makes achieving "flow," a hyperproductive mental state, almost impossible.

Self-objectifying women also have greater difficulty recognizing changes in their own bodies. If they experience an increased heart rate or muscle contractions as the result of feeling angry, for example, they lose the ability to recognize those physiological changes and their meaning. Women who score high in self-objectification have difficulty even counting their heartbeats. So, self-objectification reduces both awareness of anger and the ability to respond with anger.

Anger, however, is the dark matter that permeates these daily experiences. Even small doses of exposure to sexually objectifying images result in strong negative emotions in girls and women. After looking at pictures of other women in sexually revealing clothes, women report higher levels of aggression, anger, body dissatisfaction, and sadness. Not only do women feel strong negative emotions and unhappiness with their bodies, but also they report feeling less able, effective, and competent. More than half of girls who have low esteem and body confidence are markedly less likely to assert themselves.

The immediate and temporary impacts of objectification, however, pale in comparison to the long list of what are typically thought of as women's "mental" problems, many of which reside squarely at the nexus of objectification and anger.

———

Women and girls experience anxiety, depression, self-harm, eating disorders, a desire for body modification, and sexual dysfunction at substantially higher rates than boys and men do. Three themes run like underground rivers through all of these phenomena: self-surveillance, self-silencing, and suppressed anger.

While there is no direct causation between objectification, anger, and these ailments, combining measurements of a person's self-objectification and internalized anger results in the most accurate predictive diagnoses of the likelihood that a girl or woman will develop one or more of the aforementioned psychological conditions.

An inability to articulate anger is recognized as a significant component of both depression and anxiety. By itself, self-silencing is understood as a central aspect of depression. Before puberty, the incidence of depression in American children is roughly equal. Between the ages of twelve and fifteen, however, the number of girls reporting depression triples. Girls are also significantly more likely than boys to be diagnosed with anxiety-related disorders.

People with eating disorders also record high levels of self-silencing, as well as a markedly high propensity to prioritize the needs of others over their own feelings. In particular, studies in multiple countries confirm the ways in which the imposition of thin, white beauty ideals affects girls and women around the globe. Every decade since 1930 has seen a rise in anorexia in teenage girls. Today the female-to-male ratio of clinical eating disorders is 9 to 1. Roughly one in three to two in three teenage girls, depending on the study, report using laxatives and pills, or fasting and dieting, to control their weight. Fewer than one-third of boys report the same, though that number is also increasing. In adulthood, half of all women say they have used laxatives to meet "quick weight loss" goals, even though almost 60 percent said they knew it was "bad for my health." Women who are angry or sad also eat impulsively more often than men do.

Social discrimination hasn't been related to eating disorders that are emaciating as frequently as it has been to those related to obesity. While obesity is linked to poverty and diet, research confirms that obesity can also frequently be a stress response to discrimination. African American girls and women have particularly high rates of obesity. High measures of internalized anger and body surveillance are seen across the spectrum of eating-related poor health outcomes.

The relationship between one's body image, shame, and inadequacy are similarly reflected in increased chances of depression or eating disorders in the LGBTQ community. Societal and religious pressures that generate conflict in a gay, lesbian, or trans person are often internalized and manifested in self-objectification and shame.

Girls and women also make up the vast majority of people reporting self-harm. A 2017 study of more than 15,000 people between the ages of fifteen and twenty-four found that girls are more than three times as likely to hurt themselves deliberately than boys are. Self-harmers use words such as *broken*, *defective*, and *deserving* of pain to describe themselves. The desire to inflict pain on oneself is tied directly to self-disgust, a sense of worthlessness, and unexpressed rage. A 2016 report in the United Kingdom concluded that one in six teenage girls had cut herself.

Suicide is also infused with anger. Girls think about killing themselves almost twice as frequently as boys do, but boys have traditionally used more dangerous and lethal methods, succeeding at four to five times the rate of girls. US suicide rates for girls between the ages of ten and fourteen, however, tripled between 2000 and 2015, driving the overall increase in teen suicides during that period. While many mainstream media outlets talk about possible reasons for the spike in overall suicide rates—ranging from opioid abuse to economic stress, depression, and poor impulse control—few if any relate the phenomenon to gender or to suicide's clear relation to anger.

When we talk about low self-esteem, a girl's unhappiness with her body, or emotional distress or malaise, what we mean, but are loathe to say out loud, is that so many girls and women feel inferior and insufficient. Those feelings drive distress.

Women make up the vast majority of people with "issues" and, not surprisingly, they are more likely than men to seek psychological or psychiatric help. Like girls, women suffer higher rates of illnesses in which anger mismanagement figures centrally. Also like girls, many women are consumed by feelings of inadequacy, and many exhaust their mental resources being aware of how they look at all times. Women are prone to what's called imposter syndrome, which is characterized as insecurity about their abilities, and feeling less competent, prepared, and accomplished than their peers. They are less likely to believe they "deserve" good things, including the rewards of their work. Some of the gender imbalances in reports of mental distress result from men being less likely to admit vulnerability and seek help, but rigorous research indicates consistently that women are experiencing higher rates of mental distress because they are experiencing more stress and anger.

Depression has been described as a "silent temper tantrum." Globally, women experience depression at seven times the rate that men do. Anxiety disorders affect 33 percent of women during their lifetimes, compared with 22 percent of men. Being trans and nonbinary, gender nonconforming and gay make the likelihood of mental distress much higher. Whereas 7 percent to 20 percent of the general population report anxiety and depression, almost 50 percent of gender-nonconforming people do. Rates of suicide for members of the LGBTQ community are nearly nine times the national average.

Sociologists Robin W. Simon of Wake Forest University and Kathryn Lively of Dartmouth College, coauthors of a 2010 paper titled "Sex, Anger and Depression," believe that the anger women have tied up in anxiety, depression, and self-harm is rooted in steady experiences of inequality both at home and in the world at large. Mental distress has been linked to stigma, discrimination, and abuse, all of which generate stress and profound feelings of anger. In women, that anger, constantly self-restricted, loops back on itself.

Gender gaps in the incidence of depression, anxiety, and self-harm are preceded by measurable gender gaps in levels of childhood self-objectification, shame, and internalized anger as discussed in chapter 1. These habits share the quality of rumination: persistent, looped, and usually negative thinking. A tendency to ruminate is a clinically understood antecedent of depression. But rumination is also how many girls and women learn to deal with their anger. Rumination is why women report having more intense and persistent feelings of anger. In other words, feminine norms encourage behaviors that result in a higher likelihood of mental distress, feelings of powerlessness, and inadequacy, all of which amount to shame.

Women feel shame more than men, who are more inclined to say they feel guilt. Guilt is the response of a person who feels he had some control but failed to exercise it properly. Shame, on the other hand, reflects no expectation of control. It is a feeling that you, your essence and being, are wrong.

Anger and shame often work dynamically, with anger masking shame, and shame generating more anger. Descriptions of this relationship in research are rich with broader meaning. Here is a description from one detailed study of people who feel shame: They "tend to suffer from persistent, oppressive appraisal processes in which all interactions are rigidly assessed in accord with the degree of perceived criticism, ridicule, judgment, or outright humiliation experienced." Shame-prone patients have "resentful feelings of being unappreciated, insulted, mistreated, or humiliated," contributing to "hostile, hypervigilant states of mind . . . The shameful self is experienced as small, weak, and bad." Treatment of anger and shame-proneness includes helping the person experiencing them to "feel whole, adequate, and essentially deserving to exist." These descriptions are a veritable hit list of states induced by objectification and traditional feminine socialization.

Shame infuses women's most intimate experiences, from menstruation to sex. Women who internalize objectified ideas about their bodies often feel intense disgust with bodily functions—even pregnancy. Objectification and self-surveillance also put women at higher risk of sexual dysfunction. Rather than enjoying sex or engaging with their partners to ensure sexual satisfaction, women, distracted by what their bodies smell, feel, and look like, become unable to think about their own pleasure.

Age shame is also a problem primarily for women. As women approach and go through menopause, naturally gaining weight as fat-to-muscle ratios shift, they exhibit many of the same anxieties and symptoms that teenage girls do. The process of growing older makes women's "flaws" more visible and acute; thus, aging, a natural process, becomes frightening, disorienting, and difficult for many women. Suppressing anger and internalizing objectification are as linked to middle-aged drops in self-esteem and increased mental distress as they are in younger girls and women.

The anger and aggression that women feel, however, can always be abated by an infinite list of beauty products, some of which have the added benefit of eliminating the appearance of anger entirely. Even if a woman *is* angry, no one should know it by looking at her face—optimally lineless, expressionless, and, in some cases, actually paralyzed.

In 2015, news outlets announced a plastic surgery that promised to fix women with "resting angry face," popularly known as Resting Bitch Face. Plastic surgery, facial exercises, and even "facial yoga" hinge on the idea that showing strong, particularly angry, emotions is bad and makes women undesirable. Antidepressant advertising targeting menopausal women encourages them to be tranquil, sedate, and, essentially, nice to look at. Lotions, creams, and injections are "soothing" and "calming." Good skin care, the way to overcome "angry" rashes or textures, has become a matter of carefully managing not just the feel of the body but also the disciplining of emotions.

Even crying is plagued by these expectations. The wikiHow article "How to Cry Without Looking Unattractive" explains, "Why not try to look pretty when you cry?" "Smile and be happy," "try to be quiet," and "giggle."

The belief that women should be babyish and childlike means that women physically infantilize themselves. The physical and emotional softness, smoothness, and suppleness that women pursue isn't only a matter of attractiveness. Looking perennially young means not looking as though we have successfully weathered life in such a way that we might have authority or have developed expertise, wisdom, and skills that are of value to us or to the people around us.

Sociologists Dina Giovanelli and Stephen Ostertag describe media as a "cosmetic panopticon," which encourages women to discipline themselves. Philosopher Sandra Lee Bartky similarly explained, "This self-surveillance is a form of obedience to patriarchy. It is also the reflection in woman's consciousness of the fact that she is under surveillance in ways that he is not, that whatever else she may become, she is importantly a body designed to please or to excite."

Because women themselves pursue body adaptations that make them "feel better," critiques of beauty and cosmetic culture are often themselves critiqued. There is no avoiding the fact, however, that despite a growing focus on men's appearance, women make up the vast majority of people whose day-to-day existences are most shaped by these norms and by industries that are managed largely by men who profit from them.

Few women, particularly those living in the United States or other industrialized countries, escape the press to be eternally dewy and lineless. Indeed, they are rewarded for conforming to standards, in other words, being "good." According to a recent study in the journal of *Research in Social Stratification and Mobility*, the more time and money a woman spends on grooming, the higher her salary at work, regardless of how well she rates on job performance. Prior theories have focused on the benefits of being attractive, but this study teased out the difference between attractiveness and *investment in appearance*. Researchers speculate that women who use makeup signal that they are responsive to social norms, gender stereotypes, and society's greater propensity to police women's behavior, "in ways that keep women distracted from really achieving power."

Even though I know this intellectually, I am not immune to any of it. I love makeup, femininity, and appearing attractive. On a good day, I can "look thirty-five" even though I actually look like the fifty-one-year-old that I am. When I was twelve or thirteen, people often assumed I was nineteen or twenty, which I took as a compliment. In between those ages is the "sweet spot" of evident fertility. On any given day, I swing wildly between the desire to both confront ageism and adapt to its demands. Even as I am aware of what the dread of looking older means, I recently started dying my hair. It was something I considered in terms of media appearances, but I also like looking younger. Sometimes I leave the gray for months, embracing aging with glee; then, on a whim, I change it. Demands like these wear on us in ways that we aren't even conscious of—or find difficult to acknowledge.

It is notable that anxiety, depression, and concerns about weight and appearance tend to cluster around puberty, pregnancy, perimenopause, and menopause. These stage-of-life changes, we never cease to be reminded, involve hormones, but they are all also times in which girls and women find themselves in the crosshairs of objectification, social inequality, and, often, intense and unacknowledged anger.

Therapeutic approaches to managing emotional distress focus mainly on "fixing" the individual through behavior modification rather than addressing considerations of anger and power. I have read hundreds, maybe thousands, of articles by teachers, therapists, doctors, researchers, counselors, and parents about teenage girls' emotional issues and ailments, and I can count on one hand the number of times that contorted anger, cultural denigration, and social inequality have been primary considerations. The same is true in many conversations about other transitions, such as menopause.

Currently, some variation of girls' inability to cope with "unprecedented social pressures" is the most facile explanation for a constellation of anger-related ailments that surface in adolescence but, in truth, linger throughout our lives. Social media. Cell phones. Porn. Girls are dating too early, are the children of divorce, have single mothers, absent fathers, are too sexy. Maybe it's drugs. Too much schoolwork. Not enough schoolwork. Music videos. Too many friends. Not enough friends.

So what? This is life; get over it. The problem is too big. There are more serious issues. Besides, it's puritanical to critique sexualization. Girls are embracing their own bodies, and they get positive feedback when they post sexy photos and report a sense of worthiness associated with that feedback. It's empowering, pleasing, mutual, and consensual. Any wet-blanket critiques are slut-shamey and unpleasantly bitter. Anyway, men are also being objectified now.

In fact, what is pleasing and instills a sense of control in girls *and women* isn't sexualization, but the *power* it brings. Studies show that the positive emotions experienced by women who self-sexualize in social media, for example, are not actually correlated to the degree of self-sexualization but to a specific motivation: being admired, attracting attention—the likes and followers of social media. Those are symbols of influence and status. That is a far more accurate reflection of what women are reporting, as is the fact that sexualization remains the most available, albeit very narrow, path to power for girls.

Power and empowerment are not the same. Neither are sexual objectification and sexuality, which are often confused. And pretending that men are affected by objectification the same way women are, individually or collectively, is just that: a pretense. Women don't own the media and marketing companies that profit from their images, and they don't lead the religious and educational institutions that dictate what constitutes obscenity—currently considered inherent in women's naked bodies. Men can opt out of sexualization if they choose, but women, given history, have few options. Which brings us, inexorably, to pornography.

By the time I met Toaster Boy during my college presentation that day, pornography was part of everyone's day-to-day life—from the students to those of us standing in front of the classroom—whether we consume it as a product or not. Nine out of ten young adult men, and one in three women, report using pornography. It is difficult today for a girl or a woman to encounter male peers who have not been exposed to or are relying on pornography for regular sexual gratification.

The past two decades of pornography's explosive production has led to an overall increase in its social acceptability, but this shift has come with a rarely noted and steadily increasing gender divide over this acceptability. In 2015, University of Maryland sociologists Philip Cohen and Lucia Lykke found that between 1975 and 2012, general opposition to pornography among men and women decreased, but men's opposition declined precipitously, whereas women's didn't. They attribute the gap to "increases over time in men's actual consumption of pornography, and its increasingly degrading depiction of women."

Porn is no longer something you have to seek out. It's ambient. It finds you. Forty years ago, a child might have found a copy of the relatively mild *Playboy* under an uncle's bed. Today, explicit and graphic video pornography is a quick click away on a phone or a computer. In porn, as elsewhere, women appear as "flavors," a riff on our consumability. Stereotypes in porn are eroticized distillations of the same stereotypes that girls see about "womanhood" elsewhere. Poet Adrienne Rich described these tropes as "white goddess/black she-devil, chaste virgin/nigger whore, blonde blue-eyed doll/exotic 'mulatto' object of craving."

The porn industry, which makes more money than all sports industries combined, is clearly driven by demand, mainly heterosexual men's demand. Studies reveal that after watching mainstream porn, men and women both are more likely to express adversarial beliefs about sex and gender, express negative opinions about the impact of sexual harassment, be more accepting of interpersonal violence, and are demonstrably less likely to support policies and programs designed to meet women's needs. There are interpersonal impacts as well. According to studies of college-aged women, those who are aware of former partners' pornography usage exhibit higher rates of self-objectification, as well as body and sexual dissatisfaction. Women and girls are not *supposed* to be angry about pornography and its impacts, but women, when asked, report feeling anger about porn. They often keep it to themselves because to say so immediately turns a person into a prude and a scold.

Toaster Boy's dilemma was not, on its surface, blatantly pornographic, but it seemed informed by a particular logic of much of contemporary pornography, the heterosexual male sexual entitlement and the denial of women's experiences required to fulfill that entitlement. The invisible power imbalance in the classroom relied on this assumption.

Additionally, the classroom conversation was preoccupied with "blame" in assessing his example of sexting and sharing a photo without consent. His question was essentially an argument for his innocence and her responsibility for the outcome. One of the most powerful effects of learning to prioritize other people's perspectives above your own is that you lose the ability to see others as blameworthy, even when they are openly acting as aggressors. In the classroom, it was almost certainly the case that the women were managing a double bind that we face constantly: conform to traditional gender expectations, stay quiet and be liked, or violate those expectations and risk the penalties, including the penalty of being called puritanical, aggressive, and "humorless." The men could quickly pinpoint their resentment at being considered sexist or their anger at being thought of as violent, but the women were less likely to feel anger and, if they did, to recognize and call it anger.

Women live their lives trying to create bodies of *deference*. And anger is not compatible with deference. Objectification denies us subjectivity, and anger is *all about subjectivity*. You can't express anger without asserting *I* and your own perspective. In the "cosmetic panopticon," expressing anger is disobedient and rebellious, powerful and threatening, because it is the seed of aggression and collective action.

ANGRY BODIES

Been programmed to self-destruct!
—Kathleen Hanna and Bikini Kill, "No Backrub"

had a headache that lasted for years. It was there when I opened my eyes in the morning and there when I went to sleep at night. Some days my face hurt so much when I woke up that I could barely move my jaw or facial muscles. I got used to this pain being the wallpaper of life. It wasn't until the day that my husband was seeking relief for a rare headache that I realized the exceptional day, for me, was one when I *didn't* have a headache.

The doctors I consulted were full of speculations and even prescriptions, but none helped. Eventually I was diagnosed with "stress," which, in my case, meant my jaw muscles were in a near constant state of clenching. In the end, I did what most women not only do but also are encouraged to do: live with the pain and discomfort. While most of the doctors I spoke to acknowledged that managing work and family life were contributors, no one, not once, specifically delved into the relationship between stress, pain, and anger.

Researchers attribute differences in feelings and perceptions of pain to a combination of biology, hormones, genes, and socialization. For example, the female sex hormones estrogen and progesterone have been shown to amplify pain sensations while testosterone reduces them. What is generally agreed upon, however, is that in order to treat and understand pain, we need to give up our cultural commitment to the division of body and mind. In pain, the same dualism that defines our approach to sex, gender, social organization, and labor is hurting our ability to address physical and mental health.

These persistent divides mean that the way we think about women's pain is stunningly similar to the way we think about women's anger. As with anger, women report feeling pain in more sustained ways—more acutely and more frequently, including following medical procedures—than men do. As with anger, women's pain is frequently minimized and ignored. As with anger, gender roles, and often racial stereotypes, shape pain.

Women are expected to accept physical pain as a normal part of everyday life, whereas for men, stoicism is expected in the face of pain that might be experienced sporadically. Men demonstrate higher thresholds and tolerance for certain types of pain; women, for others. However, women, socialized to be more expressive in general, are more likely to talk about their pain. When pain is induced as part of a study, for instance, they record greater physical reactivity and sensitivity. A willingness to report pain is correlated with lower pain thresholds, so much so that a person's openness to say that he or she is hurting eliminates what are thought of as biological sex-based differences. People who score high in "masculine" behaviors—even women—display higher pain tolerance than those who react in a more "feminine" manner, while people who score higher for femininity and feminine behaviors exhibit less pain tolerance. These findings are particularly insightful because they clearly and compellingly demonstrate that behaviors many people learn to think of as "natural" ones stemming from biological sex are actually fluid and relate, instead, to socially constructed gender norms and expectations.

For example, the study found that even the gender of the researcher matters to how men with traditional expectations think about and experience pain. Men who scored high in traditional, binary gender beliefs demonstrated higher pain tolerance *when in the presence of women dressed in ways that emphasize their femininity.* Pain tolerance was highest in men who were told that women are more tolerant of pain.

Regardless of sex or gender, research shows that anger is the single, most salient emotional contributor to pain. The relationship is particularly close in women because we consistently say we are feeling more stress and are less likely to externalize our anger.

Anger is not the first thing we think of when we feel stress or pain, unless there is an immediate anger-producing incident. If you trip, break a bowl, or hurt yourself exercising, your immediate response might be anger—and, accordingly, you might curse or scream loudly. Most of us understand that when we have a sharp and immediate cause of pain, we respond with anger that says that pain is wrong. But what most of us don't think about is that when we have anger, we respond, often unconsciously, with *physical pain.* Unaddressed anger affects our neurological, hormonal, adrenal, and vascular systems in ways that are still largely ignored in the treatment of pain. It's hard to overstate what this means in terms of women's health.

All over the world, women report much higher rates of both acute and chronic pain than men do. Of the more than one hundred million Americans who report living with daily pain, the vast majority are women. (A comprehensive study involving more than 85,000 respondents in seven developing and ten developed nations found that the prevalence of chronic pain conditions in men was 31 percent but in women it was 45 percent.)

Researchers believe that the role of anger in persistent pain is probably difficult for patients to admit because of widespread denial of feelings of anger. Women in pain are often women enraged but incapable of communicating that rage constructively.

Even when we do express ourselves, gender norms shape responses. Consider cursing, something many of us who are angry or in pain, do. In her book, *Swearing Is Good for You: The Amazing Science of Bad Language*, Emma Byrne explains pain mitigation as one of the many benefits of swearing. Among other benefits she cites, for example, are that workplace teams who use swearing, banter, and friendly insults are more productive and cohesive. Swearing also often means a person is more respected by those around them. It is also a more direct way to communicate. When a man and a woman use the same curse words, however, the woman's words are considered more offensive. In an effort to avoid swearing, women often fall back on euphemisms and *indirect* communication. Byrne posits that gendered approval and disapproval of swearing is based on social understandings of "male power and female purity." When women curse they tilt toward the "impure," and, in essence, are tacitly assumed to deserve punishment.

How is this tied to anger and pain? Cursing numbs pain. The relationship between pain and cursing is not one-way (for example, stubbing your toe and letting out a stream of expletives in rage). Those expletives, in turn, affect our perceptions of pain. Through a series of creative experiments, scientists have found that the stronger the curse words people use while experiencing pain the higher their tolerance for that pain. Byrne notes, depressingly, that women who curse when in pain, however, are *less* well cared for by those around them.

A whole spectrum of health issues is now clearly linked to how people feel and express anger, which directly affects our hormonal system, immunity against disease, heart function, muscles, and skeleton. The headache that I experienced is the result of what is called somatization, in which a mental state such as anxiety—or anger—expresses itself physically, despite there being no evidence of a known medical condition. It is particularly common in women who ignore, divert, or otherwise minimize their anger. Over time, those mismanagements are almost always unhealthy, and they frequently become physically painful.

Anger releases specific stress hormones, such as adrenaline and cortisol, in the body that have a direct impact on health. Both of these hormones provide important clarity and energy that is useful in short-term stressful or threatening situations; however, long-term elevated adrenaline and cortisol are distinctly unhealthy. Cortisol results in increased blood sugars (glucose), affects the immune system, alters digestion, and influences growth and the reproductive system. Mood, behavior, motivation, and desire are all affected. Our bodies and brains process what we think of as irritations and daily hassles in the same way they process threat.

Women who repress their anger are twice as likely to die from heart-related disease. Responding with extreme rage, however, is similarly problematic. Two hours after a vitriolic outburst, the risk of a heart attack increases fivefold, and the chance of suffering a stroke, fourfold. People with chronically elevated blood pressure, or hypertension, have a notable inability to express anger confidently and effectively.

Likewise, strong, unprocessed negative emotions negatively affect our immune systems. Studies have shown that even *remembering* an angry experience results in a decline in antibodies, the first line of defense in fending off disease. One study concluded that within three to four days of an anger incident, people are more likely to develop the common cold.

Repressed anger is now considered a risk factor for a panoply of other ailments. Women are three times more likely to develop disabling and painful autoimmune illnesses, those in which the body, in essence, attacks itself by producing self-damaging anti-bodies, than men are. For example, women suffer from chronic fatigue syndrome at four times the rate men do, and they are twice as likely to develop the neurodegenerative disease multiple sclerosis. They also make up more than 90 percent of people suffering from fibromyalgia, which causes sleep and mood disruptions and widespread musculoskeletal pain.

Certain cancers, particularly breast cancer, and particularly in black women, have been linked to what researchers describe as "extreme suppression of anger." In black women, who suffer some of the highest rates of breast cancer, the illness has been correlated with perceived experiences of discrimination and the anger they cause. A twelve-year longitudinal study, which assesses change over time, found a 70 percent increase in cancer-related deaths in people with the highest scores for suppressing their negative emotions. A follow-up to a landmark 1989 study on this topic found that the survival rate for women with breast cancer who expressed their anger was twice that of women who kept their anger to themselves.

It is important to be clear that anger does not *cause* these illnesses, but studies repeatedly suggest, and in some cases confirm, that its mismanagement is implicated in their incidence and prevalence among women. Emotional distress is linked to multiple behaviors that, together, create a complex matrix of cause and effect that, for example, predispose a woman to have a heart attack or develop breast cancer. Improved survival seen in studies about women who expressed anger does not prove that saying "I am angry" effects a cure, but rather that the ability to think and talk about emotions, and, in the case of anger in particular, feel control over factors in one's life, might lead to deeper understanding, more aggressive approaches to treatment, and overall healthier decisions. Women who are more expressive are also more assertive—and therefore more likely to research their treatment options and to follow their physicians' recommendations, and so on.

The complicated nature of the problem is evident in the degree to which experiences of anger and stress, like other health issues, are racialized and classed. Economists Anne Case and Angus Deaton of Princeton University captured a lot of attention in 2015 when they described dramatically rising rates of mortality among middle-aged non-Hispanic whites. They described the primary causes—suicide, drug and alcohol abuse—as "deaths of despair."

People with incomes below the poverty line are two times more likely to be living with chronic pain and three to five times more likely to experience regular extreme pain and mental distress. People with so-called anger issues are also at higher risk for substance abuse. Suicide, like substance abuse, is closely tied to shame. Suicide is, according to Dr. Michael Lewis, an expert in emotional and intellectual development, "likely to be the result of shame associated with rage directed inwards." This news was treated as explosive when the research was released, but for years researchers and members of the medical profession have argued for a greater understanding of how identity—class, gender, ethnicity—profoundly impacts health. Harvard public health sociologist David R. Williams has created a scale that measures how systemic discrimination generates health inequalities. When it comes to the intersections of gender, class, and ethnicity, women of color are living with significantly degraded health and care.

HOW WE THINK ABOUT ANGER MATTERS

Ruminating on negative feelings, which accounts for women's longer-lasting and intense experiences of anger, increases the chances that women "catastrophize": imagining and anticipating negative outcomes. Ruminating and catastrophizing, as previously discussed, more cultivated and common in women, intensify feelings of pain. One response is substance abuse. At least one study has linked the tendency to ruminate and catastrophize to an increased likelihood of taking prescribed opioid analgesics. That likelihood, in turn, brings an increased risk of addiction. Patients who are legitimately prescribed drugs such as OxyContin can quickly develop dangerous tolerances and a greater chance of overdose. Similarly, in terms of pain, rumination, and catastrophizing, being sexually assaulted also puts a person at higher risk of substance abuse, so much so that it is a known risk factor. Unaddressed anger in the wake of assault, which tends to be processed in silence and often with shame, contributes to that likelihood.

Given the overwhelming numbers involved, it is easy to think that the root of the problem of pain differentials resides in women's "natural" makeup. However, interesting outliers refute that idea. In her comprehensive book on the subject, A Nation in Pain, writer Judy Foreman cites a particular example: in almost all countries, women are up to three times more likely to develop irritable bowel syndrome (IBS), suggesting a biological propensity. In India, however, the ratio of men to women suffering IBS is inexplicably reversed. Men in India are not more "womanly" than men elsewhere. Differences like this one highlight inadequacies in arguing that women are biologically prone to specific ailments in the absence of social considerations.

Not all pain is created equal. In many families, as in many institutions and in the law, physical harms are "real" and count for far more than emotional and psychological ones. As the mother of a childhood friend used to say, "If there is no blood, don't call for me."

Deborah Cox, Karin Bruckner, and Sally Stabb, coauthors of The Anger Advantage: The Surprising Benefits of Anger and How It Can Change a Woman's Life, describe the ways in which anger in women changes in form, meaning, and effect. They describe women's anger as moving "sideways"—diverted into relational and passive aggression, physical symptoms, and, for some people, what amounts to constant low-grade and hard-to-describe irritability. In their book, the three researcher-clinicians propose that many of the diseases and physical discomforts common to women are transformations of anger into "socially acceptable forms of distress."

Unmanaged anger makes us "feel bad."

Such an interesting double entendre.

———

Hormones, genetics, body weight and size, and psychological makeup all affect the incidence and intensity of pain. They do not, however, determine how we make meaning of our own pain or how our pain is treated socially and institutionally. Social understandings of gender turn complicated pain gaps into preventable suffering gaps.

When a woman says she's in pain, the person listening to her might respond in any number of ways. Ideally, the person would offer solace or, if in position to, solutions. However, he or she might also laugh at her; or tell her no, she's actually not in pain; or say the pain isn't "real"; or describe ways that it's all in her head; or suggest that she's too pretty to be in pain; or explain that pain is "just part of being a woman."

Studies in implicit bias consistently show that most people, including, importantly, medical professionals of all genders and ethnicities, have a difficult time taking women's pain seriously. Men are, for example, treated more quickly in emergency rooms. In one study that looked at people with abdominal pain, men waited roughly forty-nine minutes, compared with women's sixty-five minutes, before being treated by doctors. Men are also sent to intensive care units more quickly and frequently. Medical professionals spend more time with male patients than with female patients who have the exact same symptoms. One analysis revealed that women even have longer wait times before they get doctors' appointments.

Distressed patients in high-income areas are treated more quickly than those in low-income areas. Wait times for blacks and Hispanics are 13 percent and 14 percent longer, respectively, than those for whites. Heart disease is now the primary killer of women in the United States, yet women are twice as likely to die from heart-related ailments as a result of dismissal and misunderstanding of their pain and symptoms. Physicians are twenty-two times more likely to suggest that men suffering knee pain due to arthritis have surgery, the most trusted protocol for treating arthritis pain when other approaches have failed. Differences like these are seen globally.

Overlapping biases about the "inherent" pain resistance and angry affect of black women yield consistently painful, dangerous, and sometimes lethal outcomes. In the United States, the medical profession has an ugly history of using black bodies for brutalizing scientific experiments, based on the belief that black people can't feel pain. This was the premise of experiments conducted in the mid-nineteenth century by Alabama surgeon J. Marion Sims, the "father of gynecology." Sims invented the speculum, an instrument that looks like a prototypical tool of torture, and pioneered several landmark surgical techniques. His expertise and fame were gained at the expense of enslaved black women on whom he performed experimental surgeries without anesthesia. Anarcha Wescott, who was seventeen at the time of the first experiments, survived thirty of these gynecological procedures.

We see the long tail of this history today. Early in the summer of 2017, Yunique Morris, a healthy fifteen-year-old African American girl in California went to an emergency room with strong chest pains. She was misdiagnosed not once, but twice. Doctors initially declined to do a chest X-ray, despite her anxious mother's request. "She felt nobody is helping her, and she didn't really understand what was going through her body, but she knew something wasn't right," her grandmother explained to local media after doctors found multiple blood clots in her lungs hours before she died.

A 2016 University of Virginia study found white medical students and residents held "fantastical" ideas about black people's bodies, thinking, for example, that it was possible or probably true that black people really are less likely to feel pain, as well as to have blood that clots more quickly. The belief that white patients are more fragile and in need of care even infuses the treatment of newborns in neonatal units. A 2017 Stanford University study involving more than eighteen thousand low-birth-weight babies treated over four years in California hospitals found that doctors' and nurses' racial perceptions of parents affected their treatment of babies in distress. Black and Hispanic babies received fewer tests and time-sensitive examinations and were more likely to develop infections resulting from sloppy care.

Sexist and racist stereotypes about melodramatic women and pain immunity not only affect perceptions but also behavior—including that of women. Many women internalize the same stereotypes and, not wanting to be seen as angry, hysterical, and demanding, opt for unhealthy and risky stoicism. They second-guess themselves, delaying care and discounting symptoms.

The male body and men's experiences are still frequently the defaults for what constitutes "real" in terms of symptoms, "normal" physiological functioning and pain. This bias, a symptom of broader cultural androcentrism (male-centeredness), reaches a particular peak in the case of menstruation. The assumption that period pain is not "real," "bad," or debilitating is reflected in the near complete absence of serious research about it at all. One in five women have menstrual pain severe enough to interfere with their normal lives, and yet there is very little recognition of this pain as legitimately stressful or deserving of mitigation. For example, one study found that women are between 13 percent and 25 percent less likely to be prescribed painkillers when they describe the same symptoms of abdominal pain that men do. The period pain that women have, for example, at work, is often either treated like a contagious disease or a minor irritation that women should shut up about. Period and period-pain stigma go hand in hand. Forty-three percent of women who participated in a 2017 Australian survey reported that they lie about period pain and, when it was bad enough to affect their work, provided another reason for being "sick."

Doctors who gloss over women's menstrual and abdominal pain will also frequently fail to examine women thoroughly, dragging out discomfort and resulting in misdiagnoses. In a recent survey of more than 2,500 women in the United Kingdom, 40 percent of those diagnosed with endometriosis reported being evaluated by doctors more than ten times before the disease was identified. Ten times. That means visit after visit after visit. Weeks and months and years. Countless money and endless time wasted. Lives derailed and lost. In 2015 twenty-one-year-old Kirstie Wilson died from undiagnosed cervical cancer after being told by doctors that her pain was not serious, just "growing pains or thrush."

Among the more insidious stereotypes surrounding pain is that an attractive and, usually, young, woman can't possibly be sick. Her pain, when she says she has it, must be some sort of exaggerated delusion. In my early forties, a doctor waved away my concerns about physical discomfort and excessive, spiking anxiety with this: "You're too young, and you look great." Studies show that overcoming what is called the "beautiful is healthy" problem requires that a woman provide her own medical evidence and signs of disability for doctors to believe them. "Attractiveness, a contextual variable unrelated to the pain experience," researchers have concluded, "exerts an even stronger effect when there is less objective information available."

In 2014 a survey of more than two thousand women found that more than half had a physician say some variation of, "You look good, so you must be feeling better." My personal favorites among some of the actual comments women had received for their literal pains, were "You can't be too sick because you have makeup on," and "You are not in your sweatpants," and "You are too pretty to have so many problems." Three-quarters were told at least once by a doctor that nothing could be done to alleviate the physical hurt for which they sought treatment. Fifty-seven percent were told, "I don't know what's wrong with you."

Men, too, are hurt by the assumption that "looking good" might prevent them from receiving proper medical treatment. They are also specifically expected to be stoic, to "man up" and "work through the pain." However, when they do say they are in pain, they are less likely to be dismissed. It's not only a matter of what men say. When girls and women say they are in pain, people not only struggle to recognize their pain in an abstract way but in an *actual* way: on their faces. When a woman's face exhibits signs of pain, it is incomprehensible to some viewers. This is also the case when a white person is showing pain versus a black person. As is the case with "seeing" anger, studies show that people reflexively recognize pain when a man's face reflects it but not when a woman's does. As with anger, when a person's face is androgynous and shows clear signs of pain, observers identify it as male.

In their 2001 study "The Girl Who Cried Pain: A Bias Against Women in the Treatment of Pain," Diane E. Hoffmann and Anita J. Tarzian pointed out that women are "more likely to have their pain reports discounted as 'emotional' or 'psychogenic' and, therefore, 'not real.'" This invalidation parallels the invalidation of women's anger, which is similarly often reduced to proof of women's mental weakness. One study of postoperative pain relief for patients who had undergone coronary artery bypass surgery revealed that men in pain were given pain relief medication, but women were given sedatives. Sedatives aren't pain relievers, or analgesics. They're calming and dulling agents that "take the edge off." But for whom, exactly? A sedated patient is quiet and docile, not angry or demanding. Men may be treated more quickly because they are more comfortable asserting themselves with doctors and other hospital staff. That women are socialized as children to be more deferential puts them at a particular disadvantage in medical settings, where status, like that of a doctor or other medical professionals, matters. People who communicate anger are treated more quickly than those who wait politely.

While careful studies and analyses of how women feel or what they do after experiencing medical dismissal are rare, I have found moving accounts written by women. They consistently describe the indivisibility of their pain and anger under these circumstances. In June 2017 writer Anne Wheaton found herself in an emergency room with blinding pelvic and abdominal pain. A doctor thought she had kidney stones and sent her home to "wait it out." After several agonizing days and another emergency room trip, she was eventually diagnosed, by a woman doctor, with ovarian torsion, a potentially fatal condition if left untreated. Ovarian torsion produces what is often described as the most extreme pain a woman can experience. Not only did several doctors, all male, miss evidence of her condition, but, at one point, she was tested for pregnancy, despite *having no uterus.* "I think of the unbearable grief my children and my husband would have experienced if I had died as a result of this negligence," Wheaton wrote, after finally being properly treated. "All of it preventable, if these doctors had just taken the time to figure out why there was darkness where there should have been an ovary, instead of deciding I had something that no tests had confirmed." She went on to file complaints against the medical staff that misdiagnosed her and with the state medical licensing board, asking that hospitals take concrete steps to ensure that busy staff aren't defaulting to male anatomy, something that continues to happen in possibly life-threatening cases.

Similarly, in a collection of essays titled *Pain Woman Takes Your Keys,* Professor Sonya Huber writes movingly about what it is like to live with chronic pain and have it routinely ignored and dismissed. "I was so angry at every limb, the way each joint refused to do my bidding," she writes. She, too, was told that she "looked great" and had nothing to worry about. Another doctor suggested she was lying in order to get painkillers. She describes crying, screaming, yelling, breaking things, and quivering with rage. She was treated as though she were an addict, a child, or insane. As Huber recounts, "I had been beyond the brink of fear into anger . . . but anger and rage brought me back to panic." Stories like these attest to why 60 percent of chronic pain sufferers say they feel intense anger toward their medical care providers.

Obviously, thinking about anger, being angry, or writing about anger will not eliminate pain, illness, discrimination, or death. Neither will hostile lashing out, behavior that often alienates others. However, expressing anger in specific ways measurably reduces the pain that chronic sufferers experience and improves mortality rates. Research has shown that a person's degree of expressed anger singularly explains the success of pain-mitigating interventions. People who articulate their emotions and in a way that "makes meaning" out of strong negative feelings of anger and resentment, are better able to adjust to pain. In particular, research has found that writing about emotions in a way that makes sense of them can result in significant improvements in pain relief. This relationship is, again, a type of feedback loop with inhibited anger, higher pain levels, and, often, stronger feelings of depression, feeding off of one another. Studies have shown that in people with less severe pain "no such relationships were found."

Internalizing and diverting anger, which women are prone to do, transforms our minds and bodies into material objects of our own rage. By the time a woman reaches midlife, the most significant predictors of her general health are her levels of stress and where she ranks in terms of keeping her "anger in."

As discussed above, social position affects pain and anger. It's not only a matter of social position, however, but of how that position is understood. Clinicians now understand anger as a mediator between the perception of injustice and the intensity of pain. People who perceive injustice experience greater pain, both mental and physical, and those who experience the most chronic pain have the highest rates of inhibited anger and depression. Feeling socially powerless, which often manifests in low self-esteem, is a known contributor to poor pain regulation. Feelings of self-efficacy, on the other hand, improve pain regulation. Achieving the mental state that enables a person to reduce pain is not only a matter of "self-help" habits. It requires social, communal, and cultural support.

When, as women, we say, "My body hurts," we are actually conveying not only our individual subjective experiences of pain but also the social reality that having a female body hurts and endangers us. It is a statement of unaddressed injustice that, studies show, is masked by pain and anger. Women cannot, by themselves, remedy this situation. We can, however, deliberately and methodically set out to grow people, build families, communities, institutions, and societies that take our concerns seriously and recognize that what happens to us is important. Not because we are enraged or suffering, but because we are *valued*.

How many times does a woman say, "I'm so tired," because she cannot say, "I am so angry!" How many times is women's anger deliberately miscast as exhaustion? Rosa Parks, whose refusal to give up her seat on a segregated bus in Montgomery, Alabama, in 1955, became a catalytic event in the civil rights movement, is a famous case in point. Jeanne Theoharis, author of *The Rebellious Life of Mrs. Rosa Parks*, describes Parks's family deliberately teaching her a "controlled anger, a survival strategy that balanced compliance with militancy." Theoharis describes how, as Parks's public persona grew, she was almost always denuded of her rage. "In nearly every account, [she was] characterized as 'quiet.' 'Humble,' 'dignified,' and 'soft-spoken,' she was 'not angry' and 'never raised her voice.'"

"People always say that I didn't give up my seat because I was tired," Parks explained once, "but that isn't true. I was not tired physically, or no more tired than I usually was at the end of a working day. I was not old, although some people have an image of me as being old then. I was forty-two. No, the only tired I was, was tired of giving in."

THE CARING MANDATE

I've got a thick skin and an elastic heart.
—Sia, "Elastic Heart"

y mother wasn't born with an innate desire or skill for plate flinging. She modelled the era's feminine ideal. She was a wife, daughter, and mother *as a firstborn girl*, a Catholic, a polite and "good" person. She was eternally kind, seemed effortlessly nurturing, consistently sweet natured, and almost always put together and pretty. Patience was her greatest virtue. To her, as is the case for many girls and women today, the term "angry woman" was an oxymoron or even an insult. An angry mother and wife was even more transgressive. What kind of woman resents taking care of the people around her? How selfish is a woman who has her own desires and, worse, puts her own interests first sometimes? Not a "good" one.

From watching her, I learned that her needs and anger—and, by extension, mine—were not important enough to be disruptive. What she felt, she felt in isolation. She would not bother my father, my siblings, or me if she was not happy. This didn't mean she didn't get impatient or discipline us, only that she never seemed outwardly mad. She was clearly angry, though, and occasionally her anger would bubble over in random and sporadic incidents, fits of irrational rage or paralyzing anxiety.

Despite the fact that traditional heterosexual marriage is no longer dominant in US society, the values my mother embodied as a heterosexual married woman in a traditional relationship and marriage still are. Even though most women work, and work for pay, regardless of marital status or sexual orientation, they continue to carry the burden of responsibilities for chores, child care, elder care, and emotional labor—both in and out of the workplace. This tacit, and sometimes explicit, mandate that women care has remained remarkably inflexible in the face of other societal changes related to gender roles. The caring mandate is stressing us out and making us angry, sick, and tired.

We all have stress, but the word is an anodyne, gender-neutral one that masks what is going on in day-to-day life. A 2016 study found that women in the United States and Western Europe have twice the levels of daily stress that men do. Women describe being under constant, intense stress as the result of workplace hostility and disproportionate responsibility for caring. Inadequate social support means that women, often thinking about a wider range of people and possible harms, experience higher levels of vicarious stress, reporting that they feel the impact of life events intensely.

In the United States, women between the ages of eighteen and forty-four are nearly twice as likely as men to say they feel "exhausted" or otherwise worn out every day. A meta-analysis of almost two hundred studies conducted in more than fifteen countries found that women are more physically and emotionally exhausted than men, accounting for their higher rates of burnout in many sectors, such as media. "An awful lot of middle-aged women are furious and overwhelmed," wrote Ada Calhoun in a 2016 article titled "The New Midlife Crisis: Why (and How) It's Hitting Gen X Women." "What we don't talk about enough is how the deck is stacked against their feeling any other way."

Women make up 47 percent of the American workforce; 42 percent of mothers with children younger than eighteen were the sole or primary breadwinners for their families in 2015, and another 22 percent are members of dual-income households. Today more children live with single mothers (23 percent) than in families with a woman homemaker and male breadwinner (22 percent). Slightly more than one-third of children now live in dual-income families, 3 percent with single fathers, and 7 percent with cohabiting but unmarried partners.

Nonetheless, housework and care continue to be done mainly by women. On a typical day in the United States, 85 percent of women do housework, cooking, home maintenance, or care work related to health or finances, compared with 67 percent of men. Married mothers do almost three and a half times as much "core housework"—cooking, cleaning, child care—as married fathers do.

Annual surveys show that statistics like these are similar across developed nations where women, on average, spend two hours more on unpaid work per week, whereas men, on average, have two more hours of full-time paid work and leisure. Data from the US Department of Labor show that while the gender chore gap is slowly shrinking over time, it remains large and debilitating to gender equality more broadly.

Leisure time highlights the problem. In the United States, a recent survey revealed that men engage in relaxing and entertaining activities 35 percent of the time that women are doing chores. For women, that number is almost half, 19 percent. The presence of children is an accelerant, particularly on nonworkdays. Whereas parents came closer to spending equal amounts of time in child care activities during workdays, fathers engage in leisure 47 percent of the time that mothers are taking care of kids. Mothers, on the other hand, relax only 16 percent of the time that fathers engage in child care. A survey conducted by the United Kingdom's Office for National Statistics yielded similar findings in 2016. It found that women have five hours less leisure time a week than men do. Furthermore, since 2000, men's downtime has increased, while women's has shrunk. These metrics persist even in the most gender-egalitarian nations, such as Norway, Sweden, and Denmark, where men do just over a third of unpaid work. In Ireland, Italy, and Portugal, women do 70 percent. Italian women continue to do more work than women in other European countries. Gaps in paid, unpaid, and leisure time are greatest in Arab and sub-Saharan African countries.

In Australia, Canada, Finland, the Netherlands, and the United Kingdom, men have increased the amount of time they spend doing unpaid household work, but in the United States, this shift stalled in the 1990s.

Men are often still thought of as "helping" at home. The majority of Americans still believe that chores, domestic work, child and elder care are "women's work" regardless of whether or not a woman is the primary or even the sole wage earner. Eighty-two percent of more than a thousand Americans surveyed in 2015 said that women should take responsibility for children's emotional and physical needs. Respondents assigned men to one primary child-related task: discipline. As a result, on any given day in 2016, 83 percent of American women reported doing domestic work, compared with 65 percent of men.

While it would make sense to think that the work is distributed according to who has more time at home or earns more money, traditional gender expectations trump both. This is true even in same-sex couples, where the partner who is considered more "feminine" does more unpaid work. Almost 75 percent of people surveyed believed that women in straight couples should be responsible for the inside of the home, and almost 90 percent thought men should take care of the outside, such as auto maintenance and yard work.

Much of the additional time that women spend on care work specifically involves child care that is *unrelated* to the biology of birthing and breastfeeding infants: bathing, feeding, and dressing, for example. The work that men do tends to be more sporadic, on an as-needed basis, optional, and more enjoyable. A father, for example, might bathe a baby or play with kids as opposed to managing the logistics of child care or pulling together a meal for four people, three of whom have dietary restrictions, in thirty minutes. Two-thirds of cooking for families is done by women.

Child care is not only time-consuming and often time sensitive, but it has a higher stress quotient than maintenance work and isolated chores. Forgetting to give a child critical medication or accidentally feeding a child with allergies life-threatening food is an order of magnitude more consequential than not remembering to replace light bulbs or changing tires. By one estimate, minor distressing events involving young children occur at the rate of one per three minutes, while major incidents of potentially greater risk happen three times every hour.

When our three children were babies, my husband worked full-time, and I worked part-time. Having three children under the age of three was overwhelming, and my work, which I did at night after everyone was asleep, was a welcome respite. Before my husband came home, I had an evening routine that enabled me to make sure no one died before he arrived.

I would sit on the floor and read to my older child, who was tucked under my right arm, while I breastfed each of our twins sequentially. If I could get everyone into position, we happily sat on a blanket on the floor, leaning against a sofa. Our dog stretched out nearby.

We were peacefully ensconced one night, when my two-year-old announced she had to use the bathroom. This was great news on the toilet training front, but very bad on the breastfeeding-twins-near-dog front. I was patting one baby, lying face up between my legs, and breastfeeding the other. Leaving two infants alone with a high-energy terrier during a mad dash to the bathroom didn't seem wise. I was paralyzed. I announced a game in which I'd close my eyes, and my toddler could "surprise me" by tapping my head as she went and when she came back. She thought it was exciting and leapt up, but as she bolted, she tripped over the dog, and her foot, and full body weight, landed on the chest of the baby on the floor. I scooped her off the screaming baby, dropping the baby I was breastfeeding on the floor, headfirst.

In three seconds, we went from peace to pandemonium. A panicky call to a doctor revealed that one child could have ruptured her spleen, the other might have a concussion, and, undoubtedly for my older daughter, years of therapy might ensue. Twenty minutes later, when my husband walked in, everything was calm. Luckily, no one was actually hurt despite all my worries. Several years later, I wrote what happened into a movie script. The producers removed it because, they told me, it was "not realistic or believable."

No amount of work stress, or anger that I felt related to work, came close to the stress I felt at home. In 2014 a trio of researchers at Penn State measured people's cortisol levels and found that they went up significantly when people returned home from work, with women's stress-hormone level skyrocketing.

Chances are good that no one in your family sat down to make sure that the women do more unpaid work. Mainly, everyone is trying his or her hardest to manage work, families, income earning, and care. But global studies show that women, and girls, are consistently doing at least an average of two hours more unpaid domestic work a week. Many boys and men, trying to do their best and also feeling tremendous time pressure, believe instinctively that this information is wrong and that they do their "fair share." However, studies show that men reliably overestimate their domestic contributions. Many men also undermine efforts at equalizing the distribution of work. In one 2014 study (conducted in the United Kingdom by a large retailer), 30 percent of surveyed heterosexual men admitted to purposefully doing household work *poorly* so that their partners would stop asking and do the work themselves. The increase in men's domestic labor commitments during the past thirty years amounts to a whopping one minute more per day per year.

While chore and care disparities are apparent in all demographic groups, marital status, race, sexuality, and class make marked differences. In the United States, for example, African American couples, married or not, are less gender polarized in terms of family roles and responsibilities than couples of other ethnic and racial categories. African American fathers spend the most time on child care, followed by white fathers and then Hispanic fathers. In lesbian families, egalitarian divisions of labor are prioritized consciously. Single parents have to, by necessity, do most things by themselves.

In my own family, what made a beneficial difference in our allocations of time was something we had no control over and did not think about until after the fact. When our oldest child was two, her twin sisters were born. Three children under three means all hands on deck at all times, so my husband had to participate in day-to-day care and logistics in ways he might not have otherwise. In the constant chaos that was our house for several years, it often seemed that only our shared sense of humor kept us sane. Otherwise we were like partners on a relay team, only we had children instead of a baton.

Under the circumstances, we actually operated much more like gay and lesbian couples do: more likely to explicitly discuss child care, elder care, domestic care, emotional labor, and the needs of professional life instead of defaulting to women, or more-feminine people, taking on the bulk of the work. An influential twelve-year study comparing lesbian, gay, and straight relationships found that heterosexual couples have higher levels of stress, greater sensitivity to insult, and less ability to use humor to enhance their relationships. They demonstrate more hostility toward each other, including using tactics of interpersonal control and domination. In heterosexual marriages, women report feeling that they have less voice and influence in their own marriages. Overall, same-sex couples tend to have happier and more egalitarian relationships that, research finds, results in less aggravation, frustration, aggression, and rage.

We had only our children to care for and were not responsible for extended family or a family member with a disability or special needs, both of which exponentially increase household stress, not only in terms of worry but also by shifting how family members relate to one another. Already demanding situations become even more so, and parents often experience anger, resentment, and frustration.

Two-thirds of the people taking care of rapidly aging populations are women, specifically daughters. Women in the United States spend more than twice the average number of hours per month taking care of parents than their brothers do. "Whereas the amount of elderly parent care daughters provide is associated with constraints they face, such as employment or childcare," explained the lead researcher of a study of gender and care labor, Princeton University sociologist Angelina Grigoryeva, "sons' caregiving is associated only with the presence or absence of other helpers, such as sisters or a parent's spouse."

Even in China, where sons taking care of parents is the reason commonly cited for extreme birth sex imbalances, women provide the lion's share of parental elder care. In the United States, those most negatively impacted are lower-income women, 54 percent of whom spend more than twenty hours a week on unpaid care work for families.

Gender gaps in time are even wider than statistics suggest because women take on emotional labor. Whether a woman is parenting, spousing, caring for elders, working for or without pay, she is still expected to think about, if not actually do, care work, and to be content while doing it, as though we are perpetually accompanied by sweet music, birds, and tiny woodland creatures that help us assess everyone's moods, the tone of interpersonal dynamics, the demands of social life, and the intricacies and niceties of workplace politics.

As children, we learn that the realm of "feelings" is feminine, so it is easy for men and boys to fall into a habit of outsourcing relationships, social networking, and the emotional work that comes with them. Women will spend time and effort sending holiday cards and gifts to family members, arranging teachers' presents and coaches' retirement parties. We are often busy not only managing our own feelings but also for regulating the feelings of others.

Feminine care subsumes us and our bodies. Even sex becomes infused with the expectation. For many men, the expectation that women be eternally engaging in their emotional management turns into the expectation that they provide sex to do it. The two become entangled routinely in the prioritization of men's sexual pleasure.

Faking orgasms, which up to 80 percent of women say they do, is a good example of how the belief that men are owed nurturing, emotional protection, and niceness from women plays out in intimate ways. A massive 2018 study found that heterosexual women have fewer orgasms than any other sexual demographic, and substantially less than heterosexual men. Women say that they fake orgasms primarily to protect the feelings and egos of their male partners. Of those women who fake orgasms, 92 percent say that they believe it contributes to higher self-esteem for their sex partner, the primary reason that 87 percent of them did it in the first place. Being careful with other people's feelings is generally good, but not when it becomes one-way sexual entitlement.

In a searing 2018 piece titled "The Female Price of Male Pleasure," writer Lili Loofbourow relentlessly described how normalized prioritizing male sexual pleasure is and how it relates to ignoring women's needs and even pain. She pointed out that 30 percent of women experience vaginal pain during intercourse, 72 percent experience pain during anal sex, and yet "large proportions" never say anything to their partners. "A casual survey of forums where people discuss 'bad sex' suggests that men tend to use the term to describe a passive partner or a boring experience . . . But," she goes on to say, "when most women talk about 'bad sex,' they tend to mean coercion, or emotional discomfort, or, even more commonly, *physical pain*."

What does this look like in day-to-day life? Five times as many clinical trials have been conducted on the topic of male sexual pleasure, such as for erectile dysfunction, as on female sexual pain. What does this look like in terms of resources? Loofbourow, putting a fine point on the topic, looked at Pubmed, which publishes medical research studies and found 446 studies of dyspareunia, vaginismus, and vulvodynia, all highly painful conditions affecting women's ability to have sex. Studies of erectile dysfunction? 1,954. As one doctor she quotes explains, women will silently provide sex "with their teeth tightly clenched."

This intersection of sex, pain, and emotional labor also has an impact on how women think about and respond to rape. "This need to protect men from the truth of *my reality* if it will hurt them," explained writer Emma Lindsay in 2017, "has extended so deeply that I have laughed off sexual assault so that I would not hurt the feelings of the man who assaulted me."

Gritting teeth is something people do when they are in pain. But it also happens to be something they do when they are filled with rage.

THE SEEDS WE SOW

Families with two working parents have already broken ranks with the traditional family; this does not, however, automatically result in egalitarian homes. Traditions, gender-role demands, and the need to be efficient almost always confirm conservative gender norms and their inequalities.

Today girls, like women, perform an average of two hours more domestic work a week than their brothers. Starting at a young age, girls around the world do roughly 30 percent more unpaid work than their brothers. That percentage is 50 percent by adolescence. They are laundering, vacuuming, clearing dishes, and more likely to be helping with the care of younger siblings. Boys may do these things too, but they are still more likely to be taking out the trash, washing cars, mowing lawns, and doing general maintenance work. When asked what they are responsible for, boys list almost 50 percent fewer chores than girls do. Sometimes physical size differences and strength matter, but most of the time—particularly when it comes to taking care of siblings or housekeeping—gender role makes the more significant difference.

There's also a wage gap. Boys are 10 percent more likely to be paid for their time and effort at home. In 2016 an annual "pocket money" survey of more than 1,200 children and almost 600 parents found that boys were paid 13 percent more than girls. Shoveling a snow-covered driveway might yield more cash in hand than emptying the dishwasher. Because boys' work is more likely to be compensated and more profitable, they save more. Sociologist Yasmin Besen-Cassino has tracked adult wage gaps to the type of work (and compensation for that work) done by teenagers. Parents, implicitly associating wage earning and financial acumen with masculinity, also give boys credit cards and talk to them about finances more regularly.

Girls and boys aren't only doing traditional chores but they are also still playing with traditional toys that reinforce these practices. Stroll through any toy store—brick-and-mortar or digital—and games and toys continue to be marketed along stereotypical gender lines. Girls are engaged in beauty and domestic pseudoplay, whereas boys' play is more likely to be linked to competition, jobs, and money. Girls can play doctor, and boys can "cook," but studies show that even young children feel already that they are crossing established and definitively marketed gender lines.

People have sent me death threats for suggesting that boys be allowed to play as girls do, with toys that encourage them to express "feminine" traits. Many boys are mocked, shamed, and bullied for even trying. In many families, dolls, amazingly, are still controversial toys for boys. What girls are doing when they mother dolls is modelling nurturing behavior and unpaid care work. They dress them. Push toy strollers. Change toy diapers. Feed them "mush" made in toy kitchens.

Many people are comforted by the thought that boys aren't "naturally" interested in caring, nurturing activities and that they are born, instead, with visions of trains, planes, and automobiles filling their heads. Boys, do, however, show gender flexibility and nurturing instincts. In a study of children's toy and television preferences, researchers Isabelle Cherney and Kamala London found that, when left alone, half of boys ages five through thirteen picked "girl" and "boy" toys equally—until they thought they were being watched. They were especially concerned about what their fathers would think if they saw them. Over time, boys' interests in toys and media become more rigidly masculinized and codified, whereas girls' stay relatively open ended and flexible.

When girls play with dolls (that is, mimicking unpaid care work) and boys practice professions (earning a salary), adults don't talk about wage imbalances. Instead, they speak in platitudes. In one high school classroom I visited, a seventeen-year-old wanted to know if I agreed that "motherhood is the most important job in the world." In my mind's eye, his words floated out of his mouth and arrayed themselves vividly in a glittering semicircle above his head.

Only minutes later, a classmate, unaware that what he was about to suggest is illegal, explained why employers should be allowed to fire pregnant women: they are a waste of time and money, will inevitably not work to full capacity, and will have to leave eventually because they will want to take care of their children. As a society, I explained, we love motherhood, but not mothers, especially those who operate independently of men. We are happy to say "parenting" but not to extend institutional support to people who parent. My suggestion that men could also leave work to take care of their children, particularly if supported in the workplace, was taken as seriously by these students as if I'd said pixies would make up this new ideal workforce.

The lack of institutional support for women's wage earning makes clear that we are supposed to care in ways that do not infringe on men's ambitions, success, or earning potential. Masculinity and men's caring is affirmed in moneymaking, whereas women's isn't. So boys and men are taught that the way to demonstrate care for their loved ones is to provide and protect. Making money is the primary way that men are expected to do this.

There is nothing constitutionally or biologically barring men from being nurturers as a primary social function. American anthropologist Professor Barry Hewlett has for decades studied the Aka Pygmy people of central Africa. Men and women are equally fluid in their abilities and responsibilities, and Aka fathers parent like few other men in the world do. Children are within their reach 47 percent of the time during infancy. Women take care of children and cook, but they also hunt and explore. Hewlett was stunned when he realized that Aka fathers even suckle babies to soothe them in the absence of their mothers. Biology, here, is clearly adapting to social norms, not the other way around.

The caring mandate is implicit in the pressure on girls and women—tacit or overt—to define *themselves* relationally. We've even convinced young women that keeping their own names when they get married is selfish, damaging to their families, and a social affront. Today only an estimated 8 percent to 10 percent of women in the United States keep their names after marriage, down from a mid-nineties peak of 23 percent. Three in five Americans think that women should take their husbands' names, and more than half believe it should be enforced *legally*. There is nothing intrinsically wrong with a woman deciding to change her last name. The problem is that most men are not comfortable reciprocating and often consider it an insult when a woman chooses to keep her name. A survey conducted in 2013 by *Men's Health* magazine found that 63.3 percent of respondents would be very upset if their wives didn't give up their birth names. There is no title for a man that identifies his marital status as the first and most important aspect of his identity, the way that *Mrs.* and *Miss* do. *Ms.* is a word meant to, as the 1901 coiner of the term put it, be "a more comprehensive term which does homage to the sex without expressing any views as to their domestic situation." *Ms.* is still not in common use—nor, it seems at times, is a social acceptance of common honorifics traditionally reserved for men. In England in 2015, for example, a woman doctor was denied access to the women's changing room at the Cambridge gym that she'd joined. The fitness company's automation system was programmed to code any customers using the prefix *Dr.* as male.

Overall, women report feeling and expressing anger more in the context of domestic life and intimate relationships than in other arenas, but married women in heterosexual relationships, across socioeconomic groups, report some of the highest levels of anger, especially those who don't work outside of the home.

When asked what makes them angry or depressed in intimate relationships, women's most common responses—including betrayal, condescension, and unwarranted criticism—cluster around men's negative behaviors. Men, on the other hand, report getting angry at women's negative responses *to those behaviors*, describing them as women's "self-focused behavior." "Women tend to be angered by the negative actions of men," explains Professor Ann Kring, chair of the University of California at Berkeley's Department of Psychology, in a paper on gender and anger, whereas "men tend to be angered by women's negative emotional reactions and self-focused reactions."

In the summer of 2015, the American Sociological Association released the findings of a longitudinal survey of more than 2,000 people, ages nineteen to ninety-four, all in heterosexual relationships. Between 2009 and 2015, 371 of the respondents had either divorced or broken up nonmarital relationships. The study highlighted a major difference between people who are married and those who are not: women initiate 69 percent of divorces, compared with men's 31 percent. In cohabitating relationships, there was no gender gap in who initiated separations.

Most husbands don't enter marriage thinking about embedded gender privileges. They also don't consciously think they have higher status and deserve, in their marriages, the deference that comes with it, but for many men, marriage means just this. Unreformed, marriage, explains sociologist Lisa Wade, is "a moment of subordination for women more so than men, [because women] subordinate themselves and their careers to their relationship, their children, and the careers of their husbands." Single, childless women are the only women who report that they have the time and freedom to pursue interests, ambitions, and hobbies at the same rate as married heterosexual men do. After divorces, men are twice as likely to remarry, whereas women are less likely to want to remarry.

Just because men don't *think* they enjoy higher status does not mean that they don't enjoy higher status. The anger that men report aligns with the emotional responses that people with higher status feel when they perceive *insubordination*. The divorce/separation statistics indicate that inequality in marriage is a significant driver of anger in women, and that anger is an emotion that women recognize and act on.

Feminism is often blamed for "destroying marriage" and for reducing women's overall subjective sense of well-being, but those claims invalidate women's anger over being expected to fulfill outdated and unfair gender roles. Feminism isn't ruining marriage— sexism and the persistent expectation of masculine entitlements are.

It's easy to assume progress in gender attitudes over time. Until I was hit over the head with how *not* assured this progress is, I know I certainly did. Many men who support gender equality and gender-role flexibility in principle have a difficult time in practice. It is surprising to many people I talk to, for example, that many studies reveal that millennials hold more gender conservative beliefs when it comes to domestic and work life than prior generations do. While men and women support the idea that women should work—and, indeed, women are demonstrably more ambitious—they are less likely to embrace domestic egalitarianism. A pair of studies published in early 2018 suggest a less dire picture, but highlight how slow the pace of change is. "We've been getting a lot of mixed messages recently," explains Stephanie Coontz, director of public education at the Council of Contemporary Families. While noting the long trajectory of shrinking gender gaps, she cites, as a concerning example, a 2014 survey of high school seniors that found pronounced support for the idea that men should have authority over their wives.

The addition of children to a relationship generates even more traditional attitudes. Today 40 percent of millennials are parents, and, as parents, many hold neotraditionalist views of gender. Among millennial men *without* children, 35 percent believe women should "take care of the home and children," a nine-point increase above Gen Xers and a fourteen-point jump above men older than forty-five.

Prior to having children, 24 percent of millennial men report expecting to have equal responsibility for child care. Among those with children that number plummets to 8 percent.

In what is surely a recipe for stress, anger, and frustration, there is no similar drop for millennial women in heterosexual partnerships. Before or after having children, women assert consistently that their spouses will be equally responsible. Their work ambitions do not recede commensurate with their spouses' expectations that they will stay home and take care of children. Millennial mothers, particularly the college educated, who spend twice as many hours on child care as their male counterparts do, are reluctant to leave the workplace. Working-class women who lack options (including a man who earns a higher wage) face a difficult economic road and higher likelihoods of divorce.

A number of factors contribute to this generational shift toward more gender-stratified and conventional roles. Sociologists Besen-Cassino and Dan Cassino describe men's reluctance to take on chores in terms of a masculinity backlash. In what they note is an American phenomenon, one study they conducted reported 77 percent of men doing no daily housework compared to more than half (55 percent) of women. Men do one-third the amount of work of what women do at home. Contrary to what might seem sensible, men whose wives earned more did even less than those whose wives did not. This behavior was not a reflection of relative income but of a woman's high-earning status.

Stubborn workplace obstacles to gender-flexible roles often force people into conventional roles, despite their best intentions. Changing demographics also affect how gender is managed. A growing Hispanic population, today representing 22 percent and growing, brings with it a higher acceptance for traditional gender norms. Hispanic men are more likely to support traditional gender roles at home and are likely to want binary divisions of family and work responsibilities more often than other young adults. Choice feminism, which posits that decisions women make are feminist simply because women are making them, researchers believe, also enables women to adopt homemaker roles more readily than their mothers did.

It should come as no surprise that millennial women report feeling more constrained by gender stereotypes and having more stress than any other demographic group in the United States.

"Caregiver syndrome" is a term used to name the stress women feel. For tens of millions of people, caregiver syndrome, which is also referred to sometimes as "caregiver stress," is actually "debt stress." But because money = men in the cultural imagination, this connection is often ignored in considerations of care.

Women have stress related to wage earning and health concerns, but what they also have, so easily and casually dismissed, is the *economic burden of care*. Regardless of age, most people report that worrying about money is their biggest cause of stress. Care is expensive, so care often comes down to money. No one wants to think of caring in monetized terms because attaching actual money to care sullies our gender ideals. But all caring is monetized, and for women, negatively so, particularly in consideration of long-term financial security. Not only is caring expensive and financially risky, but this gendered care mandate continues to be the major roadblock to virtually every established path to financial stability and leadership that women might pursue.

Women continue to cluster in lower-wage sectors where they have minimal or nonexistent institutional support, scant benefits, and reduced opportunities to accrue wealth. A 2015 analysis of women's labor between 2006 and 2010 found that, despite women's academic successes and legal victories, the top job for women in the United States was what it was in 1950: secretary/administrative assistant. It was followed closely by two other "maternal" jobs: teacher and nurse. Women compose the majority of low-wage service workers, workers in the food service industries, and sex workers. Women make up more than 90 percent of paid domestic and health care workers in the United States.

This sex segregation of labor even makes its way into our language. In 2017, people began noticing that when Google was used to translate words from nongendered to gendered languages, it did so using gendered assumptions. Bankers were "he," and teachers were "she."

The jobs that women tend to do are intensely emotionally demanding and require suppressing negative emotions such as anger.

Teachers, nurses, administrative assistants, and service workers all record high rates of burnout, and emotional exhaustion is one of the primary reasons for this. An in-depth 2014 study of secondary schoolteachers in Germany, for example, revealed how closely burnout and anger suppression are related. Similar studies in countries across the globe reveal what experts describe as an "epidemic" of exhaustion, stress, anger, anxiety, and excessive work demands.

In her book *Transforming Nurses' Stress and Anger: Steps Toward Healing*, Professor Sandra Thomas found similar themes in nurses' job-related dissatisfaction and reasons for their high rates of anger—repressed anger in particular. Nurses often work in environments where gender, power, and injustice are life-or-death issues. One in four nurses leave their chosen field because of burnout and "moral distress." In several studies nurses show significant risk of depression, the main predictors of which were fatigue, stress, and unexpressed anger.

Teachers and nurses are saying many of the same things when they describe being burnt out and angry about their working conditions. "I feel overloaded and overwhelmed." "I am not treated with respect." "I am blamed and scapegoated." "I feel powerless." "I am not being heard." "I feel morally sick." "I am not getting any support." These will sound familiar to any mother or caretaker. The work that nurses and teachers do is hard, stressful, and undervalued specifically because it is *women's* work.

Feelings, like anger, are difficult to categorize for the purposes of personnel policies and they don't constitute recognizable discrimination. Rather, these are the costs of being women who are expected to efface themselves in the service of others. Women are aggregated in sectors where being cheerful, accommodating, flexible, and patient, no matter the circumstances, are job requirements. These are idealized maternal qualities that, when fulfilled on demand, require constant suppression of negative emotions and trigger high stress.

Twenty-five years ago, sociologist Arlie Hochschild coined the term *emotional labor* to describe the work done by people who have to express emotions they don't truly feel while suppressing those they do. Workers, she explained, who are expected to hide their own feelings or generate desirable ones become alienated from their own authentic selves. Emotional labor has become a central tenet in understanding many industries, particularly the service industry, in which women are overrepresented and poorly compensated.

When women at work don't provide this labor—when they aren't maternal, nurturing, and centered on others—people's expectations are dashed. A "no-nonsense" woman is "cold," "bitchy," and disliked. If she expresses frustration or anger at being treated unfairly, or even asks for help, she is considered less competent and less deserving of pay or reward. In men, people understand anger as a response to a provocation, but in women, it is seen as an unpleasant characteristic, as in "She is an angry woman."

The belief that women will happily, willingly, and freely provide care means that women's time and work are chronically undervalued and underpaid. Even if women choose to work in specific care-intensive sectors, they are not choosing for their wages to be low. Despite ardent deniers, the wage gap is alive and well. "At the current rate of change, and given the continued widening of the economic gender gap already observed last year," concluded economists at the World Economic Forum in 2017, "it will now not be closed for another 217 years."

A 2016 study conducted by researchers at Cornell University determined that job type is one of the single greatest contributors to an enduring gender wage gap. The more "feminized" a job, the less people will pay for someone to do it. Comparable pay for qualitatively different but comparable work remains elusive, with female-dominated occupations remaining chronically undervalued. In category after category, when women migrate into a field, median salaries drop. When men go into a field, salaries go up. Women are working in lower-pay sectors—sectors that pay lower *because* women dominate them. According to the Bureau of Labor Statistics, twenty-six of the thirty highest-paying job categories are male dominated, while twenty-three of the thirty lowest-paying categories are female dominated.

To overcome these wage gaps, many women seek out higher education, meaning that they incur more student loan debt. Women hold 65 percent of student loans. These loans, in turn, are harder to repay *because* of wage gaps and because women have to be more responsive to unplanned pregnancies, child care, elder care, and medical emergencies, all of which make saving money virtually impossible.

Even more infuriating, male wage earning continues to be institutionally prioritized and in ways that impede women every day. In 2018 social scientist Dr. Heejung Chung, analyzing data from twenty-seven European countries, found that men have greater access to flexible programs, while women in female-majority workplaces had the *worst levels* of access. A 2013 study conducted in the United States revealed that employers distrust women when they ask for workplace flexibility.

"Women employees are suspected of divided loyalties between home and work and seen as more likely to use time off for personal, rather than career, reasons—no matter what justification the women give for their requests," explained Jennifer Glass, a coauthor of the study. "We were surprised that status and reason made no difference in the strength of the gender difference, which shows you how strong the distrust of women workers actually is among ordinary managers."

Even as women continue to struggle financially, emotionally, and physically to personally rectify "second shift" (working for pay, then getting home and doing the bulk of unpaid care and domestic work) impacts, they are now also engaging in a powerful "third shift." To make ends meet, women are side hustling. A recent survey revealed that more than forty-four million Americans have at least two jobs, and the majority of them are young women caring for parents and children.

Few developed nations are as hostile to women entering and staying in the workplace as the United States, the only peer nation that does not require employers to offer paid family or maternity leave. Many people continue to believe that money, as conservative Wisconsin state senator Glenn Grothman argued when voting against equal pay legislation in 2012, is "more important for men," whom, he added, "may be a little more money conscious." Given the reality of our lives, this seems like a mind-numbingly stupid assertion, but it is a belief that millions of people incorporate into their lives every day.

Since 1999, while women in other countries increased their participation in market economies—supported by pro-family and woman-friendly corporate and government policies—women in the United States have continued to drop out of the workforce. Certainly it is important to frame solutions to achieving work-life balance in terms of both sexes. But it is equally important to understand that the discrimination men and women face in their capacities as caregivers results directly from the *devaluation of women* in the society.

Women's unpaid and undervalued care work stands as the single greatest wealth transfer in today's global economy. Without this provision of care, markets would crash, economies would grind to a halt, and men could not continue to dominate entire job sectors and institutional hierarchies. Without it, "the masculinization of wealth," as writer and activist Gloria Steinem called it long ago, would be impossible.

Rising income inequality has meant increased financial vulnerability and insecurity, as well as health and retirement risks for everyone, but most acutely for women. Making money, saving money, keeping up with daily expenses, paying off student loans, and paying for medical care are the reasons cited most often for women's daily stress. One survey analyzing financial anxiety found that women had higher debt stress and are especially worried about "unexpected crises" and saving for retirement.

None of this means that the average man feels rich and all-powerful or that all men are mean-spirited chauvinists and supremacists out to oppress the women around them. There are always some women higher on the totem pole than some men, and most men are trying their hardest to provide and care for their families. However, while masculinity brings with it its own costs, the assumption of feminized and largely unpaid care is a very specific tax on women and their families. Within like groups, men's ability to work full-time, uninterrupted and for higher wages, is greater and, significantly, made so by women "not working" and providing them with unpaid care resources.

And yet being angry about this is so, well, *ugly*.

Saying that life is "stressful," and leaving it at that blithely dismisses women's anger and the inequalities that contribute to that anger. Statistics about wages, time distributions, stress, and wealth gaps do a poor job of accurately portraying the day-to-day lives of hundreds of millions of women. They don't capture how emotionally draining, physically demanding, financially damaging, and mind-numbingly boring caring for people is, even when you love them—which sometimes you don't. No one wants to acknowledge that taking care of the people we love sometimes makes us angry. We don't want to as individuals, because of guilt, and we don't want to as a society, because the entire economy depends on women's assuming this responsibility for this work without complaint and for no wages or little to no institutional benefits.

Primary caretakers, regardless of sex, are at high risk for anger-related mental health issues such as anxiety and depression. Women who care for the elderly or their spouses, such as stay-at-home wives and mothers, record greater incidences of depression, sadness, and feelings of hostility, in addition to less life satisfaction. According to one four-year study, middle-aged and elderly women who were caring for disabled spouses developed anxiety and depression at six times the rate of women who did not shoulder similar responsibilities. Women taking care of parents were two times more likely.

In another study, researchers compared dual-income families where both parents worked roughly equal hours and for similar wages with families where one parent (almost always the woman) worked part-time. The rates of stress and depression were similar for the dual-earner parents but significantly higher in the mothers working part-time. The wage gap seems to directly produce greater depression in women. A 2015 Columbia University study of more than twenty thousand found that when women and men have equal incomes, or in situations where women have higher incomes, gender gaps in depression were virtually eliminated. Rates of stress and depression were similar in households with similarly situated parents. Mothers who worked part-time, however, reported significantly higher rates of strain and depression when compared to fathers in similar families.

Many mothers are plagued by exhaustion, stress, anxiety, and depression, all of which are exacerbated by sleep deprivation. Research reveals that a household with children leaves men's sleep relatively unaffected but increases a woman's risk of sleep interruption and deprivation by 46 percent.

While the wage gap's direct connection to caring and anger hasn't been explored in depth, anger and depressive symptoms have been described by sociologists as "the cost of caring" for women.

Whether at home or at work, caretakers often feel resentful, powerless, and insignificant—despite their undertaking such a crucial task. Powerlessness contributes to stress and depression. The sense of lacking control and being vulnerable also provoke anxiety. Sometimes caretakers respond to this stress with explosive anger. This may dispel negative feelings but usually only fleetingly. In taxing circumstances, it is important to distinguish between anger and resentment. Anger is a forward-looking emotion, rooted in the idea that there *should* be change. Resentment, on the other hand, is locked in the past and usually generates no meaningful difference in the situation.

The coup de grace? Women don't age out of these gaps until they are in their mid-eighties. An annual health study of more than eight thousand people in the United Kingdom, like similar studies in the United States and other countries, found that women are consistently less satisfied and happy than men are over multiple life stages. Women surpassed men in terms of life satisfaction and happiness only in their eighth decade. In other words, until they are no longer responsible for caring for other people.

WHO THINKS MONEY IS MORE IMPORTANT TO MEN?

Much of what I have described regarding women's disproportionate responsibility for care is the legacy, in the United States, of a historical cult of domesticity or the "cult of true womanhood," a term used by historians to describe a particularly relevant nineteenth-century ideology. This ideology placed women—idealized as frail, feminine, caring mothers who embodied "womanly virtues"—squarely in the home as carers, helpmeets, and sex providers. "Woman" in this estimation meant white and upper-middle class. Working-class women, black women, brown women, Asian women, and immigrant women were, by default, not "real" women. They worked, as slaves or often in jobs that were physically demanding and that required them not only to leave their own children in the care of others but also to take care of other people's children and homes when they did.

This history infuses our lives as carers and the structure of our economy today. We see women divided by class, race, and ethnicity fulfilling different roles along similar lines, regardless of whether we are talking about caring for children, men, and/or homes, providing sex, or giving birth. The "natural" desire to care is supposed to subsume any anger we feel about its provision, despite the stress and economic vulnerability it cultivates.

My mother was a good girl who became a good wife who then became a good mother who was never supposed to be angry or demanding. As she read to, cooked for, hugged, and played with us, and as she cared for my father after *his* long days, enormous quantities of her boundless energy went into staying calm, pleasant, and supportive. She worked every day for long hours, earning no money, no recognition, scant thanks, and experiencing the "normal" stresses of being a homemaker. And she was privileged, compared with many other women, by status, class, and ethnicity. She ran a household in which other women, economically and socially vulnerable, worked as maids and helped with child care. Nonetheless, her stress was real and abiding. So, too, is the frustration that many women have when they feel that they are being taken for granted. As mothers, or potential mothers, we often come to terms with what feels like dismissal. As mothers, women aren't supposed to care if they have status or not. Which is good because, despite so much vacuous political blather about how important this work is, our society demonstrably does not support us and, indeed, sees motherhood and care work as low-status pastimes.

The anger we experience as the result of demands that we care and care and care runs through our bodies like a current.

Sometimes we throw plates. What we should be throwing are people with retrograde ideas out of office.

MOTHER RAGE

With what price we pay for the glory of motherhood.
—Isadora Duncan

At the end of 2014, women around the world dissolved into sidesplitting laughter after hearing news reports that a clinical trial testing a male contraceptive had been brought to an early close because men in the study didn't like the side effects. These included acne outbreaks, mood swings, low libido, depression, and weight gain. For a solid two days after the initial media coverage, wherever I went, I heard women referring wryly to this story. Soon reporters, mainly men, were writing about how terrible and cruel women's responses were.

Women weren't jeering at men because we didn't take the adverse side effects of hormonal birth control seriously. We were (most of us) laughing because we were dumbstruck. We were angry. I wrote about how irritating it was to realize how little so many men knew or cared about this aspect of women's lives, and within hours of my posting the article, it was shared more than thirty thousand times.

"When you laugh with people, you show them that you like them, you agree with them, or that you are in the same group as them," explains Sophie Scott, a neuroscientist who studies laughter at University College London. Laughter enhances relationships by buffering tension and anger. Like crying, it can be a palliative behavior when we feel ire or disappointment bubbling up. Giggling, guffawing, smirking, and rolling our eyes are all socially palatable substitutes for something people might really not like: namely, outright aggression and anger.

As the episode played out in media and across coffee tables and conference tables, it became apparent that most men really *don't* know much about birth control. Not about the side effects of the most commonly used methods, how much it costs, or how complicated and time consuming it is to obtain. A 2017 survey found that only 37 percent of men believe affordable birth control for women makes a difference in their lives.

Maybe read that last sentence again. I had to when I first saw the number. In a 2016 survey of more than 1,200 men, a majority said they "never or rarely" worry about unplanned pregnancies. It's easy to extrapolate from this that they haven't had the surge of white-hot fear that comes from thinking you might be pregnant, or the panic from realizing you forgot to take your daily pill, or the frustration of being denied access to emergency contraception or a safe abortion. They are almost certainly unaware of how excruciatingly painful having an IUD inserted can be or what it feels like to have your period for a year straight as a side effect of hormonal patches.

When I used birth control pills, I regularly stared at the endless pages of small print describing the risks. Each month for years, I weighed them: potential vision problems, mood swings, weight gain, vaginal discharge, erratic periods, reduced libido, breast tenderness, and nausea. Those are the minor ones. The serious possible side effects include heightened risk of blood clots and stroke, sustained anxiety and depression, painful yeast infections, bone density problems, migraine headaches, infertility, gallbladder and heart disease, and possibly elevated odds of developing cancer of the cervix, breast, and liver. The possibilities were frightening to consider. They still are for tens of millions of women.

Occasionally, I would hand my spouse the package insert, folded and refolded like origami, so that he also had to consider the warnings. Other forms of birth control, at least those with comparably high rates of efficacy, have similar and sometimes even more risky and undesirable side effects. The IUD, for example, can perforate a woman's uterus or bring about a systemic blood infection (sepsis), which can be fatal.

These potential, albeit rare, life-threatening dangers aside, birth control is expensive and, for women, often requires multiple trips to a clinic or doctor and a pharmacy. Even more time and money are needed if one method doesn't work out and a woman has to try others. At any point in the process, multiple people that a woman will never have sex with, or even see again as long as she lives, have the power, based on their own opinions, to deny her effective and safe choices. Outright denial, such as cases where pharmacists refuse to fill prescriptions, happen but are relatively rare. More common is making access difficult, costly, and possibly embarrassing. Consider Plan B, a popular emergency contraceptive. A 2015 study revealed that only 14 percent of stores actually sell it on store shelves, preferring, instead, to dispense it from behind a counter or display it in a lockbox. Why? Because women. Sex. Babies. *Control.*

Most prescriptions for birth control still have to be filled by pharmacists. Being shamed, denied, or having to ask for emergency contraception instead of simply grabbing it off a shelf might seem like slight inconveniences—after all, women can always go to other stores—but, in fact, these effect specific harms. Denying or controlling access are intrusions against a woman's interests, disparagements of her moral character, refusals to acknowledge her autonomy, and violations of her privacy and even safety, all part of a denser matrix of obstacles. And, of course, there is the inevitable indignation and deep anger that accompany these interactions.

As for men, the most trying obstacle that they usually have to consider if they want condoms, the primary male contraceptive, is whether or not the latest version of a twelve-thousand-year-old sheepskin technology is worth the $2 price tag and a trip to the corner store.

Women understand birth control. We understand the risks, and we understand the costs of unwanted pregnancies. What we don't understand is people who refuse to think about the lives we lead and the calculations we make. This level of blithe ignorance not only affects us personally, in terms of our relationships and sexual lives, but politically, in terms of gross negligence and cluelessness shaping public policy.

At the heart of the caring mandate is the particular entanglement of "woman" and "mother." Do you want children? Can you have children? Can you afford children? Do you want to be pregnant? When will you become pregnant? Do you want to avoid pregnancy? Who decides if and when you do? Who decides what risks you take? Are you child free and tired of other people judging your choice? Are you a surrogate? Will you use a surrogate? Will you adopt? Will you give a child up for adoption? Will you have an abortion? Are you a mother? Are you an ambivalent mother? Do you worry about your ambivalence? Are you regretful? Would you ever say so? Do the people around you assume you will "mother" them?

Regardless of whether or not a woman ever has a child, ideals of motherhood shape our identities; our economic, political, and social lives; and our emotions. Maternity—and our relationship to it— informs many of the most important decisions we make as women and many of the most important decisions that are made *for us* as women. The demands of motherhood, as an ideology, frame the thirty to forty years an average woman spends managing her fertility, if she is lucky enough to be able to manage it at all. Each decision she makes—or, even more importantly, is socially prohibited from making—affects her body, her relationships, her ability to earn a living, and her sense of herself.

Just a woman's *potential* for pregnancy affects how the people around her think about her and her capabilities and responsibilities. It also provides dangerous rationales for paternalistic male oversight. It's traditional.

My father was in his late seventies, when, having just arrived for a family visit, he began to talk about how physically uncomfortable he was. As a function of his age, his back hurt, and sleep was often elusive. Certain foods, just the smell of some, could make him nauseous and sick. Sometimes, for no reason at all, his gums would bleed. He could not drink or exercise as he used to and had to make sure that he was alert to food-and-drug interactions. It made him anxious and vigilant. It was exhausting.

I tried to make him comfortable, saying that I understood how hard it was to experience his body in this way. He insisted that I couldn't possibly know what he was going through, because I was much younger. I smiled and suggested that maybe now he could better appreciate how pregnant women feel. His wife, for example, went through four pregnancies, and between his mother, sister, four daughters, and daughters-in-law, we'd had at least another eighteen among us. Though long accustomed to my pointed commentaries on gender, my father still looked shocked at being compared with a pregnant woman, and then *he* started laughing.

He was blindsided by the comparison because for almost eighty years he had lived in a socially entitled way that shielded him from this information. In practical effect, his symptoms were indistinguishable from a pregnant woman's. They differed only through interpretation. He held deeply the common belief that, as women, we are all mothers in waiting, and that, as mothers, we will happily sacrifice our bodies, health, work, and sense of selves. The pain that comes with being pregnant is "natural," as he put it.

When women talk about their pregnancies, they often say that they wish someone had explained more about the experience, beyond platitudes and attempts at humor. I remember this feeling acutely: of not knowing what was happening to me, and wondering why the women I knew—the mothers I knew; my own woman relatives—hadn't talked openly about this. I was frustrated and angry that such a major life event, one involving daily physical changes and emotional adjustments, could be so smothered in silence. I was surprised, too, by my own silence.

As a pregnant person, I was as much an object of reproduction as I have ever been an object of sex. Whereas I had long been aware of the latter, the former caught me off guard. The physical transformation of a person's pregnant body, in a rapid and highly visible way, is a material objectification. Pregnant women are stared at, commented on, and touched; we belong to everyone. Even strangers feel free to comment on our weight or size and tell us how to eat, what to drink, and how to move. Pregnant women are, studies show, associated with mindlessness, meaning lacking in thought or consciousness, or, at least, a *different kind* of mind, one with less agency. Either way, when women themselves perceive that they are being objectified, which happens every day to a visibly pregnant woman, they act *more* like objects, moving less and speaking less. How we act when we have ultrasound exams, for example.

Ultrasounds are often a source of great happiness and excitement to parents and vital as diagnostic tools, but the way that they are framed actively contributes to minimizing potential harms related to pregnancy and maternity. In a standard ultrasound, we see a fetus, but no woman. A developing fetus could be adrift in the sea, a jar, or empty space, as opposed to inside its mother. This isn't an accident. When, in 1965, *Life* magazine published its iconic photo of an eighteen-week-old embryo hovering in a transparent, oval-shaped bag against infinite darkness, it was mirroring equally new and startling pictures of Earth in the void of space taken by the early astronauts and cosmonauts. The fetus image was part of a dramatic photographic essay by Swedish photographer Lennart Nilsson called, "Drama of Life Before Birth."

Few people then, as now, seemed to consider that the absence of women's bodies mattered. If you look for other representations of pregnancy—for example, searching online for "images of embryos" or "fetus pictures," (which actually, inaccurately, yield the same images)—more isolated baby pictures are the primary result. Either that or photographs of women, their abdomens protruding enormously, about to give birth. The "drama" is women's, but in Nilsson's photos, as in today's pictures, women are erased.

As a result of images such as these, in the cultural imagination, women are either invisible in gestation or they magically go from not pregnant to the very precipice of delivery. And yet the intervening period is one in which a fetus isn't only gestating in a woman's body but *is* the woman's body. Each stage, from zygote to newborn, materializes *from her body*: particle by particle, cell by cell, hair by hair, bone by bone. Her cells, her blood, her plasma, her placenta, her hormones, her water, her digested food, her movement, her anxiety, her fear, her pain, her discomfort, her joy, her wonder, her hopes, and her labor.

This is the time when women experience the happiness of feeling a baby kick, but it is also the time when they have bone-crushing fatigue, escalated risks of hypertension, stroke, diabetes, hair loss, nausea and vomiting, dehydration, painful and swollen extremities, sleeplessness, the routine poking and prodding of medical tests, endless bodily surveillance, anxieties, and, tragically, miscarriages and stillbirths.

When we erase women in our images of pregnancy, we erase

how women feel and what they need physically and emotionally. When we erase women, we can more easily ignore their rights and the enormous costs they bear when they bring new humans into the world. Our legal and ethical considerations still do not address adequately women's experiences of being both one and two (or more) at the same time, and images depicting growing fetuses as separate individuals perpetuate that problem.

For the record, being treated like a fetal container is enraging.

Motherhood is central to our social perception of women and our notions about motherhood—nurturing, forgiving, sacrificing—and it is also central to how we think about women's anger. When we feel anger related to expectations or pressures of being mothers or not, that anger is often accompanied by guilt.

In pregnancy, women are often taken aback by strong feelings of anger—anger generated by shifting relationships—with spouses, siblings, other children, friends, employers—and, for some women, a newfound awareness of double standards and discrimination.

The minute a woman announces that she is pregnant, the perceptions of the people around her, and her relationships, begin to shift. Faced with the physical demands and economics of pregnancy and parenthood, couples, particularly heterosexual couples, can find themselves in conflict over expectations and beliefs. Women are sometimes surprised by their spouses' previously unaired expression of traditional gender roles. Intimate relationships and sexual and familial roles are redefined by pregnancy and impending childbirth.

Beyond changing relationships in her life, a pregnant woman is also experiencing a changing relationship with herself, unanticipated transformations in identity that are difficult and unsettling.

The number of people struggling with pregnancy-related stress, pain, and anger at a time that we collectively pretend is the happiest of their lives is staggering.

Pregnancy-related depression affects 37 percent of women in the United States. According to the World Health Organization, 10 percent of pregnant women and 13 percent of those who have given birth worldwide report postnatal distress, primarily depression. In developing countries the averages are higher: 15.6 percent of women are depressed during pregnancy and 19.8 percent after. In the United States, both African American and Latina women experience significantly higher rates of both pre- and postnatal depression and anxiety compared with their peers of Asian and European descent. These experiences can be deeply unsettling and shameful to women. After all, what kind of woman isn't filled with boundless joy at the thought of a baby that will, by some people's genuine estimation, rationalize her existence?

Until relatively recently, there has been very little open discussion about what happens to a woman during pregnancy, childbirth, or after childbirth. Men in particular are frequently left entirely in the dark about changes that women go through. A recent medical survey revealed that more than a year after giving birth, 77 percent of mothers endured back pain related to gestation and birth, 49 percent suffered urinary incontinence, and 50 percent lived with persistent pelvic pain. After childbirth, almost 30 percent of women are left with undiagnosed pelvic bone fractures, while 41 percent have tears in their pelvic floor muscles. For almost a quarter of all women, sex is painful even eighteen months after giving birth. If suturing is necessary following labor, due to vaginal tearing or because an episiotomy had to be performed during birth, some doctors still add a "husband stitch": an additional closure to "tighten" the vaginal canal and thus enhance the woman's partner's sexual pleasure. I. Kid. You. Not. Some women learn that they have this extra stitch only *after* enduring intense pain during sex.

For many women, admitting to discomfort, resentment, and anger in these circumstances is shameful and embarrassing—as if they're admitting, in a deep sense, to failure. Because these feelings are tied to motherhood, a role that is *supposed* to make us happy, peaceful, grateful, and fulfilled, they are doubly stressful and anger provoking. Motherhood, the ideal, renders these feelings illegitimate.

From 2006 to 2010, 85 percent of women in the United States between the ages of fifteen and forty had given birth, the highest percentage since the early 1990s. Conceptually, we think of each experience as a private matter. However, the life changes a pregnant woman or new mother face are hardly limited to her own body and her personal relationships. In the current environment of gender backlash, each instance is intensely public and political.

At work, pregnancy generates biases about women's abilities, competence, and commitment, and sheds light on deep prejudices. Some women continue to hide pregnancies from employers as long as they can in the knowledge that, despite the law, pregnancy discrimination remains a potent reality and is, in fact, the leading edge of wider maternity discrimination. Pregnancy often comes with anxieties about demotion or firing.

A good example of this comes from the medical field. One-third of physicians in the United States are women, as are half of medical students. In a 2017 survey of more than five thousand women doctors, nearly four in five (77.9 percent) reported discrimination. Of those, 66 percent said that they had experienced gender-based discrimination in the form of disrespect, exclusion, and wage-parity issues. When asked about the nature of that discrimination, 35.8 percent said it was related to their maternity and particularly acute during pregnancy (89.6 percent) and maternity leave (48.4 percent), both in terms of needing to take leave and being out for leave.

Becoming a parent is the riskiest financial decision a woman can make. Compared with childless women, mothers are offered an average of $11,000 less when they get a new job. For every child a woman has, she faces a wage decline of −7.8 percent per child, and it's cumulative. These well-known erosions of wage earning are known by economists as "motherhood penalties" and they have a gender-flipped corollary in the "fatherhood bonus." Becoming a father makes a man *more likely* to be hired—even more likely than a childless man. Also, for every child a man has, his earnings increase 6 percent.

Divorce with children is a close second in terms of financial risk. Divorced women often find themselves with huge gaps in their resumes, primary and unsupported responsibility for child and elder care, and no way to earn enough money. This is acutely the case for middle-lower and low-income hourly wage earners, who for a variety of reasons are more likely to divorce. Many women in this situation are severely limited in their ability to access credit or emergency supplemental income. Women's long-term security is in real peril when they adapt their work to be flexible because "someone" has to.

Even women who intend never to have children may become ensnared in the same net: if you are thought to be in the "fertile zone," your work, salary, and tenure are indexed to employers' perceptions of your *potential* to give birth. Employment benchmarks: salary, recommendations, time, job titles, and promotions. A 2014 survey conducted in the United Kingdom surveyed five hundred managers. Two in five admitted to being "wary" of hiring women of childbearing age. Fully one-third said that they would prefer to hire men in their twenties or thirties in order to avoid the costs of women's potential maternity leave. The same reasoning meant that equally high numbers were reluctant to employ women who already had children, including for senior positions. Single and child-free people may experience unfair distributions of time and effort when they work alongside parents, whom, it is often felt, aren't pulling their weight, but the problem is not parents; it's ideologies about motherhood and gender that shape workplace norms.

Beyond the impact on women's careers and salaries, the difficulties and expenses of medical care, often in situations with very few workplace protections and in the absence of broader economies of care, can be overwhelming.

In the United States, just thinking about the costs of childbirth is a tremendous source of tension for parents, increasingly women on their own. Insurance coverage for pregnancy, childbirth, and newborn care was not mandatory in the United States until the passage of the 2010 Affordable Care Act (ACA). But its benefits are hardly assured. One draft of the Republican Party proposed ACA replacement was called, ironically, the Better Care Reconciliation Act, which would have increased both the costs of women's pregnancy care, as well as the cost of contraception. The bill, defeated multiple times during 2017, would have allowed states to define independently what constituted ACA-mandated essential health benefits in their Medicaid plans—in many cases, eliminating coverage for pregnancy, labor, and neonatal care.

Even though these are still covered by law, women and families in the United States pay more for pregnancy and childbirth than anywhere else in the world. By an order of magnitude. A natural birth brings a bill of $30,000, on average. A Cesarean section often sends the cost soaring to more than $50,000. Insurance will cover roughly 50 percent of these expenses. In most countries around the world, there is no cost or next to no cost to being pregnant or giving birth. This is only one reason why deciding to become a mother in the United States is among the worst financial decisions a woman can make.

———

Virtually all societies glorify motherhood and yet, in a reflection of what this means for *women*, every ninety seconds a woman dies from a preventable pregnancy-related complication.

According to the World Health Organization, 99 percent of maternal deaths occur in developing countries in sub-Saharan Africa and South Asia. However, the United States has the highest maternal mortality rates in the developed world and is the only country in which that rate is growing. Today it is safer to give birth in Bosnia or Kuwait than in California, and a woman having a baby in the United States is six times more likely to die than one in Scandinavia. According to the CDC, black mothers in the United States die at three to four times the rate of white mothers, one of the widest of all racial disparities in women's health.

In 2017 an in-depth investigation conducted by the nonprofit news company ProPublica and National Public Radio found that only 6 percent of funding grants targeted for "maternal and child health" in the United States are allocated to the health of mothers. Doctors in training for maternal-fetal medicine can be certified without ever having had a rotation in an actual labor and delivery unit. Maternity wards are being closed in hospitals with little or no provisions being made for women in distress. When Providence Hospital in Washington, DC, closed its maternity ward in 2017, laboring women, unaware, continued to arrive and were either sent away or directed to the emergency room, where staff had only minimal training in obstetric emergency care—training that included watching YouTube videos. Higher rates of complications and mortality are emblematic of a lack of access and resources at every stage of life: from adequate sexual and reproductive health education, to care prior to and during birth.

According to a recent national childbearing survey in the United States, 21 percent of black mothers and 19 percent of Hispanic mothers hospitalized for pregnancy and childbirth-related problems complained of degraded treatment related to ethnicity, language, race, or identifiable cultural background. Women in rural areas, in addition to poor women and those who are incarcerated, face the highest risks. The shackling of jailed women during labor is a violation of their human rights, yet only ten US states expressly prohibit the practice.

Childbirth complications, despite their disparate impacts are, nonetheless, a great equalizer of women. After giving birth to her daughter in September 2017, tennis champion Serena Williams spoke and wrote openly about her emergency C-section and possibly deadly risks that cascaded in its wake. The day following giving birth, she began gasping for breath. Years before, she'd suffered a pulmonary embolism—a blood clot, typically formed in the lower extremities, that dislodges and finds its way into the artery leading to a lung—and she immediately recognized the same symptoms.

When Williams informed a nurse, her concerns were dismissed. She insisted on a CT scan and asked that a blood-thinning medication be administered. After some resistance, the imaging procedure was performed, and, sure enough, she had accurately self-diagnosed her condition. Meanwhile, the anticlotting medication heparin caused a hemorrhage, and coughing caused her Cesarean incision to reopen, resulting in yet *another* operation. Upon returning home, she was bedridden for several weeks. Williams described what happened to her and the immediate demands of then going home to care for her newborn: "I've broken down I don't know how many times. Or I'll get angry about the crying, then sad about being angry, and then guilty, like, 'Why do I feel so sad when I have a beautiful baby?'"

Similarly, in 2003 philanthropist and supermodel Christy Turlington Burns almost bled to death from postpartum hemorrhaging. "A woman can bleed to death within two hours," explains Burns when she talks about why providing competent maternal care is so vital. She went on, in 2010, to found Every Mother Counts, a nonprofit that works to improve maternal health globally.

Improving maternal outcomes means valuing women not only as reproductive engines but also as human beings—something that is still, quite apparently, a problem. A 2015 report looking at more than sixty studies across thirty-four countries concluded that women around the world experience "poor treatment during childbirth, including abusive, neglectful, or disrespectful care" because of a pervasive "lack of respect for women." Pregnant women, trans and gender-fluid people all approach maternity in this environment of underlying carelessness and dehumanization.

I do not mean to imply that doctors, nurses, and the literal armies of people that can contribute to bringing a baby into the world consciously hold women in contempt or deliberately provide shoddy care. But the culture that we *all* operate in does not adequately recognize what it means for us to be both women and human, and, in pregnancy, to be both ourselves and another. An ethos of maternal sacrifice, largely religiously derived, underlies our social and institutional interactions.

I have had two pregnancies and given birth to three children, and in both instances, I was both well cared for *and* endangered. My first baby was breech, and I gave birth to her after a nerve-wracking and physically intensive three-month period of high risk that involved almost daily medical tests and bed rest. On the day I went into labor, in an effort to prevent a breech delivery, five doctors and nurses surrounded me and tried to turn the baby from the outside by pressing their hands in a clockwise motion on my abdomen. This was excruciating, and after three attempts, they gave up. Like one-third of women in the United States, I ended up having a Cesarean. My husband and I shared the surreal experience of going into an operating room, with me, naked from the waist down, legs splayed open on a table, surrounded by total strangers who barely acknowledged me in any way. I was awake and shaking violently, as a doctor I didn't recognize, since my regular physician was unavailable, cut through seven layers of my abdomen and pulled out my daughter.

A Cesarean may have been mercifully quick compared with a protracted labor, but recovery took more than a month and was grueling. In addition to all of the regular messy, uncomfortable, and wet realities of giving birth, it is hard to handle and feed a newborn while recovering from major abdominal surgery. It's harder still if you are breastfeeding and develop mastitis, a common mammary gland infection related to breastfeeding. I tried to avoid pain relievers because I was worried about their presence in breast milk.

Two years later, my second pregnancy was also high risk, as I was carrying twins. Twenty-four weeks in, I began contracting. At twenty-eight weeks, I developed tachycardia. My at-rest heartbeat raced at between 120 and 140 beats per minute. The only meaningful improvement would come once I gave birth, but, in the interest of having babies able to breathe on their own, labor had to be forestalled until as late as possible. By the end of my term, I had gained more than half of my prepregnancy body weight.

Every day, twenty-four hours a day, I wore both a contractions monitor and a heart monitor. Small electronic boxes, wires, and fabric straps covered my body, which made holding my two-year-old challenging, let alone bathing, changing, working, using the bathroom, and sleeping. The prescribed anticontraction medication, the side effects of which included anxiety and paranoia, made the tachycardia worse and regularly set off the heart monitor, necessitating routine trips to the emergency room and overnight stays. My cardiologist and ob-gyn were not communicating. I eventually took myself off the anticontraction medication because I could no longer tolerate my heart beating wildly or the paranoia I was, indeed, developing.

I worried every minute of every day that something life altering and potentially tragic could happen to me, the babies, and my family. This wasn't an abstract fear. In between my pregnancies, my cousin had died while giving birth to her third child in a major US hospital. And only months after this happened, a close friend developed massive hemorrhaging as the result of giving birth and had to be raced from one DC hospital to another. A woman I worked with was mourning the full-term stillborn deaths of her brother's twins. Every time I visited the hospital, which I was doing two or three times a week, there were pregnant women experiencing everything from healthy pregnancies to scary and often physically traumatizing ones.

I was fortunate in that I had a supportive spouse, health insurance, and access to good care, but I was also in a Catholic hospital, which, studies show, might put women at greater risk when they are pregnant and going through childbirth. I liked and trusted my doctors, but I knew that they were beholden to the Catholic Church's Ethical and Religious Directives (ERDs), guidelines based on beliefs that I find deeply hostile to women. A patient's preferences might end up taking a back seat to ERDs that have developed culturally—even if women are part of review boards—in the near-complete historical absence of women or ethics informed by women's experiences. In the United States, many women have no choice but to go to Catholic hospitals, which currently make up 12 percent of all the hospital beds.

In 2009 Sister Margaret McBride, a Roman Catholic hospital administrator in Phoenix, was caught in the crosshairs of this reality. She saved the life of a twenty-seven-year-old woman who arrived at the hospital three months pregnant and suffering from dangerous pulmonary hypertension. McBride, on the hospital's ethics committee, approved a procedure that would save the woman's life but ended the pregnancy, arguing that abortion was not its primary objective. The young mother of four lived, but McBride was excommunicated.

"The mother's life cannot be preferred over the child's," read the bishop's statement in explaining why both the mother and McBride were excommunicated.

According to a 2016 Merger Watch and American Civil Liberties Union report, Mercy Health Partners, an Ohio- and Kentucky-based Roman Catholic health organization, endangered the lives of women by forcing them to undergo dangerous miscarriages in lieu of safer and healthier options. Similarly, a Catholic hospital in

Michigan refused to induce labor for a woman exhibiting symptoms of a life-threatening infection. In another case, a woman in distress was sent home twice, having been given nothing more than an over-the-counter fever reducer. She miscarried in her toilet, by herself. None of these women, all of whom were less than twenty-four weeks pregnant, was informed by her hospital that she had medical options. Instead, they were left in medical limbo to experience protracted, painful, and dangerous miscarriages or, eventually, surgery that could have been avoided.

Religious preferences and a willingness to sacrifice women, not the word of God, are what overruled sound medical protocols that would have saved Savita Halappanavar, a thirty-one-year-old pregnant woman who died in an Irish hospital in 2012. Her husband's harrowing account detailed the days leading to her death by septicemia. The hospital refused to perform a life-saving pregnancy termination, despite the couple's pleas. When I first learned of her death, I assumed that the hospital was Catholic, but I was wrong. It was not, which was almost *worse*. "This is a Catholic country," Halappanavar and her husband were told. Is this a good place to mention that thousands of priests who have molested children are still Catholics in good standing?

A gestating girl or woman is perceived by many people as a carrier, a baby machine, a vessel, or, as an Oklahoma state representative asserted recently, a "host" who "invites" a baby in. Women are not hotels, or inns, or beakers, or vials, either, even if they are treated as though they are. In March 2017 E. Scott Lloyd, director of the US Office of Refugee Resettlement, decided that an undocumented teenage girl, "Jane Doe," who had been raped and impregnated, should not have an abortion. He was convinced that, despite her wishes, "assisting with an abortion in this case is not in her best interest." One man had raped the seventeen-year-old, and now another was denying her the right to terminate the pregnancy. After Doe and three other girls in similar circumstances took the administration to court, it was revealed that Lloyd, a longtime antiabortion crusader, had discussed subjecting the teen to a scientifically unproven and highly controversial procedure meant to "reverse" a medically induced abortion midway by administering progesterone against her will.

"Seriously. Understand what this means," tweeted reproductive rights expert Robin Marty at the time. "The Trump administration had discussions about performing medical experiments on an undocumented minor simply because she was in their custody and they thought they could."

I challenge anyone to argue that the hundreds of millions of girls and women being treated in these ways because they are girls and women aren't seething with frustration, resentment, and anger. They are rarely asked how they feel about motherhood and its violent coercion. How many times, in article after article, pundit-fueled debate after pundit-fueled debate, have you actually heard girls and women say how this treatment makes *them* feel?

How is anyone supposed to feel when women are at the mercy of people, mostly men, who quite literally know nothing about women? In 2012 a "pro-life" Ohio state legislator was asked why he thought a woman might want to have an abortion. He replied, mystified, "It's a question I've never even thought about." Another male state representative, this one from Georgia, argued for a bill that would make it necessary for some women to carry stillborn or dying fetuses until they "naturally" go into labor—which he rationalized while describing pigs and cows on his farm. In 2014, ignoring the thirty-two thousand US women impregnated through rape each year, yet a third pronounced, "If it's a legitimate rape, the female body has ways to try to shut that whole thing down." Not to be outdone, in 2015 a man trying to legislatively ban telemedical abortions (in which patients consult with a remote, not an in-person, doctor) wondered if a gynecological exam could be performed by having a woman swallow a small camera. A doctor testifying at the legislative session had to explain that women's stomachs and vaginas aren't actually connected. These examples may seem like outliers, or even funny, but they are emblematic. Treating women in these ways generates cruel injustices on an unimaginable scale.

Access to abortion, and also birth control, as the standard bearer for reproductive rights, is vitally important, but insufficient. A reproductive *justice* framework is more robust and comprehensive. "[Reproductive Justice] is a political movement that splices reproductive rights with social justice," writes scholar-activist Loretta Ross, who coined the term, working with a group of women of color who recognized the limitations of a rights framework. (Ross is also cofounder of the SisterSong Women of Color Reproductive Justice Collective.) The historical focus on abortion as the central reproductive rights issue in the United States reflected fairly narrowly defined issues of "choices" that were mainly prioritized by white, heterosexual, cisgender women. "Reproductive rights" has and often still fails to recognize the needs and rights of women whose choices are sometimes severely constrained by race, class, gender identity, economics, or disability. This framing also enabled politicians to more easily reduce the conversation, dominated by abortion, to a debate over women's "choice" and people's *opinions* about those choices.

"This myopia not only alienated women of color," writes Dorothy Roberts, author of *Killing the Black Body: Race, Reproduction, and the Meaning of Liberty*, "but also failed to address the connection between criminalization of pregnant women and abortion rights." Reproductive justice, not reproductive rights, asks us as a society to recognize the full context of women's rights and, as Roberts explains, "the right to have children and to raise them with dignity in safe, healthy, and supportive environments."

Reproductive justice should be at the very core of any political agenda that claims to be progressive and that aspires to promote social equality. In the wake of the 2016 US presidential election, conservative and liberal pundits alike called into question support for abortion rights, claiming that this support made it impossible for Democrats to win over moderate voters and to be a truly national party. This signaled a willingness to ignore a woman's human rights, a basic prerequisite to any other objective of a progressive agenda. Ignoring these connections amounts to a foolish and dangerous game in which women become not players but pawns. Abortion, as many advocates point out, cannot and should not be a bargaining chip in legislative and policy making spaces that are, still, remarkably devoid of women in anywhere near parity numbers. Ensuring that women are secure in their fundamental rights, including bodily integrity and autonomy, is a moral imperative that animates all others.

An estimate of 60 percent of women in the United States who have abortions are already mothers, a fact that makes it difficult to argue that women who seek abortions are craven, immoral, selfish baby killers. In this reality, motherhood, for many women, is rooted in the choice *not* to have more children. Most women, with a clear-eyed understanding of what having a child entails, are responding to their circumstances and experiences. They often grapple with work or educational commitments, the financial stresses of low income and poverty, medical costs, and existing child and elder care responsibilities.

Women may seek opinions, medical advice, spiritual guidance, but the decision to continue or terminate a pregnancy is a woman's alone. And it should be a decision that her community supports *because she is making it.*

When women are forced to give birth, there is a far higher likelihood that they will feel anger related *to being mothers.* A 2015 study found that more than 95 percent of women who had ended pregnancies didn't regret their decision. Only 5 percent reported feeling guilt, sadness, or anger. Giving up a child for adoption is significantly more stressful and traumatizing to women, with 95 percent of those who gave up their babies experiencing sadness, guilt, and grief that persist for decades.

Studies conducted in multiple countries show that women who were denied the right to decide if and when to become mothers experience greater sadness, stress, anxiety, anger, and guilt. They are two to three times as likely to develop depression and anxiety. Women denied abortions are far more likely to live in poverty and with long-term economic insecurity than women whose desire to end a pregnancy is respected.

The anger women experience over being forced to give birth against their wishes is often expressed as resentment of their unwanted children. One study found that one-third of women who were prevented from terminating their pregnancies describe long-term resentment of their offspring and were aware that these feelings were related to neglect and poor parenting. For example, they are less inclined to show affection. Children who were unwanted are also more likely to have cognitive developmental issues and are more inclined toward delinquency and bullying other children.

Many women don't want to get pregnant, have babies, or be mothers, and for this, they are considered freakish, incomplete, unfeminine, and even ignorant about their "real" desires. Doctors, for example, sometimes actively resist patient requests for sterilization because they believe that they know better than women themselves do. (That resistance is, however, infused with institutional racism when you consider repeated incidents of women of color being sterilized nonconsensually in hospitals and prisons, a practice only, for example, barred in California in 2014 after an investigative report found that nearly 140 women were sterilized while incarcerated, without consenting properly, a practice with an ugly eugenics history.)

Despite pressures and objections, more women today are deliberately choosing not to have children than ever before. A child-free woman is never given the freedom from social opprobrium that a child-free man is, however. The choice not to have children inevitably means being shamed, insulted, and even bullied, often by family members. Women who make this decision have to deal with insensitive "jokes," most hiding a genuine discomfort and hostility, about ticking clocks, being cat ladies, or not being "real" women. And people, apparently unable to see themselves clearly in a mirror, ask why more women today are choosing to be child-free.

Women who openly share their misgivings with being mothers, even if they chose to do so, are treated with even more suspicion than women who have chosen to be child free. In 2015 Israeli sociologist Orna Donath published a study of two dozen women who were willing to discuss maternal regret. Motherhood, she wrote, "may be a font of personal fulfillment, pleasure, love, pride, contentment, and joy," but it can also "simultaneously be a realm of distress, helplessness, frustration, hostility, and disappointment, as well as an arena of oppression and subordination." The women Donath spoke to consistently made the distinction that many people don't—and don't want to—namely, between their children and the experience of motherhood and the essentialist views of female identity that come with it. Donath sees maternal regret as an essential addition to our understanding of what it means to be a woman and a mother. Regret, she believes, plays an important role in challenging embedded ideologies and systems of power.

Women in Germany, interestingly, given their greater historic comfort with expressing anger, compared to American women, have grabbed the topic of mother regret by the horns. In *The Mother Bliss Lie: Regretting Motherhood*, author Sarah Fischer examines the disparate impacts that parenthood has on mothers and fathers and expresses the anger women feel over the imbalances. In *The Abolishment of the Mother*, Alina Bronsky and Denise Wilk talk about how motherhood ideals undermine women's ability to function as full citizens and workers. After these books were published, a German columnist described "regretters" who share their feelings as child abusers.

Mother regret sounds like a luxury to women who struggle to have children or have no choice but to leave their children. Indeed, mothers who express frustration, regret, and anger might anger *other women*.

When my aunt and her husband moved to the United States from Haiti, they had to depart the country in pressing circumstances that required leaving their three young children in the care of her parents for several years. Later, my aunt became a nanny to other people's children. She was smart, soft-spoken, curious, funny, sweet, well read, and intelligent. She missed her children but did not pour sadness or resentment into her caring for others. She did not distribute her affection on the basis of how much she was being paid, but cared deeply for her charges, staying in touch with them long into their adulthood. Like all child care workers, she forged a complicated relationship with them and their parents, primarily their mother.

Most people, needing help raising their children, don't want to think of this kind of child care in terms of the commodification of maternal ideals. And yet we as a society often demand that immigrant and impoverished women meet these ideals while simultaneously denying them the ability, by socially maintaining their low status, low wages, and lack of benefits or childcare support, to mother their own children. I have often heard people express love for the women who care for their children and then, in the same sentence, admit to not even knowing if they have their own. The emotional labor and emotional costs of this work can be immense.

The pressure women feel to be mothers or to fulfill ideals of maternal care, however, is perhaps most powerful, onerous, and painful for women who experience infertility, pregnancy loss, or the death of a child. These experiences can be filled with sadness, exhaustion, guilt, and remorse that are compounded by crushing social silence around loss.

Roughly 10 percent of women in the United States experience infertility, and a large number pursue lengthy, physically grueling, and expensive procedures to conceive. Anger can feel like a constant companion in the face of frustration with your body, financial stresses, and the unintentional insensitivity of friends, family, and strangers. It is an almost certain and predictable outcome of dealing with endless tests, schedules, sex on demand, insurance requirements, and interference with work.

Addressing an enduring concern, researchers have found that suppressed anger and stress negatively affect the efficacy of fertility treatments. One study of women in California revealed that women who reported higher levels of anger and depression had fewer fertilized eggs. Women with polycystic ovary syndrome (PCOS), a prevalent cause of infertility, report more difficulty labelling and sharing feelings of anger and suffer from higher rates of depression. Powerful negative emotions alter brain chemistry and hormone production in ways that reduce the likelihood of implantation. Again, this is not, of course, to say that anger causes infertility, but unrecognized or unaddressed anger interferes with conception. "Reduce the stress in your life" is common advice that rarely goes to the heart of what is generating the stress that women feel.

Women often endure infertility, pregnancy, infant loss, miscarriages, and stillbirths in isolation, because while sadness is a socially palatable response to these often life-altering events, rage, frustration, jealousy, and guilt are not. Some women are able to respond to miscarriages with little or no grief. However, many feel deep despair, with some saying that their feelings of anger and sadness far exceed what most people understand. It is common for women to feel as though they are careening between anger, envy, and sadness from day to day. It is very difficult to talk about how angry and full of shame these losses can make us. When having a baby is seen as a type of success, then not having a baby is a failure that can fill us with feelings of inadequacy.

A typical social response to a woman who has miscarried, had a late-term pregnancy loss, stillbirth, or lost a child soon after birth is that she "try again." This strikes me as heartless and tone-deaf advice.

My sister was two weeks overdue with her second child when she experienced almost 100 percent placental abruption, a potentially deadly condition in which a woman's placenta detaches from the uterine wall. Prior to conceiving, she was, at five foot five, a scant 105 pounds. A week after her due date, and carrying a fully developed baby weighing more than 9 pounds, she asked to be induced, but her doctor felt that labor should happen "naturally." It had been a very difficult pregnancy in which she was sick almost every day. She was huge, hugely uncomfortable, unable to sleep, taking care of her toddler and husband, and exhausted. She felt strongly that she needed to have her baby as soon as possible. What she thought, what she knew, and how she felt, however, were not, in the end, what mattered. What her doctor considered natural is what mattered. A woman's confidence in the sense she has of her own body and needs is, in fact, what ends up seeming unnatural.

"Naturally" ended up meaning she woke up one night bleeding excessively. It meant that she had an emergency C-section after the administration of only a local anesthesia. It meant that she lost massive quantities of blood and almost died. Her baby did. This was what is called a "traumatic birth," words that simply cannot capture what happened to her and her family. The only small grace is that she cannot remember much of these details.

Thirty hours after she gave birth, learned of her loss, and was finally asleep, a man walked into her room, unannounced. It was two in the morning. He turned on the lights, waking her and my brother-in-law. Ignoring her, he arrogantly told her husband to expect strange behavior because, "Women sometimes lose their minds." He was the hospital therapist.

Words escape most of us in the face of tragedies like this. Dr. Jennifer Gunther, a physician and reproductive rights activist who similarly lost a son, describes belonging to "the saddest sorority of mothers: those who gave birth but have no baby."

Every year, tens of thousands of women have stillbirths, and thousands more have babies that do not live beyond the first week or two of life. A lack of openness and social support frequently leaves women to their own devices, in grief, bewilderment, and anger, and still experiencing the aftereffects of pregnancy and childbirth. "Moms who lose their babies are not able to show the world their mother-ness," explains Kate Kripke, a clinical social worker who specializes in the prevention and treatment of perinatal and postpartum mood and anxiety disorders.

What my sister needed was not people urging her, as so many did, to get pregnant again as soon as possible, but acknowledgment of her loss and the violence that she experienced in that loss. She needed to know that this was not a failure or that she was a bad mother. She needed to be allowed to be not only sad but also, in her grief, to be angry. But as Gunther explained, "Society does not like to hear from us castaway mothers."

Motherhood is central to our social perception of women: single women, childless women, wives, mothers—all women. As a life experience, it is complex and joyful, life altering in virtually every way imaginable. But this ideal is often used as a cudgel, and that has to stop in order for women to be free.

In motherhood, we can find joy, love, security, community, and, for many women, life's greatest purpose. It is not and should not be, however, the inevitable path for all girls and women; the standard against which we are all measured. It is a basic human decency to create a society in which motherhood is not wielded as a weapon against women, in which it is not coerced, forced, punishing, violent, and life threatening.

The immense social expectations of motherhood can power-fully choke the anger they provoke. Do women have the right to be angry at being denied the right to control what happens to and in their own bodies? Do women have the right to be angry when they are forced to undergo dangerous and humiliating procedures? Can we openly share our resentments and frustrations with the pressure put on us to give birth and sacrifice in silence?

So much mother-related rage comes from desires that we have as *nonreproductive* people. If we are mothers, we are allowed to be angry about what happens to our children and families, we are allowed to be angry *at* our families and children as mothers and partners, but we are not allowed to be angry about what happens to *us* in the experience and expectations of motherhood.

If we can recognize the common experience of intense anger after a person experiences stress or trauma, or even the anger that might come from slamming a finger in a car door, why can't we admit to feelings of intense anger related to the circumstances of pregnancy, childbirth, and motherhood? Or anger related to being treated as a vessel or a baby-making machine? Or anger related to suddenly knowing that your primary intimate relationship is not as egalitarian as you think? Or anger related to being thought of as less committed or capable at work? Or anger that might come from shock at the aftereffects of giving birth? These are issues we rarely discuss openly, particularly in mixed gender company, as though talking about them is shameful or weak. As if to say that to admit to these shifts and injuries is to admit that we aren't "woman enough" or "mother enough."

For women who have children, motherhood becomes defining, and the love that we feel for our children is often overwhelming. We care in so many ways, but for motherhood to be truly dignified, compassionate, purposeful, and fulfilling, it must presume a woman's right to freely choose to be a parent. Unfortunately, this is not the world we live in. Instead, motherhood, the ideal, smothers women's ability to protest unfairness and injustice. The challenge we face is in being unapologetic about our desires and decisions and in not judging other women's choices. It is in rechanneling the anger, guilt, and shame that we often encounter into creating a culture that no longer conflates the word *woman* with *mother* and the word *mother* with *sacrifice*.

SMILE, BABY

Anger is one letter short of danger.
—Eleanor Roosevelt

On a recent fall day, I found myself in New York's Penn Station having an experience familiar to most women. I had missed a train to DC by what felt like seconds. As I stood in the midst of a jostling crowd trying to figure out what to do next, a man passed his hand along my upper arm and whispered the classic chestnut, "You'd be prettier if you smiled." I was forty-eight at the time and could not remember a time or place where I hadn't experienced intrusions like this, many of which were far more threatening.

What if I didn't smile? What would he do? Would he mutter "Bitch" as he brushes by? Or scream "Fucking cunt!" at the top of his lungs? As I stood in Penn Station, frozen, dozens of prior interactions

like these flew through my mind. I was angry, but I had learned long
ago that reacting in anger might lead to worse outcomes.

I was nine the first time a boy threatened me with rape in a
schoolyard, telling me that no one was there to help me if he did.
When I was fourteen, a man grabbed me by the arm and jerked
me around sharply so that he could "get a good look." When I was
twenty, a group of men pulled my boyfriend's arm off of my shoulder
so they could grab my bottom. Only weeks before the train incident,
a man had followed my daughters and me up the front stairs of our
house. I noticed him only after unlocking the door, when, standing
right behind us, he said, "Can I come in with you?" I've lost track,
there are so many stories.

In cases like these, I usually freeze—like many of us do. My brain
and heart race to determine the nature of the risk and calibrate my
response. However, on the day when I was fourteen, and the man
grabbed my arm, I didn't freeze: I punched him hard in his windpipe.
This was my first memory of blinding visceral rage in these circumstances. He yelled, cursing as I ran. It was the first and last time I
allowed my anger to overcome my fear. I was acutely aware of the
danger. It was also an important marker in my life, one I distinctly
remember as a building block in the self-limiting wall I constructed
around my freedom of speech and movement.

Most of these incidents occur in broad daylight, in spaces filled
with people, but it is so normal in some places that no one stops,
says anything, or pauses to intervene.

Everywhere, we learn to adapt to boys and men hissing obsceni-
ties, making sexual suggestions, touching us intimately, lurking on
stoops, staring from benches, following us on foot and in cars, and
generally refusing to keep their hands, thoughts, and desires to
themselves. I'd grown up seeing this happening to my mother, aunts,
and grandmother my entire life, yet no one ever talked about it.

Anger is typically considered the "fight" instinct to fear's "flight"
in the face of a threat. But to juxtapose anger and fear in this way

suggests that they are isolated from each other, which is a misrepresentation. In moments like these, anger and fear are indistinguishable, stewed together with confusion and humiliation.

It is absurd that every day women have to contend with the possibility that they will be attacked verbally or physically. When women leave their homes, they consider the possibility, however remote, of being mutilated, terrorized, or killed for not acceding to the demands of aggressive men. As women, we can lose our dignity and any sense of safety or feelings of rights to public space that we might have—all on someone else's whim. This is how we come to accept the harsh fact of our violability. We bite our tongues, sometimes until they bleed.

To be sure, there are pleasant and friendly exchanges to be had with men who are unthreatening and flirtatious. Even at young ages, many of us create our own screening mechanisms: some men are dangerous, some men are simply flirting. I know many girls who are flattered when they are first harassed and even more women who bemoan the loss of attention as they age. But behind it all, we can't truly know which men are harmless. And the cost of being wrong is high. Everyone has her own reaction. But I am personally so fed up with this continued harassment that I can barely contain myself when it happens. And I shouldn't have to.

"God should have made girls lethal / when he made monsters of men," writes poet Elisabeth Hewer. A world full of women who smile on demand is a world where women's anger is irrelevant and where the threat of male violence is legitimized. That's why no woman ever wants to hear the two little words "Smile, baby . . ."

According to multiple large-scale studies conducted and compiled by the nonprofit organization Stop Street Harassment, between 65 percent and 98 percent of women worldwide have experienced persistent street harassment that alters the course of their day. In the United States, 65 percent of women reported being harassed. A similar study, conducted by Cornell University and antiharassment advocacy group Hollaback! found comparably high rates globally, including the finding that more than 50 percent of women representing twenty-two countries have been groped in public. In Germany, that number is 66 percent, with 71 percent of women reporting being followed—the majority more than once. More than half of women who say they have been harassed in the United States remember being younger than seventeen the first time it happened. Across Europe, more than 81 percent of women report being harassed before the age of seventeen. Globally, 84 percent of women say the same, many also citing ages as young as nine and ten. In India, 47 percent of women have had a man expose his genitals. One in sixteen women in that country say they don't like to go out at night for fear of harassment and assault. In Nassau, Bahamas, where I grew up, unrelenting street harassment continues to plague girls and women.

For women with disabilities who frequently navigate difficult public space, street harassment is cruelly adaptive, with men, for example, positioning their crotches in the faces of women using wheelchairs. Rubbing salt in the wound is the idiotic suggestion that women with disabilities should *appreciate* the attention because it is humanizing in the sense that they are often not seen as sexual beings. "Sexual harassment when coupled with disability does not actually reinforce a disabled sexual identity in a culture that continues to ignore that disabled people are sexual beings," explained disability critical studies PhD candidate Kim Sauder after the publication of a related 2016 *New York Times* article. "Downplaying the harm of street harassment not only erases the real harm it causes nondisabled women who experience it regularly but also ignores that some disabled women do experience it and that it only makes them less safe not more fully human."

Gay, lesbian, nonbinary, and trans people also suffer high rates of street harassment, often physically violent. In 2013 the European Union surveyed almost ninety-five thousand LGBTQ people. Fully half said they deliberately avoided public spaces because they feared being harassed. In the United States, similarly high rates have been documented.

Sexual harassment and violence are so normalized among girls and women that they don't often consciously register them as abusive behaviors. In a study of teenage girls, one fifteen-year-old responded to questions about harassment by explaining, "I pretty much expect to be groped and touched by random guys every time I leave my home in the morning." In this environment, many of us are happy that there is no "real" violence. But some of us don't escape its threat.

In 2003 twenty-nine-year-old Richard McCullough stabbed fifteen-year-old Sakia Gunn at a New Jersey bus stop after she rebuffed him. Gunn told McCullough she was gay. He was charged with a bias crime. In the summer of 2013, twenty-one-year-old Islan Nettles, a transgender woman in New York, was killed by a group of men in what *New York* magazine called a "come-on gone wrong." Nettles's brutal murder, investigated as a hate crime, was one of the more visible in a steady stream of similar attacks on black trans women that continues today. Lesbians, gay men, and trans people in South Africa are often, like Gunn, "correctively" raped and killed.

My husband and I are often acutely aware of how differently we are experiencing the same space. During a recent trip to an unfamiliar city, we set out early one morning with our daughters for a daylong walk to a landmark. As we got closer to our destination, we realized that we couldn't possibly make it in the time we had designated. He looked at a map, we chose a faster and less scenic route, and set off anew at a quicker pace. As he walked, my daughters and I, without speaking, began to slow down and cluster together. Somewhere along our route, women had slowly disappeared. Now none was visible anywhere, and men were standing in twos and threes in doorways and narrow alleys, staring at us. We shrank ourselves in to a dense hub of femininity.

In my experience, most men don't learn, as boys, to think about how different their experiences are from those of the girls and women around them. Men learn to regard rape as a moment in time; a discreet episode with a beginning, middle, and end. But for women, rape is thousands of moments that we fold into ourselves over a lifetime.

It's the day that you realize you can't walk to a friend's house anymore or the time when your aunt tells you to be nice because the boy was just "stealing a kiss." It's the evening you stop going to the corner store because, the night before, a stranger followed you home. It's the late hour that a father or stepfather or brother or uncle climbs into your bed. It's the time it takes you to write an email explaining that you're changing your major, even though you don't really want to, in order to avoid a particular professor. It's when you're racing to catch a bus, hear a person demand a blow job, and turn to see that it's a police officer. It's the second your teacher tells you to cover your shoulders because you'll "distract the boys, and what will your male teachers do?" It's the minute you decide not to travel to a place you've always dreamed about visiting and are accused of being "unadventurous." It's the sting of knowing that exactly as the world starts expanding for most boys, it begins to shrink for you. All of this goes on all day, every day, without anyone really uttering the word *rape* in a way that grandfathers, fathers, brothers, uncles, teachers, and friends will hear it, let alone seriously reflect on what it means. This is not to say that boys and men cannot or do not suffer assaults, because they certainly do. It is, instead, to clarify the ways in which the reality and threat of male-perpetrated sexual violence is normalized in the lives of girls and women as a restrictive force.

Sometimes there is a dawning realization, and it is painful. One father I know whose daughters were on the cusp of leaving for college said to me one day, "If you think about rape, it will drive you crazy." I don't know if he was more upset before or after I told him that they were already past a red zone—that 44 percent of rapes occur before victims are eighteen.

That day on our family trip, when I explained to my husband that we needed to take the longer way around the neighborhood, he was flummoxed and exasperated. We said we would meet him, but we wouldn't continue. Together we rerouted the rest of the walk. It was interesting, though, that his initial reaction, irritation, I felt, was directed at me and not at the fact that this was a common inconvenience in our lives. I, too, was irritated and angry, but who was I going to be angry with? The men in the alley? The women who raised them? The religions that empowered them? The laws that failed to protect women from being harassed? I couldn't do any of those things.

Street harassment, a situation that highlights the fact that women can't say "no" to men and be safe, is routinely minimized despite known harms, two of which are increased anxiety and hypervigilance.

Researchers at Virginia's University of Mary Washington wanted to understand the effect of unwanted sexual advances and the increased self-surveillance that comes with sexualization. They looked at the relationship between harassment, objectification, body evaluation, and depression and shame, and discovered that a large number of women experience what the study's authors called "insidious trauma" over time, leading to the development of symptoms associated with post-traumatic stress disorder. If a woman had been sexually assaulted, the results were much stronger. These dynamics can also often leave the victim feeling disassociated from her own body. When I read this study I had a genuine *aha!* moment. It was not until I was well into my forties that I realized how, in response to learning to think of my body as a source of danger and vulnerability, I had come to feel it was not "mine."

Doctors have long puzzled over why, if some women don't go to war, they exhibit higher levels of post-traumatic stress than men. Unwanted sexual advances, objectification, and persistent harassment are partially to blame. But so too is a cultivated awareness of threat and elevated anger. Media rarely link street harassment with greater crimes, even when the connection is vivid. Publicized but decontextualized cases are routinely in the news: for example, a man hurling a bowling ball at a woman's head after she declined his offer to buy her a drink or another who smashed a glass over a woman's head when she wouldn't dance with him. In 2014 a Florida man in a car offered a fourteen-year-old schoolgirl $200 to have sex with him; when she refused, he pulled her by the hair into his car, choking her until she fainted. He then threw her out of the car and ran over her several times as people nearby watched, stunned. She lived to identify him to the police. In 2009 a woman died when catcallers in a van drove up onto the sidewalk, striking her and her friend. Only weeks before, another woman was run over by a man after she turned down his offer for a ride. In San Francisco, a man stabbed a woman in the face and arm when she rebuffed him. Women runners and bikers, those at bus stops and bars, all know the hazards. These stories are easy to find.

Girls and women adapt to these intrusions, usually by not talking about them, blaming themselves, or doing their best to ignore what is happening around them. There is an additional aspect, however, that often goes unremarked upon. "I've been taught there are greater needs in the community. Perhaps this is part of the reason studies indicate only one in fifteen African American women reports being raped. We've seen the unchecked power of white men ravish our communities, and we carry the message of 'not right now' when it comes to addressing our pain if the offender is black," explained writer Shanita Hubbard in late 2017. Hubbard was talking about how awareness of the threat to black boys and men, of violence and incarceration, inhibits black girls and women who have been harassed and assaulted from coming forward. She was writing specifically about #MeToo, a global movement revealing the reality and effects of male-perpetrated harassment and assault, but this issue is applicable to other contexts. "When your community fights for those same people who terrorize you, it sends a very complicated and mixed message . . . that your pain is not a priority."

In the early days of 2016, twenty-nine-year-old Janese Talton-Jackson was approached outside of a Pittsburgh bar by a man who asked for her phone number. When she wouldn't give it to him, he shot her to death on the sidewalk. Months before Talton-Jackson was killed, another man, angry that a woman had refused his advances, broke through the front door of the woman's apartment and, when he found she wasn't home, threw her puppy out of a third-floor window. Meanwhile, in Florida, police were trying to find a man serially harassing women real estate agents.

Of course, it's not only street harassment or strangers. The same male entitlement behind these propositions and the violent retaliation when men are spurned is what lies behind obfuscating language about "unrequited love," "teenage passion," and boys who "snap." For example, in 2014 sixteen-year-old Maren Sanchez was killed by a classmate whom she'd turned down for the high school prom. As I wrote this chapter, police revealed that, in 2016, sixteen-year-old Shemel Mercurius of Brooklyn was shot by a twenty-five-year-old man who wanted to date her. When she refused, he shot her three times with a submachine gun.

"Vulnerability is not an inherent characteristic of women's bodies," explains Sara Ahmed in *The Cultural Politics of Emotion*. "Rather, it is an effect that works to secure femininity as a delimitation of movement in the public and an overinhabitance in the private."

Harassment and the ever-present suggestions of violence at this scale constantly reminds women and girls of their place. For the most part, girls' and women's experiences with harassment are still cloaked in silence, and we continue, as a global society, to peddle dangerous advice to girls about "staying safe." This isn't about safety. If it were, we'd teach boys, who are also subject to childhood molestation and risk, the same lessons, but we don't. It's about social control.

ANGER, HARASSMENT, VIOLENCE, AND HYPERVIGILANCE

There is deep cultural resistance to taking women's fears of male violence seriously. Ultimately, in the face of what is clear social, legal, and political inequality, it is rape that keeps women, women's physical freedom, and women's rage, in check. Women's experiences of harassment carry the psychological resonance of actual rape threats, a proposition that strikes some people as ridiculous.

A 2015 study found that women's fears of crime are made worse by exposure to sexually objectifying experiences and media, and amplified by the awareness that, whatever crime they might be victimized by, they might *additionally* be raped. African American women experience higher rates of street harassment and sexual objectification, as well as higher levels of fear related to crime, which they are exposed to more.

In 2016, Australian researchers asked women to record instances of harassment or witnessing harassment over a one-week period. The tally, on average, came to one episode every other day. They witnessed other women being targeted 1.35 times a week. These incidents, consciously or not, contribute to women's awareness of vulnerability.

Women are almost twice as likely as men to worry that an incident of harassment will escalate into a more dangerous situation. When people roll their eyes at the suggestion that women's brains go so quickly to rape, or, say, make jokes about women going to the ladies' room together, I'm the fun-killer who snarkily reminds them that we are taught to do this as girls, so that men can't rape us.

Ask a woman if she has been harassed, or if she thinks about rape regularly, and she will almost always say "no" initially. Who wants to think about rape? Ask her, however, if she makes eye contact when she walks down the street, where and when she loiters for pleasure on a warm day, if she runs by herself at night, or if she pays for cabs instead of peacefully strolling home. Then ask her why. We are taught to fear rape but not to question its pervasive threat or doubt how "natural" it is or isn't. I realize that this is an idea that even many women, loath to associate themselves with "victimhood," reject.

Every woman has a rape story, whether she has been sexually assaulted or not. Probably more than one. In a 2014 essay, writer Leslie Jamison described a college classroom discussion prompted by the instructor's asking the students, all women, to share their worst fears. "So the first girl said, 'Getting raped, I guess,' which is what we were all thinking. The next one upped the ante: 'Getting raped—and then killed.' The third paused to think, then said: 'Maybe getting gang-raped?' The fourth had had time to think and had already anticipated the third one's answer. She said, 'Getting gang-raped and mutilated.' I can't remember what the rest of us managed to come up with (Sex trafficking? Snuff films?), but I remember thinking how odd it was—how we were all sitting there trying to be the best kid in class, the worst-rape fantasizer, in this all-girl impersonation of a misogynistic hate-crime brainstorming session. We were giggling. Our giggling was—of course—also about our fear."

When I started discussing rape openly and writing about it in explicit terms, many people I knew seemed horrified. After a while, however, they got used to it, and after a while longer, they started to talk about it as well. Women I'd known for years shared incidents from their pasts that they hadn't consciously linked to rape. One had fought off an ex-boyfriend who had climbed into her college dorm room through a window. Another, at a crowded party, had locked herself in a bathroom and climbed *out* of a window to avoid someone's relentless pursuit. A third described an assault but couldn't say the word *rape*. A fourth described sitting in a subway car that emptied out. "I would never have gotten on if the car had been empty," she said. After a man got on and sat in the seat next to her, she got off of the train, which meant she was then left on an empty platform in the middle of the night.

At one point, I was talking to a woman who claimed rape wasn't a problem where she lived. I pointed out gently that she lived in one of at least ten countries in the world, the Bahamas, where marital rape is not illegal. (In the United States, marital rape was still not illegal in some states until 1993.) Her response was, "Oh, well, in that case, absolutely. I'm one of those." One woman, in her sixties, wrote to say that her brother's two best friends had raped her on a footpath fifty years earlier. After the incident, she'd had to sit with them regularly at dinner, petrified. The first time she'd said anything to anyone about what happened was in her email to me. Every one of these women, once she voiced what had happened to her, also talked about her anger. Often, they were explicit about the way that shame and self-silencing had allowed those feelings to fester, with corrosive effects on their lives. The most common thread in these conversations, for women, is, "I didn't tell anyone," and "Why did I put up with this?" For men? "I had no idea that this is happening," or, conversely, "You're exaggerating."

Women spend insane amounts of time and money avoiding rape, fearing it, experiencing it, and denying what it means. In what may be the perfect example of a "good" rape joke, one that punches up, comedian Wanda Sykes sums up how so many of us feel: "I would like a break. . . . Wouldn't it be wonderful if our pussies were detachable?"

Give it time; I hear robots are coming to save women from rape.

LOOKING UGLY TRUTHS IN THE EYE

In the United States, a person is sexually assaulted every two minutes, women making up the vast majority of targets. A woman's chance of being sexually assaulted in her lifetime is one in five. For men, it's one in seventy-seven. Assaults of male victims, even more underreported than those of women and girls, take place primarily before adulthood. New research and definitions of rape (which include, for example, anal and oral rape) reveal higher rates of male victimization than previously understood. Current data, however, indicate that more than 80 percent of juvenile victims are girls, while 90 percent of adult survivors are women. Perpetrators are overwhelmingly male. Three-fourths of rape victims know their assailants. Additionally, the prevalence of sexual assault on college and university campuses is a worldwide phenomenon. Decades of work support the finding that, on average, one in five women undergraduates experience sexual assault, with LGBTQ students suffering the highest rates.

The role that structural discrimination plays in sexual violence is evident in patterns of rape. Indigenous women report the highest levels of assault globally. One in three Native American women in the United States will be sexually assaulted in her lifetime, for example. Native American girls and women are the only demographic cohort more likely to be assaulted by men outside of their own ethnic group. Almost 60 percent of young black women have experienced some form of sexualized assault, usually before they turn eighteen. "Many girls who experience sexual abuse are routed into the juvenile justice system because of their victimization," concluded a 2016 report. "Indeed, sexual abuse is one of the primary predictors of girls' entry into the juvenile justice system."

Women in prisons are more likely than men to be targets of inmate-on-inmate sexual assault. However, given the disproportionate number of males in US prisons—despite women being the fastest-growing segment of the American prison population—it is possible that more boys and men are sexually assaulted in jail than are all women in the United States. Very little attention is paid, in media or socially, to what these assaults represent or the havoc they wreak on the assaulted. Mainly, however, rape is a problem in families: 43 percent of all reported sexual assaults happen before victims are seventeen, which means that a significant number of them involve incest.

These are statistics, but each and every data point is a person who, willingly or not, almost always feels intense anger at his or her violation and society's carelessness.

Conservatives like to debate rape statistics, which has always made me wonder, what is their Goldilocks number? What exact number of rapes is not too high, not too low, but *just* right? What makes a rape "legitimate" in the eyes of conservatives? Certainly not victims' anger, suffering, or ideas about assault. Mainly, it is some throwback idea tied to notions of property violation or a moral infraction on the part of the victim. Today there is no law giving rapists the right to rape, but fewer than 3 percent of rapists, the overwhelming majority of whom are men, are ever prosecuted and imprisoned. More than half of US states allow rapists to sue for custody of children born of their raping. Rape laws have always reflected how we feel about people's relative citizenship rights.

Rape is the most underreported crime in the world. It's a problem in schools. The Catholic Church. Synagogues. Mosques. In Buddhism. Hollywood. The Military. Sports. In homes. In war. A problem at borders. A problem in street gangs. A problem in elder care and institutions. There are virtually no institutions that don't exhibit high tolerance for sexual harassment and assault. And while the rapes of boys and men are far more profuse than anyone is willing to seriously consider, rape is perpetrated, regardless of who is assaulted, overwhelmingly by men and adjudicated in places where men hold far more power. This is not to say that women can't or wouldn't, if granted power and status, assault, but studies show that societies where women have public authority are neither prone to rape nor tolerant of it.

POWER, STATUS, AND HIERARCHY

Ask a man what his greatest fear is about serving jail time, and he will almost inevitably say he fears being raped. What can we deduce from the fact that jail is to men what life is to so many women?

Men's vulnerability to assault in jail is similar to that of boys in now-infamous cases involving the Catholic Church, the BBC, the Boy Scouts, and Penn State. It is much harder for people to ignore allegations of rape when they involve children, particularly boys, or involve men as victims, such as in the military. Prior to October 2017 and the flurry of #MeToo sexual harassment and assault allegations, cases that pitched mainstream media into more aggressive and accurate coverage of sexual violence in the past decade almost all had to do with the rapes of boys, not girls or women. Many of the most shocking and high-profile cases involve all-male or heavily male-dominated hierarchies in which more powerful people use their status and credibility to rape less powerful people. In these institutions, the situation that boys find themselves in is one that is common to women around the world: less powerful, physically smaller, and in dependent positions where higher status and cultural authority give assailants valuable credibility.

Most college students surveyed, for example, believe that up to 50 percent of women lie about being raped. Other studies similarly show that police officers with fewer than eight years of experience also believe roughly that percentage of those alleging rape are lying. As recently as 2003, people jokingly referred to Philadelphia's sex crimes unit as "the lying bitch unit." This doubt remains true despite studies, conducted across multiple countries, consistently finding that the incidence of false rape claims ranges from just 2 percent to 8 percent, approximately the same as it is for any other crime. This myth is one of the more powerful inhibitors of making meaningful change to prevent and reduce rape. Another is the insistence on "staying safe" rules for girls, precautions that routinely limit freedom of movement and expression, that are based on stranger danger beliefs, even though almost 80 percent of victims know their rapists and are attacked in familiar places where they feel safe.

In 2012 the world was forced to pay attention to sexual violence against women by three particularly shocking rape cases: one in India, one in the United States, and a third, less publicized, in Brazil. In December of that year, in the city of Delhi, twenty-three-year-old Jyoti Singh Pandey was tortured on a moving bus by six men who beat, gang-raped, and penetrated her with an iron rod, perforating her colon. She died from her extensive injuries two weeks later. Protest exploded all over the world.

In August 2012, in Steubenville, Ohio, an incapacitated high school girl was carried from one party to the next over the course of several hours by two boys, aged sixteen and seventeen, who assaulted her in various ways. Teenagers posted thousands of images, texts, and comments on social media. A viral photo showed the two boys carrying the unconscious victim by her wrists and ankles through a room. Evidence included a video in which a boy joked, "You don't need any foreplay with a dead girl."

In Brazil, only a few months later, in 2013, a man raped a tourist woman on a busy bus as it drove through Rio de Janeiro. Because she was a tourist, there was global coverage, but stories of women being raped this way on public transportation in country after country are regularly in the news. In April 2016, for example, a man raped a woman at knifepoint on an empty Washington, DC, Metro subway car during a 10 a.m. commute. Four years after the Brazil case, the research institute Datafolha conducted a survey: 35 percent of women said they'd experienced physical, verbal, or other types of sexual abuse on public transportation.

"Anger is a very natural reaction to these situations," explained ElsaMarie D'Silva, an award-winning antiviolence innovator, when I interviewed her about her culture-shifting work. She was one of many women who, in the wake of the assault in Delhi felt the need to "do something." She quit a lucrative corporate job to start Safecity, a crowd-mapping application that lets people track all forms of sexual harassment and violence against women in India.

"I had experiences of gender-based violence when I was growing up," says D'Silva. "I always knew I would do this work, but the clarity came only after this gang rape. Anger played a big role. If it wasn't such a strong emotion, I would not have been courageous enough to take up this work. I have reached a stage where I am slow to anger. I channel it in positive ways. I express it now, but I feel—maybe it's maturity and time—I choose my actions strategically." Her work, and other efforts like it are generational investments, the effects of which will take time to come to fruition.

Rape continues to be pandemic globally and victims still have good cause to be skeptical of institutional commitment to justice. All over the world, sexual violence often seems to be treated, in public as well as in courts, as a matter of opinion and bad behavior, instead of profound violation that has a terroristic effect. In 2018 in London, John Worboys, known as the "black cab rapist," was set to be released from prison after having served his 2009 sentence for multiple assaults. He'd been convicted of nineteen crimes against twelve women, drugging and raping them in his taxi, and he was linked to more than a hundred others. Victims protested Worboys's release, and, as of this writing, he remains in jail.

Women are frequently encouraged to go to the police, but for women, especially women of color, this isn't usually helpful advice. Biases against people reporting rape are well documented, and police officers are sometimes themselves harassers and attackers.

A few years ago, I went for a walk along the Potomac River in Washington, DC, only to be followed, for more than an hour, by a police officer on a motorcycle. He repeatedly drove back and forth alongside the path where I was walking, slowing down as he passed. I took a detour, going out of my way to find a quiet place to sit. Ten minutes later, he drove up and stopped, because he "wanted to talk." He stayed and talked to me for fifteen minutes, asking me my name and where I lived. He ignored every nonverbal cue I sent: I was reading, wearing dark sunglasses, listening to music on headphones, answering in monosyllables, and had, as he knew, left a busy public path to sit quietly alone. He was not threatening, but he was using his position as a police officer in a way that crossed a line.

Only a few years earlier, another officer pulled me over in my car purportedly to show me how to properly set up my children's car seats. I had three children under four and they were tightly squeezed in the back seat. We were on our way home from a community pool, and I was wearing only a bathing suit. He insisted I get out and show him how I strapped the kids in. What was I going to do? I had three tired and cranky babies, it was dinnertime, and we needed to get home. I demonstrated the seat buckling, and he left. It was embarrassing and humiliating. I have no idea why I didn't report him, but I knew that I expected so little.

These were minor incidents, albeit, disturbing. For black women and women of color in particular, however, interactions with law enforcement, sometimes sexualized, sometimes not, can quickly become dangerous, degrading, and even fatal. In early summer 2015, Texas deputies pulled over twenty-one-year-old Charnesia Corley for running a stop sign, a fineable misdemeanor. Their car's dashcam video recorded what a local news report described as an "eleven-minute body cavity search" in the parking lot of a convenience store. According to the lawsuit Corley brought against the county, the officers, three women and a man, stripped off her pants and, spreading open her legs as they flashed a light into her genitals to search for marijuana, "penetrated her vagina." This case was not the first of its kind. In another, officers did not even stop to use clean gloves. Three years later, also in Texas, twenty-eight-year-old Sandra Bland was pulled over for a minor traffic infraction. A dashboard camera showed that the officer failed to adhere to the proper procedures. She was arrested and taken to jail. Three days later, she was found hanging in her cell, in what was ruled an apparent suicide. Her family eventually won a wrongful death lawsuit.

Sexual misconduct is the second most common type of police misconduct in the United States. Sometimes it spills over into gross perpetration. Women of color, trans women, sex workers, and immigrant women, already more vulnerable to violence, are subject to constant overpolicing that almost always itself carries the threat of violence.

In 2015 former Oklahoma City police officer and serial rapist Daniel Holtzclaw was convicted of more than thirty counts of rape, sexual battery, and other related crimes. (He was found guilty of eighteen out of thirty-six.) He identified vulnerable targets, many of whom had criminal records, so their credibility was called into question more easily. Eventually thirteen women, out of an unknown total assaulted, testified against him. He was sentenced to 263 years in jail. Crimes like these exist alongside the fact that in city after city across the United States hundreds of thousands of rape kits, gathered over decades and critical to identifying serial offenders, continue to sit, languishing, untested, and rotting, in police facilities across the country.

Women in other countries face similar mistreatment. For example, a 2017 report in India found that women who report rape continue to be harassed and sometimes even assaulted by police, who then intimidate women into silence.

Domestic violence is also a notable problem in policing, highlighting the dynamics of larger social issues. Some estimates put the incidence of intimate-partner violence among police families at two to four times the national average. Officers have access to national databases, making abuse of spouses easier and escape infinitely more difficult. They also have guns. They are able to track women's movements, finding personal details. Advocates who help abused women create new identities and find safe places to live are finding doing so increasingly impossible given the use of integrated agency databases and access that officers often have to those databases. Women also understand, intimately, the power of fraternal orders to protect their own if reports are made. All of this makes it extremely difficult for women expected to turn to the police for help when they are being assaulted in their own homes.

One out of four American women live with domestic violence, a ratio that translates into 4.8 million physical assaults annually. Domestic violence injures more American women annually than rapes, car accidents, and muggings combined. More than half of all women murdered in the United States are killed by men they know, just under three (2.5) women a day. (Currently, 5 percent to 7 percent of men killed are murdered by intimate partners.) Because of a lack of gun regulations, an American woman is sixteen times more likely to be shot than a woman in another developed country. Approximately four in five Native American and Alaskan Native women have experienced violence. One out of every six American women has been stalked.

Worldwide, the prevalence of intimate-partner violence, rape, and sexual assault are staggering. At least one in three women has been beaten, coerced into sex, or otherwise abused during her lifetime, overwhelmingly by men they are related to, be it a father, brother, spouse, or domestic partner. As many as one in four women are assaulted while pregnant.

The most dangerous man a woman will encounter is the one sitting at her own dinner table, yet media continue to focus on horrific crimes perpetrated by strangers and acquaintances. This violence should be treated seriously in and of itself, but it is also meaningful to understanding public violence. The single most accurate predictor of violent crime is a man's felony domestic violence conviction. For instance, 58 percent of mass shooters have histories of domestic violence. Nine of the ten most lethal mass killings in the United States involved men with histories of domestic abuse. Three of the deadlier mass shootings of 2017—one in Plano, Texas, in which seven were killed, another in which eight people died in rural Mississippi, and a third in which twenty-seven were killed in Sutherland Springs, Texas—were committed by estranged husbands enraged that their wives had chosen to end their marriages. Killings like these are not considered political or terroristic, even though in effect they are both.

Killing is one dimension of violence. According to the World Health Organization, more than two hundred million girls and women live with the lifelong and often painfully debilitating effects of female genital mutilation. Every year, more than sixty million girls are "child brides," a ridiculous euphemism. The only thing that might be more ridiculous is "child prostitutes." It is estimated by demographers that femicide, the killing of female fetuses and babies, has led to a deficit of more than a hundred million women on the planet. The gap is already resulting in the global escalation of trafficking of women to meet demand. Women and girls compose 80 percent of the estimated eight hundred thousand people trafficked annually, with 79 percent of them trafficked for sexual exploitation. Pornography, in which abuse and trafficking are often implicated, is also problematic. There are pornographers working to produce ethical porn that does not denigrate people, eroticize violent male domination of women, or profit from abuse, but much of mainstream porn does. The commercialized trade in children's and women's bodies cannot be separated from women's political and economic marginalization and vulnerability.

Everything I have described is based on data from countries during "peacetime." In militarized and war zones, civilian women are automatically made into combatants by the simple fact that men weaponize their bodies. Rape, even when women are involved as perpetrators or men as victims, degrades victims by feminizing them through penetration and is meant to degrade men by violating what is "theirs."

All of these forms of gender-based violence have been given new life by technology. Intimate-partner abusers can cheaply and easily use spyware, cell phones, texts, and email to cyberstalk, impersonate, defame, and threaten—and in ways that law enforcement is woefully unprepared to handle. The trafficking industry has also moved online, generating revenue downstream that pulses through global economies.

It's impossible to measure the impact that stories about gender-based violence have on women's psyches. It's even harder to measure what it means in terms of lost lives and opportunities.

In early August 2017 Swedish freelance journalist Kim Wall went missing while in Denmark to interview inventor Peter Madsen. She was last seen on board Madsen's mini submarine, which, authorities were led to believe, sank in Køge Bay under mysterious circumstances. After an eleven-day search, Wall's torso, dismembered, washed up on a nearby beach.

"I didn't see her die by any deliberate act," Madsen told the authorities. "I saw her die of something completely different. I saw her fall down." He was charged initially with negligent manslaughter, but an autopsy revealed that before being dismembered, the thirty-year-old woman had been stabbed more than fourteen times in the genitals alone. Madsen's computer contained videos of violently tortured and murdered women, described by one official as "some very grave videos with women recorded abroad." Eventually he was charged with murder and "sexual relations other than intercourse of a particularly dangerous nature." Graphic descriptions like this one filled the news for months. Many people could not stomach them. In fiction, however, these treatments of women and their bodies fill our screens and make millions of dollars in profit. Entire franchises are built around violence against women as entertainment.

In news coverage of violence such as this, one aspect is conspicuously absent: How do average girls and women feel about what is happening around them? Once in a while, I will read an article by a woman at her limit, sickened by images of misogynistic violence used for casual fun. She might swear off of certain movies or products. But, in truth, there is no escaping them. All you have to do is glance at a newspaper or online news source. We are reluctant to connect the dots, and so ignore what we see and go about our lives. How this actually makes us feel, the knowledge of it, the trepidation, anger, and frustration, are rarely investigated seriously.

What do we say to our children about misogyny and violence? Wall was a brave and acclaimed journalist who had worked in China, Haiti, North Korea, Cuba, and Sri Lanka, among other places. She died interviewing a prominent, wealthy Danish man a few miles from her home in one of the most gender-egalitarian countries in the world. As women, we wrap ourselves in the belief that something like this will not happen to us, as journalists that it won't happen to us in the course of our work. We bury these unnerving stories deeply. Two-thirds of women journalists report work-related threats, sexist abuse, intimidation, and harassment. Personally, I've developed an absurd skill, that of being able to weaponize virtually anything. I wear thick, heavy, and sharp-ended metal hairpins. I order hot tea when I travel alone on airplanes, easily spillable on a handsy neighbor. The list goes on and on.

We take risks. Like walking around our own communities. In 2013 a man named Ariel Castro was arrested for having kidnapped, enslaved, and tortured three girls he abducted right off the street in his friendly west Cleveland neighborhood. They grew into women locked in his house over the course of ten years. He physically assaulted and brutally raped the girls countless times, keeping them chained, and allowing them, according to some sources, outside only once or twice over the years. At least once he induced an abortion by pummeling one girl's abdomen.

During two years of this ten-year period, eleven black women in another Cleveland neighborhood were slaughtered one at a time by convicted sex offender Anthony Sowell, in what came to be called his "house of horrors." Sowell, dubbed the Cleveland Strangler, was charged with murdering these women, as well as two rapes and one attempted rape. There were more than seventy related charges. Sowell, like many others, knew that by targeting the people least valued in society—runaways, drug addicts, black women who were trafficked or were sex workers—he could easily fly under the radar. In Sowell's case, police who came to his door failed to act on the fact that his house smelled like rotting bodies. Still, the haunting question remains: How could so many women disappear without anyone noticing?

There are reasons why, for years, Gallup has found double-digit "safety gaps" between men and women. "Most Americans continue to feel safe in their immediate communities," researchers at Gallup explained in a 2014 release of an annual crime survey. "With 63 percent saying they would not be afraid to walk alone there at night." That number masks the reality that half of women, 45 percent, say they *do not* feel safe compared to 73 percent of men reported that they *do*.

After Ariel Castro's arrest, I contacted the Cleveland Police Department to ask if, in cases like his and Sowell's, gender-based hate crime reports had been filed. The police responded that they had "no responsive documents to this request."

According to the FBI, which uses a series of questions and a scale to assess incidents, hate crimes apply in situations where people are victimized, sometimes subtly and other times overtly, because of their identity. Hate crimes, however, are often not prosecuted for multiple and overlapping aspects of identity. For example, a crime targeting black lesbian women might be categorized as a racist crime, or a homophobic crime, but rarely as a racist or homophobic *and* gender-based one.

In 2015, the *New York Times* published an op-ed on the relationship between anti-Muslim searches on Google (such as "kill Muslims" and "I hate Muslims") and violence on the ground. The authors cited the example of twenty-three-year-old Asma Mohammed Nizami, who was driving home one night in Minnesota when a man yelled, "Muslim bitch!" and attempted to run her off the road. "While the vast majority of Muslim Americans won't be victims of hate crimes," the authors explained, "few escape the constant sense of fear and paranoia." That "constant sense" is not familiar to cisgender, heterosexual, white men, but it is to many women and to men of color.

Nizami was called a "Muslim *bitch*." The overlap in marginalized identities—for example, black and a woman, Jewish and a woman, homosexual and a woman, is significant. As writer Mona Eltahawy explained after an anti-Muslim attack in the United States, for the almost 25 percent of American Muslims who are black, Islamophobia, racism, and misogyny are "the brutal trifecta." In the wake of a 2015 terrorist attack in Paris, assaults of Muslim girls and women in the United Kingdom made up the vast majority of the 300 percent spike in anti-Muslim hate crimes and yet governments and the media continue to ignore the impact of gender when categorizing hate.

Women are more likely to be targeted with hateful violence simply because they are women, every day.

"A simple double standard is at work here," explains political theorist and legal scholar Catharine MacKinnon. Violence against men is "torture" and "political" because, she explains, it is about when "men control and hurt other men—meaning persons who are deserving of dignity and power." We are supposed to accept that gender-based violence, a violence that inhibits women every day, is not political in its intent or effect.

WHO DEFINES RISK?

Most of us learn to think that boys and men are the world's risk-takers, but that is only because we don't seriously address the risks women must take as they navigate boys and men. We take risks when we post our profiles on dating websites and meet up with strangers. We take risks when we can't pay for gyms (in lieu of exercising outside), taxis or car services, and other pricey "safety" measures. We take risks every time we get pregnant. We take risks when we report sexual harassment, assault, and domestic violence. We take risks when we go to the police. We take risks when we send our children into schools where we are expected to treat as reasonable the suggestion that teachers should be armed with guns. Risks abound.

We are experts at risk taking. We are also experts at setting aside our pride, hiding our humiliation, shrinking our ambitions, and carefully calibrating our resentments.

—————

Teaching girls to "stay safe" early in life, while simultaneously discouraging anger and aggression and cultivating physical fragility, all contribute to the association of weakness and fearfulness with femininity. Anger and aggression do not fit easily with these lessons. If we say we are scared, it is understandable and easy for others who can focus on what we, as individuals, can do to avoid feeling fear instead of what they, communally, can do to stem threats.

Studies show that fear differentials between men and women regulate our expressions of anger. When women display anger, men are more likely to respond with anger, but when men show anger, women respond with fear. Women, more fearful, are less likely to respond to anger in situations when men might. The degree to which these differences are underappreciated is obvious in questions such as "Why didn't she fight back?" "Why didn't she say 'no'?" "Why didn't she just leave?"

In the face of threat, we often learn that the "normal" physiological response is fight-or-flight. This description reflects men's experiences, not women's. In 2000, UCLA professor and social psychologist Shelley Taylor and her colleagues showed that when men and women encounter stress and threats, their actual physical reactions differ. Men's bodies release the chemicals norepinephrine and cortisol, which prompt fight-or-flight behaviors. Women, too, experience faster pulses and elevated blood pressure, but their bodies, instead, produce two different chemicals: endorphins and oxytocin, which lead to "tend-and-befriend" behaviors. Women become more affiliative and appear to be friendly. "Fight or flight" is the "normal" response . . . if you are a man, yet it is the standard to which women are held.

We learn as girls to read faces and other body indicators, and we develop tactics for lowering the temperature of encounters, a process known as de-escalation. The ability and inclination to take this approach is supported by socialization and the practical reality that women are often physically smaller than the people threatening them. Gender is also a factor: people who identify with feminine gender roles are also more attuned to facial expressions and also feel fearful more often. So, for example, a man who stays home to take care of his children is far more likely to display the higher risk perception and greater fearfulness that people assume are inherent in women.

Simply "leaving" or "walking away" is often not a rational option. When we feel fear, or anger, or a combination of both, we often freeze, act confused, and stop talking in order to think. We become still and quiet, and we smile. We make our rage small; we acquiesce, deflect, soothe, and shrug. Giggling is sublimation. Laughing is a path to survival. And if smiling and laughter are not options, we cry: a self-silencing deferral that is often misinterpreted as weakness.

Women in heterosexual relationships, more likely to follow traditional gender-role expectations, are more prone to display traditionally feminine traits, like crying, and silence their anger than women in egalitarian relationships are. Feminine anger is particularly difficult in more conventional frameworks because the expression of anger itself is conceived as a failure to be a "good" woman. Women in traditional relationships also express fear and sadness more when they are angry. Studies show, however, that self-silencing is not only a function of femininity but also is directly related to women's perception of *potential intolerance and anger* from their husbands and fathers. Men in traditional relationships are more aggressive, angry, and contemptuous toward women than those in more egalitarian unions.

The dynamics of gender and gender expectations about power and control are heightened in situations of intimate-partner violence. According to one detailed study of intimate-partner arguments in abusive relationships, fear was *the* distinguishing factor between how men and women expressed themselves. When couples enrolled in the study fought, women were consistently scared that men's anger would spiral into physical assault. Men did not have the same fear in terms of women's anger.

"Your abusive partner doesn't have a problem with his anger," writes Lundy Bancroft, an expert in the dynamics of power and control at the heart of domestic abuse. "He has a problem with your anger."

It is estimated that 68 percent of women in situations of intimate violence are almost strangled to death by their partners at least once. Seven in ten of these women believe they will be killed, either in the moment or eventually. A woman killed by a man she knows has, on average, been strangled seven times prior to her murder. Yet only thirty-eight US states have laws that recognize suffocation and strangulation as attempts to kill a person. Even if physical violence is not present in a relationship, male abusers are able to leverage the threat of physical violence and the fear it elicits to engage in emotional abuse.

The way anger and fear are mismanaged in abusive families lives on in children, millions of whom grow up with family violence. They live in fear of violent, manipulative, and threatening parents, mainly, though not exclusively, fathers, whose anger can infuse almost all interactions. Children living with domestic violence simultaneously see, in these interactions, the denial, erasure, and invalidation of their mother's anger as she avoids threat. Depending on their gender, these children learn that anger is dangerous and to be avoided at all costs or that their own anger is a powerful tool for controlling others. Children often blame themselves and, as adults, are at least three times more likely either to be abusers or abused.

If a woman is in a relationship where her expressing anger endangers her, she will suppress that anger. Her inability to say what is bothering her should be an early warning sign of damaging inequality in a relationship. Depression related to anger is by far the most common "side effect" of domestic violence for victims.

A recent report on gender equality, conducted by the consulting firm McKinsey & Company, cites harassment and violence against women as one of six primary and structural obstacles to women's equity and equality. The report goes further than many similar ones in directly linking gender-based violence to the economic disadvantages and manifold ills that come with it. Women who are disadvantaged by bias, street harassment, and sexual harassment in the workplace, are more vulnerable to intimate violence at home. Financial dependence is a near constant issue for women victims of domestic violence who must be able to secure, at the very least, housing if they leave, particularly with children.

Sixty-three percent of homeless women in the United States are survivors of intimate violence. Among those with children, 93 percent report trauma. A one-day census of shelters conducted in 2016 concluded that more than 40,000 people were seeking help across the United States and that there were more than 12,000 unmet requests, most of them from women seeking housing, child care, legal help, and transportation.

We tend to admire women's onscreen anger, physical aggression, and vigilantism, in films like *Kill Bill* or *Mad Max: Fury Road*. However, when women act in these ways in life, they face particularly harsh and disproportionate punishment. In May 2012 Marissa Alexander, a thirty-one-year-old African American woman, fired a warning shot at the ceiling as her husband was threatening to kill her. The bullet hit the wall behind him. The Florida resident was charged with aggravated assault with a lethal weapon. Thinking that her case was a textbook example of the state's Stand Your Ground law, which protects homeowners who defend themselves against an attack in their own homes, she rejected a plea bargain that would have resulted in a three-year sentence. Despite the law, the fact that she was in her house, had fired into a wall, and that no one was hurt, *and* despite her having no criminal record and a concealed weapon permit, she was found guilty of assault with a lethal weapon and sentenced to twenty years in prison. Every woman in Florida facing similar circumstances understood that Stand Your Ground laws would not apply to them in similar circumstances. Alexander's sentence was overturned eventually, but only after several years of relentless activism on her behalf.

The quintessential blame-the-victim approach is institutionalized in laws that not only inadequately take into account the complex dynamics of domestic violence and women's specific survival adaptations but also hold women accountable *for another person's crimes.* When men abuse children, women, who are often themselves victim, are sometimes prosecuted for not sufficiently protecting their children from a violent partner.

Sometimes children protect their mothers.

In July 2016 fourteen-year-old Bresha Meadows was charged with murdering her father, a man who had terrorized his family for years. "In the 17 years of our marriage," wrote her mother in a 2011 protective order filing, "he has cut me, broke my ribs, fingers, the blood vessels in my hand, my mouth, blackened my eyes. I believe my nose was broken." She concluded, "If he finds us, I am 100% sure he will kill me and the children." Prosecutors wanted Meadows tried as an adult, and she faced a life sentence if found guilty. She pleaded to manslaughter and was sentenced to a year in a juvenile facility, six months in a mental health care facility, and two years' probation. Activists fought for her release, and she returned home in early 2018.

Myrna Dawson, an associate sociology professor at the University of Guelph, has studied what happens to men who kill women family members and found that they receive shorter prison sentences compared with men who kill strangers. She calls this an "intimacy discount." Reasons why this is the case include the notion that men are provoked into spontaneous violence, a "crime of passion" defense. Dawson, however, also describes that what the leniency may reflect is that, across the criminal justice system, "women murdered by male partners are seen as property." Property can't fight back.

In 2012 a London woman named Laura Bates was walking home one night when a group of men started verbally harassing her from a car. Later that week, as she stood on a bus, she realized a man was rubbing his hand up her leg toward her crotch. She was on the phone with her mother and started to explain loudly what was happening, something she wouldn't have done if she hadn't been on the phone. Despite people hearing her, no one interceded.

Describing the scene later, Bates said that the passengers on the bus looked at her as if to say "Why are you making a fuss about it?" She wondered if she shouldn't have been wearing what she was wearing. She went home and said nothing. Two days later, two men standing only a few feet away from her began their conversation with "Look at the tits on that."

"At first, I felt fear, I felt embarrassment, shame, anxiety, all these other emotions that we feel when we are experiencing these things," explained Bates when we spoke. "I didn't feel like I had the right to be angry at the time."

She began talking to other women about harassment and assault and eventually set up a simple website where women could share their stories, dubbing it the Everyday Sexism Project. In the first year alone, more than forty thousand women submitted entries and continue to every day using the #everydaysexism hashtag. Within two years, there were Everyday Sexism websites in countries around the world.

"We are so socialized to accept this treatment that we don't realize we have the right to anger in the moment. I thought, 'This is the way things are. This is what it means to be a woman. I just have to deal with it,'" she said, describing exactly how I, and many women, respond. "It wasn't until I realized this is a collective experience that I began to feel anger. Anger always came later for me, and I think that's very significant for women. Only afterward do we realize how denied and pushed down that anger is."

Once in a while, I let myself think about what it would be like if girls and women could walk alone at night without fear. What would it represent in terms of change? How different would life be if we were not subjected to the risk of male aggression and violence? If we accept the interpretation of life as we know it, *we make it acceptable*. So I refuse, which makes me seem angry and aggressive simply by existing.

Women should be angry about the violence and fear that inform so much of our lives. So should men. Anger is the emotion that best protects us against danger, unfairness, and injustice. Understanding it and learning to think about its methodical uses in response to threats like these allows girl and women to move from passivity, fear, and withdrawal to awareness, engagement, and change. This doesn't mean acting in ways that might put you in immediate danger but developing an understanding of your own feelings and how to best use them to alter the space around you. The shift cultivates communities of resistance.

And if we smile, it should be because we want to.

THE DRIP, DRIP, DRIP

Who in the hell set things up like this?
—June Jordan, "Poem About My Rights"

In 2017 my writing partner, Catherine Buni, and I were nominated for a prestigious journalism prize. We were thrilled, not only because we were nominated but also because in more than four years of writing together, talking almost every day, we had met in person only once, and briefly. We met for dinner the night before the awards ceremony, which was being held in Manhattan, and, in the morning, made our way over together.

We were directed to a sign-in table and given lapel clip name tags. Catherine had on a sweater, and I was wearing a high-necked dress. We held the tags up to our collars and laughed at how ridiculous we looked with name tags pinned under our chins. People wear name tags at work events for a reason. It makes connections easier and helps with introductions and remembering people. Considering that women don't often wear lapels, I asked the man who was helping us get set up if we could get lanyards like the ones the event staff had. He obligingly went off to search.

As we stood waiting near an elaborate backdrop, industry pundits had their pictures taken. I moved over slightly so that a group of backslapping men making their exit from the ten-foot patch of red carpet could go by. As I did, one of them turned to me, beaming. "Where are you whisking me off to next?" he asked, assuming I was a hostess. I smiled and, explaining that I was not a whisker, suggested that he talk to the man handing me the lanyard. I *wanted* to say, "Oh, I'm sorry. You must have mistaken me for another brown woman," but I didn't.

His assumption was implicitly sexist and maybe even racist. Like the lapel name tag, it was another instance of subtle bias— discrimination that is often, but not always, unintentional.

Women contend all the time with people assuming we are assistants. If we are black or brown, we are further assumed to be "cleaning ladies" and janitors. A 2016 study of ethnic minority women scientists revealed that 48 percent of those who were African American had been confused for cleaning staff and administrators.

Sometimes these assumptions about women's "helper" status are obvious; other times, while consequential, not so much. In 2017 Heather Sarsons, a PhD economics candidate at Harvard University, published her analysis of twenty-nine years' worth of publications produced by economists at a top US university. She found that women who wrote on their own had the same chance of receiving tenure as men, but that women who collaborated with men had poorer prospects. Men who collaborated, on the other hand, were four times more likely to succeed. Women were not recognized for collaboration but, instead, were seen as helpers to the men. This finding is related to another, known as the Matilda effect: the attributing of women's discoveries and research to male peers. A similar preference for male status recognition is also evident in citation patterns, particularly among men, who are more likely to reference other men's work.

In the field of economics, the word "helper" is good compared with the alternatives being used. In 2017 Alice H. Wu analyzed a database of millions of comments from a popular economics job market forum. She was curious to find out how economists thought about gender and what ideas, in daily conversation, they associated with men and women. What a grim task that proved to be.

She found that the top thirty words most uniquely associated with women were, in order of prevalence: *hotter, lesbian, bb* (internet speak for *baby*), *sexism, tits, anal, marrying, feminazi, slut, hot, vagina, boobs, pregnant, pregnancy, cute, marry, levy, gorgeous, horny, crush, beautiful, secretary, dump, shopping, date, nonprofit, intentions, sexy, dated,* and *prostitute.* This language is environmentally toxic to women working in this field. But what do I know? I'm just a humorless feminist with an overdeveloped sense of why this matters.

What happened at the awards ceremony was the slightest and most inconsequential of interactions. Whisk Me Away Man was harmless in the sense that he had no ability to affect my work life, but biases such as his are pervasive and damaging and affect women's well-being every day.

There is probably not a woman alive today who doesn't know what it feels like to be incessantly and disruptively interrupted, talked over, and ignored.

At home and in schools, adults encourage boys to share their opinions more freely and to develop more complicated ideas verbally. Teachers, for example, ask boys more open-ended questions and look directly at them when they do. When boys speak out of order in class, which they do at eight times the rate that girls do, they are not reprimanded as frequently or told to raise their hands and wait their turn. In one of the more granular analyses of class-room dynamics conducted to date, Professor Allyson Jule of Trinity Western University in British Columbia found that boys speak nine to ten times more. Her work examining the gendered construction of speech in early childhood confirms earlier findings that, in West-ern classrooms, boys are allowed by adults to consume five times as much verbal space through, as she puts it, "imperceptible signals of significance over girls." Observations of children on playgrounds also show that despite girls' earlier language acquisition, by age six, boys dominate chatter with adult encouragement.

Girls' higher grades in school are as tied to their being "good," meaning quiet, as they are to mastery of subject matter. This com-pliance puts girls and women at a disadvantage as they move into college and the workplace, where disruptive speech is an element of competence, self-promotion, and competitiveness. One study of Harvard undergraduate classrooms found that male students speak *at least* three times more than female ones. Another revealed that women are 50 percent less likely to talk in law school classes.

In mixed-gender groups, men tend to take up inordinate "speech space," yet stereotypes continue to portray women as the world's motormouths. Both men and women are more likely to interrupt and talk over girls and women than they are boys and men. This is true even in scripted television shows and movies, where male actors engage in more disruptive speech and garner twice as much speaking and screen time as women do.

Linguistic patterns also reflect differences in ethnicity and class, but gender trumps status. For example, male doctors will interrupt their patients, especially if they are women, but patients don't inter-rupt or talk over doctors unless they are women. In corporate set-tings, subordinates, particularly men, are less deferential to women bosses. Linguists have studied the role of gender in speech and speech distributions for decades, concluding at one point that "women's speech"—frequently more submissive and less assertive—is a specific genre of speech. Crosscultural analyses suggest that "women's speech" is actually "powerless speech," employed by lower-status people, regardless of sex.

Stanford University scientist Ben Barres, a trans man, said one of the benefits he associated most with his transition was speaking "without being interrupted by a man."

Credibility and authority are also gendered. A man who introduces a topic on a LISTSERV gets higher rates of response and debate than a woman does. On Twitter, men's tweets are retweeted twice as often as women's. The issue is captured succinctly in a pithy and popular cartoon depicting one woman at a table full of men. The caption reads, "That's an excellent suggestion, Miss Triggs. Perhaps one of the men here would like to suggest it."

Professors Christopher F. Karpowitz and Tali Mendelberg study and write about gender and racial dynamics in professional and political spaces. One of their studies of legislative deliberations shows that women need to constitute a supermajority, or roughly 70 percent of a room, in order to achieve parity and influence. If they don't, they have a difficult time being perceived as powerful, influential, or important speakers.

A few years ago, I wrote about ways to teach girls how to navigate social disapproval for their powerful speech in an article titled "10 Simple Words Every Girl Should Learn." The ten words are: "Stop interrupting me," "I just said that," and "No explanation needed." I was genuinely overwhelmed by responses. The article was immediately translated into more than a dozen languages and continues to be shared widely. Women from all over the world still write to me about their frustrations in meetings, in schools, and at home, and they are often thankful simply for the recognition of the problems they encounter trying to be heard.

Women, for the record, also interrupt and talk over other people, but the quality of interruptions differs. For example, men use interruptions more disruptively to shift the direction of conversation, while women might interrupt in ways that prompt more conversation in the same direction.

One of my daughters tends to engage in simultaneous speech, topic switching, and persistent disruptive interruption. When she was a child, it was hard to balance teaching her to be polite while at the same time ensuring that she remained assertive and confident in her opinions. Some studies indicate that parents interrupt girls at almost twice the rate at which they interrupt boys. Excessive politeness norms for girls have real impacts on them as women, who, ironically, are told constantly to override childhood socialization and learn to "talk like men" to succeed.

The most fundamental bias we face—the one underlying all the others—is the belief that we are inherently less worth listening to than men are. Ben Barres, for example, noted that his work was less respected when he presented as a woman. After having completed a complex assignment as Barbara, he was told by a skeptical professor, "Your boyfriend must have solved it for you." Years later, Ben gave a lecture on his research. Afterward, he overheard an audience member exclaim, "His work is much better than his sister's."

Women with tenure, expertise, and knowledge are routinely passed over in favor of mediocre men with less of all. Across industries, endless parades of all-male panels (or "manels," as they are not-so-affectionately called) suggest that women are incapable of simultaneously sitting in chairs, thinking, and speaking out loud.

There is virtually no vital issue or topic (climate change, war, peace, authoritarianism, white supremacy, immigration, poverty, famine, refugee crises)—not one—in which women don't have expertise and in which gender does not play a central and pivotal role. And yet men continue to sit in womenless rooms, confident that they can create lasting solutions to humanity's most serious problems. If ever there was a mass delusion, that is it.

Corporate indifference to women's thinking and work is evident in everything from the fact that influential tech leaders don't find women interesting enough to follow on Twitter, to womanless Nobel Prizes; from women-bereft gender-equality conferences, to all-male women's reproductive health panels. Consider, for example, that between 1992 and 2011, more than 94 percent of people conducting peace negotiations around the world have been men, even though it is a long-standing and well-established fact that gender-inclusive negotiations result in more successful and lasting peace. Bodies of men acting in the absence of women is unethical, and it's dangerous.

The most common responses to the problem of marginalized women's participation in expert discussions are: "We tried but couldn't find women" and "We are gender blind and chose the best speakers." Both demonstrate a lazy, self-protective inability and unwillingness to understand the dynamics of structural discrimination. In 2015 mathematician Greg Martin conducted an in-depth statistical analysis showing how overwhelmingly improbable it is today that all-male panels occur randomly. An unbiased process would actually ensure that conference planners are significantly *more* likely to produce an overrepresentation of *women*.

All-male panels are organized "mansplaining." Like infinite numbers of other women, I have countless stories of men arguing with something I've said by sending me my own work.

In September 2016 Jessica Meir, a NASA astronaut and a physiologist, tweeted a video of herself in a space simulator replicating conditions aboard a spacecraft in the upper reaches of the atmosphere. "My first venture >63,000' [feet], the space equivalent zone, where water spontaneously boils! Luckily I'm suited!" A beaker of boiling water sat on the surface next to her. Within minutes, a man who was neither an astronaut nor a physiologist explained to Meir why the water boiling wasn't "spontaneous." As one Twitter wag immediately quipped, "Why listen to the female astronaut when there's a shirtless guy?"

Interactions like these are condescending and costly not only to women but also to the people around them. For example, in October 2016 Dr. Tamika Cross was on a flight from Detroit to Houston, when she heard a woman two rows in front of her screaming that her husband was unconscious. A flight attendant shouted, "Call overhead for a physician on board!" Dr. Cross raised her hand. Here's what the flight attendant said to her: "Oh, no, sweetie, put your hand down. We are looking for actual physicians or nurses or some type of medical personnel; we don't have time to talk to you."

Meanwhile, the ailing passenger remained unresponsive. He could have been dying. Dr. Cross flagged down the attendant again.

"Oh, wow, you're an actual physician?"

"Yes."

Instead of escorting Dr. Cross to the man in distress, the attendant proceeded to interrogate her: "What type of doctor are you? Where do you work? Why were you in Detroit?" By now, another physician, who happened to be a white man, had come forward to volunteer. "Thanks for your help," the attendant told Dr. Cross dismissively, "but he can help us, and he has his credentials." According to Cross, the man was never questioned, nor did he show any credentials. After she shared her experience on Facebook, many other women and black men came forward with similar stories.

Even when we are accepted as authoritative, we are often reminded that male validation is preferable. In 2015 the hashtag #AddMaleAuthor trended after Fiona Ingleby, a geneticist, publicly shared an absurdly sexist peer review of her work. The reviewer, a man, suggested that adding a man as a coauthor to a paper she'd coauthored with another woman would "serve as a possible check against interpretations that may sometimes be drifting too far away from empirical evidence into ideologically biased assumptions." He elaborated with confidence that this would also improve the paper overall because men "on average work more hours per week than women, due to marginally better health and stamina."

Humor as a response to claptrap is always welcome, but tongue-in-cheek slang such as mansplaining, manterrupting, hepeater, and manvalidation—words that give us a way to describe common experiences—mask the corrosive belief that women are less credible and less knowledgeable than men are, all strengthened by racist, ethnocentric bias.

While both men and women share these biases, the idea that women are less capable of complex thought is more common among men. In 2016, researchers asked 1,700 students in an undergraduate biology class to rank their classmates based on what they knew of their knowledge and class performance. (The study looked only at gender.) Men overwhelmingly rated male peers as more capable and knowledgeable than female peers, even when women obviously performed better in class. Researchers found that the antiwoman gender bias among men was nineteen times that of the women. A 2018 follow-up study of men in science, technology, engineering, and math revealed similar male overestimation of intelligence and underestimation of women.

"As a graduate student, a fellow male student said, to my face, that he had no idea how I was admitted to the program because I clearly wasn't smart enough to be there," remembered Gwen Pearson, a PhD in entomology, when interviewed about the study's findings. "He said having me as a fellow graduate student 'lessened the value of his degree.' Direct quote. He seemed to think that I should leave for the good of the other students. It was pretty devastating." The article didn't mention if this made her angry.

We learn to expect women to speak less, so when we talk, it always seems like we are talking too much. Women are supposed to be quieter and, when they speak, apologetic. Being closemouthed is a feminine quality. Once in a while, some absurd manifestation of these beliefs bubbles to the cultural surface in interesting ways, like hamburger wrappers for women, produced by a Japanese fast-food restaurant, printed with smiles on them, so that women won't be seen opening their mouths in public, a taboo. Burger sales in Japan went up 213 percent after the mouth masks, called "Liberation Wrappers," were introduced. In 2014 Turkey's then deputy prime minister, Bülent Arinç, condemned the act of women smiling in public (in other words, opening their mouths) as a sign of "moral decline of modern society." Women's open mouths and their higher-pitched voices have long been represented as indicators of madness, danger, chaos, and decay.

Women are especially not supposed to question or publicly shame men for their behavior. If they use their public voices to address topics that go beyond their gender roles, families, and appearance—particularly if they challenge that limitation—they can count on public hostility, off- and online.

In the spring of 2017, Minnesota state representative Melissa Hortman (who happens to be white) initiated a call of the House: a procedure that forces absent legislators to return to the chamber. "I hate to break up the one hundred percent white male card game in the retiring room," she announced during a public safety budget debate, "but I think this is an important debate."

Two of the absent legislators demanded that Hortman not only apologize but also resign. The majority caucus of Minnesota's state legislature at the time was 72 percent white and male, as were the heads of nineteen of the House's twenty-eight committees. These were, indeed, the people missing from the floor when Hortman asked that they return to hear women legislators speak. "I have no intention of apologizing," she responded.

Episodes such as this sound like something out of sixteenth-century England, where there were actually "common scold" laws—under which a bothersome and insistent woman could be charged legally for being, by dint of speaking, a public nuisance. Three centuries later, the famed American novelist Henry James described women's "thin nasal tones," their "twangs, whiffles, snuffles, whines, and whinnies," sentiments echoed by Rush Limbaugh when he referred to Hillary Clinton as "a screeching ex-wife." During the entire 2016 presidential campaign, while her male counterparts boomed, swaggered, and diatribed to accolades, the former US senator and secretary of state was criticized for being "shrill," "inauthentic" (if she was quiet and calm), and for "shouting" (if she used her voice clearly, loudly, and confidently). "Angry" is a common addition to condescending and sexist stereotypes like these, used to further dismiss women.

Discomfort with women speaking authoritatively is universal. In a 2014 interview on Australian TV, former Sex Pistols front man Johnny Rotten, who in 2010 settled charges of having punched a woman in the face, lost his composure with the woman host. "Shut up," snapped the aging punk rocker. "Whoever you are, shut up. Shut up. Shut up. Now, listen, when a man is talking, do not interrupt." During a 2015 on-air broadcast, a Lebanese TV host and university professor, Rima Karaki, was interrupted by her guest, an Egyptian scholar: "Are you done? Shut up so I can talk . . . It's beneath me to be interviewed by you. You are a woman." Karaki shut off his microphone. In 2017, in the midst of an on-air discussion with Symone Sanders, Bernie Sanders's former campaign spokeswoman, Republican politician Ken Cuccinelli exclaimed, "Can you just shut up for a moment?" Sanders, an African American, had been asserting that the combative Cuccinelli was "dismissing" the idea that white supremacy was a national issue.

The fear of emasculation and loss of control runs through responses to women's speech and anger. Nagging wives, shrews, and harridans, to make the association clear between women and men who aren't able to "control them," are *ball breakers*. Of all of the responses to my working on issues related to women's rights over the years, one of my favorites is when people ask my husband, "Are you okay? How are you holding up?"

THE CREDIBILITY GAP

These tendencies extend way beyond classrooms or social media to include, notably, courtrooms, where a woman testifying is more likely to be interrupted by a judge or counsel and to be doubted. Breaks in cadence and narrative contribute to women being considered less credible by a jury. These speech dynamics buttress other biases. Male jurors, for example, struggle to accept that women lawyers can advocate as convincingly and competently as men. Juries trust women in expert testimony, unless the topic is complicated. Jurors, particularly men, may be less likely to find a defendant guilty if the prosecutor is a woman. And listen to this: if a woman defendant is overweight, male jurors are, additionally, more likely to find her guilty.

Women of color and working-class women, who use language in ways that are more likely to defy mainstream norms about femininity, victimhood, and anger, are also disadvantaged disproportionately. The adversarial framework of judicial proceedings and the parameters of traditional due process linguistically favor higher-status people by assuming that all speakers are equal and that socialization, incorporating as it does inequalities related to race, class, and ethnicity, is irrelevant.

The problem of credibility, expertise, interruptions, and women's inability to use their words effectively, continuously, and convincingly exists even at the highest levels. An in-depth study published in 2017 in the journal *Virginia Law Review* revealed that male justices on the US Supreme Court interrupt their esteemed female colleagues roughly three times as much as they do one another. The court's latest addition, Justice Neil Gorsuch, proved himself up to the task, repeatedly interrupting women senators who questioned him during his 2017 nomination hearings.

Women have to work doubly, triply hard to be considered credible and authoritative. Studies show that women are more likely to be doubted when we speak in the workplace, in courts, in politics, in situations involving the police, and in medical consultations with doctors and hospital staff. People would rather have men be their bosses, their pilots, and their employees.

Gender expectations shape ideas about credibility and lying. In surveys, more people say they trust women more than they do men, but dig deeper and the reality is less appealing. They are more likely to trust women when women talk about themselves and not about other people. When women don't conform to social-role expectations, the doubting effects are magnified. In addition, a majority of people will assert that women are more honest as individuals, yet—incoherently—cannot be trusted to lead in the same way that men can. Women's displays of anger, seen as gender transgressive, can exacerbate all of these biases.

These prejudices are reinforced by ageism. The notion of older women's anger is even less appealing than girls' nascent rage. Older women are supposed to disappear or, if not, at least be quiet and take care of others. Although women over fifty-one make up the largest percentage of women in the world, in films they are the least likely to be seen. Similarly, women newscasters pay professional penalties for aging in ways that male newscasters don't. In 2013 when I googled "venerable men," I got picture after picture of older men held in esteem. "Venerable women," on the other hand, prompted the question "Do you mean *vulnerable* women?" This was aggravating yet insightful because, in fact, where *only men* are venerable, *women* are vulnerable.

———

In 2015 novelist Catherine Nichols, tired of having her manuscripts rejected by literary agents, decided to change her name to a man's. "I sent the six queries I had planned to send that day," she wrote about her experiment. "Within 24 hours, 'George' had five responses—three manuscript requests and two warm rejections praising his exciting project. For contrast, under my own name, the same letter and pages sent 50 times had netted me a total of two manuscript requests." Nichols's experiment is depressing, but its results are predictable. Women still hide their gender when they write, using initials or gender-neutral names. J.K. Rowling is one of the world's most famous examples. Her publisher thought boys would be less likely to read her books if the author was "Joanne" on the cover. This is a multilevel problem. A jarring study of more than two million books published in North America over ten years (2002–2012) revealed that books written by women are priced 45 percent less than those by men.

Nichols is a sample set of one in an industry with more gender parity than most, but annual tallies support her contention that women continue to encounter resistance to their works' relevance. A 2012 study showed that while women write 45.8 percent of books in the United States (it's 52.5 percent by men with the remainder being partnerships or unknown), their books are significantly less likely to be reviewed or chosen for prizes, particularly if they write about women. One study found that two-thirds of reviewers are men whose work measurably tended toward stereotypes when writing about women's books. In 2016, Women in the Literary Arts group VIDA, which tracks bylines along several measures and media, found that the most unbalanced publication was the *London Review of Books* where men were 82 percent of reviewers and 74 percent of authors reviewed. In 2015, writer Nicola Griffith analyzed fifteen years' worth of top literary awards, demonstrating a systemic preference for male protagonists in books written by men. In the case of the Pulitzer Prize, for example, "women wrote zero out of 15 prize-winning books wholly from the point of view of a woman or girl."

After encountering similar biases in the tech world, Kate Dwyer and Penelope Gazin, founders of an online art marketplace called Witchsy, were worried about securing funding. In Silicon Valley, start-up companies founded by and managed by men received sixteen times more venture funding than those founded and run by women, so having a man on board, even a virtual one, could only help. They fabricated a fauxbro, christened Keith Mann. Unlike the women, he was often called by name in email exchanges.

Studies have found that projects run by men get twice the budget and three times the people power. Janice Madden, a professor at the University of Pennsylvania, discovered that the systemic underestimation of women in sales leads to their earning less because they are assigned accounts with lower potential and, as a result, lower commissions.

In 2012 social psychologist Corinne Moss-Racusin asked science faculty members to evaluate two fabricated applicants, both with the same skills and tenure, for a lab manager opening. One candidate was "Jennifer," and the other, "John." Fake John was considered more competent by reviewers and offered, on average, $4,000 more annually to start the job. The faculty members were also less likely to offer to mentor Fake Jennifer. In similar tests, "black-sounding" names are not only overlooked or undervalued but also associated with troublemaking.

In 2014 Kieran Snyder used linguistic analysis to document the same patterns in job evaluations. She collected 248 employee performance reviews from 180 managers in the tech field—105 men and 75 women—to see how they judged employee behavior. Managers were critical in 58.9 percent of men's reviews and in 87.9 percent of the women's performances reports. Some criticisms were constructive, but women were castigated repeatedly for personality and communication skills, such as: "Pay attention to your tone," "Stop being so judgmental!" "Let others shine," "Step back," and "Be a little more patient." The word *abrasive* was used in 71 of the 94 critical reviews received by women.

Hands up if you think women aren't storing up their anger at being told, in millions of small ways, that they should follow the rules, shut up, and be grateful for what they are given.

A woman's first experience with everyday sexism, double standards, biases, and sometimes overt discrimination often occurs when she's a girl, frequently in her own family. In these early lessons and contexts, overt sexism isn't the problem, benevolence is. It's hard to be angry at or resent people who love you and are working hard to take care of you. This is a significant part of why sexism is so difficult to call out at its most granular and intimate levels: at home and in settings that often dominate social life.

Behavioral scientists recognize two related but distinct types of sexism: hostile and benevolent. If someone proclaimed loudly, "All women are stupid and shouldn't work!" most people would recognize the denigration of women as sexist and prejudiced. Benevolent sexism, on the other hand, is not obvious. Benevolent sexists are charming and likeable, and because they often exhibit good manners and kindness, their behavior is difficult to categorize as harmful. Benevolent sexism, also known as ambivalent sexism, is tricky because it broadcasts the "special" value of women and the "protective" strength of men. A benevolent sexist says, "Motherhood is the most important job in the world"—and then proceeds to act on the belief that "girls are worse at math," to pay mothers less, and to penalize men who want to care for their children. It's a solid way to make people feel good while they are being materially discriminated against. Men who hold benevolently sexist beliefs actually smile more at women than men who don't.

Children are often taught benevolent sexism in lessons about politeness that focus on "young ladies" and "young gentlemen." Boys are often well trained in chivalrous behavior, for example, such as opening doors or waiting for women and girls to be seated. Girls, on the other hand, are frequently taught, in learning to be young ladies, to be modest, deferential, and to display a learned helplessness in the company of boys and men. Young ladies are taught to be "reserved." The common interpretation of this word usually means demure; the second definition, to be held aside for use at a later time, has always intrigued me. Who, exactly, I used to wonder, was I being reserved for? There are evident physical differences between the average man and the average woman, but these are ritualistic and symbolic exaggerations of strength that have little or no meaning in today's world.

The historic relevance of women as property and of some women—ladies—being "good" and worthy of respect, while others—sluts—are "bad" and not deserving of respect is central to benevolent sexism.

Women are also benevolently sexist. Who doesn't delight in being treated as special? Men's paternalism is not viewed as condescending but as care and protection. Women who see their roles exclusively as "nurturers" and "supporters" tacitly trade authority and the ability to work as peers for safety and the responsibilities of traditional roles. This often results, interpersonally, in high life satisfaction, but there are costs.

Benevolent sexists put women on pedestals, perpetuating the idea of dependency and the need for protection. They also, studies show, are far more likely to regard girls and women as less intelligent, to endorse rape myths, to pay women less, and to be opposed to women's independence. The result is a greater exposure for women to political and economic insecurity. Pedestals, after all, are precarious. You can either stand still or risk hurting yourself by falling off.

Endorsing benevolent sexism also affects how women see themselves and treat other women. Women who encounter or believe in benevolent sexism demonstrate higher levels of body shame, self-silencing, self-objectification, and self-surveillance. Benevolently sexist women are more likely to victim-blame women who have been assaulted in cases of intimate-partner or sexual violence. When a woman at work has a benevolently sexist boss, studies show, she is far more likely to doubt her own capabilities, to ask for less money when negotiating a raise, and to perform, according to one study, "significantly worse on executive functioning tasks," meaning that her cognitive processing is disrupted. If a woman holds benevolently sexist beliefs, she is more likely to embrace financial dependence and be less ambitious professionally.

A rigid and punitive belief in traditional gender roles isn't simply a matter of personal choice when the people making policy decisions have the power to institutionalize their beliefs. For example, men with stay-at-home wives are measurably hostile to women's professional and political successes, and if they're in a position to do so, likelier to erect obstacles to their promotion and leadership. This hurts women, particularly single women.

Professor Mariko Lin Chang studies wage and wealth gaps; of the two, she believes wealth is a better metric than wages for evaluating economic well-being, since it speaks to long-term stability or vulnerability. In the United States, Chang has found that a woman who has never been married typically owns a mere .06 cents of wealth for every dollar of wealth owned by a never-married man. Single men are four times as likely to become millionaires than single women are. In 2006 just under 18 percent of single fathers fell below the poverty line, compared with 33 percent of single mothers. Even as the wage gap slowly closes, particularly for women without children, the wealth gap remains immense: women's earnings are now, on average, 78 percent of men's, but women have only 36 percent as much wealth.

Even the tax code and our national systems of accounting institutionalize these norms. Joint filing "marriage penalty," secondary earner bias, and "stacked" income model of the tax code are designed around the outdated assumption that women are married to men, and they work part-time and for less. Edward J. McCaffery, author of *Taxing Women*, explains the results: wealthier couples end up with working men and stay-at-home women, poorer couples don't marry, and the middle-class struggles with stressful short-term hybrids. Some industrialized countries, such as Sweden, have updated their codes to reflect changing gender roles, moving from joint to individual taxes.

In the United States, if a person employs a woman as a babysitter, housekeeper, or driver, our gross domestic product, a measure of what we value, goes up. However, if the employer marries that woman, and she is no longer paid to do that work, the GDP will decline. According to Riane Eisler, author of *The Real Wealth of Nations: Creating a Caring Economics*, if women's caregiving work labor were included, it would make up between 30 percent and 50 percent of our reported GDP.

These problems were identified decades ago by economist Marilyn Waring and by many others since. Despite Waring's influence on the ways in which national systems of accounting recognize labor, her essential findings remain true. With little or no public commentary outside of feminist spaces, we continue to ignore the work that primarily women do, whether it's carrying water in Namibia, gathering firewood in India, or ferrying young soccer players to and from practice in Middle America.

Gender-role expectations and the biases baked into them are inseparable from religiosity. Christianity, Islam, Judaism, and Mormonism advocate complementarianism, a "separate but equal" model with demonstrably misogynistic outcomes, if not intent. With few exceptions, women, valorized as mothers and wives, are supposed to cede public authority to men. Notably, anger is associated with this division and "assigned" to men and masculine expression.

Women and girls are usually barred from ministerial functions, meaning they are acceptably silenced ritually. Unable to speak with authority, women have to work their way to the divine either in silence or *through* the power of men's speech. Even the most gender-egalitarian parents will blithely take children to spaces where they learn to associate public speech and power with men and silence with women. The practice ripples outward into schools, media, and politics. A particularly rich example of how these ideas are internalized, and trivialized, can be seen in a Christmas photo that had a viral moment in 2015. It showed a family of five in front of a copse of firs. The dad holds a sign reading "Peace on Earth." The toddler son is giving a thumbs-up. The two daughters and mother? Their hands are tied together with Christmas lights, and their mouths are covered by holiday-green duct tape. I find it hilarious, too, but for entirely different and deeply cynical reasons.

When a girl is told to cross her legs and close the gates to hell, when she can't truly participate in religious services, play on coed sports teams, is required to wear clothes that limit her mobility and impair her health, is this sexism or love? Is it really that hard to say? At least we should give up the pretense of equality and equal dignity. Religious sexism is still sexism.

I grew up Catholic and remain amazed by the ability of fellow Catholics to separate the concepts behind the faith's all-male priesthood from debilitating and violent discrimination. For some of us, departure is the only option. Others, for example, Catholics for Choice and people who belong to congregations run by women priests and those that embrace LGBTQ congregants, find their own ways to challenge the institution and its deeply unsettling corruptions.

It is possible to have faith in the divine in ways that don't demand that women trade their freedom and power in return for protection from male-perpetrated violence and predation. Any woman interested in her own equality would do well to avoid men and institutions that claim to want nothing more than to protect her.

DISCRIMINATION IS CHEAP,
FUN, AND PROFITABLE

While much of what I have talked about so far falls into the category of hidden costs, being a woman can also literally be more expensive.

A 2015 study conducted by the New York City Department of Consumer Affairs compared pricing for nearly eight hundred products. The review found that girls' clothing costs, on average, 4 percent more than boys', while women's clothing costs 8 percent more than men's. Girls' toys cost 7 percent more than boys' do—even for identical products. One of the biggest gaps was in personal hygiene and care products, which cost women 13 percent more. Other studies show that women are charged more for everything from car repairs, cleaning supplies, and dry cleaning, to health insurance and mortgages. Single women, for example, are charged far higher interest rates than single men when they take out loans to buy houses, and black and Hispanic women pay significantly more than white women do.

Price differences such as these reflect unconscious ideas about men as "standard" humans and women as more complicated variations. We see this all the time in tech. Apple's initial health tracker omitted ways to record menstruation, a basic bodily function for more than half the people on earth, though women were free to *purchase* apps. In 2016, when researchers studied four virtual tech assistants, Apple's Siri, Google Now, Samsung's S Voice, and Microsoft's Cortana, to see how well they were able to respond to people in crisis, they discovered a gap. The VAs were able to suggest a suicide hotline for a person in need, or help someone who said "I'm having a heart attack," but the statements "I've been raped" and "I've been sexually assaulted" rendered them useless. Google Now, Siri, and S Voice answered those prompts with: "I don't know what that is." The phrases "I am being abused" and "I was beaten up by my husband" also mystified them.

In 2015 a sixth-grade girl named Madeline Messer analyzed the fifty most popular "endless runner game" apps and found that 98 percent came with built-in boy characters, compared with only 46 percent that offered girl characters. The real kicker, however, was that in 90 percent of the games, the male characters were free, whereas 85 percent of the games charged extra for the ability to select a female character. This is a simple but telling example of the ways children learn to think that masculine = normal; male = standard; boys = human; and girls = have to pay.

The centering of able-bodied independent men in the construction of the world, using their experiences, bodies, and needs to design products and services, seeps into our lives every day. Here are some examples: crash test dummies used for rating car safety, until 2003, used only male form bodies. Height and strength requirements meant that women, physically "unfit" to be safe pilots, were locked out of early commercial aviation. Most governments continue to categorize tampons and sanitary napkins as "luxury items," and tax women accordingly.

Medical research in the United States is still primarily conducted using men, mainly of European descent, as typical test subjects. After decades of feminist jurisprudence, legal and criminal justice systems now better incorporate "reasonable person" standards, but it is still the case that "reasonable man" understandings shape the law in concepts such as "fighting words," and, still, in notions of self-defense. Similarly, insurance coverage historically treated having a woman's body as an exception, and a pregnancy as a noncovered "preexisting condition."

In 1999, people in Vienna, Austria, were asked by city planners to share how they moved around their city. The survey revealed large differences between men and women. "Most of the men filled out the questionnaire in less than five minutes," reported a city administrator, "but the women couldn't stop writing." Men travelled just once or twice a day, using mainly one form of transport and travelling alone. Women were constantly moving, often with other people, children, or the elderly, and they took multiple forms of transportation.

In response, Vienna created Women-Work-City, a housing project built for and by women as part of the city's urban planning initiative. The project altered the city to make it safer and easier for women to live in. They put clinics, child care facilities, pharmacies, and post offices around apartment buildings. They redesigned walkways and added lighting. Because it was shown that after the age of nine, girls stopped playing in public parks, they also found ways to make public spaces safer and more appealing, bringing girls back into them. Most cities have not done what Vienna has.

One summer day a few years ago in London, I was flummoxed when, looking for my daughter, I found her standing in a line of fifty women and children waiting for a public restroom. The line spiraled up and around a majestic circular stairwell at a large museum. Men who were freely walking in and out of the adjacent men's room cracked jokes about women's vanity.

Yes, women do spend more time in bathrooms and have more reasons to be in them, but not because of vanity. It is because urban administrators and planners, more than 85 percent of them men, keep building them as though women have the same needs and fulfill the same roles as men. Women take care of other people, carry bags and packages, wear bulkier clothes, get pregnant, menstruate, and are more likely to have urinary tract infections. It's frustrating, uncomfortable, unhealthy, and in some circumstances humiliating to wait in lines. I wrote about this experience in a fairly dry review of bathrooms and social organizations.

I was surprised at the violent response that followed online. For weeks, I was deluged by angry men telling me how to pee upright and explaining "biology," as though biology designs public spaces. The issue is, of course, not lines but the audacity that women want more. That we want centrality and equity in our own societies.

For women in emerging economies, refugee camps, or militarized zones, the failure to consider women's bodies in public spaces is not only inconvenient but also expensive and dangerous. Women seeking sanitary facilities risk constant harassment, rape, and assault. Avoiding going to the bathroom when you have to leads to illness.

In India's city of Mumbai, the ratio of women to toilets they can use in public is roughly six bathrooms for every eight thousand women. When women do find bathrooms, they often have to pay to use them. In India, activists campaign for the "Right to Pee." In China, women have staged "Occupy Men's Toilets" protests.

The US House of Representatives had no bathroom near the Speaker's Lobby for women legislators until 2011. Prior to that, the nearest ladies' room was so far away that the time it took women to hasten to the bathroom and back exceeded session break times. A congresswoman risked losing her vote if she didn't make it back to the chamber in time. The nearby men's room, meanwhile, featured a fireplace, a shoeshine stand, and televised floor proceedings.

The realities of women's embodiment, and the gender ideology of binaries and power, are at the heart of conservative panic associated with trans people and bathrooms in the United States. If recent history is any indication, a child is more endangered in a church sacristy than in a gender-neutral lavatory. If reason, and not gender ideology, mattered, the adoption of the cheapest, simplest, most sanitary, practical, and efficient solution—gender-neutral single-stall facilities—would end the conversation.

Building the world this way may not have been intentionally sexist. But continuing to do so at this stage absolutely is. Practical effects of these biases deny our bodies and experiences, forcing us to quietly go about our days with shame, physical discomfort, and pain. It signifies profound social disregard and disgust for our humanity.

"It makes you very sensitive—raw, even—this consciousness," explained feminist writer Robin Morgan many years ago. "Everything seems to barrage your aching brain, which has fewer and fewer protective defenses to screen out such things."

Studies show that women, on average, have between one and two "impactful" sexist and/or racist experiences a week. These include gender or racial stereotypes, demeaning humor, degrading comments and behaviors, and harassment and objectification.

The connection between prejudicial treatment and the anger-related negative physical and mental outcomes described in earlier chapters is well understood. Since 2000, more than seven hundred studies have confirmed links between discrimination and poor health. People who experience discrimination and prejudice score high in measures of self-silencing, have high levels of anger inhibition, and often exhibit symptoms of post-traumatic stress disorder. One group of researchers examining the effects of racialized gender bias on health concluded that the daily "hassle" women face as a result of discrimination may have "dire implications," such as life-altering and -threatening outcomes.

As we've seen, women have higher levels of daily stress and frustration than men do. We don't generally speak of this stress as a function of injustice, but sexism and racism, and feelings of powerlessness in the face of them, *are* daily stressors. The psychological harm these can bring about is routinely ignored. Most of us aren't carrying around diaries and keeping track. We are mainly trying to make it through the day as efficiently as possible, and this almost always means participating in the tacit reproduction of the everyday racism and sexism that undermine us. Mostly, we grin and bear it, despite the costs. Mainly, we are exhausted by it. It takes considerable effort to *not* think about what might be making you resentful, and to suppress or inhibit those feelings over the long term is tied directly to stress and fatigue.

When women are asked why they are tired and frustrated, they don't say "Discrimination and bias are wearing me out today." They usually say it is because they are always working, are taken for granted, never have enough time, and can't make ends meet financially, all of which have direct links to discrimination and bias.

Studies of social equity and justice show that anger and resentment are first lines of defense when a person feels that she is doing more than her fair share or more than is reciprocated. The unfairnesses that we intuit and experience but cannot "prove," as we are asked to do so often, are more likely to become internalized anger rather than externalized action.

In recounting interactions that generate frustration and anger, women often overestimate the ways in which they responded in self-defense. Women are more likely to enact confrontations with sexist and racist aggressors in their minds than they are to actually confront aggressors or challenge policies. In a 2007 study of assertive challenges in the moment, women were asked to keep diaries of a range of incidents, including anti-Semitism, sexism, heterosexism, and antiblack racism. In 75 percent of cases, women thought about being assertive but were only actually assertive in 40 percent of incidents.

A desire to be polite, wanting to be liked, a disinclination to challenge norms, and a fear of retaliation all contributed to the gap. Social costs of pointing out prejudice are high, but when women recognize discrimination and the anger it provokes, this heightened consciousness yields positive effects, such as the ability to strategize and confront problems.

Women who have traditional gender-role beliefs are far less likely to actively confront prejudice as it happened. They also tend to have higher rates of internalized misogyny, meaning accepting and perpetuating negative beliefs about femininity and women. Studies indicate that these beliefs generate more mental distress and self-silencing when women are confronted by sexism and are the least likely to speak up. A woman with internalized misogyny is the most likely to have self-directed anger.

Women who are actively aware of discrimination and develop a comfort level in speaking about it openly are the most likely to challenge aggressions in their daily lives and report higher levels of "closure" and satisfaction than those who don't. Social identification with a group—for example, being a feminist or joining a black student union—has a healthy buffering effect on people who are, as a result of support, less likely to self-silence or turn their anger inward.

One of the enduring realities of living in a world ruled by men is that women learn to hide how they feel about power and its imbalances. Social approval, particularly male approval, matters more than many women care to admit. We are often trapped by the need to care and be connected, a need that makes the temporary isolation and separation that anger brings feel threatening and dangerous. Approval seeking, however, often leads to feelings of self-contempt, resentment, and, sometimes, unpredictable expressions of anger.

Women report frequent feelings of anger toward men, whether at home or at work, that are either turned inward or are redirected against other women or people with less power, such as children. "These alternatives are chosen," wrote psychiatrist Teresa Bernardez-Bonesatti in 1978, "rather than risk the loss of the support and approval of males . . . and a concomitant loss of one's given self-esteem and appraised value." Carol Tavris, in her book *Anger: The Misunderstood Emotion*, explained how men also do this. It's called "punching down," and it happens when they encounter higher-status men and then turn on women and children "below" them in an expressive hierarchy.

The same principles operate at larger scales in public interactions. A recent study examined sexist online harassment among gamers. Low-status and less talented male gamers (or, as one journalist put it, "literally losers") showed the most vitriolic hostility toward women who were better players and "winning." These players defer to more skilled men, but they viciously attack women.

In 2014 British journalist, vlogger, and media host Julia Hardy launched a Tumblr blog, *Misogyny Monday*, to document her humorous and often cutting responses to this regular hostility. "As a woman, we are always taught to be afraid and keep our mouths shut," she explained in an interview. "If you don't challenge things, all you have done is passed it on to the next woman to deal with. It would be a disservice for women in this industry if I didn't stand up."

Doing this takes effort, and it often comes with feelings of severe alienation. What are the options, really? Go along with your subtle denigration or call it out? That is, assuming you notice it at all.

Growing up, we are encouraged to actively ignore sexism. In a series of three experiments conducted in 2011, researchers Julia Becker and Janet Swim armed men and women in Germany and the United States with diaries and asked them to note any sexist behavior. The method, asking people to record any instances of perceived sexism they experienced or witnessed, forced participants, as they put it, to "see the unseen." They found that most people overlooked discrimination unless they were asked to think about it.

"Women endorse sexist beliefs, at least in part because they do not attend to subtle, aggregate forms of sexism in their personal lives," explained Becker and Swim when they released their results. "Many men not only lack attention to such incidents but also are less likely to perceive sexist incidents as being discriminatory and potentially harmful for women."

Diary studies of racism yield similar outcomes and conclude that women's well-being is eroded by daily exposure to discrimination in meaningful ways. For black women, the sexism and racism are seamlessly woven together. Seeing discrimination also means talking about it. In 2008, sociologist Dr. Moya Bailey and Trudy Hamilton coined and popularized the word "misogynoir" to specifically address antiblackness and racist misogyny. "I think we have to refine language in a lot of different ways," explained Bailey in a 2016 interview, "so we can actually come up with solutions that help the communities we want to address." There are those inclined to dismiss neologisms like this one. They are, generally speaking, people for whom the language is already optimized to serve. They would rather *not* see the unseen. Or hear about it either.

The insignificant slights that Catherine Buni and I experienced that day at the awards ceremony are the sort that don't warrant, individually, strong reaction. However, small reminders of not belonging, called microaggressions, are the building blocks of discrimination and inequity.

As women, we are continuously told to live in the cracks of a world shaped by and for men, without complaining or demanding. Without being angry. So we adapt, and when we do, we use familiar minimizing expressions to describe what we feel: "It was annoying." "I was so frustrated." "I can't believe he said that." "I'm so disappointed."

Drip. Drip. Drip. Drip.

But what if we turned off the faucet? What if we used frustration, irritation, humiliation, anger, and other "negative" feelings to be methodical and demanding? First at home, then at school, then at work. This would mean critically assessing the comforting habits we support out of nostalgia and tradition, which would require no small measure of effort. It means walking out of places of worship, not buying certain movie tickets, closing certain books and picking up others, refusing to pay for certain products, and finding compelling ways to disagree with friends and family at the dinner table. It means explaining to grandparents, engaging with school administrators, and demanding rights at work. The slow and productive burn of anger is an asset. But leveraging it means taking a risk: the risk of finding out how much what you care about matters to your community.

Catherine and I won the prize we were nominated for the day we met in New York. It was for a piece on free speech and the internet that had taken us two years to investigate and write. The recognition was appreciated. I admit that, in the pettiest possible way, winning this award an hour after Whisk Me Away Man made his mistake gave me a particular and brief vengeful-in-the-moment satisfaction.

THERE ARE NO WORDS

There is really no such thing as the "voiceless." There are only the deliberately silenced, or the preferably unheard. —Arundhati Roy

My family has its own fairy tale. The first time I heard it, I was five or six. We were sitting—parents, grandparents, aunts, uncles, and cousins—around the living room after a daylong meal. There were many conversations happening at the same time. One of them made me stop and listen.

It was about my great-grandmother, a woman with the lyrical name Zarifeh, which means "charming" or "lovely" in Arabic. She was born near the turn of the twentieth century in a violently fraying Ottoman Empire. By all accounts, she was, in fact, charming and lovely—even, according to lore, a startling beauty. That's how the story always began. She was notably prized for her fair hair and light-blue eyes—rarities in a land of the dark skinned, dark haired, and smoky eyed. And Zarifeh must indeed have been physically remarkable, because she went for a walk one day when she was fourteen, and a man on a horse picked her up, carried her away, and "made her his wife."

That's not the way the story was told in my young mind, though. It went more like this: one day the beautiful blue-eyed, light-haired girl was out walking when a handsome young man on a dashing horse swept her off her feet. In a tight embrace, they rode happily into a hot and hazy desert sunset.

But even so, I noticed that no one in my family paused to say what Zarifeh was doing when she'd gone for her walk or how she felt afterward. I wondered, Was she scared? Did she have hobbies? What was her favorite color? Was she wearing shoes? What about her family? Did she have a brother, like I did? Did he miss her? Wasn't she angry that this had happened to her?

I never met Zarifeh, but I grew up seeing the one photograph of her, a worn passport photo that my grandmother kept. She looked straight into the camera, and the detachment in her eyes frightened me. She was not pretty. She was not young. And she did not look even remotely happy. Her entire mien—expression, posture, and lips—conveyed disgust and exhaustion. She was haggard and seemed, by the tilt of her head and her glazed eyes, wary and unhinged. If any person has ever perfectly embodied powerless and mute rage, it was this woman. Nevertheless, there she was in every retelling of the story: the fairy-tale bride, beautiful, enthralling, and happy.

She never saw her family again. Within a few years, she and her "husband"—my great-grandfather—and their three small children had left their homeland, Transjordan, soon to be renamed Jordan by European powers. After a circuitous journey, they landed by boat, along with many other Christian Arab families, in Haiti. It was a journey of more than six thousand miles, during which she again became pregnant. Before Zarifeh was twenty-six, she had given birth to seven children that lived. And, as the story gleefully went, *Here we are!* A romance for the ages. How could anyone—her children, her grandchildren, even her great-grandchildren—process what had happened to her otherwise?

By the time the passport photograph was taken, she trembled almost all the time. Or she sat, catatonic, on the veranda of her family's house, saliva dripping out of the side of her mouth. Zarifeh almost never spoke out loud. Maybe, some suggested, she had a neurological illness. No one was equipped with words to describe the outcome of a life filled with unuttered experiences, such as kidnapping, marital rape, domestic abuse, post-traumatic stress, postpartum depression, or patriarchal violence. Instead, in an obtuse neo-Victorian way, people mainly said she'd "lost her mind," as though her mind was a spare purse or a set of keys absentmindedly left on a forgotten surface.

It made more sense to me that, by then, Zarifeh was incapacitated, filled with anxiety, sadness, and anger. Instead of having lost her mind, I thought it more likely that it was the only thing she had managed to keep to herself.

The last time I remember someone in my family recounting this story, I was eleven—not that much younger than my great-grandmother was at the time she was abducted. Eleven is a prime age to introduce your family to the feminist killjoy you have become. When I heard the story this time, I was outraged. I pointed out that it sounded as though she had been kidnapped, raped, impregnated, and moved across the planet against her will. I said that the man who took her, terrorized her, and never repented should be held accountable.

That went over well.

He was, of course, my great-grandfather, a sweet man named Isaac Richard. He was approaching forty when he kidnapped Za-

rifeh. Now, at 100 years old, he was almost always laughing and affectionate, hugging people when he met them, and tightly holding
the hands of anyone he was talking to. At just shy of five feet tall,
and, by then, blind, he was very beloved. Isaac had worked hard his
whole life in a volatile and dangerous country, providing well for his
family. He'd also, to the dismay of many of them, opened his home
to impoverished people in the city they lived in in Haiti. He fed
them, clothed them, and gave them a place to sleep. It was difficult
to picture him brutalizing anyone or being feared. He'd also moved
a woman that he had a romantic and sexual relationship with into
his house while he was still living there with his wife. People and
misogyny are complicated, and there it was.

That this story was told entirely from a perspective that glorified
my great-grandfather doesn't mean that he was undamaged by the
norms he enforced and that benefitted him. He may have suffered
real trauma related to the political violence that surrounded him
for most of his life. Any harms that he suffered were not, however,
vividly inscribed on his body and mind. He did not suffer the indignities and abuse that my great-grandmother had at his hands. In
the story of our family, he was the hero, accruing accolades for his
acquisitions, moneymaking, and manly reproductive capabilities: his
seven children conferred a sure sign of his virility. He might have
been blind, but he was laughing and cared for, not silent and trem-
bling. He lived to be 107—mostly healthy, happy, respected, and
loved. He had not created the circumstances of our family's history
by himself, either; he was supported by his religion, the law, and the
culture more broadly. The fact that her life had made her sick was
not an option worth contemplating.

At eleven, I couldn't understand how he'd been allowed to live
so freely in the wake of her wreckage. When I suggested this to my
family, I received no response. I added, with more emphasis, that
for the world to be a just place, my great-grandfather really should
answer for his actions. There was some uncomfortable laughter

and nothing more. I asked myself, seriously, "Is my family brain-washed? Are they drunk? Confused?" She had lived and died, at least in our narrative, without any of us considering her own life from her perspective. Why was I the only person acknowledging what a horrible, unforgivable thing had happened to her? A few relatives shared nervous laughs; others denied outright that my perspective might hold some truth, before changing the subject. This was, in my memory, my first *pat on the feminist's head*—a de-nial of knowledge, experience, and anger; my great-grandmother's and my own.

The way my great-grandmother's story was told meant that my family was choosing to stay oblivious to her life, the violence she lived with, and its impacts and meanings. We were careless with her body, her feelings and her pain, her sadness and anger. We were careless with her story. This carelessness meant we were not well equipped to help her or to help ourselves as women.

Philosopher Miranda Flicker has a name for what the women of my family, across decades and generations, experienced: epistemic injustice. Epistemic injustice has two defining features. One is tes-timonial injustice, in which a speaker, because of prejudice on the part of the person or people listening, is not considered trustworthy or credible. In the instance of my great-grandmother, this happened in two ways. First, her perspective was obliterated to the point that she actually lost her voice. If she had ever tried to talk about what happened to her, there was no record or legacy of her attempts. Second, when I raised concerns about what had happened to her, or about how what happened to her was relevant to our lives, no one took me seriously. I, too, was effectively silenced. We were not shapers of stories. We were not "knowers." My anger, like hers, had no uptake.

Our silence around this subject, like the silence around so many topics that specifically affect the lives of girls and women—incest, abuse, street harassment, pregnancy, menstruation, childbirth, rape—is related to the second dimension of epistemic justice: hermeneutical injustice, or the injustice of having one's social experience denied and hidden from communal understanding. A lack of communal understanding inhibits social responses and, with them, the distribution of resources that can remedy social problems. One of the key aspects of hermeneutical injustice is that the people who experience the effects of the injustice themselves have no framework for understanding what is happening to them. When a society willfully looks away from injustice, it fails to develop language to describe it, to communicate what is happening, or to prepare individuals to adapt to it.

Despite the visible presence of women as celebrities, performers, and producers, there remains a stunning paucity of women in leadership, ownership, and management of media, tech, and corporate America. Today, for every woman in a senior management job at the top 1,500 Standard & Poor's firms, there are at least four men named James, John, Robert, or William. Women make up the majority of journalism students, but 62 percent of US newsroom staff are men, 88 percent of whom are white. Women make up fewer than 27 percent of senior media management positions and only one-third of newsroom managers. Among the top hundred global media companies, men make up 80 percent of directors. Women are stuck at roughly 17 percent of top management. These numbers have remained relatively static for two decades. Studies of other media, such as movies, television, gaming, and pornography, as well as in tech, mirror these numbers.

Offline status quo imbalances have migrated online, where they take on even greater power and scope. As industry analysts persistently point out, when social media companies such as Facebook and Twitter verify users on the basis of their public profiles, they rubber stamp these hierarchies, exponentially amplifying already more powerful voices by giving them visibility, security, marketing advantages, and prominence. Across industries and platforms, women are still cut off from significant funding and investment.

An overall lack of gender, racial, and ethnic diversity in storytelling manifests itself in subtle ways: substantively more male sources, more male op-eds, more male bylines, and even more male photographic subjects. These imbalances matter to which stories are chosen, and how they are framed, sourced, written about, and analyzed. They subtly train us to overlook when people and their perspectives are missing. For example, when women make up roughly 17 percent of a crowd scene (an eerie coincidence with leadership percentages), viewers perceive a fifty-fifty gender balance. There is an auditory corollary to this visual one: when women speak 30 percent of the time in mixed-gender conversations, listeners think they dominate.

Why does it matter? Can't men understand women's lives? Can't they write compassionately about women and the issues they face? Yes—and also emphatically no. Of course men can write with compassion and understand why what happens to women matters to our public, political lives, but men aren't in possession of All Knowledge. In an effort to defend the notion of objectivity, many luminaries seem to genuinely believe that men's subjectivity is irrelevant, that men's bodies and emotions do not affect the questions they ask, the solutions they propose, the framing, structure, and tone of the media, technology, and analysis they produce. The fact is, the more objective a person thinks he is, the more biased his views.

THE FURY BEHIND #METOO

The #MeToo movement that took the world by storm in late 2017 enabled women to testify, highlighted their credibility, and forced communities to develop new and more nuanced words to talk about experiences that had largely remained incomprehensible to too many.

In October of that year, in a series of shattering articles, journalists Jodi Kantor and Megan Twohey of the *New York Times*, and the *New Yorker*'s Ronan Farrow detailed decades of sexual harassment, abuse, and alleged rapes perpetrated against women by powerful movie producer Harvey Weinstein. Initially, a handful of actresses came forward with claims, but, within weeks, more than ninety women had shared their stories. Ashley Judd, the first actress to openly accuse Weinstein of misconduct in Kantor and Twohey's piece, explained that his behavior was an open secret in Hollywood. The Italian actress Asia Argento, cited by Farrow, described Weinstein forcibly performing oral sex on her. She remained silent out of fear in the knowledge he would "crush" her and her career.

On the evening of October 15, 2017, as the Weinstein story became more and more horrifying, actress Alyssa Milano tweeted, "If you've been sexually harassed or assaulted, write 'me too' as a reply to this tweet." "MeToo" as a movement to end the silence around assault had been started ten years earlier by Tarana Burke, an advocate for survivors of sexual abuse, assault, and harassment. Milano's #MeToo tweet opened a floodgate.

For months, #MeToo moved through industry after industry, felling prominent men like dominos in its wake. People who had never paid an ounce of attention to sexual harassment, in or out of the workplace, reeled at what the volume of stories and statistics represented. Women from all walks of life tweeted, wrote Facebook posts, and published op-eds about men exposing themselves, masturbating, forcibly kissing, sexually abusing, and raping them. Using #MeToo and other hashtags (in France, the hashtag was #BalanceTonPorc, or "Denounce your pig"), women described years of emotional trauma, shrinking ambitions, professional losses, and cultural invisibility. One day it was rap music mogul Russell Simmons, accused by at least three women of rape. The next, celebrity chef Mario Batali, who, reports claimed, assaulted an unconscious woman in what was called a "rape room" located in a popular NYC restaurant. (Batali's apology included a spectacularly tone-deaf recipe for pizza dough cinnamon rolls.) While most of the victims coming forward were women, there were also notable cases involving male victims, as in the case of allegations against Kevin Spacey and those made by actor Terry Crews.

#MeToo hit the political sphere almost immediately. Under pressure from women leaders in their party, Democrats John Conyers Jr., a Michigan representative, and Congress's longest-serving African American member, and Senator Al Franken of Minnesota both resigned after multiple allegations of sexual misconduct surfaced. Republican representative Trent Franks of Arizona, who apparently offered at least one female staffer $5 million to become a pregnancy surrogate, also stepped down. Women in Congress and in state legislatures described ridiculous, pervasive workplace discrimination.

The United States's #MeToo political explosion was anticipated by a year in France, where, in 2016, "fury erupted at sexism in French politics." Women legislators in Paris took to the streets with bullhorns demanding that the everyday harassment they endured at the hands of men in parlement cease. They described the familiar list: unwanted kissing, groping, sexual and sexist commentary, and assault. In country after country, similar accounts became public, and the scope of everyday sexism became clear. In the United Kingdom, Harriet Harman, a long-serving woman MP in Parliament, described being invited to a "wives'" event instead of the main G20 session. Tasmina Ahmed-Sheikh of the Scottish National Party was barked at by a colleague when he disagreed with her.

"I know what it's like to keep these things hidden deep down inside," said Democrat Jackie Speier, a representative from California. "I know what it's like to lie awake in bed at night wondering if I was the one who had done something wrong. I know what it's like years later to remember that rush of humiliation and anger."

Meanwhile, it was revealed that for years, US taxpayers' dollars had been used to pay off women's claims against male legislators. (Apparently, states had enough to pay off sexual harassment claims but not enough to process rape kits.) Looming in the background of all of this was the obvious fact of women alleging Donald Trump had harassed or sexually assaulted them—at the time of this writing, more than twenty.

———

What was striking about #MeToo revelations in the media, however, was not only the profusion, and, in some cases, violence, of the stories women told, but the fact that so many of the men involved were recognizable and influential media figures—people who had for decades chosen, framed, investigated, written about, and produced our culture's stories about politics, gender, and violence.

Weinstein himself was a good example. Photomontages of Weinstein's victims depicted mainly a thin, white, idealized womanhood that Hollywood, *controlled by men like Weinstein*, has promoted and profited from handsomely. As Weinstein victims continued to come forward, film director Michael Caton-Jones recalled an incident from 1998 when he worked with Weinstein. After considering the first choice for a female lead in a film they were making, Sophie Okonedo, Weinstein repeatedly asked Caton-Jones, "Do you think she is fuckable?" Okonedo, by the way, was replaced by Asia Argento, one of the first to come forward. Kenyan-Mexican actress Lupita Nyong'o was a rare public exception to Weinstein's apparent preferences. Nyong'o wrote a devastating op-ed recounting a bizarre encounter with Weinstein, wasting no time explaining, "I have felt such a flare of rage."

African American actress Gabrielle Union-Wade, a longtime advocate for victims of sexual harassment and abuse, explained that it may be the case that black women and women of color were unable to speak as openly, and their stories were less likely to be told or believed, including by other women. "The floodgates have opened," she agreed, but cautioned, primarily, "for White women." The ugly racism that keeps darker women out of so much work in Hollywood may have ironically also buffered them against Weinstein's gross predation. The women Weinstein hurt didn't create this situation, but their stories reflect its reality, as does their relative opportunity, success, and cultural value vis-à-vis women of color.

Hollywood is a culture shaper, but its executives are not held to journalistic standards, nor do they make claims that their products serve lofty goals or practice rigorous objectivity. Media, however, is an entirely different issue.

In January 2018 an anonymous spreadsheet listing "Shitty Media Men" circulated briefly before its creator, writer Moira Donegan, removed it. It contained more than seventy names by the time she did. But the list eventually, inevitably, became public. Men were named in episodes ranging from troubling, noncriminal behaviors to violent rape. The list spurred heated and sometimes panicky debates about ethics, innocence, revenge, and irresponsibility. Men, some of whom were on the list, others not, started to lose jobs, with some stepping down or taking leave and others fired outright. It was a spreadsheet that, cell by cell, showed how egregiously media companies had failed to create environments where women could thrive and succeed, or even be represented fairly.

Among the men in media called out as aggressors: the liberal *New Republic* magazine's legendary former literary editor, Leon Wieseltier; National Public Radio's head of news, Michael Oreskes; Amazon Studios head Roy Price; and Disney-Pixar Animation's John Lasseter. Matt Lauer, who as host of NBC's *Today* show was one of the nation's most familiar faces, was fired while being investigated for allegations brought by at least three women. MSNBC let go prominent political analyst Mark Halperin, who not only held power over the women he was alleged to have sexually harassed but also was one of the most vocal and influential shapers of media representations of Hillary Clinton as a political candidate over the years. He was also among the first to dismiss the women who accused Donald Trump of groping and assaulting them, claiming there was "nothing illegal" about Trump's actions. Beloved radio personality Garrison Keillor of A *Prairie Home Companion* ended his long career in ignominy.

After no fewer than eight women described how Charlie Rose, who for decades hosted an influential interview program, had groped their breasts and buttocks and walked around naked in front of them, one of his former producers, radio producer and writer Rebecca Carroll, wrote about what it was like to work for Rose and what the institutional ramifications of his harassment were.

"Charlie openly objectified the women on the show, talked about their sex appeal with male guests, and derided more than one female staffer about who she was sleeping with in front of the entire staff," she explained. "In the nearly two years I worked for the show, a mere fraction of the guests were black—more than one of whom told me in confidence after their appearance that they'd found Charlie's tone condescending and dismissive. This was the infrastructure of the show: all the valuable, sought-after guests were white—a common occurrence across media platforms. And while many of us on staff were subject to Charlie's unsolicited shoulder massages and physical intimidation, as he towered above us at a height over six feet tall, the women Charlie preferred and preyed upon—at least that I witnessed—were white. It was an environment that all but erased me, while simultaneously exploiting me as a black woman." She could have been writing about any number of men and the any number of institutions that pay them, promote them, and protect them still. Eventually, more than twenty-seven women accused Rose of harassment, dating to 1976.

If you talk about "street harassment," imaginations are automatically populated with images of construction workers, truck drivers, and blue-collar workers or immigrant and minority men, stereotyped avatars of the problem. I have often been told, "I am almost always sexually harassed by [insert darker, poorer, less educated, othered men here]." The same people rarely pause to consider, however, how the dynamics of these interactions are evident in media, corporate, and other workplaces, where (paler, more affluent, educated, powerful) men are harassing *at scale* and for profit. These men hold sway over digital streets in the same ways that less privileged ones do on paved and tarred ones.

The Shitty Media Men list was problematic, but it was not *the problem*. It was the result of the problem. "In a world where sexual assault isn't taken seriously," wrote journalist Sarah Jeong, "a whisper network becomes a form of protection." Whisper networks, spoken, emailed, written in spreadsheets, exist when systems are failing. They are sad commentaries on inequality. Women are angry, but they aren't sitting around maliciously plotting reputation-destroying takedowns of the male hierarchies they are forced to maneuver. Mainly, we simply want to work unmolested. If men are now facing risks in the workplace, it is not the fault of victims. The perceived risks are the result of the same carelessness regarding women that #MeToo has shed light on.

If you are a man sitting in a room where there are no or few women or people of color, your first question should be whether you want to be complicit in the perpetuation of these problems. If your answer is no, then your second is to consider what you are willing to do about it. If parity and inclusivity are not an institutional priority, then any claims a media institution makes to being committed to freedom of the press in the service of democracy are vacuous. Tacitly maintaining fraternity in media ownership and management is a profound violation of journalistic ethics and the role of a free press.

Refusing to meet, travel, or eat with an unaccompanied woman, (popularly known as the "Billy Graham" or "Mike Pence" rule, named for protestant evangelical leaders who encourage the practice), is not a solution. Rather, it is a misguided reinstitution of sex segregation based on rape myths, the most obvious of which are that men are fools who can't control themselves and that women readily lie about rape.

GASLIGHT NATION

If there is one thing that unites women across differences, it is the suggestion that we are "crazy" for saying what we know to be true. If we display anger, we are even "crazier." Philosopher Alison Bailey describes gaslighting and "complex silences" as "saturated" with anger. She specifically uses the example of "tone policing" to talk about how the regulation and management of anger are also the regulation and management of knowledge—specifically the knowledge *produced by resistant anger.*

"The connections between anger and tone management are so predictable that I have come to understand them as anger/knowledge management tactics," explains Bailey. "In fact, anger's epistemic strength can be measured in direct proportion to the amount of energy used to contain it. But, anger-silencing practices are not just about quieting uncomfortable tones as a parent hushes a child at a movie. There is power in the hush. The hush reasserts dominance: it restores the audience's own epistemic and psychological comfort."

Celebrities who spoke openly about their harassment and assault have wealth, visibility, and resources that most women do not. Nonetheless, the emotions and conflicts that they displayed in their public appearances and statements, particularly around their use of anger, were remarkably familiar to women broadly.

A few weeks after the Weinstein revelations, actress Uma Thurman, another of the producer's victims, was asked what his decades of abuse meant about her industry. "I don't have a tidy sound bite for you," she said through gritted teeth, "because I've learned—I am not a child—and I have learned that when I've spoken in anger, I usually regret the way I express myself. So I've been waiting to feel less angry. And when I'm ready, I'll say what I have to say." Thurman not only tone policed herself, she *talked about* tone policing herself.

Her anger was reined in, and, as she explained later, she was trying not to cry. This is a good illustration of the awareness we all have of how easily and quickly our fury, if expressed, can be twisted against us. Thurman's posture, her face, her voice all thrummed on screen, belying the composure of her words. The actress's sense of her own position reflected the precariousness of women, even powerful women, when they have this anger. And Thurman is not only a celebrity but also an actress who is recognized specifically for her representation of powerful, angry, vengeful women in films such as *Kill Bill*.

Two months after Thurman spoke, in another pitch-perfect example of what Bailey describes in her work, Salma Hayek also shared her experiences with Weinstein. She'd never publicly come forward, she explained, because "I didn't consider my voice important, nor did I think it would make a difference. . . . Women are talking today, because in this new era, we finally can." She describes Weinstein's "Machiavellian rage" and "attack of fury" and his "terrifying words." However, even in describing several humiliating episodes, she didn't once mention her own anger.

Actress Rose McGowan was a central figure in Weinstein's downfall. McGowan, whose unorthodox childhood included growing up in a cult, regularly brandished her fury and aggression in public appearances, appearances that seemed to fill other people with discomfort. *Vanity Fair* described her as the "white-hot voice of rage." Her public engagements in the wake of the revelations were complicated by her unwillingness to de-escalate hostile exchanges and, instead, respond aggressively to critiques and challenges.

I asked Judd, whose career, she soon revealed, had been blackballed by Weinstein, how she thought about her anger over the years of silence. "By the time I was talking about Harvey and being heard, in 2016 and 2018, I had long ago coped with the anger," she explained. "Learning how to express carried, suppressed anger is definitely a process. It festers and becomes toxic rage and fury. It requires so much adrenaline and dumps cortisol into our systems." Her response has been to use her body to fend off the possible ravages of rage. "Running, movement, drawing . . . cathartic arts," she said, "helped to physiologically transform roiling anger into strength, energy, and motivation." This body competence made it possible for her to talk about her childhood sexual abuse, dysfunctional family dynamics, and workplace sexual harassment with determination and control.

All of these women were actresses, asked to play the role of leaders and activists for a cause that they mainly seemed to have come to through personal pain. The work involved in doing this is exhausting and often enraging. Some people collapse in on themselves. Others draw strength and expertise from their own anger and the communities that they build. Tarana Burke did this. For decades before being catapulted onto a national stage by Alyssa Milano's tweet, she worked with survivors of sexual assault and violence in marginalized communities.

The #MeToo movement "started in the deepest, darkest place in my soul," she writes, describing an early encounter with a girl, "anger-filled," whose detailed story of assaults emotionally overwhelmed her. "I watched her put her mask back on and go back into the world like she was all alone, and I couldn't even bring myself to whisper . . . me too."

I have found that it is difficult to admit, even if only to myself, how hurtful, degrading, and humiliating sexual harassment and assault really are. In terms of harassment, the intrusion is—while never quite surprising at this stage—still shocking. The anger that I feel comes slowly and steadily. I wonder, like many women that I have spoken to over the years, "Why didn't I do something?" Among my friends, almost all of whom have similar experiences, we've talked about what so many described in the wake of #MeToo: warn one another, avoid aggressors, and, if necessary, leave jobs. I can think of only two women I know who took legal action, with mixed outcomes. Most women won't even contemplate it.

A landmark example is Ellen Pao. In 2012, after working for many years at Kleiner Perkins Caufield & Byers, one of the tech industry's leading venture capital firms, Pao filed a gender discrimination suit. During a courtroom trial covered extensively in media, Pao described hard-to-capture instances of bias, sexual harassment, and retaliation. Like many women who took on pioneering gender discrimination proceedings in other industries, Pao did not win her suit, but she inspired other women to come forward and also take legal action. The "Pao effect" is credited with contributing to both Chia Hong and Tina Huang filing racial and sexual discrimination lawsuits, the former against Facebook; the latter, Twitter.

A scant few weeks before the Weinstein expose, Pao wrote a *New York Times* op-ed in which she talked about the dozens of women she had spoken to in the year since her case closed. Has anything changed, many of them wanted to know? She noted presciently, "The huge change is that people now acknowledge the problem. Women telling their stories are believed, for the most part, and by the press." This simple quality, of being believed, is one we can never take for granted.

FROM BEDROOMS TO BOARDROOMS AND BACK

The more vulnerable women are, socially and economically, the harder effecting this change will be. Depending on which survey you read, anywhere from 40 percent to 90 percent of women working in the restaurant and hospitality industry report persistent unwanted violations, including invasive and denigrating language and humor, as well as unwanted touching, hugging, kissing, and questions about sex. Almost half of this harassment comes from owners, managers, and coworkers—the rest from customers.

During the past several years, women in the field sciences, tech, philosophy, astronomy, economics, academia, financial sector, political arena, military, trucking, construction, sports, retail, and restaurant industry have come forward to detail the costs of harassment. Women truckers, firefighters, migrant farmers, hotel workers, and construction workers, all working in heavily male sectors, report excessively high levels of sexist hostility. The same is true in science and tech. A 2014 survey of 666 scientists, 516 of whom were women, revealed that 64 percent had been sexually harassed. Half of women in tech report unwanted sexual behaviors and one in ten leave their jobs because of harassment.

The position women workers find themselves in speaks directly to their vulnerable economic position in the much-touted "gig economy" that will supposedly free us all.

A 2016 report from the US Equal Employment Opportunity Commission (EEOC), titled *Select Task Force on the Study of Harassment in the Workplace*, concluded that 75 percent of cases of sexual harassment or assault in the workplace go *unreported*. Only 6 percent to 13 percent of people actually file complaints because they fear reprisal. Their fear is justified: 40 percent of women reporting sexual harassment at work to the EEOC said that their employers retaliated after they came forward. Another study put that number at 75 percent. The primary legal mechanisms available to employees who do take action focus overwhelmingly not on the behavior of aggressors but on whether or not the woman responded and how. There are good reasons why the leadership of today's labor movements are filled with women seeking better working conditions and leverage in the workplace.

In November 2017 the Alianza Nacional de Campesinas, which represents the interests of roughly seven hundred thousand women farmworkers in the United States, published an open letter of solidarity with #MeToo actresses. Two months later, a coalition of industry heavyweights launched the TIME'S UP Legal Defense Fund in reciprocal solidarity. The organization raises money to support lower-income women facing discrimination, lobbies for better legislation, and engages in activism.

Harassment is never an issue solely of individual experiences. Environments that tolerate harassment are, almost always, more broadly hostile and toxic. People who harass in the workplace are not sex ad-

dicts or people with poor dating skills; they are abusers of power and
of people. They badger and cajole, joke and flatter, trade in unnerving
hints and innuendo. They rely on gender-role expectations, silence,
and status gaps, as well as their targets' economic and professional
needs, to ensure a lack of consequences. Mainly, however, they leverage widespread social tolerance for their behavior and their ability to
flip the switch on multiple overlapping networks that institutionalize
perpetrator perspectives: the law, religion, media, and schools.

To wit, backlash to #MeToo was swift. As man after man re-
signed or was fired in the closing months of 2017, people voiced their
fears that "innocent" men were being punished for "flirting" and that
boys and men, falsely or irresponsibly accused by vindictive women
or wilting violets, would suffer and lose their reputations and jobs.
This happened even as it was obvious that the men who were actually fired or sanctioned were powerful abusers whose employers, in
virtually every case and in order to legally protect themselves, acted
after investigating allegations.

Advocates were criticized for going too far, infantilizing women,
"witch-hunting," and ruining lives. They were taken to task for being
angry harpies. The subtitle of an *Atlantic* magazine article, "The Humiliation of Aziz Ansari" read, for example, "Allegations against the
comedian are proof that women are angry, temporarily powerful—
and very, very dangerous." The episode in question involved an article, authored anonymously, in which a woman detailed a sexual
encounter with Ansari, a popular comedian and actor. The woman,
who called their date "the worst night of my life," described an evening that included her performing oral sex. The next day, she texted
Ansari that she felt violated by the exchange. He explained he was
blindsided and apologized. Discussion around the article involved a
mess of overlapping social, ethical, and moral issues that threw many
people into an anxious frenzy. It begged complicated discussions
about gender, socialization, entitled sexual behavior, the nature of
coercion, and the definition of violence.

Unlike hundreds of other #MeToo cases that came to light, this one did not involve comfortably black-and-white transgressions that hinged on legalities. Instead, it revealed acceptable and legal behavior that many men uncomfortably recognized in themselves, and it directly linked behavior men may have themselves engaged in with women's unhappiness, acquiescence, pain, and sense of violation. This was, perhaps, an even more harrowing example than the typical workplace examples that #MeToo had heretofore surfaced. Key distinctions faded away for people whose bar seemed to come down to "He didn't rape her." What was notable was how little middle ground there was. So few shared words were available to discuss intimate interactions. Fewer yet to convey women's perspectives in ways that were understood by everyone as legitimate. The whole episode was unsettling in new ways.

Just as much as in more clear-cut cases, the conversation around Ansari highlighted the tremendous power—in this case articulated in social norms, sexual mores, and intimate interactions—that men can wield over women, overtly or not. The piece was disturbing because it put men's entitlements to sexual pleasure and priority on the same spectrum as violent assault and men's institutional power, suggesting that "radical" feminist social critiques of masculine power are as relevant in bedrooms as in boardrooms. Gender conservatives are not interested in this idea—never have been. Instead, as is often the case, attempts are made to pivot the conversation to "personal responsibility," mainly the woman's. The reality of being taught to please others, to not say "No!," to ignore your own discomfort, to be aware of the possible threat of physical harm are all washed away in the ultimately denialist question, "Why didn't she leave?"

No one wants to deliberately hurt men or, a silly suggestion, "criminalize flirting." Women make distinctions between work and play. We can tell the difference between welcome and unwelcome sexual advances. So can men, even when women express their lack of interest and lack of consent nonverbally. The "miscommunication model"—the idea that men and women simply don't understand each other—is a bankrupt one. The problem isn't that some people don't understand. It is that they *understand too well, and what they understand is that they can get away with predatory abuse.*

Weinstein knew. He knew that women were his to do with as he wished. And decades of silence on the part of his friends, the men and women who worked for and around him, his industry, financial backers, the criminal justice system, and the media confirmed, loudly and clearly, that he was right in thinking he could get away with it.

If #MeToo has made men feel vulnerable, panicked, unsure, and fearful as a result of women finally, collectively, saying "Enough!" so be it. If they wonder how their every word and action will be judged and used against them, *Welcome to our world.* If they feel that everything they do will reflect on other men and be misrepresented and misunderstood, take a seat. *You are now honorary women.*

Calling for consideration, compassion, and accountability isn't revenge. It is a demand that systems be put in place that create safer and more egalitarian workplaces for everyone. Most people who took issue with the movement or with discussions after the *Atlantic* Ansari piece seemed unwilling to address the negative space of women's lives: how many women have been lost and damaged over decades, how much creativity and accomplishment has been derailed, how much poverty and pain results. Women who come forward are not to blame if the system that so egregiously ignored discrimination against them is now also failing to provide adequate institutional protections for those accused. The ugly truth is that more people are still motivated by the desire to prioritize men's income generating and reputations than they are by the desire to ensure women's rights and safety.

If, instead, women's words and bodies mattered and our justifiable anger was respected and allowable, it would not have come to this. As feminist writer and activist Ijeoma Oluo eloquently put it: "If you wanted to avoid our rage, maybe you shouldn't have left us with so little to lose."

Women may not have cultural parity in mainstream storytelling, but we have alternative ways to tell stories today that never existed before. Stories that, until relatively recently, would never have been told—certainly not in a woman's own words. And, with this change, women are beginning to openly express rage, anger, aggression, and outrage in their own defense.

Over the course of several weeks in January 2017, more than 156 women stood in a courtroom and described, in relentless, graphically detailed, and powerful public statements, how former USA Gymnastics and Michigan State University doctor Larry Nassar had sexually abused them. Nassar's trial, both horrifying and mesmerizing, was televised, and millions of people tuned in to watch the women describe, clearly and mercilessly, what Nassar had done to them. On the one hand, I wished that the women did not have to pour their trauma into the world to be recognized, but on the other hand, as the women themselves realized, it was important for them to be heard.

Many of the women were young children when Nassar's abuse began. He was a trusted authority, and the girls' complaints to adults were repeatedly dismissed. They recounted being violated by Nassar even while parents, friends, and family members had been in the same room. They shared their humiliation, fear, anxiety, and pain. They revealed how much loss—of parents, friends, and religious communities—they experienced as the result of trying to convince people that he had hurt them. One woman, Kyle Stephens, recounted being made to apologize to Nassar by her father. "His belief that I lied seeped into the foundation of our relationship," she explained. "Every time we got into a fight, he would tell me, 'You need to apologize to Larry.'" She was twelve.

During the trial, Nassar wrote a letter to the presiding circuit court judge, Rosemarie Aquilina. "Hell hath no fury like a woman scorned," he said, going on to say that the women were lying and that the judge was craving attention and the media were "sensationalizing" his case. It was too hard, he said, to have to listen to all of his victims.

The last person to speak in Nassar's trial was Rachael Denhollander, the first woman to come forward with allegations. "How much is a little girl worth?" she asked, directing her comments to Judge Aquilina. "How much is a young woman worth?"

Nassar was found guilty of criminal sexual abuse, and Aquilina sentenced him to 40 to 175 years for sexual abuse, on top of a prior 60-year sentence for child pornography. The judge's clear contempt for Nassar during sentencing was criticized by many people who felt she'd been "inappropriately," well, *judg*mental. Judges make strong and angry statements every day. Critiques of Aquilina betrayed a deep unease with women passing judgment *on men*. (In 2016, in what must have put fear in the hearts of many, a panel of three International Criminal Court judges convicted, in a historic first, a Congolese military commander for rapes committed by his soldiers. All three judges were women.)

Some believe that the kind of anger the women showed in the courtroom—anger that was often blunt, vengeful, and retributive— is destructive; that knocking down one person does nothing to actually lift up another person, in this case Nassar's victims. Their anger was the kind described during the same time frame in dull critiques of women's #MeToo public outrage as "hard to engage with." You know what's *really* hard to engage with? Armies of abusive, entitled, predatory men with social influence and credibility that both Nassar and #MeToo put on display.

If these women could—after years of people calling them fabulists and decades of sexual assault and trauma—reclaim their dignity, strength, and satisfaction, while holding not just Nassar but also the people around him accountable, then this kind of anger has a place. "Little girls don't stay little forever," Kyle Stephens asserted in her final statement. "They grow into strong women that return to destroy your world." Stephens and her "sisterhood of survivors," as the judge called them, did something remarkable: they reversed the traditional trajectory in which shame accrued to rape victims and anger was re-served for the defense of "wronged" and "misunderstood" aggressors.

These women's courtroom statements followed in the wake of another gripping public testimony. In 2016 an unnamed eighteen-year-old woman, raped behind a university campus dumpster by a male student whom the media described as the "Stanford swimmer," published her courtroom letter online.

"I wanted to take off my body like a jacket and leave it at the hospital with everything else," she wrote. "After work, I would drive to a secluded place to scream." The letter was clear, calm, and detailed. Every word was constructed, letter by letter, from her immense rage and contempt. Within hours of the letter being published, it had been read by millions.

Her assailant was sentenced to just six months in jail by a judge who explained that anything longer would have "a severe impact on him." His father asserted that this was "a steep price to pay for twenty minutes of action." He was out of jail in three months, his name put on a sex offender registry. At one point he offered to go on a college speaking tour to lecture college students about the dangers of "drinking and promiscuity."

"When I read the probation officer's report, I was in disbelief, consumed by anger, which eventually quieted down to profound sad-ness," the victim wrote. "My life has been on hold for over a year, a year of anger, anguish, and uncertainty, until a jury of my peers rendered a judgment that validated the injustices I had endured . . . The probation officer's recommendation of a year or less in county jail is a soft timeout, a mockery of the seriousness of his assaults, an insult to me and all women."

WOMEN'S FREEDOM OF EXPRESSION? MEH.

When I wrote about this Stanford rape case for *Rolling Stone*, editors closed the comments section because anonymous commenters were doxing her (sharing her name and address with malicious intent). For days, advocates played whack-a-mole across media platforms, trying to protect the young victim's identity and ensure her privacy and safety.

By sharing their stories, women become whistle-blowers. They enter into a world familiar to women journalists, writers, and politicians, all of whom are particularly exposed to being extorted, threatened, stalked, impersonated, doxed, and sent graphically and sexually violent material. Attacks are not only anonymous or perpetrated by individual people, as is often assumed, but are also perpetrated by acquaintances, coworkers, government actors, and former intimates. While everyone can encounter harassment online, the harassment that women face is more intense, more sexualized, and tied to higher levels of offline threat and violence. It also leverages women's offline wariness and safety concerns for greater emotional resonance.

Journalists and politicians, women claiming public space with authority, elicit particular vitriol. Women journalists on Twitter record three times as many abusive comments as male counterparts, for example. A detailed 2016 analysis of more than seventy million reader comments on the *Guardian* news website revealed that of women writers, a disproportionate number—eight of the ten—were the most harassed on the site. The ten least-harassed writers were all men, a group that makes up 68 percent of the media company's bylines. The topics that garnered the most abuse? Feminism, rape, and the Arab-Israeli conflict.

Once in a while, a male peer feels compelled to explain to me, in a fabulous example of false equivalence, that he, too, receives harassing emails and messages. Anyone can, and men often do get harassed. Some studies show that men are harassed more often. But the quality of harassment differs vastly. Nothing will ever convince me that the intent and effect of being called an asshole are the same as opening your in-box in the morning to dick pics, cannibalistic rape porn, racist gore, and videos of men masturbating.

The intention of this harassment is pretty straightforward: to make women shut up. The desire for women to stop talking is profuse in the language and imagery of harassment. Hanging, strangulation, forced fellatio, decapitation, and choking women with objects are all common themes. "Women that talk too much need to get raped," wrote one of the thousands of men who threatened British activist Caroline Criado-Perez with rape after she successfully lobbied to have the novelist Jane Austen put on UK banknotes in 2014. "Shut your whore mouth now," demanded another, "or I'll shut it for you and choke you with my dick."

The "just words" objection to taking these threats seriously ignore the offline gender-based violence that women have to take into consideration. In 2014, a feminist organization at University of Mary Washington, a school in Virginia, protested a popular rugby team song that sometimes went by the name "Fuck a Whore," a "fun" chant about humiliating and raping women, including dead women. After some students protested, arguing that the song normalized violence against women, the administration disbanded the team. The women who led the challenge were shunned, harangued, and threatened in social media. Five months later, one of the group's members, twenty-year-old Grace Mann, was killed by a male roommate: he'd bound her and shoved a plastic bag down her throat.

There's a lot of scoffing about women and our "victim mentalities." Most of the women I know consciously or unconsciously assess and reassess. They are not alarmists, but smart, determined, and thick skinned. This doesn't mean they don't feel anxious or angry, but, as they do offline, they weigh the costs and benefits. Women can't afford to either "get offline" or ignore the connection between online threats and offline violence. The "choices" women have are limited, and women are often forced to silence themselves.

"What I couldn't say is, 'Fuck you,'" explained media critic Anita

Sarkeesian during a 2015 speech. Sarkeesian was one of three women who were the primary targets of a multiyear campaign of misogynistic online harassment called Gamergate. At one point, her face was used to create an online game, played by thousands, in which users could beat her up until she appeared bruised and bloodied. "To the thousands of men who turned their misogyny into a game . . . My life is not a game. I have been harassed every day for going on three years, with no end in sight, and all because I dared to question the self-evident, obvious sexism running rampant in the game industry."

Sarkeesian, along with writers and developers Brianna Wu and Zoë Quinn, was hounded by cyber mobs and threatened with rape and death. She was forced to cancel an appearance at a university after administrators received emails from an anonymous person threatening "the deadliest school shooting in American history" if she appeared. All three women had to leave their homes.

The treatment of these women was an expansion of another instance of planned, networked abuse that targeted black women writers and activists in what was dubbed "Operation: Lollipop." In 2014, harassers, primarily men's rights agitators organizing on the forum 4Chan, began impersonating feminist women of color across multiple social media platforms. The impersonator accounts posted abusive and hostile commentary and content designed to provoke discord and embarrass the women who were targeted. The campaign, planned over a year was revealed when women fought back using #YourSlipIsShowing. In 2017, this incident, like parts of Gamergate, were shown to have been a leading edge in what has come to be understood as a full-scale attack on the integrity of US elections. Mainstream media, despite many efforts, seemed unable or unwilling to recognize threats against women online, abuses that presaged the meddling and propaganda related to the 2016 presidential election, as fundamental threats to free speech or the proper functioning of democracy.

Sarkeesian went on to describe how intentional she must be

about every word choice and about the decisions she makes about where to speak and to whom:

> Every day, I see my words scrutinized, twisted, and distorted by thousands of men hell-bent on destroying and silencing me. What I couldn't say is that I am a human being. I don't get to publicly express sadness or rage or exhaustion or anxiety or depression . . . I don't get to express my feelings of fear or how tiring it is to be constantly vigilant. In our society, women are not allowed to express feelings without being characterized as hysterical, erratic, highly emotional, or overly sensitive. Our expression of insecurity, doubt, anger, or sadness are all policed and often used against us. By denying ourselves the space to feel and to share those feelings, we perpetuate this notion that we should suffer alone. That we should toughen up or grow a thicker skin, which we should not have to do.

Aware of foul treatment like this, women often withdraw, stop writing and speaking, or change what they write about. They police their own voices and move to sex-segregated places, leaving the theoretically gender-neutral public forum for men. One-third of women report shuttering their opinions because they fear threats and violence. And yet this issue never seems to take priority as a problem that undermines our work, freedom of expression, political engagement, or the proper functioning of democracy.

"What I couldn't say is, 'I'm angry,'" said Sarkeesian. "I am angry. In fact, I'm furious . . . I am angry that I am expected to accept online harassment as the price of being a woman with an opinion."

Politicians are women with opinions. The numbers of women in world governments are slowly increasing, but at radically inconsistent rates. In the United States, women make up just less than 20 percent of Congress and an average of 24 percent of state legislatures. During the past twenty years, as other countries have made strides toward women's political efficacy, the United States went from being 52nd in the world for women's representation to 104th. In the United Kingdom, women's increasing participation in government was marked by gains during the 2017 general election. Women now make up 26 percent of the House of Lords and have the same percentage of cabinet posts, both record highs. However, in Germany, the percentage of women in the Bundestag is the lowest in twenty years.

Women are nowhere near the supermajorities they need to be heard and to achieve influence in shifting policy and resources.

What this also means is some frankly surreal exchanges in public forums: exchanges that vividly shed light on how important it is for women to have parity in office. In 2013 Michigan State House representative Lisa Brown was barred from speaking on the floor for having used the word *vagina* to make a point during an abortion-access debate. "It was so offensive," said her male legislative opponent, "I don't even want to say it in front of women. I would not say that in mixed company."

In 2015 New Zealand's prime minister used the specter of rape during a heated parliamentary debate about a migrant detention center. When women legislators responded by talking about their own rapes, not perpetrated by migrants, they were removed from the legislative chamber for "flouting the rules" of parliament.

During her 2018 hearing on a proposed bill to increase menstrual supplies to women inmates in Arizona prisons, state representative Athena Salman understandably used words such as *menstruate* and *heavy flow* while presenting testimony to an all-male panel of colleagues. "I didn't expect to hear *pads* and *tampons* and the problems of periods," said one of the men. "Can you keep your conversation to the bill itself? Please?" Women in jail were turning maxi pads into tampons by squeezing them into cylinder shapes, risking infection and toxic shock syndrome.

Salman's proposal touches on a worldwide "debate" in legislatures and city councils over whether or not menstrual supplies are a "luxury." Most governments categorize tampons and sanitary napkins this way and tax women accordingly. There have been some successful challenges to this gender tax—in France in 2015, for example—but most countries continue to impose this cost on women. In December 2017, teenage girls and women in the United Kingdom took to the streets in a #FreePeriods protest, demanding that the government provide period supplies in schools for girls who receive free meals.

Is it possible to read a book about anger and not get mad? I haven't found it possible in writing one. What are we doing? Why does anyone think that men who cannot say the word *period* and do not know that the vagina and the stomach are not connected are competent and trustworthy leaders?

Angry, assertive, and persistent men are noble and can engage in theatrical posturing in a way that women rarely can and, indeed, in a way that women are censured for. In 2016 Planned Parenthood president Cecile Richards was relentlessly hectored by members of Congress during hearings on Planned Parenthood funding. A deliberative body made up almost entirely of men talked over and interrupted her more than forty times. A year later, during Senate Intelligence Committee hearings about Russian interference in the 2016 US presidential election, Senator Kamala Harris was cut off by committee chair Senator Richard Burr, who castigated her for not being polite enough. In another hearing, Senate Majority Leader Mitch McConnell, using an obscure parliamentary rule, silenced Senator Elizabeth Warren. "She was warned. She was given an explanation. Nevertheless, she persisted," he declared famously, propelling a deluge of memes and merchandise bearing that phrase. The popularity of "Nevertheless she persisted" as a meme was outdone a year later by "Reclaiming my time," the phrase calmly used by California Democratic representative Maxine Waters during a congressional hearing as she turned the tables and shut down Treasury Secretary Steven Mnuchin's attempts to avoid answering her questions. The internet went wild with glee.

In the midst of these episodes, doing *his* best impersonation of a malevolently lurking domestic abuser, Donald Trump interrupted Hillary Clinton fifty-one times during the first presidential debate in 2016, as he appeared to stalk her on stage. "For more than 90 minutes on a national stage," wrote the Associated Press's Tamara Lush, "Trump subjected the first female presidential candidate from a major party to indignities [women] experience from men daily, in the workplace and beyond." Following a pattern familiar to most women, Trump talked over or interrupted Clinton three times as frequently as she interrupted him.

While many criticized Trump's troubling behavior, media went on after the election in a silencing vein rarely if ever applied to male pols. "Hey, Hillary Clinton, shut the f— up and go away already," was the opening line of a *New York Daily News* op-ed titled, "Hillary Clinton Shouldn't Be Writing a Book—She Should Be Drafting a Long Apology to America." It was one of many with a similar message: "Dear Hillary Clinton, Please Stop Talking About 2016." As one former male candidate after another tried to outdo the next in announcing future political ambitions, Clinton was expected to fade into the ether. This diffuse hostility is the icing on a very big cake.

"When women in office start speaking truth to power," wrote Rhode Island state legislator Gayle Goldin in late 2017, "power talks back—by killing your bills, changing your committee assignments, and smearing your reputation." When sexual harassment is involved, she explained further, "an elected woman must face a harsh truth: questions about the credibility of her story often lead to questions about her credibility as a legislator."

A 2016 report by the Inter-Parliamentary Union revealed that more than 44 percent of women parliamentarians around the world have been threatened with death, rape, beatings, or abduction. One-third are harassed through exposure to persistent unwanted and intimidating messages.

"I've had people tweeting that I should be hung if they 'could find a tree big enough to take the fat bitch's weight'" said the United Kingdom's Diane Abbott, MP and shadow home secretary. "I've had rape threats . . . and n*gger, over and over and over again." A 2016 analysis of six months' worth of tweets revealed that 45 percent of malicious tweets sent to women MPs in the United Kingdom targeted Abbott.

Italy's speaker of the house, Laura Boldrini, has spoken extensively about the graphic sexual content and threats that she has received and now works to ensure women's public freedom of expression. After that country's Cécile Kyenge became the minister of integration in 2013, she did not anticipate the river of racist threats. In one instance, another politician suggested that Kyenge should be raped so she "understands" what it felt like.

In 2016, after five women city council members in Seattle voted against an ordinance to approve a new basketball arena, they were overwhelmed by messages of sexist rage. "You cunt. You whore. You bitch. You don't know anything," showed up in media as "vulgar language." One woman was assigned a police escort.

Massachusetts congresswoman Katherine Clark was a victim of swatting, a dangerous "prank" in which someone anonymously contacts the police with a false report of a shooting or bombing so that heavily armed officers, such as a SWAT team, are sent to a person's home.

In 2016, the president of the Big Country Oilmen's Association, in Canada, organized a golf tournament and set up a cutout of Alberta premier Rachel Notley so that golfers could smash her "face" with golf balls. In September 2017 President Donald Trump retweeted a mocked-up video of him hitting a golf ball so hard that it knocked over Hillary Clinton.

The survey of parliamentarians also found that 42 percent of women reported "extremely humiliating or sexually charged images spread through social media." When men want women to stop talking, they send them porn.

Nonconsensual sexualization of prominent women in politics is "normal" in ways that male politicians usually never have to think about. Graphic sexualizing of woman politicians and candidates isn't "harmless" fun, it's a political strategy. Research shows that sexual objectification sullies a woman's reputation, degrades viewers' perceptions of the person's moral standing and competence, and demonstrably hurts her chances of being elected. A 2009 study found that Sarah Palin supporters asked to focus on her appearance decreased their willingness to vote for the McCain-Palin ticket. During the 2016 presidential campaign, pornographic memes, fake videos, and sexualized images of Hillary Clinton were used to portray her both as a violable slut and as frigid and undesirable.

It is noteworthy and, if you can keep your sense of humor, funny in a wry way, that four of the top six terms searched by American millennial men on the website Pornhub in 2016 were *mom*, *stepmom*, *MILF*, and *lesbian*. What does it say that these men got their kicks sexualizing these particular women? Women who represent taboo violations, but it is clear, too, women with power over them as boys and men, or women who reject men outright.

In 2012 the sexist abuse of former Australian prime minister Julia Gillard was so extensive that the country's *Macquarie Dictionary* updated its definition of *misogyny*. Sue Butler, who was editor of the dictionary when the decision was made, explained that an accurate contemporary definition of misogyny would mean "entrenched prejudice against women," as well as institutional and pathological hatred and the persistent exclusion of women from positions of leadership and authority.

Sexism is usually discrete, in that a person can act in sexist ways or experience incidents of sexism. Misogyny is systemic. Sexism is interpersonal, misogyny is structural. Sexism might alter your day, but misogyny and the power behind it will alter your life outcomes and shape the world around you at every level.

Today, globally, there are two hundred million fewer girls and women online than men. That gap, which reflects structural discrimination on multiple levels, is expanding.

———

#MeToo represents a turning point in how willing women are to admit their anger. It seems more evident that, for many of us, the display rules have changed.

"I am not a cool, chill girl anymore. I am a woman who is very angry and very tired. I know that that makes me unlikeable," explained writer and activist Andrea Grimes. "I know this will literally cost me money in lost bylines and recognition and respect from men who decide who gets hired to write what and when, who decide not to recommend me for a gig or who tell their buddies to steer clear of this particular gal, because she's crazy about this thing, she'll nag the shit out of you, man—she'll fuckin' tag you in a tweet about rape culture on a Friday, dude."

The importance and visibility of women's collective anger can't be overstated. This anger takes determination, thoughtfulness, and work. It means respecting *our own* anger and being willing to respect the anger of other women.

Women's experiences of anger are often lonely ones, focused internally and diverted into other feelings and behaviors.

It's also easy to feel isolated when you are a lone voice—maybe in your house, or school, or at work—but remember: you are never alone with this anger. "On the night of May 25, 2014, I curled up in bed and waited to die," wrote the woman who started the #YesAll Women hashtag, one year after she had created it to express that all women are affected by misogyny even though all men are not sexist. "I was a Muslim woman who had dared to start a viral hashtag that laid out the fears women faced—while men shamed and accused them of generalizing against an entire gender for the sins of a perceived few."

I remember that day. She was angry. I was angry. Millions of women were angry. She was sitting in space, alone, but she knew the value of creating a place where women could go "to breathe, to vent, to empathize." She also knew, as she put it, that her "voice had power and potential. It could be raised. It could be heard."

We had never met, but we corresponded briefly that morning, and I remember the moment, later in the day, when she closed her account. Those of us who were aware stopped tagging her and encouraged others to do the same. Threats were profuse, and the hatred evident.

The tension lasted for days and then weeks as she was assailed not only by an army of #NotAllMen-ers but also by divisions among women who were using her hashtag. "An author I knew and mutually followed deemed me a man hater and claimed that she always knew I had the potential to be one," she explained. " 'She's just so angry, you know?' she tweeted."

It is difficult to express exactly how anxiety provoking and physically sickening being at the heart of a trending hashtag can be. Absorbing millions of people's emotions is overwhelming, and absorbing their anger is frightening. The first time it happened to me, I had a full-blown anxiety attack that felt like it lasted for days. Once a movement like #YesAllWomen begins, it takes on a life of its own and has unpredictable and unintended consequences.

"You do dwell on that a lot, after the death threats start pouring in," the woman said of her experience. "I regret the death threats. I regret the media attention. I regret the pain and the tears, and the hatred I held for myself for so many months afterward. But I do not regret giving women a place to speak and be heard and acknowledged on a worldwide scale."

She closed her recollection with an affirmation that I often draw on:

I am here. This is my mouth. This is my voice.
You cannot silence me.

———

Every story counts, yet we are only just really being able to tell ours. We are still not allowed to say, from positions of communal respect and authority, what is unjust and unwarranted. Women's judgments, thoughts, work, and contributions are constantly ignored, abbreviated, and squelched by a dense matrix of violence and discrimination. In the face of erasure, we are forced to reconcile our identities, hopes, and ambitions with a constant awareness of threats to our safety, humanity, and dignity.

Critics of #MeToo and similar hashtag movements hold that they "don't really do anything." Tens of millions of women have used hashtags such as #MeToo, #TimesUp, #NotOK, #Everyday Sexism, #aufschrei, #Fasttailedgirls, #thisisrapeculture, #ChurchToo, #WhyIStayed, #YouOkSis, #YesAllWomen, #YesAllWhiteWomen, and others to create something vital: language and communal understanding. These are forays into epistemic *justice*. They are assertions that we, too, are knowers. That we deserve the privilege to speak, to be heard, and to be believed. Choosing to ignore this function betrays a certain smugnesss with power and the hold it has over what is deemed "truth" and "objectivity."

We need diverse stories to proliferate across media, in our classrooms, and at our dinner tables. We need to hear women's stories, in *their own* words. Women are sharing the obstacles we face, talking about the social norms that undermine us, and the ways in which we are constantly adapting. We need to do these things in spaces where men will engage with us willingly and with trust, learning from us without threatening to rape and kill us, just as women have been engaging with and learning about men's experiences for all of recorded history.

Part of the injustice of my great-grandmother's life was the retelling of her story in a way that further oppressed her and her descendants. Retelling it in a way that illuminates Zarifeh's experiences so that others can contemplate what they meant is a way to remedy that injustice; to bring to light the injustice of her life and her almost certain crushing anger.

THE POLITICS OF DENIAL

The problem with the Enlightenment was not its belief
in understanding, but its failure to understand a culture
whose civilized veneer concealed mass . . . frustration
and rage.   —Ellen Willis

On a Friday night in Isla Vista, California, in 2014, twenty-two-year-old Elliot Rodger killed six people: four men and two women. Prior to his well-planned shooting spree at three locations, Rodger had written a detailed tract and created several YouTube videos describing his intent to, among other things, kill every "stuck-up blond slut" at the sorority house he attacked. He talked about quarantining, raping, and breeding women. In his writings and videos, he used denigrating language that women hear every day. The fact that Rodger killed more men than women is irrelevant. Men are often targeted and caught in the crossfire of violence centered on a hatred of women.

The morning after Rodger's mass killing, I found myself sitting at breakfast with a group of garrulous friends in the middle of Pennsylvania. As I ate, I reluctantly kept up with news of the shooting and watched, horrified, as US media ignored Rodger's aggrieved entitlement. Initial coverage followed the predictable path, describing a mentally ill "lone wolf" shooter. The more I learned, the angrier I got. Every woman I know who was paying attention grew, over the day, increasingly, unbelievably enraged. As the day went on, media began to report on Rodger's "issues" with women but continued to see these as disconnected from narratives about guns and mental illness, as though guns aren't related to masculinity and the manifestation of mental illness happens in a cultural vacuum. Rodger was affiliated with "incel" groups online. "Incels," originally a benign description of involuntary celibates, is now commonly understood to represent a subculture of profoundly misogynistic and, increasingly visibly violent, communities of men. (In 2018, a man drove his van into a group of people on a sidewalk in Toronto, killing ten people. He'd made a pledge to the "Incel Rebellion.")

As the day progressed, I did something common to many women that I know who do similar work: I split my consciousness in two. As we enjoyed our morning, I tried not to think about Rodger, his caged women, murdered roommates, and mourning families. When we drove past a Mennonite community on the way to lunch, I didn't talk about a Mennonite friend, a survivor of childhood sexual abuse. She'd come to understand that the justice, peace, and nonviolence of her faith did not extend to her or her mother when her father raped them repeatedly throughout her childhood. Words like these, spoken out loud, are in and of themselves considered angry and aggressive.

In an effort to manage similar feelings and, attuned to the rage so many women felt, I tweeted the following message, using the hashtag #YesAllWomen: "#NotAllMen practice violence against women but #YesAllWomen live with the threat of male violence. Every. Single. Day. All over the world." It was retweeted more than five thousand times in a matter of minutes.

It was soon lunchtime, and so, eating with my friends, I put away my ire and my phone. Talk soon turned to a discussion of Amish life and whether we should visit a settlement. Like a stone across water, my brain skipped to Charles Carl Roberts, who, in 2006, had walked into a one-room Amish schoolhouse a few miles away from where we sat. He sent the boys out of the room, tied up the girls, and shot eight out of ten of them in the back of the head, killing five. The youngest was six; the eldest, thirteen. I didn't want to take my children there.

The topic of the shooting came up, and several of the men at the table expressed a relief that they weren't in Isla Vista and subject to the randomness of Rodger's violence. The words "blonde sorority sluts," "everything I hate in the female gender," and "I will destroy all women because I can never have them" hadn't made it into the mainstream news. When I began to describe his misogyny, the almost uniform reaction among the people was that I must be wrong and, if not, certainly exaggerating. There was widespread skepticism and, in at least one conversation, a flat-out denial that this was the case. I struggled to describe how what appeared to be Rodger's internalized racism (he was Anglo-Asian) was related to his violent ideation.

I was angry, and, to my community, it was an unseemly and unwelcome emotion. My barely bridled hostility felt raw and personal and, I am sure, to anyone who noticed it, "over the top." None of the people I was with argued strenuously against the idea that Rodger's violent misogyny was relevant to understanding his actions or those of other mass killers. Instead, the general vibe was that I was taking it all too seriously. Most of this came from men, intentionally or not. I spent a long time thinking about why I cared not to be categorized as angry.

In the meantime, Rodger's rambling hate-filled manifesto was uploaded to Rap Genius, where the website's cofounder Mahbod

Moghadam, in a vile annotation to the text, complimented Rodger's writing style and suggested that his sister was "smokin' hot."

Rage became a layer of my skin.

Denial of women's experiences and the anger they can provoke is complicated. It's not the same as silencing. It's an active response that stems from feelings of threats to identity, a knee-jerk expression of sexist beliefs that is itself deeply sexist in that it is frequently rooted in the idea that women are too emotional, less intelligent, and in need of guidance.

Bear with me.

The truth of women's lives can be difficult to see and unpleasant to accept, for men and women both. According to the Pew Research Center, 56 percent of American men think sexism has been eradicated from American life. By comparison, 63 percent of women say it affects them on a regular basis. That gap makes a monumental leap to 78 percent of conservative men who, essentially, don't believe the 75 percent of liberal and progressive women (sometimes their own wives, mothers, sisters, and daughters) who say that sexism presents real and daily obstacles. It's not only older men, however. Men between eighteen and thirty-four are also likely to say that sexism does not affect women's lives—38 percent of them, compared with the 63 percent of their female peers who say that it does significantly. While the majority of the people surveyed agreed that masculinity is favored culturally, men were far more likely than women to attribute behaviors that women think are socialized to biology. In other words, they are more likely to think men's dominance is natural and immutable.

Nearly 50 percent of men without high school diplomas and 25 percent of those with college degrees believe that women fall back on using gender discrimination as an excuse for workplace outcomes that they don't like. What does this look like in your day-to-day life? Do you say, "Gee, I cannot believe my boss took credit for my work *again!*" or do you keep it to yourself? If you say something, does the person you are with—a spouse, a sibling, a coworker—respond by saying "Are you sure? Maybe it was a mistake?"

Men's support for mechanisms for achieving gender parity is consistently lower than it is among women, and men are more likely to say their workplaces are both more balanced and equitable than in the past. Even when presented with personal experience and irrefutable evidence of bias and sexism, many men refuse to admit what the women around them are experiencing. One study, mirroring others cited earlier, found that science professors at major research universities rate applicants whose names are male as more able, skilled, and competent. They also felt that people with identifiable men's names deserved higher incomes and assigned equally prepared and skilled women lower salaries. When presented with these outcomes, many men dismissed them by questioning the study's "objectivity" or rejecting them as unimportant.

A 2017 Pew Research poll found that 42 percent of working women reported at least one of eight types of discrimination on the job related to their gender. Almost one in four women, 23 percent, said they were "treated as if they were not competent," compared with 6 percent of men.

Each of these gaps contributes to women feeling unprepared and uncertain, and adds to stress, fatigue, frustration, anxiety, and anger. This is doubly true if women raise the topic and what they say is rejected out of hand. If women internalize these perspectives, when they self-blame or divert their anger, the impacts are even worse.

CONSTRUCTING MASCULINITY FROM WOMEN'S VULNERABILITY

After making a speech about stereotypes in media to a roomful of older teenage students in 2016, I was invited to stay for lunch. As we ate, the conversation turned to how difficult it was to confront classmates about difficult topics such as racism, heteronormativity, gender identity, and sexism. "What do I do," asked one girl, "when boys I've known since kindergarten are standing next to me in the hallway laughing at a rape joke? Worse, when they do it standing next to a girl who they know has been assaulted?"

We went over some strategies: for example, cultivating a network of boys who understood the importance of bystander intervention and could use the fact that they were boys to speak to their peers in a way that girls could not. There was, in the group of more than three dozen students, only one boy. He raised his hand. "I think you would convince more boys if you said things in a nicer way," he suggested. "I just think that you sound too angry." His was a typical rerouting from discussing the cause of our anger, which he undoubtedly felt uncomfortably implicated in, to condemning our expression as counterproductive.

In 2016, researchers Octavia Calder-Dawe and Nicola Gavey from New Zealand's University of Auckland worked closely with a group of teenage students to learn what they thought about everyday sexism. They concluded that the adolescents lived in a general environment in which "gender equality is taken for granted and the possibility of enduring sexism is firmly rejected." If asked directly, students described sexism as affecting men and women equally. The students they surveyed went out of their way, regardless of gender, to stress symmetry in sexism's effects. But despite the drive to make things equal, boys and girls parted ways when asked to describe actual incidents of sexism or violence.

Sexism against boys and men was discussed primarily in rhetorical, theoretical, and speculative ways, whereas sexism against girls and women was shared in painful individual or witnessed incidents. When students were asked "Where, if anywhere, does sexism come up in your everyday life?" girls told personal stories of sexual harassment or violence, denigrating humor, and demeaning stereotyping.

The boys, however, provided mainly hypotheticals. All of the students reported witnessing acts of sexism against girls and women. There were virtually no actual examples of antimale sexism. Instead, students focused, for instance, on stereotypes in advertising.

People who deny sexism will always be more hostile to your anger than to what is actually causing your anger. A lot of the difficulty of denial is that women's inequality is woven into men's identities in early childhood. Teenage boys are heavily invested in masculinity and achieving it. They can and do suffer real penalties when they don't.

Earning money and keeping people safe are basic responsibilities of manhood. Women's equality—in the form of work, sexual liberation, public power—generates gender-role stress. Four in nine men say that because of greater gender equality and labor competition, it's harder to be a man today. Men whose wives threaten to earn as much or more than they do, work more hours. When women make more money, they do less housework. Men with higher-earning wives are more likely to have erectile dysfunction and depression.

It's not only money, though, but the idea that men are supposed to protect. Hearing about street and sexual harassment and threats of assault directly challenge a man's ability to keep "his" woman safe. This triggers not only confusion, doubt, or anger but also stress and feelings of inadequacy. When women are honest about these issues, their honesty can be experienced as a threat to masculine identity. The core issue is that, no matter where you may live in the world, dominant norms of masculinity are actively constructed out of women's vulnerabilities. What are "real men" if they can't protect women? What are "real men" if women can provide financially for themselves and their families?

In addition, talking about sexual harassment and violence means that men have to face *their own* vulnerability—and, sometimes, their own sexual assaults as boys. Most assaults that men experience happen in childhood, and they are smothered in shame and trauma, not in the least because being violated is considered feminizing.

Much of the denial we encounter is constructed to protect these masculine ideals. Even when men overcome these threats to their identity, masculinity and male centrality reassert themselves. Fathers are often particularly surprised when they learn that their daughters will face sexism and that their own privileges or attempts to protect them will not be sufficient to offset the impacts. A common response is to empathize by defining women, the ultimate in unhelpful patriarchal thinking, relationally: "My daughter, my wife, my sister, my mother." This defines women not by their rights or as individuals but as extensions of men and *their* rights. Women have a right to walk, go to school, look nice, and work unmolested by entitled bores, independent of their relationship to a man.

This frame of reference is also apparent in denials that almost always begin with "Women over there . . ." That might mean across town or in another state or country. Instead of listening to what is being said to them, people who have probably rarely before expressed concern about "women over there" respond by pointing out that there are women who are poorer and sicker. Who have acid thrown on them. Who are more likely to be abused, raped, and beaten. Without fail, when women and girls point to forms of oppression in their lives, someone has this response—a polite way of saying, effectively, "Shut up, and be grateful we treat you as well as we do." This line of thought is, at its foundation, an argument about men, not women. It asserts the superiority of some men over others who treat "their" women less well, as in, "Consider yourself lucky that we are not selling you on Amazon."

Women are not in competition with other women for their human rights. My rights are not relative to another woman's pain and vulnerability. They should not be contingent on affiliative male status.

Centering men and masculinity in these ways invades women's experiences of anger. Men's stress over roles and identity is frequently a factor in how women express anger and how men receive it. Both men and women respond with anger when another person acts in critical, aggressive, and controlling ways, but many men exhibit those behaviors as a function of being adequately masculine. The behaviors that women say cause them to feel intense anger are often those that men display as aspects of traditional masculinity. In women, on the other hand, the controlling and aggressive behavior that men might find enraging indicates that a woman is *not* conforming to traditional norms.

A similar justifying pattern is evident in how anger can affect relationships between women of color and white women. "To hold somebody else's anger involves being able to hear and listen without being defensive," explained psychologist Robin Cook-Nobles in 1977. "Since a great deal of black women's anger is directed at white women, both past and present, this can be hard for white women to do." This is no less true today than it was forty years ago.

On average, people are angered by the same things: unfairness, perceptions of injustice, and threats to safety, family, and status. But men get angrier when challenged by women than they do by other men—in other words, when their "natural" higher status is questioned. Studies show that men are particularly bothered when women do not prioritize *their* needs, for example, and, instead, express their own needs or discomfort or desire for change. Men report feeling the greatest anger when women display negative feelings, have angry reactions, and make "selfish" demands. Men describe the problem in terms of women's "moodiness" and "self-absorption."

Even when tropes of masculinity are obliterating men's personal lives, many men will not consider sexism a legitimate issue. For a couple, the more the husband believes in gender stereotypes that generate male privileges and the less the wife does, the more likely they are to divorce. As discussed earlier, women are significantly more likely to initiate divorce. For men, the institution of marriage comes with the assumption of certain privileges. It seems to generate male confidence in gendered and ultimately sexist roles that the insecurity of cohabitation doesn't. Women cite inequality in their personal relationships as the reason why they seek to end their relationships, a reality verified multiple times over by surveys and studies.

In 2017, for example, a Minitel study found that 61 percent of British women are very happy being single, compared with 49 percent of men. Women cite onerous demands of domestic and emotional labor as the reasons why they would rather not be in relationships. Many men are brought up to expect this labor.

A 2015 survey of heterosexual American men revealed that only 34 percent wanted a romantic partner who is "independent," compared with the 66 percent who said the same of daughters. Men also favored intelligence in daughters more than in spouses. In other words, they want wives who are more dependent, obedient, and less self-sufficient, but daughters—extensions of themselves in ways that wives aren't—to be smart, ambitious, and independent.

If more men asked women the question "What is making you angry?" and cared about the answer, then maybe divorce initiation would even out. It is a particularly delicious irony that conservatives who bemoan declining heterosexual marriage can best prop up the institution not by doubling down on traditional binary gender roles, but by embracing their fluidity.

———

The degree to which you agree or disagree with binary ideas about gender roles depends on where you fall in terms of separate spheres ideology (SSI), the underpinning of benevolent sexism. In this framework, women and men are strictly segregated in terms of their roles and responsibilities, capabilities and "natural" interests. Women restrict their power and influence primarily to social life, religious life, churches, schools, and parenting, while men do the same in the public sphere: moneymaking, lawmaking, and media. These two worlds are, in theory, separate but equal. In practice, however, it is obvious that they are neither, a false equivalence fundamentally irreconcilable with democratic ideals.

The higher a person's separate-spheres beliefs, the more negative his or her attitudes toward gender-equalizing changes. This is not only a matter of roles and responsibilities but also, eventually, it affects cognitive ability. Women in communities with greater gender equality, for example, have superior cognitive skills, while men in gender-unequal communities underperform in social sensitivity. A 2017 study of more than two hundred thousand people in twenty-seven countries showed that abilities were the result of a lifetime of "biopsychosocial" conditioning. In other words, as the researchers titled their work: "As you sow, so shall you reap."

High SSI scores also predicted income differences between men and women in families; a couple's allocation of paid and unpaid work; political participation; and the endorsement of discriminatory attitudes in the workplace. When these attitudes move into the public sphere, unlike in most homes, they intersect with other forms of discrimination and denial. For example, 55 percent of white Americans believe that there is more discrimination against white people in America than against blacks and other minorities.

In the world of separate spheres, as long as women follow the rules and are "good"—a sensible course of action when there are few other options—they will be cherished. A common way of managing these beliefs is to sort girls and women into groups: evil tempting hussies or good and almost always happily maternal figures. The "whore" deserves what she gets, while the "Madonna" can't possibly be victimized because she would never do anything to deserve punishment. Layered on top of this are the racism and ethnocentrism that historically and enduringly restrict the meaning of "real woman" to stereotypes of white women and, for example, reduce black women to undeserving and violable Jezebels, Hispanic women to salacious tarts, Asian women to passive and pliant dolls, and working-class women to sexless drones.

Psychologists Andrea Miller and Eugene Borgida call the belief in separate spheres for men and women a "motivated, system-justifying ideology." System justification is the name given to the emotional and cognitive process that kicks in when a person encounters information or behaviors that challenge their sense of self and their worldview.

According to system justification and what is called just-world theory, when evidence suggests the world is *not* a just place, people with this orientation seek to reassert fairness either by ignoring dissonant information or by blaming people for the ills that befall them. Poor people are lazy and don't work enough. Black people are more likely to be criminals. Women who go out, drink, and have sex are culpable for their rapes.

These ways of thinking divide people into "in groups" and "out groups" in order to attribute deservedness and vindicate hierarchical, and often violent, domination over others, including in homes. In this schema, a woman who renounces traditional gender roles and acts in anger is particularly problematic. Simply by speaking in anger, she violates powerful rules. Her anger is a strong reminder of social imbalances, and the denial of her anger is a defensive system-justifying response. So, mockery, trivialization, suppression, and denial often ensue because denial is psychologically assuaging—an effective managing of "feelings of dissonance" and "anger related to unfairness."

WOMEN ARE ALSO SYSTEMS-JUSTIFYING

It is, of course, not only men who believe in separate spheres, or who deny women's words and anger. It's often, sometimes much more often, other women. Studies show that women who adhere to conservative gender ideologies are more likely to deny their own anger and to respond poorly to other women who display anger, particularly in ways that highlight failures in comforting social systems. When women who hold just-world views are angry in response to criticism, that anger often masks confusion and fear. For example, the fear that discrimination is real and that violence is not something they can control by following rules. Sometimes, depending on the context, there is fear of competition and what other women's success says about gender and gender roles. For example, studies indicate that women with benevolently sexist beliefs are the most hostile to other women when they demonstrate raw ambition or display political power.

During a recent television panel discussion, I was surprised to find myself in a debate with a conservative writer who felt that #MeToo had "gone too far." Men and boys were being hurt and oppressed, she claimed, and women were equating clumsy flirting with crimes, or they were weak and oversensitive, or vindictive and lying. Laws, she argued, served citizens well, and innocent men were going to have careers destroyed because of missteps. The primary thrust of her arguments was that, in her experience, most women do not face #MeToo problems, and those that do bring them on themselves. My responses to her fell on deaf ears. Although this was an on-air conversation, I could have found myself mired in the same debate at a family reunion, a school meeting, or a casual dinner party.

Thinking that the world is just and hoping that it can be more just are very different orientations. Studies show that women will maintain beliefs in separate gender spheres and a just world, supporting patriarchal norms even when it puts them at a clear disadvantage. Denial and diversion allow people to maintain psychological equilibrium and stave off feelings of powerlessness in the face of emotionally disruptive and anxiety-provoking information. Indeed, in our TV debate, while I rattled off statistics, the other woman kept repeating, "This is not a world I recognize."

Her response was a good example of what social theorists call identity protection cognition, the process by which people "selectively dismiss asserted dangers in a manner supportive of their preferred form of social organization." So her falling back on benevolent sexism by blaming female victims and defending and prioritizing male wage earning probably made the dissonance of having to think about what women's harassment represented in terms of her own inequality easier. The whole discussion frustrated me, and she, undoubtedly, was angry as well, because what I said seemed alien, angry, and confrontational.

Denial is rarely based on facts or reasoning. It is a visceral emotional defense that overrides reason, critical thinking, and deliberation. It is evident, for example, in conservative white men's stark outlier perceptions of risk in regard to everything from climate change, food and environmental toxicity, gun violence, and abortion in the United States. In these cases, this very narrow cohort of people, most of whom appear to be part of Donald Trump's administration, has outlier risk assessments, seeing little or none of the dangers or rights infringements that almost everyone else does. Social scientists call this the "white male effect" and describe it as a mechanism for protecting status. While powerfully descriptive and accurate in the United States, this is, in fact, an unhelpful misnomer for what the researchers describe more accurately as identity-protective cognition. In countries such as Sweden, where women enjoy higher status, the effect is seen in relation to ethnicity, with both white men and women assessing risk differently than other, lower-status ethnic groups do. Men who believe in separate spheres and adhere to benevolently sexist beliefs don't "see" women's anger as legitimate because to see the problems, and risks, that women face as real would require status-threatening change.

Women who believe in separate spheres and adhere to benevolently sexist beliefs also become some of the strongest enforcers of discriminatory norms. As members of juries, for example, women who score high in benevolent sexism and just-world beliefs are the most likely to harshly judge rape victims or women who have been abused by intimate partners. They will overlook the broader meaning and context of male perpetration and its prevalence. None of this is to excuse racism or sexism or other forms of bias and overt prejudice, but, rather, it is to point out why anger, and arguing on the basis of facts, so often fail to change minds.

Unfairness and facts aren't what provoke anger; people like me who point them out do.

⸻

A conversation like the one I had with the woman on TV is often cast as a difference between our "choices" as women, as though we make these choices in a social, cultural, and political vacuum. This is based on the weakly constructed notion of "choice feminism," which can be summed up by the fatuous idea that every choice a woman makes is a feminist choice because a woman is making it. Feminism is public and political by definition, and the term "choice feminism" rings hollow for many reasons, not the least of which is that it depoliticizes women's thinking and decisions, and contributes to women blaming themselves, feeling depressed, and being quiet when they witness or encounter discrimination.

The girls included in Calder-Dawe and Gavey's study described this result in terms of the "unspeakability of sexism." It is a significant problem that makes it difficult for girls, and women in adulthood, to talk openly about double standards, bias, and discrimination or the anger associated with them. This silence, combined with the lack of a language or structure to understand disturbing day-to-day interactions, means that many girls learn to think of their experiences as the result of their isolated choices. They are actively encouraged by adults to see sexism as a matter of their personal responsibility, not as a social wrong and an institutional inhibitor to equality. Every chance I get, I point this out.

⸻

The woman I debated on television was the perfect example of the Trump voter that mystified some pundits: a college-educated white woman who acted "against her own best interests" by voting for Donald

Trump and not Hillary Clinton. This was a spectacular example of how intersectional forms of discrimination and oppression work. In this case, yes, there were economic concerns but what this voting bloc did was leverage racial privilege to maintain status, even if their gendered rights were being degraded. Institutional white male supremacy means that white women benefit from access to patriarchal norms (for example, systems that continue to favor white men in power) in a way that other women don't, but it requires a trade and comes at everyone's expense.

In the buildup to Trump's election, conservative white women were the angriest people in America. A January 2015 *Esquire* magazine survey of three thousand Americans found that of every demographic group measured, white women reported the highest levels of anger and aggression, especially conservative ones. White women voters for Trump reasserted racial supremacy, but they were doing it in the face of overwhelming evidence of their own relative gender inequality and lower status.

Donald Trump was a "broad-shouldered" paternalistic candidate who ran on a platform of "othering" entire groups of citizens, employing the language of contempt and disgust that fuels authoritarian beliefs. Women supporters could engage enthusiastically with his hateful rhetoric, but they had to contend with the fact that Trump's campaign was also a carnival of misogyny. Every Trump appearance, every news story, every tweet, every utterance he made highlighted his ugly attitudes toward women.

Anger and disgust have been categorized by social scientists as dimensions of the same human emotion. Trump's disgust with women and their bodies, his anger toward them, was a powerful force. One Clinton-Trump debate was a specific masterclass in the relationship between gender anger/disgust. Midway through the December 19, 2015, Democratic debate, presidential hopeful Hillary Clinton was late returning to the stage after a five-minute bathroom break. Almost immediately, the media reported that she was delayed because of a line at the women's bathroom. As the break came to a close, with Clinton nowhere in sight, the moderators started without her. Within minutes, Clinton walked back onto the stage, smiling, and said, "Sorry," to knowing laughter. Women, the laughter acknowledged, live in the interstitial spaces of a world shaped by and for men. Was she angry that they'd started without her?

Afterward, Trump took this opportunity to mock Clinton, saying, "I know where she went, it's disgusting, I don't want to talk about it. No, it's too disgusting. Don't say it, it's disgusting, let's not talk." For the next two days, Clinton, and the rest of us, had to endure a cadre of male politicians and reporters writing about her body and her bodily functions. Earlier in the year, Trump told a lawyer who needed a breast pump that she was "disgusting." During the first GOP presidential debate, over that summer, Fox News TV journalist Megyn Kelly challenged him on his sexist record. The candidate ridiculed her later, saying, "You could see there was blood coming out of her eyes; blood coming out of her wherever."

Men, in Trump's worldview, might do disgusting things, but noncompliant women are, themselves, disgusting. The association goes beyond just how people think about women's bodies and corrupts how they perceive women's abilities and morality. In one study, participants were asked to evaluate women's performances on certain tasks after they saw women "accidentally" drop the contents of their purses. In some cases, hair clips fell out of the bags; in others, tampons. People judged women who dropped tampons more harshly, saying that they were less likeable and competent. Some even went out of their way to avoid sitting next to them. Even more interestingly, the effect spread beyond the woman holding the purse with the tampons to feelings of revulsion toward other women.

The disgust that Trump paraded so flagrantly was easily shared by some of his supporters, who displayed their fears in calls that Clinton be jailed ("Lock her up!" became a recurrent, rabid chant at Trump rallies and continued even after he'd won the election) or even shot. "When people chanted of Clinton, 'lock her up,' at Trump's rallies," explains philosopher Kate Manne, "it obviously expressed a desire to see her punished. But it also went beyond that and seemed to express a desire for her containment." The language of containment was used by political foes and voters who seemed unable to separate their disgust for Clinton's body from their political anger and punitive agendas. In treating Clinton in this way, Trump and his voters displayed their disgust for women more broadly. Bleeding, leaking, seeping, oozing, and defecating are the stuff of our humanity and for this humanity, we particularly learn to revile women; and, as women, to hate ourselves. And we are not supposed to feel anger about this?

Even if a woman could overlook all of this, if we could set aside the public commentary on how offensive our bodies are, only weeks before the election, the now infamous *Access Hollywood* tape, recorded in 2005 showing Trump, then a real estate mogul and reality TV star, boasting to the show's Billy Bush about how his celebrity gave him carte blanche to sexually molest virtually any women who caught his eye, was aired publicly.

"I moved on her like a bitch. But I couldn't get there. And she was married." (As was Trump, to his third wife.) "Then, all of a sudden, I see her, she's now got the big phony tits and everything . . . I just start kissing them. It's like a magnet. Just kiss. I don't even wait. And when you're a star, they let you do it. You can do anything . . . Grab 'em by the pussy. You can do anything."

If the exposure to what he dismissed as "locker room talk" agitated liberal and progressive women, for conservative women, it was more threatening, to a worldview, by an order of magnitude. Here was a man who was like men they knew well, saying the same things, in the same ways, promising to be a protector and yet, right there, in plain view, being venal, misogynistic, and predatory. As if that wasn't bad enough, after the tape was released, Canadian author and blogger Kelly Oxford asked women to use the hashtag #NotOK to share the story of the first time they remember being threatened or attacked in the way Trump described. Within twenty-four hours, more than nine million women responded, describing years of psychological pain and distress. Women around the world recounted the sharp pain and anger of their own humiliations and assaults.

When people encounter overwhelming evidence of social inequality that defies what they believe about their own natures, the world, and their place in it, instead of processing facts and addressing what they mean, they *up the ante* on gaslighting, victim blaming, exaggerating the benefits of inequitable social systems, and adamantly defending the status quo. They respond in anger and are prone to shut down women's angry demands.

During these weeks, I felt overwhelmed by women who, disoriented, talked to me privately, reliving episodes that they had ignored and minimized, sometimes for years. Every picture, video, and audiotape of Trump on the campaign stump, however, dragged unwelcome memories from women's subconscious. These upsetting experiences often came as news to the men in their lives, with whom they had never talked about harassment or assault. Women learn to keep such flashbacks to themselves, often because we think no one cares. We are also taught to ignore and downplay men's aggressive harassment. Many women I spoke to also added that they were explicitly conscious of not wanting the men they loved to "feel bad" about what had happened to them. They chose, in other words, to protect them from unpleasant and difficult truths.

Every time Trump lurched, leered, and blathered on about "respecting" women, he not only stirred up trauma but, importantly, also called into question the legitimacy of his saying he was "protecting" women. What was Trump, using the familiar and comforting language of benevolent sexism, promising to protect people from anyway? Climate change? Poverty? Sickness? No, he routinely promised to protect "people" from racialized violence, mainly against white women. Mexican immigrants are rapists. The Central Park Five were guilty (except they weren't). Muslims will rape and terrorize. And China is raping (figuratively) the United States. The threat of rape was a constant drumbeat in reestablishing legitimacy for a historic and endlessly toxic border patrol masculinity inherent to white male supremacy.

True to systems-justification scripts, Trump's supporters responded to Trump's repugnant boasts with excuses such as "It's harmless." "Boys will be boys." "It's just locker room talk." Each rationale more trivializing than the next. Each irrationally bolstering an unjust imbalance in credibility and relevance. Each requiring women to ignore the plain degradation of women for his entertainment. Each, ultimately, deflecting anger into channels that would exacerbate racist and other discriminatory outcomes.

If powerful white men put predatory sexual behavior on display in a way that consciously implicated, as Trump did, the role of status and power, it gives blunt lie to the popular demonization of dark men and the laying claim to authority on the basis of protecting. GOP leaders, mainly silent in the face of Trump's disrespectful treatment of women, immigrants, Muslims, black people, and the disabled, leapt into concerted public displays of outrage in defense of their "wives, daughters, and mothers." This was not out of concern for women's rights and dignity. They exhibited a newfound outrage because Trump was talking about a white woman—one who was married, no less. In theory, a "good woman" who had "done nothing" to deserve this treatment. Like their women. They were concerned only insofar as his crass claims threatened the rationale for their power.

The Trump tape lodged itself in women's brains but was promptly evacuated from men's. During the presidential debate on October 9, 2016, Facebook analyzed millions of live comments to see what election-related topics people were prioritizing in their chatter. The Trump tape was number one of women's top five trending topics but did not even make men's list. Piled on top of the Trump tape, the memories and feelings it provoked, and the hypocrisy it revealed, women were apparently also forced to come to grips with how little sexual harassment and assault seemed to matter to the men in their lives. Deny. Deny and deny some more.

This is not only a divide, however, in more conservative households and communities. In 2017, *Elle* magazine conducted a survey, similar to the one conducted by *Esquire* magazine in 2015. This postelection poll showed that 53 percent of respondents were angrier about the state of the world than they were a year prior. No surprises there. Again, women were angrier than men, with 74 percent versus 69 percent saying they encountered, for example, enraging information at least once a day in the news. White women were also, again, persistently angrier than black women, a finding that refutes, as writer and political commentator Professor Melissa Harris Perry wrote at the time, angry black women mythologizing. This time, liberal and progressive women, 76 percent of whom said they were angrier year-over-year, had the most pronounced response. No surprises there either. However, while two-thirds of Democratic women in that survey said they believed that white men run the country, only 37 percent of their male peers agreed.

Forty-four percent of college-educated white women in America voted for Donald Trump. More than 90 percent of black women voters supported Clinton in a singularly cohesive refutation of Christian white male supremacy and its fundamentally authoritarian core.

GENDER AND ANGRY AUTHORITARIANS

Crosscultural studies reveal some universal qualities about authoritarian mind-sets: rigid adherence to rules, strict moral codes, strong feelings of contempt and disgust, obedience to social groups, an aversion to introspection, and a propensity and desire to punish others. At the most intimate scales, in families, the same can be said for rigid enforcement of gender norms. It is in families that gender binaries are established and policed through rules, moral codes, expressions of disappointment, and revulsion. There are often expectations of respect for authority that override how a child feels or what the child knows about himself or herself.

Research shows that adults who grew up in households that adhered to strict and punitive rules and philosophies translate their anger against their parents into strict and punitive politics. Studies reveal another consistent and related pattern: antifeminism and contempt for women are related directly to authoritarian beliefs.

In 2017, political scientists Carly Wayne, Nicholas Valentino, and Marzia Oceno found that sexism predicted Trump support more than economics, a person's party affiliation, political ideology, or racial attitudes. It matched the consequences of ethnocentrism and far exceeded authoritarian orientation. The researchers specifically concluded that anger around gender and gender roles makes sexism the political force it was in our politics.

For women, as with systems-justification and just-world beliefs, authoritarian beliefs and tendencies are strengthened by exposure to sexism. A 2012 study of the psychological benefits of authoritarian beliefs involving more than a hundred thousand people globally showed that women's commitment to authoritarian leaders goes up the wider the gender equality gap in their community.

For many women in the United States, inequality is normalized by religious beliefs and the way those beliefs shape family structure. In traditional family structures, more likely to be embraced by religious conservatives, gender roles are sharply and appositionally delineated in a hierarchy favoring men's final decision-making and economic power. In these families and faiths, rules about how people should look and behave, how they love, who they love, how people work, think, dress, and whom they trust with power are usually strictly imposed.

Sexism in the home is the ordinal "othering" relied on by authoritarianism. Home and family-based discrimination might be dressed up in centuries of tradition, and theological and philosophical musings, but it is oppressive nonetheless. The most powerful effect is the division of women and men in such a way that it is "natural" for women to not want, seek, or hold power. The baseline attitude of patriarchal conservative religious life is this fundamentally discriminatory treatment of women and girls. This is profoundly political.

In the United States, American Protestant evangelicals and Catholics rank among the highest in acceptance of authoritarian behaviors in leaders. In 2016, 81 percent of white evangelicals voted for Donald Trump despite his evident godlessness, bullying, and cruelty. Notably, both groups are also very accepting of punitive policies, such as torture, policing women's sexual and reproductive choices, and spanking children. They are also among the most punitive when it comes to attitudes about women, sexuality, and gender roles.

The status of women in US politics is closely related to these attitudes and social policies that institutionalize them. In the United States, a growing political divide is largely a divide over how we think about gender roles. Despite claims to the opposite, conservatives simply do not appear to believe women can or should be full participants in society. Women should do the work of caring, but not so much if that caring is expressed by public ambition or political power. One 2015 survey found that only 20 percent of Republicans wanted to see a woman president in their lifetimes. There is good news, however. Trump's election seems to have shifted that sentiment. In 2018, that number was 30 percent.

Any perceived hypervisibility of conservative women in media doesn't alter the fact that since the mid-2000s, Republican women have made almost no gains as elected officials and continue to lose ground as elected representatives. Today there are three times more Democratic women in Congress than there are Republican women. In addition, GOP women in Congress are losing leadership opportunities. The "political divide" cannot be understood or closed until we acknowledge socially acceptable misogyny.

Speaking from a position of moral authority and often with righteous anger are vital to having a public voice and holding political power. But when women assert themselves, whether they are openly angry or not, they often encounter social opprobrium, invalidation, backlash, and punishment.

"Vengeance is mine" was the leitmotif of the 2016 US presidential election. Both a rambling, shambolic Donald Trump and an unkempt, finger-pointing Bernie Sanders could be enraged at no cost to their moral standing. Just the opposite, in fact: each used anger effectively (a largely unremarked-upon gender card) to cultivate populist activism. Clinton, on the other hand, rarely displayed anger or adopted an angry tone. Even when her voice, smile, and clothing choices were being criticized unfairly, even as Trump stalked behind her on a debate stage, and men pontificated on her bodily habits, she remained calm, unruffled, and *not angry*. Others, like Democratic senator Elizabeth Warren, seemed to get angry for her. Warren rage tweeted endlessly, often with open aggression, behavior that was more palatable coming from her, as she was not perceived as acting *on her own behalf*. It was only after the 2017 publication of Clinton's raw and honest memoir about the campaign, *What Happened*, that some people started to ask, "Why isn't she even angrier?"

At the same time, First Lady Michelle Obama, on the other hand, was constantly cast in conservative (and sometimes liberal) media as an angry black woman who dangerously exercised undue influence over her husband. Additionally, this characterization of Mrs. Obama echoed the common trope that her husband was emasculated by her anger. She was cast as a "darker, continuous, and hidden side" of the chief executive, himself constrained in expressing anger in a way that a white president undoubtedly (and now, thanks to Donald Trump, blatantly) is not.

"That was one of those things where you just sort of think, 'Dang, you don't even know me,'" she explained during a 2016 interview with Oprah Winfrey. "You just sort of feel like, 'Wow, where'd that come from?' That's the first blowback because you think, 'That is *so* not me,' but then you sort of think, 'This isn't about me.' This is about the person or people who write it."

Black women are stereotyped in this way, but they are also disproportionately likely to be vocal leaders and, as such, have to use their anger particularly judiciously. They are more likely to serve in extra-institutional contexts, meaning outside of recognized and traditional institutions and hierarchies—at the forefront, for example, of criminal justice reform, reproductive and racial justice movements, disability rights, and environmental and climate change activism. In either case, they are often influential in positions that are resistant to the status quo. But expecting black women to take on the mantle of "angry black women" in defense of others is a specific problem. As writer Feminista Jones explained in 2016, the United States has a long history of expecting black women to be strong and to carry other people's worries and weight. The risk here, she explains, is that these women are "mammy-fied" as saviors for helpless white people.

If there is one benefit of Donald Trump's election in 2016, it is that no woman should ever again doubt that she is capable of running for and winning political office. The anger and depression that so many people felt upon his election generated an unprecedented spike in activism and women running for or preparing to run for political office. A Brookings Institution report on political participation published in early 2018 concluded, "This may be the first time in American history that an entire cohort of young women reports greater political engagement than their male peers."

Within six months of the election, more than twenty thousand women announced their intent to run for office. Emerge America, a training program for women who run as Democrats, saw an 87 percent increase in applications. Some 16,000 women, a jump from 920 in the previous year, contacted Emily's List, which endorses pro-choice women candidates, for support. She Should Run, a nonpartisan training organization, had an almost identical increase. New organizations and movements such as Getting Her Elected, Run for Something, and the American Women's Party were swamped with volunteers. This spike in women's political activism is driven almost entirely by progressive women, who are on the verge of forcing a serious national reassessment of women's status.

In times of political tumult, women—regardless of political orientation—are given more social leeway to be angry, and they run with it. Historically, during periods of heightened public distress, women have been the engines behind not only protests but also, even before they could vote or run for office, political policy. The Women's Christian Temperance Union, for example, founded in 1874, led the fight for Prohibition, largely as an attempt to stem domestic violence and poverty. It eventually, under the direction of Frances Willard, spread to agitate for fair labor laws, prison reform, and women's suffrage.

One of the most successful adaptations that women make in light of stubborn biases regarding their "proper place" is to filter political ambition and anger through motherhood. Mothers Against Drunk Driving, the Children's Defense Fund, MomsRising, Mothers Out Front, Moms Demand Action for Gun Sense in America, and Mothers of the Movement are examples of this approach. These organizations are, subversively, "nonthreatening" ways to marshal women's rage-fueled political energy.

"I remember being agitated and angry and sad, and feeling like I had to do something," Shannon Watts told me when we spoke in 2017. Watts is the founder of Moms Demand Action, an influential antigun violence advocacy group. She was describing how she felt on December 15, 2012, the day of the shooting massacre at Newtown, Connecticut's Sandy Hook Elementary School in which twenty-year-old Adam Lanza, after murdering his mother at home, went to the school and killed six teachers and twenty children before shooting himself.

"I think, for so many women in this country, when they are angry, there is confusion between anger and sadness," Shannon reflected. "In the wake of Sandy Hook, that is what was happening for so many women in this country. Incredible sadness, frustration, and anger all in one, and the realization that we had to get off the sidelines. I should have done it long before. As a white, suburban woman, it was Sandy Hook that resonated with me. I had not realized that ninety Americans were being killed [by gun violence] every day."

Six years later, in February of 2018, another school shooting galvanized millions when a man walked into Marjory Stoneman Douglas High School and shot fourteen students and four adults. In the wake of the shooting, well-informed students unabashed in their righteous rage organically fueled a highly visible national #NeverAgain movement, pressing for gun regulations that adults had failed to pass.

Less than five years after Watts launched Moms Demand Action as a Facebook page the day after Sandy Hook, the organization had 4,500 volunteers spread across almost seventy thousand neighborhood chapters in every US state. Organizations such as this give spectacular lie to the opinion, sounded by New York City councilman Peter Koo in 2017, that "[a]n angry mom can't accomplish much."

Women's anger over Trump's election has been the single greatest propellant of women's multifocus activism. An April 2017 poll of just under thirty thousand people showed that 86 percent of those who had taken steps to protest his administration and its policies were women; 28 percent were between the ages of thirty and forty-five; and 50 percent were between forty-six and sixty-five. In Texas, a state whose patriarchal tradition is equally met by one of resilient and progressive women's movements, a postelection movement is being led almost exclusively by women. Women were leaders of and majority participants in both the People's Climate March and the March on Science, both of which took place in cities around the country (and overseas, too) in April 2017. Women feature prominently in both urban and rural progressive-leaning grassroots resistance organizations. Some are leaving cities to go back to their homes of origin to run for office as liberals.

When Trump announced illegal immigration policies, women made up the large majority of immigration lawyers who offered their services to stranded and detained immigrants. Women started Safety Pin Box, a service created to help encourage white people to use race-based social and economic advantages to counter systemic racism. Women made up more than 80 percent of people who called Congress to protest the repeal of the Affordable Care Act. Women lawyers and judges have disproportionately challenged the Trump administration at every turn. In March of 2018, statewide teacher strikes in West Virginia, Arizona, and Oklahoma made headlines across the United States, where teachers' salaries are roughly 30 percent less than those of comparably educated workers employed in other sectors. While media touted the "historic" nature of these movements, few noted that these strikes were essentially women's strikes against their systemic undervaluing and exploitation.

Regardless of country or politics, women, whether as activists, voters, or politicians, disproportionately support dismantling traditional (male) entitlements to privacy, property, and wealth accumulation. They favor social safety nets and mechanisms that support economies of care, such as regulations for a cleaner environment, safer water, rational acknowledgment of the impacts of climate change, and legal reforms to address mass incarceration and institutional violence. In the United States, women spearhead fights against voter suppression, for bank reform, and against sexual violence in the military, prisons, and on campuses. Women founded Black Lives Matter, developing an innovative, distributed model of leadership and activism. They are leaders in the Dakota Access Pipeline protests and immigration movements. Just the fact that women are engaged in these fights makes them "elite," ugly, and angry in the eyes of people disinclined to expand their notions of citizenship to include women as equals.

Resistance to Trump takes a skill that women are familiar with: the work of building social networks with very little support or resources; of organizing, calling representatives, building communities; and of helping people process traumatic feelings productively. "Women have to get their messaging, tone, and appearance exactly right to be taken seriously," says activist organizer Emily Ellsworth. "When you have to work under those conditions daily, it stands to reason that you get good at resisting."

Women being good at resisting male power, which is significantly what we are talking about in terms of anger, politics, and denial, is often a matter of embodiment as resistance. In April 2018, for example, a now-withdrawn GOP candidate for the Maine legislature disparaged sixteen-year-old Emma González, who survived the February 2018 shooting in Parkland, Florida, calling her a "skinhead lesbian." Only weeks before the shooting she'd shaved her hair, hot and bothersome to her, off. If big hair symbolizes a certain glorification of traditional feminine norms, no hair is a clear rejection of those norms. As *New York Times* writer Vanessa Friedman pointed out, González's image belongs alongside others of loud and unapologetic women, real and imagined: actress and activist Rose McGowan; the *Black Panther* character Okoye, played by actress Danai Gurira; and *Mad Max: Fury Road*'s Imperator Furiosa, played by Charlize Theron. It is, as portrayed by Asia Kate Dillon on the TV series *Billions*, distinctly nonbinary. These women's appearance stands in stark political and philosophical contrast to, say, the extravagantly coiffed women who filled the Trump White House at the time. Friedman quoted Princeton University lecturer Erin K. Vearncombe, an expert on the cultural meaning of appearance, who explained, "absent hair on a woman's head can be read as disruptive to the politics of the male gaze."

If you can't focus on a woman's hair, it is infinitely more difficult to ignore what comes out of her mouth.

Women's collective anger is what drove them to march in worldwide protest on January 21, 2017, the day after Trump's inauguration. That day's Women's March is thought to be the largest protest in history. An estimated five million people convened in more than six hundred cities to advocate for women's human rights, workers' rights, LGBTQ rights, racial justice, immigration reform, and more. For millions of women who'd felt shocked by what Trump's election represented, this was the first time they had protested anything.

At the DC march, which I attended with friends and family, millions of women, men, and children filled main avenues, side streets, and park expanses near the Capitol. Like many who were there, I was struck by how much the organizers had accomplished. While chaotic, they had, in an astoundingly brief amount of time, brought together a sprawling coalition of varied people, organizations, and interests. The speakers ranged from six-year-old Sophie Cruz, who spoke, in Spanish, about immigrant rights, to unrelenting then eighty-two-year-old Gloria Steinem. Remarkably, there was not one reported episode of physical aggression or any arrests in any city in the world.

One of the most affective performers in DC was Janelle Monáe, a visionary Afrofuturist musician, actress, and role model. Monáe shared the stage with the mothers of African American men and women killed in acts of police violence and led the crowd in a call-and-response anthem, "Hell You Talmbout." Beginning with "Sandra Bland," each mother spoke her child's name as the crowd chanted back, "Say her name!"

Monáe's care and insistence that these women and their children be recognized was more than symbolically important in the moment, however. "We had that music for two years," she told me when we spoke eight months later. "We were sitting at Wondaland, our arts collective, and we were all so upset. We couldn't write our albums, we couldn't work. We couldn't write party songs. There was nobody who wasn't upset. The song came from a place of anger, but it was about channeling it. Let's bring attention to these people. This song is not for us. It's about us saying, 'We're playing this music as a weapon.' Music gets people involved."

This ethos of creative expression infuses Monáe's iconographic work. For more than a decade, while her industry waxed on about the genius of various (often hypermasculine) male peers, she quietly developed an avant-garde corpus of work only now being recognized for its brilliance and social and political commentary.

Monáe's performance at the march was a call to millions of women, demanding that they consider their choices: ongoing complicity in white supremacy or actively fighting against its perpetuation.

Over and over again, during the day and over the following years, I've heard people saying that raising awareness of race in the context of women's equality is "divisive." Sexism is always mediated by other factors: race, class, sexual identity, disability, gender identity. If you are inclined to think that raising the issue of race when discussing gender inequality in America is counterproductive, it can mean only that you are not "seeing" your own privileges and are unwilling to sit with discomfort.

The energy, drive, and grassroots organizing it took to pull together the Women's March were presaged by the Black Lives Matter movement, which was launched by Alicia Garza, Patrisse Cullors, and Opal Tometi. Distressed upon hearing, in 2013, that George Zimmerman was acquitted in the 2012 killing of seventeen-year-old Trayvon Martin, Garza, a community activist, wrote a Facebook post that closed with the words "black lives matter," sparking a movement. Their work established a model for what has become an expanding global network.

When I asked Garza what spurred her to action, she replied thoughtfully, "Anger at injustice is one part of what motivates me. But it is not a sustainable emotion in and of itself. It has to be transformed into a deep love for the possibility of who we can be. Anger can be a catalyst, but we cannot function on anger alone. When it's not used properly, it can quickly become destructive. That's why love is important: love connects us to what we most care about; what we yearn for."

It is frequently the case that while we recognize male leaders as representative of "humanity," we fail to do the same for women leaders. Strategists and pollsters speculated that it was unwise for the first anti-Trump march to be a "Women's March." The event may not have met the sort of criteria relevant for people with more power, people less constrained in their ability to speak freely and forcefully, both in and out of their own homes.

But the march served an important purpose for women everywhere, showing us all that we could and would defend ourselves and our interests. That we would not shut up and go away. That we would no longer put up with being represented by people who were failing us. It launched protesters into various campaigns around the country. Ten months later, the November 2017 elections were marked by historic victories for women, minorities, and members of the LGBTQ community. Voters consistently supported candidates who represented and embraced pluralism and social and economic justice.

It might make more sense for those concerned with the relevance or representation of movements like these to focus on the question of why the quiet anger and energy of women voters and politicians are so often ignored in favor of the loudest man in the room. Or to ask why the second Women's March, in which millions of people once again flooded city streets on January 20, 2018, was barely mentioned in mainstream media. It was hard not to compare this treatment to the over-the-top attention paid to Tea Party activists only a few years before. Denial and silencing take many forms.

WHAT DOES FEARING MOCKERY MEAN?

In one of the only studies I found about what women dread most in response to their anger when they express it in a close relationship, women did not say violence, harm to their connection, or retaliatory anger. They said what they dreaded and anticipated the most was being mocked. This is not an exaggerated or imagined concern, nor is it restricted to intimate interactions. Studies show that women who display or express anger in deliberative groups, for example, are taken less seriously than the men around them are.

Mockery captures the doubt, deflection, and denial that too many of us have come to expect in response to our anger. While women are aware of their anger and more comfortable expressing emotions, they are also aware—particularly in interpersonal contexts—that their anger might have very little traction.

Sandra Thomas, a professor of nursing at the University of Tennessee, spent decades studying women's anger, aggression, and emotional lives. In a 2005 review of years of research, including crosscultural studies in several nations, she found that the most consistent and prevalent theme in women's recounting incidents in which they felt and expressed anger was powerlessness. Powerlessness characterized two-thirds of situations described by women. "Women wanted someone or something to change, and they could not make that happen," Thomas wrote. "In fact, it was not uncommon for a woman to say that her significant others or coworkers were not even listening to her views or requests. Being told that your anger, and what it represents, is invalid is perhaps the epitome of powerlessness." Powerlessness is one of the reasons women cry more. It is less likely to cause an angry response in the person a woman is talking to.

Girls are constantly seeking ways to convince people they know, respect, and love that what they are saying when they describe their experiences or their anger and frustration is true, and that it is serious. Even at just eight to ten years old, young girls have been found in studies to think they will be made fun of or disciplined when they display anger. The culprits? Classmates—especially boys—but also, disturbingly, teachers. As girls move into adulthood, their awareness of the relationship between their anger and popularity becomes acute.

The gender beliefs and display rules that fuel these interactions, when discussed in terms of research or social science, can sound categorical and heavy-handed, but, in our actual lives, especially family life, they are far more subtle and invisible. The sexism we *don't see* is written in the cadence of traditions and habits. It makes its way into our identities around dinner tables, as we carpool, during school plays. It's going on when you ask only your ten-year-old daughter to set the table and send only her eight-year-old brother out to shovel snow. That's why it's important to consider that while anger-denial responses are common everywhere, they are most cutting and consequential at home, which is where the majority of girls and women say they feel and express anger most frequently. Everyday discrimination against girls and women is bound so tightly with prevailing cultural norms and "family-friendly" traditions that we barely see it for what it is: a massive social injustice perpetrated at every level of society.

We all have the right to believe what we believe and to live life as we see fit. But that doesn't mean we don't get to call what is clearly discrimination by its proper name. Benevolent sexism is still sexism. Religious sexism is still sexism. Both operate at intimate and personal levels but extend into every aspect of our lives, establishing a complex and dynamic model for difference and domination that spirals outward.

A family, the starting point of our socialization, is an initial, foundational condition, and small changes in those conditions yield enormous advantages. Our emotional divisions, the ones that discourage and punish women's anger while cultivating and often rewarding men's, generate and sustain persistent imbalances in behavior and outcomes.

When individual people are sexist at home—implicitly or overtly, with hostility or with benevolence—their communities and societies are less egalitarian. A 2012 study of gender inequality in fifty-seven countries found that the gender beliefs of individuals in their homes "don't stay confined to the person who has them, but affect how a society functions." The more sexist individuals are, the more unequal the society. Societies with high levels of household and interpersonal sexism are also the least stable and secure. Working with a collaborative team, Houston's Rice University professor of political science Valerie Hudson conducted more than ten years' worth of research definitively showing that the greatest predictor of a nation's peacefulness and security is the way that girls are treated in their own homes.

It is not just a coincidence that we are at an uncomfortable strategic inflection point for the rights of girls and women just as we face grave threats to democratic values and the health of the planet. One cannot be separated from the other. This is an era of angry women and women willing to make noise. This is not a luxury but a necessity.

Be angry.

Be loud.

Rage becomes you.

A RAGE
OF YOUR OWN

*That's what I want: to hear you erupting. You . . . who
don't know the power in you.*

—Ursula K. Le Guin

*I felt like a hand was at my throat when I first started
writing. That if I was going to be a proper writer, I'd
better be as polite as possible and as calm as possible
and as unangry as possible—and recently I've been
thinking, you know, fuck that, basically.*

—Zadie Smith

What now? What to do with all the rage? This was not
a question I could have even asked myself ten years
ago. The anger I felt was so deplorably mismanaged
that I didn't recognize it. The first time I did, it was in the most
socially palatable form: as a mother.

One day in 2010, I found myself standing, panic stricken and shaking, in a small bathroom in my house. Only minutes earlier, I'd been standing less than ten feet away in my kitchen, calmly and cheerfully making dinner and talking to my daughter, who had recently turned thirteen. It was a lovely evening, one of the first of spring. Despite having just finished two hours of soccer practice, she was bursting with energy.

This was a child who'd spent years perfecting how to climb doorframes and stair rails. She'd once disappeared, at the age of six, in the middle of a basketball court. I found her sitting in one of the hoops, twelve feet in the air. She would lie on the crossbar of park swing sets like a cat and was so full of energy that even hours of intense sports couldn't tire her out. When she was eleven she applied to a school in Italy, though we had no intention of moving. She was confident, fearless, and full of excitement about the world.

I shouldn't have been surprised, therefore, when she asked if she could walk to our local ice cream shop. I excused myself, walked out of the kitchen and, saying I'd be right back, locked myself in a bathroom. Once the door was closed, I was stunned to find myself crying, my thoughts flying incoherently. Our neighborhood did not regularly present undue threats, and her asking was unexceptional. She had walked by herself many times, but I was struck that afternoon by how "adult" she looked, a concept that I actively resented, for what that meant to her freedom.

It felt too early. I knew I would have to teach my daughters about harassment and to adjust to the constant threat of rape, but I didn't want to. Mainly, I could not imagine the sadness we would feel, in different ways, for different reasons, and in different measure. At five foot seven, my athletic and physically adventurous daughter already looked much older. Walking alone, she was certain to experience harassment, if she hadn't already. She would, from now on, have to be alert in public spaces. Vigilant. She might, as many girls and women do, turn in on herself or, without even realizing it, begin

limiting herself, her curiosity, and her exploration of life. Her openness to new experiences and natural inquisitiveness would now be
bounded by her femininity, by the reality that her gender mattered
and in ways that made her unequal in the world.

Then I realized I wasn't having an anxiety attack. Instead, anger
was washing through me like a tidal force. The wave of white heat
rippling through me, material and intense, felt like another person
in the room. Why hadn't I ever said or done anything about this?
What made me absorb my own experiences in silence?

I collected myself, went back to the kitchen and gave my daughter some simple and practical advice about what to do if a person
made her wary or uncomfortable. Walk into a store, I explained, or
look for a woman with children, or knock on someone's front door
and explain to the person what is going on. I talked to her about
her right to walk freely and look people in the eye. I explained
the dynamics of street harassment and made clear that the attention she might receive had nothing to do with her clothes or her
stride; that there was no shame in being a girl and walking with
confidence.

The rage I felt that day grew. I desperately needed to give the
memories and feelings I had context. The more I thought, the more
I shared, the more I wrote, the more I understood—and the angrier
I became. It had been years since I'd engaged in any kind of activism. I had no time. That too became an issue. I was exhausted by
the demands of wifehood, motherhood, and work, and resented the
imposition of other people's social expectations, including their gendered norms, in our lives.

When my anger began to interfere with my ability to have a
conversation about virtually anything, when my family wondered
what had transformed me into a vortex of frustration and rage, I
turned to other women. I found, if I scratched the surface of their
regard even a little bit, they were often also simmering with a low-
grade and silent rage.

"What to do? What to do with all this rage?" I kept asking myself.

—————

If you have ever looked for ways to think about anger, chances are, like I did, you immediately found advice about "anger management." It's an interesting term, as it implies we have control over how and when we *feel* anger, and that it must be controlled or reined in. The problem, however, is that anger management techniques often take into account only an excessively narrow band of anger expression recognized as problematic: destructive, monstrous rage—mainly the kind that is stereotypically associated with men.

For women, healthy anger management doesn't require us to exert more control but, rather, *less*. We are managing anger all the time without even realizing it. Even this idea of "control" and "management" is a limiting way to think about anger if you want it to be purposeful, deliberate, engaging, and change making. For so-called anger management to be truly relevant, it must focus equally on self-silencing, somatization, unhealthy anger diversion, and negative social responses.

But my research on anger yielded very little information about women and its positive uses. Almost all of the available clinical research I found focused on negative mental health impacts and, where aggression was concerned, focused on men. There was a mountain of information about explosive rage and chronic anger, but a relative molehill about silence or denial or useful expression.

What I wanted was a way to cultivate what I think of as "anger competence." I didn't want to think of my anger as being *outside* of myself. I wanted to own my anger, because it brought me back to myself. It gave me clarity and purpose.

Anger is an emotion. It is neither good nor bad. While uncomfortable, it's not inherently undesirable. Most of the anger-related problems we encounter come from its social construction and how our emotions are filtered through our identities and social location relative to others. Anger should not be an entitlement.

When women are asked why they continue to associate being angry with negative outcomes and fear, they say it is because they do not want to "lose control" and act in "inappropriate" ways. This desire not to be disliked or seen as crazy, irrational, or dangerous, masks the lack of control that *we already live with* as the result of the silencing, sublimating, denying, and social opprobrium. It is still the case that gender-role expectations continue to make anger expression taboo for women. This is truer in some cultures than in others, but within each culture, anger almost always belongs to the domain of masculinity.

In 2010, for example, a large-scale study conducted in the United States and Canada found that only 6.2 percent of people thought that women's expressing anger was "appropriate." Locating this difference in gender is descriptive but not entirely accurate, since the dynamic of who gets to express anger matters in all unequal social relationships. Among men, status related to race, ethnicity, and class also limits the expression of rage and affects the perception of risk. Within like groups, however, meaning same class/ethnicity, for example, it is generally more appropriate for women to keep their anger to themselves.

If there is a word that should be retired from use in the service of women's expression, health, well-being, and equality, it is *appropriate*—a sloppy, mushy word that purports to convey some important moral essence but in reality is just a policing term used to regulate our language, appearance, and demands. It's a control word.

We are done with control.

The ideas expressed in this chapter are meant to provide tools for developing competence. Anger competence.

For years, I was so sure of anger's negative nature that I could not reconcile it with my sense of self, my relationships, my political power, or my desire to fight social injustice. The emotion was so effectively severed from my use that, instead of being a catalyst for change, feeling angry invalidated both my confidence and my own experiences. Like most people, I had learned to think of empathy and compassion as divorced from anger, but empathy and compassion were fundamental to my anger. I have since learned that my rage is a critical part of my self, and it is a part of myself that I have grown to respect and love instead of suppress. This is not easy, and it can make for difficult situations, but my personal experience reflects the social science finding that people who allow themselves to feel the fullest range of emotions, including the unpleasant ones, are happier and lead more fulfilling lives, regardless of cultural context.

Anger is a moral emotion that hinges on our making judgments about the people and world around us. As women, we are supposed to be one step removed from both moral thinking and the authority that comes with it. Our feelings of anger, deep in our bones, our blood, and our minds, are a refutation of that oppressive standard and the control of women that comes with it. It is not only that we have the right to claim anger. It is that our anger is a moral obligation. If we are willing to spend time, money, and effort for so many other things, surely liberating our anger should make the cut.

In what they term the "anger advantage," the title of their 2003 book, psychologists Deborah Cox, Karin Bruckner, and Sally Stabb make recommendations based on an integrated understanding of anger as a complex social, emotional, physiological, and psychological phenomenon. The researchers' work focuses on addressing the ways that women bypass their own awareness of the anger they feel and, instead, find diversions and coping mechanisms that impede meaningful change. They identify four skills that are good baselines for anyone using anger productively: (1) anger consciousness, (2) anger talk, (3) listening to others, and (4) what they term "think tank," or strategizing. Below, I have elaborated on these themes to include a broader constellation of suggestions.

1. DEVELOP SELF-AWARENESS

Anger does not, in and of itself, make you "right." It is, however, explained feminist writer and thinker Audre Lorde, "loaded with information and energy." Use it this way. People who understand how they are feeling are able to be patient and thoughtful in anger. They develop a liberating detachment that enables them to decide what solutions will work for the problem they face.

In terms of self-awareness, you can take stock of your default anger settings. Are you expressive or a ruminator? Do you simmer or explode? Do you cry or calmly assert yourself? Are you diverting your anger? Do you even admit to yourself that you are mad about something or at someone close to you? What are you scared to say, even to yourself? You might tend toward getting angry quickly, known as trait anger, or you might be a person who is slower to anger even when provoked, known as state anger.

For some of us, when we are expected to be happy or cheerful or to carry other people's emotions for them, the first important step is simply the awareness that we have strong negative emotions. Admitting that you are angry—to yourself and to others—can be difficult and destabilizing, but it is urgently important, if only for the way in which it builds and maintains your self-respect and esteem.

The more you know about anger, the less you will be subject to it as a negative force. Experts agree that owning one's anger—knowing what it is and naming it—enhances relationships and intimacy.

Some people benefit also from finding "their people," the ones who will understand, listen, empathize and, often, are angered by the same issues or problems. Even if you can't act immediately on how you feel, simply talking about anger is beneficial; other people often see solutions and alternatives that you don't. Sharing is important for specific reasons. Naming, writing, and talking, known as affect labelling, is different from simply venting the way you might, for example, by throwing plates. Naming, talking, and writing, are beneficial because they actually interfere with the neurological mechanics causing anger or anxiety. They constitute a kind of anger mindfulness.

Talking constructively also means listening, which serves the dual purpose of your being able to better understand other people's anger, which makes it less threatening and less of a risk. If it *doesn't*, that, too, is valuable information. If you find you are crying and silent but seething inside, what circumstances are leading to your feelings of powerlessness? Are you scared of someone else's anger? What is the real risk? Write it down, think it over, and, when you have time, talk about it openly. An adult relationship that can't withstand your saying you feel angry is probably not a healthy one and, if that pattern is sustained, probably not worth continuing.

The key is not to use communication to catastrophize and ruminate, both of which contribute to lasting, corrosive anger, but to achieve recognition and change, if possible. Anger that anchors you in place is not helpful.

2. DISTINGUISH THE THREE *AS*: ANGER, ASSERTIVENESS, AND AGGRESSION

Anger, assertiveness, and aggression are frequently and unhelpfully lumped together, particularly when the person who is being assertive, angry, or aggressive is a girl or woman. All three are, however, related by the word *no*, and a simple, unapologetic, declarative *no* is not a word that girls and women are taught to embrace.

Assertiveness is simply the act of stating a position with confidence. It is a form of direct, clear, and honest communication that is a known and effective response to everyday stressors. Assertive women are more emotionally resilient and less likely to experience anxiety or depression.

Being assertive means different things to different people, however. For some, simply saying the word *no* is a big step. For one person, writing a polite but firmly worded email to a coworker is assertive; for another, verbally demanding that a spouse pull his weight is assertive. For yet a third, starting a petition online does the trick. It takes practice and, in some cases, years to undo socialization that might be leading you to bite your tongue or not believe that you are deserving of whatever it is that you are asking for.

Aggression is a more directly confrontational behavior, less civil, but, in many cases, respectful. It is possible to be both assertive and aggressive without being angry at all and, conversely, to be angry without being assertive or aggressive. Each, depending on context, has its place. I remind myself sometimes that the root of the word *aggressive* is related closely to the Latin word *aggredi*, meaning "to go forward."

For women, assertiveness and aggression, like anger, can be conflicting, because they suggest a woman's lack of interest in yielding. To doing what she is told. And women are supposed to yield.

Studies show that women who make demands at work acquiesce more quickly to responses than men do. In other words, they give in before they might be satisfied. Observe in your own speech how often you might be suppressing your words or demands. Ask yourself, "Does being assertive make me feel anxious?" "Do I repeatedly use minimizing words, such as *just* when I write emails?" "How frequently do I begin a sentence with *Sorry?*" Do you give in or backtrack on a demand quickly and easily?

Anger, assertiveness, and aggression also all become entangled in the word "passionate." "I'm not angry, I'm passionate" is an expression I often hear when talking about this topic. The word "passionate" always strikes me as a particularly gendered one, women being more likely to be described as passionate, whether they are angry or not, for speaking firmly and with determination. "Passionate women" are often women who have developed an exquisite ability to select their words and convey their strongest beliefs while navigating anger-averse people and cultures. Anger *is* the emotion generated by feeling passionate about an issue or topic of serious interest or commitment. Ask yourself, why might you prefer to be thought of as passionate and not angry? Being "passionate" is, almost certainly, a useful way to avoid the dismissal of stereotypes (as an angry black woman, for example, or an ugly and humorless white woman, for example) or to sidestep other negative associations with the word "angry." However, by not admitting when anger is actually the issue, when it is righteous and justified, we contribute to denying our right to use it effectively and appropriately. "Passionate" is too often a word for anger that is meant to convey that what you are feeling is not explosive and destructive, threatening or aggressive. It perpetuates the idea that anger is negative and to be avoided.

3. BE BRAVE

Be brave enough to stop pleasing people, to be disliked, to rub people the wrong way. In many environments, all you have to do to be castigated as an angry woman is to say something out loud, so you might as well say exactly what's bothering you and get on with it. This means that, usually, you have to come to terms with not always being liked. Your anger and assertiveness will make some people unhappy, uncomfortable, sensitive, cautious. They will resent you, your thoughts, your words. They will hate your willingness to risk social connections and challenge social conventions. Be prepared to be labelled humorless, difficult, a spoilsport, and a ruiner of parties, meetings, dinners, and picnics.

There is discomfort in understanding. There will always be people who are deeply uncomfortable with your anger. They will attempt to diminish what you say by disparaging your choice of expression. This is a kind of laziness and a sure symptom of dismissal and, sometimes, abuse. If someone does not care to consider why you are angry, or why anger is your approach to a specific event or problem, then that person is almost certainly part of the problem. Among women, this dismissal often comes from the desire not to identify with "victimhood," and your anger, as a marker of social difference and disadvantage, is a challenge to that concept. Demanding fairness and describing a problem doesn't make you a "victim." Silencing, denial, mockery, intimidation, and callousness might, though.

It helps, in these circumstances, to think of the difference between being nice, which girls are taught to do at all costs, and being kind. Nice is something you do to please others, even if you have no interest, desire, or reason to. Kindness, on the other hand, assumes that you are true to yourself first.

4. TAKE (DELIBERATE) CARE

It is possible to take care of others without being careless with yourself. Most women take on what they do not only because they are expected to but also because they love and care and want to. But the expectation that we do so infinitely and selflessly, and the demands that such expectations produce, exhaust us. Care with purpose. Understand that this includes taking care of your own health and wellbeing. Learn to say no and to say no unapologetically.

One of the most effective ways to address care creep is to think deliberately and to make conscious choices. It is possible to audit the paid and unpaid work you do and even the emotions that you manage for other people.

SET CLEAR BOUNDARIES. Many women resist admitting resentment about taking care of the people around them or that they feel frustrated at being taken advantage of, at home or at work. You do not have to be porous. Being porous to other people's needs will almost always exhaust and anger you. Egalitarian relationships enable better communication and emotional expression for everyone.

ASK FOR HELP. The anger that women feel at being treated unfairly, at recognizing societal hostility to their identities, is made significantly worse by low expectations. Wanting more and demanding more probably doesn't come easily because low expectations are feminine. Low expectations, feelings of inadequacy, and low self-esteem are the driving engine of the self-help industry. Do you know when you need self-help? *When no one else is helping you.* An ideology of personal satisfaction and improvement is no substitute for systemic restructuring for liberation. It is no accident that the explosion of the self-help industry, one that to a great extent feeds off of women's sense of inadequacy, coincided with the rise of choice feminism and neoliberal economics. Like choice feminism, self-help also reduced the need for social and state commitments to change by placing the blame for reduced circumstances on people who don't have the time, money, or resources to "help themselves."

SEE YOUR ANGER NOT ONLY AS A POSSIBLE SYMPTOM BUT ALSO AS A WAY TO RECOVER YOURSELF. If you are among the millions of people who have experienced abuse in childhood, for example, or physical and sexual violence in adulthood, anger is inevitable. Women who suppress this anger suffer more deleterious effects related to that suppression. Recovering from these assaults and their memories is hampered by ignoring what your anger represents as an agent of better health.

RETHINK FORGIVENESS. It is often the case that our anger comes from feeling betrayed, disappointed, and taken for granted. The feelings we have—hurt, resentment, frustration, and rage—are often portrayed as negative and not worth being taken seriously. We are often encouraged to ignore, forgive, and forget. For women whose lives are informed by faith, forgiveness is frequently prioritized over beneficial resolutions. Being forgiving in self-sacrificial ways is emotional labor par excellence.

Forgiveness is valuable and important to relationships, but if your instinct is to withhold forgiveness, it is probably a good one. The expectation of forgiveness often involves shaming you for not feeling forgiving. This is dismissive in that it ignores feelings of hurt, pain, and trauma and contributes to the sense that you do not deserve to be heard. Forgive nothing until you are good and ready to, especially if there has been no indication that the behavior causing you distress has changed.

TEACH THE PEOPLE AROUND YOU TO NAME AND TALK ABOUT THEIR ANGER. If you are a person with child care responsibilities, teaching children healthy anger habits can only improve everyone's lives and relationships. While they cannot always avoid the traps of gender stereotypes, children can learn to understand them and adapt accordingly. For girls, this means not only talking openly about anger and its relationship to other emotions and related behaviors but also modelling healthy habits. Talking openly about anger also gives adolescent girls an opportunity to participate and think about how they are able to shape their own environments. (For boys, it requires different lessons: for example, about empathy, shame, and male entitlements.) As women, we are forced to use our anger without the social benefits that many men can rely on. Talk about *that* openly and regularly when you sense that your anger is being 'splained to you.

CONSIDER A THERAPIST. Whether you are a self-silencer or a rager, it's important to acknowledge when your anger is destructive to you and others. Some women have explosive, physically destructive and unpredictable outbursts in which they risk hurting themselves or other people. Unfettered anger elicits feelings of shame and often covers deeper feelings of self-disgust. Explosion, vengeance, or retribution, studies show, doesn't uplift a person's mood, contribute to improving communication, or effect desirable change. If you often express anger this way, it is important to figure out what is going on and why.

If you find yourself easily frustrated, irritable, and stressed, the focus of your anger is almost certainly misplaced. Flying off the handle in unpredictable ways rarely makes change or makes you feel better. Anger like this is usually a symptom of unaddressed emotions and, almost always, a history of having learned that expressing your emotions is not only bad but also makes you a bad person.

Therapy, in all of its iterations, however, is also another expensive yet uncommented-on cost to women, who make up the vast majority of people seeking help for mental distress. In my twenties and thirties, paying for therapy was not even remotely an option financially. Cost is frequently an obstacle to getting care, even if insurance partially covers treatment. In addition, therapy is not automatically beneficial to women. The field has a long history of enforcing, rather than challenging, the status quo inequities that cause us so much harm. As with some medical treatments, therapy can be shaped by cultural and social norms and expectations that affect both therapists and clients, their expectations, goals, and the ways that they interact. A therapist's cultural competence or incompetence can significantly alter outcomes. Any evaluation of a therapist or treatment should include these considerations. It is always advisable to interview therapists before deciding how to proceed. In some instances, it is possible to identify the problems that you need help with, but, in others, it is not. Being comfortable with the person you will work with is an essential first step.

In some communities, people turn to religious authorities as proxies for therapy. This has similar issues related to cultural inhibitions, costs, and beliefs. And, as with therapy, religious counsel can, under certain circumstances, do more harm than good. Rachael Denhollander, the first woman to bring charges of sexual abuse against US gymnastics team physician Larry Nassar, is an evangelical Christian. Like many people, she turned to her community and church leaders for guidance and emotional support in her time of crisis. But this is not the same as going to a professional therapist. The young woman came to realize that lessons about modesty, forgiveness, repentance, and anger were enabling Nassar's abuse. Accountability did not seem to matter.

"There is an abhorrent lack of knowledge for the damage and devastation that sexual assault brings," Denhollander explained after Nassar had been tried, convicted, and sentenced. "It is with deep regret that I say the church is one of the worst places to go for help."

The day I published my first article, I made an appointment to see a therapist. She was smart, caring, and compassionate. Through long discussions with her over a period of years, the way I thought about anger and myself shifted. Weathering the vicissitudes of being a Woman on the Internet, on the receiving end of a perpetual stream of ugliness, would have been infinitely more difficult if I hadn't been able to do this.

5. CULTIVATE BODY CONFIDENCE

If your appearance is important to you (and studies show that it is for the overwhelming majority of women), it is important to consciously balance how your body looks with your body's health and competence, meaning health and functioning as opposed to attractiveness. Self-objectification makes it harder to feel your anger or do anything about it. It makes you more vulnerable to threat and assault. It contributes to low self-esteem, self-silencing, and a heightened likelihood of self-harm, anxiety, and depression. If there are people in your life telling you or girls that you know that "girls are prettier with their mouths shut," demand that they stop. Studies of athletes show a strong correlation between body competence, self-esteem, and healthier anger expression. Think about how you can develop a sense of your body's strength and abilities in order to refute damaging, pervasive messages undermining self-esteem and the almost inevitable mental distress that comes with it.

Girls who grew up in the post–Title IX era are pioneers not only in sports but also in female aggression, competitiveness, anger, and leadership. The 1972 passage of this clause in the Civil Rights Act, protecting equal rights to education, is perhaps best known for its impact on athletics. It opened the doors to girls in sports. In reality, the mass movement of girls into athletics meant that an entire generation, currently coming into its political own, was able, in unprecedented ways, to join teams, develop competitive bonds, and express feelings physically, including aggression and anger. Sports are a way of learning teamwork and developing physical prowess, but they are also important because they teach people how to regulate and channel aggression, violence, and power. Becoming proficient in self-defense has similar benefits.

Girls who participate in team sports have higher self-esteem, are more resistant to rigid gender norms, are more ambitious politically and professionally, and are more inclined to be leaders. In sports, you are able to develop mastery over a honed sense of the *potential* of aggression, with or without anger, to alter your environment as well as what professor and cultural historian Maud Lavin (the author of *Push Comes to Shove: New Images of Aggressive Women*) describes as the "sheer physical joy of exerting aggression outward instead of inward."

In her consideration of sports and aggression, Lavin focuses on women's boxing as a way to think about these themes. She writes: "Women's boxing has become—as a symbol for many and an actuality for practitioners—evidence of the will to fight without shame, and to be able to take a hit and come back."

Still, social inhibitions remain powerful. Unfortunately, in the United States today, girls drop out of sports at twice the rate of boys by the age of fourteen, and by the time they reach seventeen, more than half have stopped playing any sports. The spillover benefits of sports as an institution that teaches competitiveness, aggression, leadership, and public participation are important in ways that often remain hidden and are lost by trends like these.

"For a long time, showing obedience and good manners were considered the most important things for a girl to learn," explained Brazilian writer Vanessa Barbara in a 2017 *New York Times* op-ed piece titled simply, "Brazilian Women Can Learn to Yell." "Even now, especially in developing countries like mine, this has barely changed: the worst thing a woman can do is speak up for herself and spread ideas that are not 'appropriate,' like saying that misogyny exists in her professional field or denouncing a sexual crime committed by a powerful man. It's always better to stay quiet and just let the abuser have his way. If the woman could also manage to say 'Thank you' after that, it would be even better."

Describing a lifetime of socialization and an abusive relationship, Barbara went on to explain why she signed up for a self-defense class. "Learning how to block, evade, immobilize, and disarm potential attackers was not the hardest task. The most difficult was the yelling," she wrote. Her instructor told them to pretend they were facing an aggressor. "We should look him in the eye and shout as loud as we could. Anything, really, could work: 'No!' or 'This is Sparta!' or 'I'm mad as hell, and I'm not going to take this anymore!' Some of us simply couldn't do it, having spent an entire life being courteous and delicate."

It's not only in nations like Brazil that girls are raised this way. Parents, teachers, and media in every country cultivate risk-taking in boys, and wariness, nervousness, and fear in girls. Parents of newborn daughters, for example, take fewer risks and are almost twice as likely to be risk averse than parents of sons. Michelle Craske, director of the UCLA Anxiety and Depression Research Center, has found that, contrary to stereotypes, baby boys start off more fretful and exhibit more signs of stress and neediness than girls do. Parents will ignore fear and anxiety in boys but cultivate them in girls. By the time a girl is seven years old, her mother's anger habits and risk perceptions are passed on to her.

Taylor Clark, author of *Nerve: Poise Under Pressure, Serenity Under Stress, and the Brave New Science of Fear and Cool*, refers to this dynamic as the "skinned knee effect." "Parents coddle girls who cry after a painful scrape but tell boys to suck it up," he writes. "This formative link between emotional outbursts and kisses from mom predisposes girls to react to unpleasant situations with 'negative' feelings like anxiety later in life. On top of this, cultural biases about boys being more capable than girls also lead parents to push sons to show courage and confront their fears, while daughters are far more likely to be sheltered from life's challenges. If little Olivia shows fear, she gets a hug; if little Oliver shows fear, he gets urged to overcome it."

The route you take to body competence doesn't matter and, indeed, needs to be tailored to your health, age, abilities, and interests. The point is that you cultivate a strong sense of your body, its capabilities, and your use of it.

6. TAKE YOUR ANGER TO WORK

Anger is often part of the average workday, and occupational status directly affects how we feel and express our anger. Women are far more likely to be employed in jobs that require them to suppress anger, with spillover effects into their personal life. For example, a nurse who spends her day silencing herself with both doctors and patients is more likely to respond explosively at home to a relatively minor frustration. Women describing what makes them mad in the workplace consistently identify similar catalysts as those related to what makes them mad in other areas of life: being taken for granted, a lack of time and related stress, being disappointed by other people's failure to care or step up to the plate, and feeling abused, as well as experiencing various forms of discrimination related to race, gender, disability, or pregnancy.

Navigating anger, frustration, and resentment when their expression puts your livelihood at risk is difficult and complex. Because of the realities of workplace hierarchies and the legitimate fear of retaliation, many of us, even if we are aware of our anger, stay silent. We then tend to, in turn, punch down, taking out our ire on loved ones at home or on subordinates.

Cox, Bruckner, and Stabb point out, however, that resolving work-related anger problems can also be thought of in terms of improving relationships. When asked, women are consistent about the primary causes of anger in their lives: overwork and stress; feeling as though they are being taken for granted; other people's irresponsibility or taking credit for what they are doing; and being condescended to, humiliated, or demeaned. These are aggregated, in the literature of anger studies, as being angered by other people's irresponsibility, feelings of powerlessness, and the perception of injustice. Regardless of the context, the approach stays the same: awareness, talking, listening, and strategizing.

For most of us, anger is related to the desire for greater control in the workplace—of our own careers, our physical safety, our ability to earn a living, our health. Not expressing anger doesn't achieve any of this. This isn't to say that starting the day in an alienating diatribe is advisable. Organize your thoughts and actions with clear objectives. That may mean asking for a long-overdue raise, but it might also mean saving money to quit a miserable job and look for another one or taking the step to report harassment.

Chances are, if you are angry about a problem, so are others; this is information that you can use to your advantage. If there are issues too hot for you to confront directly, consider what Trojan horses you might be able to develop to achieve your goal. If you fear consequences or retaliation, find allies and champions who can represent your interests. If you don't have a mentor or sponsor, get one. It might also make sense to explain explicitly to your employer the positive contributions that anger can generate in a workplace, in terms of diverse ideas and outcomes. The communication of anger can improve organizational functioning and workplace environments, and can benefit not only you but also those around you.

If there is not a specific catalyst for your anger at work, such as an incident of bias or harassment, and you live instead with a low-grade irritation and discontent, consider what it means in terms of what *does* make you consistently very angry. "When I was in the workplace, my anger was misdirected," Shannon Watts, the founder of Moms Demand Action for Gun Sense in America, told me. "I wasn't fulfilled by what I was doing, and therefore it came out in my work relationships. I was unhappy, but once I realized how I could direct my anger to help other people, it was completely life changing."

7. CULTIVATE COMMUNITIES AND ACCOUNTABILITY

Anger can feel very isolating, but, in fact, it is an emotion that demands communication and conversation. It also finds strength in community.

Finding communities that validate and share your anger creates powerful opportunities for effective collective social action. In these settings, anger is often a source of energy, joy, humor, and resistance. Anger, awareness, listening, and strategizing are all key components to social movement.

Communities built by women in response to what makes them mad also have the added benefit of making women's anger and community public and visible, creating important shifts in representation and understanding. In our political and emotional culture, political anger is, as discussed, still associated with men and their rights and power.

It is often the case that while anger often brings girls and women together in resistance and protest, the political nature of that anger is routinely disregarded. It should be made explicit, however. Take, for example, a problem that is common for girls the world over: school dress codes. Girls are overwhelmingly negatively affected by dress code enforcements that institutionalize gendered and raced ideas about sexuality, shame, "modesty," and "professionalism."

When girls protest being disciplined and publicly embarrassed— sometimes pulled out of class or made to wear "shame suits"—the media often write about their efforts in trivializing discussions about "leggings" and hairstyles, instead of more in-depth and serious consideration of what is making protesting students angry: sexist double standards, racist norms, and, often, homophobic ideas that directly infringe on their civil rights.

For some of us, finding a community means expanding beyond immediate and physical circles. The internet has been a transformational space for women and for their use of anger. On a hot summer day in 2011, a fifteen-year-old girl in Louisville, Kentucky, wanted to talk to me after a speech. She waited until everyone else had left to ask what she could do about a problem that made her mad and left her feeling hopeless. Whenever she raised the issue of gender inequality in her home, she explained, her parents punished her by refusing her dinner and confining her to her bedroom.

This was strange, I thought, since they didn't shut off her access to the internet. She could, I suggested, find supportive online feminist spaces. She could reach out to others similarly isolated but engaged. Today she is able to talk to girls in places as far flung as Pakistan, Colombia, and Tibet. Thirty years ago, this girl would have lived in almost complete isolation from others who were experiencing what she was.

Girls and women today have an opportunity that those before them never had: the ability to access and build virtual and transnational relationships. The power of the internet and its networks can be immensely destructive, but it can also be freeing and disruptive. Girls and women can now transcend their historic isolation from one another. Using social media and technology, we are able to form networks and communities that span neighborhoods and cross borders. It will take decades for us to really understand what this expansion of girls' worlds means, but we can already see the effects in global feminist movements. At its heart, this technology is dissolving a public/private divide in ways that decades of activism and scholarship never could.

Lastly, seek out people with whom you might otherwise not overlap. Without effort, any community you form is almost certainly bound to be homogeneous. Studies show that racial, religious, and ethnic segregation continue to be prevalent, with negative effects for all of us. Fill your world with different voices and perspectives.

8. CHALLENGE BINARIES

Binaries make up the male-female structure of the world. They mark the differences between home and work, personal and professional, private and political, and emotional and rational, to name only a few.

In terms of anger, context often governs how you feel and express it, and for women, one of the foremost regulators of our expression is how we are *supposed* to act in public versus in private. In both places, we are more subject to being tone policed, but in public spaces, this is especially true.

The private/public divide is fundamental to keeping women isolated from one another and, historically, from engaging in politics and commerce. The divide also masks the relationship between interpersonal sexism and institutionalized discrimination.

According to Professor Aída Hurtado, this divide is not historically relevant in the same way for immigrant women of color, black
women, working-class women, and women with marginalized sexual
identities. In the United States, for example, white women were
the most likely to be sequestered in an idealized feminine domestic
sphere, and it was a private sphere that was, in defense of the rights
of white men, off-limits to the (public sphere) government. For non-
white women, the government has always been more invasive, freely
interfering with their bodies, private lives, and personal decisions.
"There is no such thing," Hurtado explains, "as a private sphere for
people of color, except that which they manage to create and protect
in an otherwise hostile environment."

A second very consequential binary to reconsider is the one that
supports stereotypes about emotions and reason, instinct and thinking. It is frequently used to invalidate women's anger and concerns.
Women are designated more emotional, but then the designation
itself is used to undermine our reason. In this framework, a man, a
thinker, can have emotions, but a woman, a feeler, *is* emotional. To
paraphrase one study, if a man gets angry, he's having an off day, if
a woman does, she's a raging bitch.

We envision our emotions battling our reason because, after all,
that's what we are usually taught. As a woman, this lesson can be
particularly insidious because, in the way of these dualisms, you fall,
like it or not, onto the "emotional" and "irrational" and, therefore,
"inferior," side of the equation. The entire setup makes it easier for
what you say to be portrayed as unreasonable. One of the most important steps you can take is to refuse to play by those rules.

When you are angry, there is no part of you that is uninvolved.
To have feelings is to react to your environment but also to your
rational thoughts. Those reactions take place everywhere: your nervous system, your cardiovascular system, your endocrine (hormonal)
system. How you respond makes up the "character" aspect of your
anger that operates in context. The more attuned you are to both,

the more likely you are to understand what you are experiencing and to consciously calibrate your affect and behavior, leading to better decisions. Ignoring the "emotional" information at your disposal does the opposite.

9. TRUST OTHER WOMEN

Sometimes we are our own worst enemies. On a personal level, it is often the case that the people or person you would most likely talk to about being angry are the ones causing you to feel angry. Being nonconfrontational is an early life lesson for many of us, particularly with other women. Instead, some of us learn to resort to cattiness, silent treatments, passive aggression, and the "mean-girl" behaviors thought to be inherent to being female. Or, in order not to threaten a relationship, we divert our anger into other channels, never finding an outlet or resolution to what is bothering us. This, however, suggest Cox et al., doesn't help deepen a friendship the way a more honest and respective exchange does.

When a friend tells you she is angry, do you ask why and listen? If you see a woman "losing her shit," do you make fun of her? If a girl is "moody," do you ask her not about what's wrong with her but about what's happening around her?

Do you even have a solid cadre of women friends? If not, if you have always thought that the vagaries of female friendship are too demanding and that male friends are "so much easier to deal with," it might be worthwhile to consider if you are the "cool girl," the "no-drama" type that some men love and what that might mean.

When other women are angry, are you very critical? As women, we are even more judgmental about other women's violations of rules about anger than men are. Before we reach puberty, we learn, as girls, to police other girls' anger. As women, we need to learn resistance to a fundamental lesson of misogyny: that other women are untrustworthy and deficient and that, in anger, they are dangerous. Call out stereotypes about "angry black women," "fiery Latinas," and "sad Asian girls." Or consider how women have to navigate them, and in ways that you yourself might not. Trust other girls and women, and give them leeway. Plenty of other people will be willing to step in to criticize them.

We are as exposed to sexist ideas as men are and often held responsible for enforcing them. Denigrating other women can be a blood sport.

This doesn't mean blind denial of egregious behavior or ignoring the ways in which another woman might be hurtful or hateful. Anger is the emotion of problem solving, and so civility matters. Empathy is critical, and kindness is usually possible. If you are angry at a friend, if she has disappointed you or acted in a hurtful way, you can incorporate how you feel into peaceful approaches that yield more effective and lasting solutions. This is not to say that aggression and hostility are always avoidable or don't have a place, but, rather, that they rarely work as sustainable options for relationships.

It's important, too, to consider whether or not you hold the women you know to a different, higher standard. I often find that I am faster to excuse my father, for example, if he does something that angers me, than I am my mother. I have higher expectations of her: that she will be patient, that she will sacrifice more, that she has more control. This is unfair, and I have to deliberately think about how I am responding to her when I find myself responding with irritation or frustration.

It is a symptom of a larger problem of sexism that one of the only acceptable and predictably talked-about forms of anger in women is a girl's anger toward her mother. This is particularly true in adolescence. It's no mistake that the time when we come to a growing awareness of our inequalities, we are supposed to focus our anger on another woman. I've lost track of the number of times I've been asked how awful it is to have teenage daughters because, the myth goes, I would find them enraging, and they would find me embarrassing and overbearing. As they approached puberty, I sat down with my children, and together we broke down stereotypes about teenage girls and mothers hating one another.

In the course of writing this book, I was really struck by a pattern that I had not thought about before: cultural silence around daughters *defending* mothers. An important part of my research was talking to women who had found ways to consciously think about their anger and its place in their political, social, and personal lives. I interviewed women from many countries who had successfully turned feelings of powerlessness and rage into social movements and influential artistic endeavors. The women I spoke to repeatedly came back to one theme: they each talked independently about fighting for mothers whom they saw, as children, experience indignity, violence, injustice, and unfairness.

Over and over again, they talked about watching their mothers survive domestic violence and described their mothers' lives in terms of frustrated ambitions and missed opportunities. They shared stories of the religious oppression, political disenfranchisement, and social prohibitions on women's rights that work their way into the intimacies and stresses of day-to-day life. Each woman clearly defined her life's work as the legacy of having witnessed the exhausting and brutalizing reality of discrimination. Each woman said, in her own way, "I was enraged by what my mother lived with, and this rage, corralled into making change, has shaped my life." For some women, they were aware of this alongside mothers who had explicitly taught them the uses and abuses of anger. For many others, though, this was not the case, and they perceived their mothers as being in need of defense.

The first women we know are our mothers, and yet we sometimes treat them, especially when they are angry, with the least compassion. That becomes a model for how we treat other women.

10. ACCEPT A DESIRE FOR POWER

Anger and power are always entangled. Women are just as motivated by the desire for power as men; it's just that our cultural ideas about power don't associate it with femininity. If you are a girl or woman, chances are you have grown up unwittingly associating ideas about power with masculinity. Our primary roles as caretakers make the idea of power, associated as it often is with masculine behaviors like competition, conflicting. Power is, for example, associated in implicit bias studies with domination and not nurturing. Powerlessness is, on the other hand, implied in femininity.

In personal relationships, imbalances in power are frequently implicated in women's feelings of anger, anger expression, and anger resolutions. For many people, admitting to differences and shifts in power in intimate relationships, no matter how subtle, can be difficult or overwhelming. When women seek more balance in the distribution of power, when they demand a more egalitarian give-and-take, they often encounter resistance. Money is often a flashpoint in these scenarios. "As the comparative economic resources of spouses become more equal," Leslie Brody explains in *Gender, Emotion, and the Family*, "so does the balance of power between them."

It's important to talk about expectations in relationships before, undiscussed, they become problematic. The association between our expectations of power and gender are worth examining openly. Both interpersonally and socially, the mockery that women anticipate and dread from men—mockery that sometimes spills into contempt—has been tied to men's attempts to justify higher status.

In cases where there is intimate conflict over gender roles, many women who seek equality in their relationships feel guilt, as though to demand more parity in expectations and care is "unnatural" and harmful. In situations like these, the result is often intense resentment. Brody cites research, for example, that shows women are angrier when they "unwillingly consent" to something to make another person happy or as the result of pressure, a demonstration of lower status, and powerlessness. Often, the way we express this is to say we feel "hurt" instead of angry. It often means that girls and women cry instead of asserting themselves verbally. This isn't only a matter of spouses but also of child-parent and sibling interactions.

"To be honest, every time I got very angry, I burst into tears," explained ElsaMarie D'Silva, the founder of Safecity, when we spoke. "Not many people understood that they were tears of frustration and anger. When you burst out into tears, it's seen as a weakness and not a strong emotional response in anger. As a girl, you are so angry and frustrated, and it comes out in tears; it puts you in a further vulnerable position."

D'Silva converted her childhood anger, which she described as always having to be in control of, and powerlessness into a powerful social movement and now works in a field that requires confrontation and direct communication with angry people. Understanding her own anger, she says, was vital. "Anger played a big role. If it wasn't such a strong emotion, I would not have been courageous enough to take up this work. First of all, putting myself out there, willing to tell my own story, switching careers at the time of its peak, giving up a cushy and comfortable life, and also listening to other people."

In more public and political terms, women also experience anger as the result of power imbalances and, more likely to be in subordinate positions, have fewer avenues for achieving institutional power and controlling social and media environments. We rarely get to express anger, and the moral judgments it implies, from a position of actual institutional power. One of the most astounding and telling features of the Women's March and the #MeToo movement is that they both illustrate *how many* angry women it takes to generate public response.

Stand up for yourself and hold the communities and institutions you are part of accountable. This isn't, despite girl-power mantras, a popular activity when it means demands for serious change. The more comfortable we become with claiming ownership of public and institutional spaces, in anger, the more effective our efforts will be.

There is creativity in anger and much anger in creativity. Women are constantly manifesting rage in creative, productive, and visionary ways. On September 15, 1963, a Sunday morning, members of the Ku Klux Klan bombed the predominantly African American Sixteenth Street Baptist Church in Birmingham, Alabama, killing four girls. Famed singer Nina Simone, born in Saint Louis but a French citizen since the 1930s, was overcome with shock and rage. "I had it in mind to go out and kill someone," she explained when describing how she came to write "Mississippi Goddamn," one of the most moving and powerful protest songs of the twentieth century. "I tried to make a zip gun." Her husband turned to her and said, "You can't kill anyone. You are a musician. Do what you do."

What you do will differ from what someone else chooses to do. There is no one, right way. For me, for example, writing has been a mechanism for converting very powerful negative feelings into immensely satisfying and productive work. Writing led me to action, clarity, and a community that was thinking and feeling as I did. In writing, the anger I felt might overcome me became a vehicle instead of a destination. The clinical term for this is sublimation, defined as a mature defense mechanism that, unconsciously, transforms socially unacceptable feelings and behaviors into socially acceptable ones. Some people might call this anger management, but it is really transformation.

While sublimation is an unconscious process, anger can also be explicitly woven into everyday life in productive ways. This shouldn't be confused with efforts to "get your rage out" in destructive acts. For example, "anger rooms" have opened up around the country as businesses. People are able to throw vases, destroy televisions, and otherwise wreak physical havoc on a useless space. While maybe fun and even humorous, and the twenty minutes of relief it provides might feel good, in reality, this kind of destruction rarely does anything to alter feelings of anger or to change the conditions that generate anger.

The key, really, is in doing what you do best and, often, in a way that creates information that can be used by others. Self-described "Chicana dyke-feminist, tejana patlache poet, writer, and cultural theorist" Gloria Anzaldúa used her anger to stunning effect in her writing. "By writing," she explained, "I put order in the world, give it a handle so I can grasp it. I write because life does not appease my appetites and anger . . . To become more intimate with myself and you."

Arizona State University assistant professor Jacqueline Wernimont maintains what she refers to as an angry bibliography. In response to constant examples of the erasure of diverse voices in academia, she updates it with information about work produced by a broad range of scholars. "If we can't see the ethical stakes and power relations in digital archives," she explains, "we are going to do violence. Do better." Sports journalists Shireen Ahmed and Jessica Luther, joined by several others, started a podcast called *Burn It All Down* to create sports media counter to the highly problematic mainstream neglect of women's voices in sports. As I researched this book, countless women shared "anger playlists" of songs expressing anger, curated to be a communal resource.

When I spoke to Janelle Monáe about the role of anger in her work, she described a clear sense of its place, role, and cultural legacy. "I have a difficult time immediately articulating 'I am angry,'" she explained. "As an artist, while performing, I don't overthink my emotions, I just 'do' them." She is aware, however, of why those emotions powerfully matter. "We are making this music as our weapon. We can get people involved. We wanted to remember these people [victims of police violence] and remember what happened. The next generation can remember that this happened. We chose to use music as a way to combat this injustice. We wanted to use our voices to deal with our anger." In 2016 Monáe launched the grassroots organization Fem the Future to advocate for women's parity in the entertainment industry.

These themes are persistent in the lives of people who make social justice a priority in their lives, or for whom social injustice is a daily reality. During the civil rights movement, for example, Dolores Huerta cofounded, with Cesar Chavez, what is now the United Farm Workers union. "You grow up with all of this racial injustice, and it just makes you really angry," explained Huerta, a lifelong activist, in a film about her life, *Dolores*, released in 2017 when she was eighty-seven. Wild destruction and rage, she says, "will get you nowhere."

I have, throughout writing, circled back to social justice and equity. Whether you are politically active or not, these are of central importance to anger and the feedback loops of which anger is a part. The chances that a person can Horatio Alger her way out of anger or inequality are exceedingly and, in our current global economic environment, increasingly, slim. No matter how resilient you are, how ambitious you are, or how well you might "manage" your own anger, it almost always has a context that far exceeds your individual control, skills, desires, and talent.

Awareness of how our culture and environment affect even our most intimate feelings and interactions, and how our most intimate interactions affect our culture and environment, doesn't happen spontaneously. With some fairly minor exceptions, those of us who seek information and change, whether from need, empathy, or because we have no choice, are seekers by dint of personal need, curiosity, experience, and hard work. If we are lucky, we have parents and teachers, friends and mentors, who teach us or at least love us unconditionally when we challenge our communities. Unfortunately, not all of us are equipped by our families and schools to understand some of our most consequential feelings and experiences as women.

We are more likely to be deliberately discouraged from seeing our experiences in social and political contexts.

Understanding the social and political issues that affect your life is a critical part of thinking about your anger. It also enables you to deal with deniers and silencers, the most stubborn of whom cannot be convinced by facts. There are people whose minds and behavior you will never change, and you can shift your efforts accordingly.

Plan how to best use the anger you feel. Focus, think, and analyze. Strategizing clearly allows you to decide when it makes sense to speak—or not—how to anticipate situations that cause stress, and to think clearly, not in the heat of the moment, about how you want to solve your problems. The more you know, the better equipped you are. The better equipped you are, the more efficacy and uptake your anger will have. Contrary to the idea that anger clouds thinking, properly understood, it is an astoundingly clarifying emotion.

A WISE ANGER

These old men have a storm coming, the likes of which they cannot comprehend. —Lorde

nger is a genealogical phenomenon. My anger was related to my mother's, Norma, and hers was related to her mother's, Julia. We each developed our own ways of thinking about what feminist philosopher Alison Jaggar described as the "outlaw emotion."

When my mother turned seventy, more than forty years after the Throwing of the Plates, I asked her if she remembered why she did it. She laughed and explained that she'd thrown many, many more plates than the ones I saw her destroy that day. For many years, my mother's life, like the lives of millions of women every day, was filled with a mute rage. It wasn't until she was well into her sixties that she admitted to a lifelong and bottomless reserve of anger that was consuming her—one that was also a response to her own mother's anger.

My grandmother, Julia, Zarifeh's daughter, died in 2015 on the night before her ninety-fourth birthday. The first thing I thought of when I heard that she was gone was that we would never hear her voice again. To her dying day, it was too loud and her voice had a rough and jarring tenor. It wasn't the kind of voice, given this description, that you would associate with affection or pride, but those were the feelings her voice evoked in her grandchildren.

Of all of the possible traits a person has, this may seem like a strange one to focus on, but not if you knew her and the circumstances of her life. She was a girl whose entire world was structured to teach her that what she said wasn't worth listening to, that she was not as smart as the men around her, and that she should be quiet and not expect too much. She categorically refused to do this and, along the way, taught her granddaughters to do the same. I say *granddaughters* because, like so many women, especially of her generation, Julia did not come into her own until she was in her fifties. Her children knew a different person than her grandchildren did.

Being a child of what she called a "hard father" and a very damaged mother might cow a person, but Julia was fierce and resilient. She didn't brood. "Po diable," an affectionate way of saying "poor devil" in Creole, was her sole summation of her mother's life. Her insistence that "I never let anyone touch me" was as close as she ever came to acknowledging her mother's experiences. It was a truth that landed her in jail one day after she fought off a Ton Ton Macoute, a member of the private militia of Haitian dictator François "Papa Doc" Duvalier. As she stood in the Port-au-Prince airport, having just sent my grandfather off on a business trip, the man sexually harassed her, caressing her hair and saying something obscene. She pushed him away and told him what he could do with himself, so he arrested her and threw her in jail. She never talked in detail about this incident, but within a month, my family had fled Haiti.

As a young woman, she was glittery, vivacious, flirtatious, and brazen. She went out unchaperoned and boasted of the delight she took in frequently smoking and playing cards with men. She never turned down a good party, and she was famous for throwing her own. That she sought pleasure, and defined what that meant for herself, was clear from the fact that when she was twenty-three, she married my grandfather Fred Smith. My tanned, blue-eyed Bahamian grandfather was the "exotic," foreign in every conceivable way, and she took a huge risk when she did this. When they met, she broke off an engagement to someone from her own community. When they married, we always joked in the family, they didn't speak any of the same languages sufficiently enough to hold a complete conversation. He was a warm and thoughtful grandfather to me, but their marriage was a forty-five-year slow-motion disaster that left wreckage in its wake. It was punctuated loudly by periods of joy, adventure, and prolonged intemperate exchanges.

My grandfather's approach to marriage was a classic rage generator. It seemed to be symbolically bookended by two phenomena: the global expansion of Pan American Airways, which enabled him to work and travel far and wide, and the wish-fulfillment of the *Playboy* empire, which gave him license to be a sexist hedonist. I was in my grandmother's kitchen one day in 1975 when she called him during a business trip to Colombia. A woman answered, and when my grandmother explained that she, his wife, wanted to speak to him, the woman replied, "*I'm* his wife." He managed, remarkably, to simultaneously be a philanderer, a bigamist, and a pious Anglican who didn't drink and who taught his children, under threat of the switch, to never lie. The charming hypocrisy he embodied must have been spectacularly exhausting.

Divorce, however, was not an option for a woman like my grandmother. She was Catholic, uneducated, and socialized to understand her place first and foremost as a wife. And, besides, she'd chosen him of her own accord. He hadn't ridden in on a horse and taken her. He'd flown in and asked nicely. But she bristled. She wore her resentment on her sleeve.

When he was just past fifty, my grandfather suffered a debilitating stroke, one of many to come. She took care of him long after he could no longer take care of himself, and she wasn't gracious about it. It was hard and thankless work that he frequently made harder. Her critics were rife, but no one seemed to consider why she seemed as angry and hostile as she did. Everyone seemed to expect her to put aside decades of hurt, hypocrisy, and humiliation and be a silent, loving, selfless nursemaid. She was considered mean spirited, hard, miserly, and uncaring.

Nurturing was never a word easily associated with my grandmother. Until late in life, her approach to my grandfather and to her offspring could be likened more to a bulldozer run amok on a construction site than a gardener's deliberate tending of a garden. For long periods, she ceded the parenting of her children to others, sending them away, one at a time, at the age of eight, for which she was thought of as callous. Only after talking to her many times did I come to appreciate the profound sadness of her "choices." My grandfather made the decisions and, given his reasoning and authority, her children were gone. She knew that her daughters, growing into girls in a place where girls were toys, were much safer elsewhere, and she couldn't, in polite society, say why. So, "angry" and "callous" she became.

As my grandfather lost the ability to be responsible for their family decisions, she asserted herself more in managing their lives. When she insisted on working for pay instead of taking care of everyone else and their children, she was considered strange and difficult. Her independence, her expectation of respect, and her refusal to provide unpaid labor that was taken for granted were all viewed as undesirable and selfish.

As a grandmother, she was not a person to take lightly or for granted. Quietly, I'd long studied her every move. When we, a passel of grandchildren, were little, a hug from her felt like a rough aggression to be strategically avoided. When she saw us coming, she would lock us out of her house with a jug of water that we had to stretch between us for the duration of long afternoons in the brutal heat of her yard. This was a person who might, if we dared to complain, hit us with a flyswatter. Though we all knew she loved us, for a long time, if you'd asked, we couldn't have said *how* we knew.

You had to pay attention. Which was precisely what she needed and loved. She not only condoned but also cultivated mischief. As a toddler, I routinely jumped off of her refrigerator, yelling "Catch me!" I have no memory of her telling me to stop, but I also have no memory of splitting my head open on her kitchen floor. She caught me every time. One day she let me comb her hair. Until then, I thought the tight, elegant black bun on the back of her head was just the way her hair grew. When I saw a black river of hair cascade down her back, I thought she'd performed magic and was amazed. She had a secret, hiding in plain sight. As an adult, I realized, she had always filled me with glee. As difficult as she could seem to her family, she was beloved by almost anyone who met her.

My grandmother had none of the expected, obligatory, and imposed traits of an older woman. She was having none of the invisibility and quiet imposed on women who have outlived their sex appeal and fertility. There was very little about her that was serene, quiet, or tranquil. She was also, everyone said, vain. But this, too, was a deliberate misunderstanding. To her dying day, she demanded to be allowed to live with dignity, which is not the same thing as vanity. While she was slowly dying, the nurses in her hospital named her "the Ninja" because she physically fought them off when they wanted to perform procedures that would make their jobs a little easier. She was only four foot ten, yet sometimes three, four nurses could not make her agree.

If she was angry, she said so. Usually loudly. But a few years after my grandfather died, when I was in my twenties, my grandmother's difficult, tough, and abrasive demeanor turned soft, generous, and considerate. She would pat your hand. She'd send you kisses over the phone. She'd say out loud that she loved you, your children, and their children. She would send great- and great-great-grandchildren she'd never know $10 in the mail. For years, this continued to surprise me.

Julia was resilient in the face of tremendous odds against her. She weathered personal troubles and colonial violence, becoming, in the process, a wise old woman who lived unapologetically. Of all the women I grew up observing, she was the freest with her anger. Like most people, as she aged, she learned to better master her emotions. She had fewer conflicts and responded to them with more equanimity. Despite the low expectations of those around her, she valued herself highly and tried to live as she wanted. She spoke her mind. She intuited the difference between being sociable and being true to oneself, being popular and not. She taught us to seek love, even if it was flawed; to work hard; to care quietly; to complain loudly; to be loyal and firm. She showed us how to be self-sufficient, something still not to be taken for granted when you're a girl basted in the corrosive juices of our culture's sexism. She did all of this without giving any of us more than a few scant words of direct advice. In other words, this old woman with no power trusted us to know what was best for ourselves, something rooms full of old men with too much power refuse to understand.

Her anger was essential to her survival. Where my father and uncles saw a penny-pincher, I saw a smart and pragmatic woman who understood her financial situation and was trying to plan for the future. Where they saw unreasonable, I saw a woman who knew she was playing a long game and would do what she had to, even if others failed to understand. Where they saw selfishness, I saw her insistence that she mattered as an individual, not as an eternal handmaiden.

When my grandmother died, her face was deeply etched with

lines. But she was beautiful, and her smile was dazzling. While I miss her presence, I can't find it in myself to be sad. Instead, I think of what it took for her to survive, intact, for almost a century, living in countries rent with violence and in a family, like most in the world, dedicated to men's rule.

As a child, in my mind, she and my mother swirled around each other in sharp contrast. In both, anger was manifest, but so differently. In one, it was expressed and disdained. In the other, repressed and damaging. In both, the lesson could have been the standard one: that anger was overwhelmingly negative. But this always struck me as wrong. Their anger was not the problem. A lack of understanding about their anger was.

After my grandmother died, in an effort to unlearn all of the negative lessons I'd absorbed about being a woman and having anger, I wrote down everything positive that anger can be:

Anger is an assertion of rights and worth. It is communication, equality, and knowledge. It is intimacy, acceptance, fearlessness, embodiment, revolt, and reconciliation. Anger is memory and rage. It is rational thought and irrational pain. Anger is freedom, independence, expansiveness, and entitlement. It is justice, passion, clarity, and motivation. Anger is instrumental, thoughtful, complicated, and resolved. In anger, whether you like it or not, there is truth.

Anger is the demand of accountability. It is evaluation, judgment, and refutation. It is reflective, visionary, and participatory. It's a speech act, a social statement, an intention, and a purpose. It's a risk and a threat. A confirmation and a wish. It is both powerlessness and power, palliative and a provocation. In anger, you will find both ferocity and comfort, vulnerability and hurt. Anger is the expression of hope.

How much anger is too much? Certainly not the anger that, for many of us, is a remembering of a self we learned to hide and quiet. It is willful and disobedient. It is survival, liberation, creativity, urgency, and vibrancy. It is a statement of need. An insistence of acknowledgment. Anger is a boundary. Anger is boundless. An opportunity for contemplation and self-awareness. It is commitment. Empathy. Self-love. Social responsibility. If it is poison, it is also the antidote. The anger we have as women is an act of radical imagination. Angry women burn brighter than the sun.

In the coming years, we will hear, again, that anger is a destructive force, to be controlled. Watch carefully, because not everyone is asked to do this in equal measure. Women, especially, will be told to set our anger aside in favor of a kinder, gentler approach to change. This is a false juxtaposition. Reenvisioned, anger can be the most feminine of virtues: compassionate, fierce, wise, and powerful. The women I admire most—those who have looked to themselves and the limitations and adversities that come with our bodies and the expectations that come with them—have all found ways to transform their anger into meaningful change. In them, anger has moved from debilitation to liberation.

Your anger is a gift you give to yourself and the world that is yours. In anger, I have lived more fully, freely, intensely, sensitively, and politically. If ever there was a time not to silence yourself, to channel your anger into healthy places and choices, this is it.

ACKNOWLEDGMENTS

I am eternally grateful for the words of the many brilliant people whose work I was fortunate enough to include here. They are too many to list, but I have tried my best to provide a useful endnotes and a bibliography in acknowledgment.

Without my brilliant friend Jaclyn Friedman, my agent, Anna Sproul-Latimer, and Simon & Schuster editor Daniella Wexler, this book would have lingered in endlessly edited proposals migrating from one computer to the next. I am so grateful for their professionalism, encouragement, and wry humor, especially during a particularly difficult and intense six months in late 2017. I will forever be thankful, too, to editor Jane Frannson for her rigor, humor, and, now, friendship. To Laura Bullard, for her rigorous fact-checking; I will always remain in awe.

In 2011, when I returned to writing after a long hiatus, I was plagued with uncertainty. I jumped blindly into social media and blundered along as best I could, undoubtedly being an unrelenting pest along the way. During that time, I reached out to many people whose thinking I admired and whose words of encouragement as allies, editors, or writers meant more than they could possibly have known at the time: Robin Morgan, Lauren Wolfe, Anna North, Holly Kearl, Julie Burton, Kate McCarthy, Jamia Wilson, Rebecca Traister, Laura Bates, Cristal Williams Chancellor, Jessica Valenti, Gloria Steinem, Avital Norman Nathman, Liz Plank, Jill Filipovic, Imani Gandy, Jodi Jacobsen, Katha Pollitt, Deanna Zandt, Lynn Povich, Zerlina Maxwell, and Rachel Sklar.

I am also indebted to wise friends and intellectual hand-holders

Danielle Citron, Susan Brison, Mary Anne Franks, Anne Collier, Susan Benesch, Shauna Dillavou, and Sandra Peppera.

My sincerest thanks, also, to the women who graciously took time out of their busy lives to answer my questions and let me tell their stories here: Laura Bates, ElsaMarie D'Silva, Alicia Garza, Ashley Judd, Janelle Monáe, Dior Vargas, Shannon Watts, and Regina Yau.

This book was borne of years of talking and thinking that involved an untold number of patient family members willing to listen and have some truly difficult conversations. This, I can say began when I was eight and my father, Edward, asked me to help my mother clear the dinner table. I'd like to thank him for many unintentional childhood consciousness-raising exercises, and my mother, Norma, for providing the spark of resolve and for allowing me to share her stories. I am indebted to your being loving and supportive parents.

Last, and critically, I could never have written this without my husband Thomas Jones's encouragement, sharp good humor, thoughtfulness, and intelligence. There are no words that adequately convey my love. I never *would* have written this if I hadn't been moved by our intrepid daughters, Isabelle, Caroline, and Noel, and my brave sister, Koralyn Sawyer. Thank you for your infinite patience and unconditional support.

In the same vein, for years of inspiration, friendship, and companionship, thank you to my brothers, Edward and Omar, and to sisters-in-spirit Beverly Frank, Jacqueline Bendy, Fanny Lim, Susan Crawford, Marya Stark, Laura Unger, Monica Spaller, Catherine Buni, and, always, my first feminist teachers Caren Kaplan and Michael Collins. And finally, no thanks would be complete without including Dr. Carla Elliot-Neely. Thank you for your infinite kindness and wisdom.

NOTE ON SOURCES

In conducting research for this book, I realized that there are not, in fact, many recent studies that deeply delve into how ideas about gender relate to specific emotions and, in particular, studies of how those ideas intersect with race, class, gender identity, and other aspects of our identities. Whenever possible, I cite specific findings and have tried to include as many related studies as possible in the endnotes.

There are certain excellent works that stand out as worthy of specific mention: *The Cultural Politics of Emotion*, by Sara Ahmed; *Gender, Emotion, and the Family*, by Leslie Brody; *The Anger Advantage: The Surprising Benefits of Anger and How It Can Change a Woman's Life*, by Deborah Cox, Karin H. Bruckner, and Sally D. Stabb; Carol Tavris's classic *Anger: The Misunderstood Emotion*. Also, in terms of political theory, both Andrea Miller and Eugene Borgida's academic work, "The Separate Spheres Model of Gendered Inequality," as well as Michael A. Milburn and Sheree D. Conrad's book, *Raised to Rage*, were particularly insightful.

In writing this book, I also made a *Rage Becomes Her* playlist on Spotify. I listen to music when I write and over the months of writing this book many people shared their favorite "anger songs." Please listen, add yours to it, and encourage others to as well: https://spoti.fi/2M7KHm3.

NOTES

With this book, I have tried to synthesize decades of research and feminist thinking across multiple fields to create a useful resource for readers. It includes references to a variety of materials, including song lyrics, lines from interviews, poems, legal briefs, research, and speeches. The bibliography contains referenced works, as well as additional books and papers that are not directly cited. I have included several meta-analyses of studies that are full of excellent sources and citations. As the endnotes are already lengthy, the publisher has decided to house the bibliography online. It can be found here: http://www.simonandschuster.com/rage-becomes-her-bibliography.

INTRODUCTION: NICE TO MEET YOU, RAGE

xiii how to express negative emotions: Dana Crowley Jack, "Understanding Women's Anger: A Description of Relational Patterns," *Health Care for Women International* 22, no. 4 (June 2001): 385–400, doi:10.1080/07399330121599.

xiv is more for exerting authority: Jiyoung Park et al., "Social Status and Anger Expression: The Cultural Moderation Hypothesis," *Emotion* 13, no. 6 (December 2013): 1122–31, https://doi.org/10.1037/a0034273.

xv longer periods of time than men do: Beverly A. Kopper and Douglas L. Epperson, "The Experience and Expression of Anger: Relationships with Gender, Gender Role Socialization, Depression, and Mental Health Functioning," *Journal of Counseling Psychology* 43, no. 2 (April 1996): 158–65, http://dx.doi.org/10.1037/0022 -0167.43.2.158.

xv proposed "anger management" solutions: Yaling Deng et al., "Gender Differences in Emotional Response: Inconsistency Between Experience and Expressivity," *PLOS ONE* 11, no. 6 (June 2016): e0158666, https://doi.org/10.1371/journal .pone.0158666.

xx and use their emotions more effectively: Brenda Mae Woodhill and Curtis A. Samuels, "Positive and Negative Androgyny and Their Relationship with Psychological Health and Well-Being," *Sex Roles* 48, nos. 11–12 (June 2003): 555–65, https://doi.org/10.1023/A:1023531530272.

xxi that we take ourselves seriously: Elizabeth V. Spelman, "Virtue of Feeling and the Feeling of Virtue," in *Feminist Ethics*, ed. Claudia Card (Lawrence: University Press of Kansas, 1991).

CHAPTER 1: MAD GIRLS

3 into preschool preparedness and gender: Shannon B. Wanless et al., "Measuring Behavioral Regulation in Four Societies," *Psychol Assess.* 23, no. 2 (June 2011): 364–78, doi:10.1037/a0021768.

4 the baby was a boy or a girl: John Condry and Sandra Condry, "Sex Differences: A Study of the Eye of the Beholder," *Child Development* 47, no. 3 (1976): www.jstor.org/stable/1128199.

4 be described as fearful or sad: Olga Silverstein and Beth Rashbaum, *The Courage to Raise Good Men* (Toronto: Penguin, 1995).

4 angrier, or more violent and hostile: Judith A. Lyons and Lisa A. Serbin, "Observer Bias in Scoring Boys' and Girls' Aggression," *Sex Roles* 14, nos. 5–6 (1986): 301–13, https://link.springer.com/article/10.1007/BF00287581.

4 "but don't know [they] are speaking differently to them": Kristina Dell, "Mothers Talk Differently to Daughters Than Sons, Study," *Time*, November 13, 2014, http://time.com/3581587/mothers-emotion-words-girls-boys-surrey-study-mothers-encourage-emotions-more-in-daughters-over-sons-study-says.

4 using a wider range of words: Ana Aznar and Harriet R. Tenenbaum, "Gender and Age Differences in Parent–Child Emotion Talk," *British Journal of Developmental Psychology* 33, no. 1 (March 2015): 148–55, https://doi.org/10.1111/bjdp.12069.

4 do the same with girls: Judy Dunn, Inge Bretherton, and Penny Munn, "Conversations About Feeling States Between Mothers and Their Young Children," *Developmental Psychology* 23, no. 1 (1987): 132–39, www.ncbi.nlm.nih.gov/pmc/articles/PMC2610353/#R17.

4 boys or telling them stories: Robert D. Kavanaugh, Betty Zimmerberg, and Steven Fein, eds., *Emotion: Interdisciplinary Perspectives* (Mahwah, NJ: L. Erlbaum, 1996).

4 perceptions of gender and emotion: Anna North, "Baseball Reveals Women Get Sad, Men Get Angry," *Jezebel*, March 7, 2011, https://jezebel.com/5778566/baseball-reveals-women-get-sad-men-get-angry; Kerri L. Johnson, Lawrie S. McKay, and Frank E. Pollick, "He Throws Like a Girl (But Only When He's Sad): Emotion Affects Sex-Decoding of Biological Motion Displays," *Cognition* 119, no. 2 (2011): 265–80, doi:10.1016/j.cognition.2011.01.016.

4 faces as less angry than men's faces: Reginald B. Adams Jr. et al., "Emotion in the Neutral Face: A Mechanism for Impression Formation?" *Cognition & Emotion* 26, no. 3 (2012): 431–41, www.ncbi.nlm.nih.gov/pmc/articles/PMC3392118; D. V. Becker et al., "The Confounded Nature of Angry Men and Happy Women," *Journal of Personality and Social Psychology* 92, no. 2 (February 2007): 179–90, http://dx.doi.org/10.1037/0022-3514.92.2.179; E. Ashby Plant et al., "The Gender Stereotyping of Emotions," *Psychology of Women Quarterly* 24, no. 1 (2000): 81–92, https://doi.org/10.1111/j.1471-6402.2000.tb01024.x.

4 labelled by participants as "cooperative" and "babyish": Adams Jr. et al., "Emotion in the Neutral Face."

5 most difficult for people to parse: Elaine Fox et al., "Facial Expressions of Emo-

tion: Are Angry Faces Detected More Efficiently?" *Cognition & Emotion* 14, no. 1 (2000): 61–92, www.ncbi.nlm.nih.gov/pmc/articles/PMC1839771.

5 expression is overwhelmingly categorized as male: Ursula Hess et al., "Face Gender and Emotion Expression: Are Angry Women More Like Men?" *Journal of Vision* 9, no. 12 (2009): http://jov.arvojournals.org/article.aspx?articleid=2122332.

5 is not necessary for sadness: W. Gerrod Parrott, ed., *The Positive Side of Negative Emotions* (New York: Guilford Press, 2014).

5 while sadness is a "retreat" emotion: Eddie Harmon-Jones and Jonathan Sigelman, "State Anger and Prefrontal Brain Activity: Evidence That Insult-Related Relative Left-Prefrontal Activation Is Associated with Experienced Anger and Aggression," *Journal of Personality and Social Psychology* 80, no. 5 (May 2001): 797–803, www.socialemotiveneuroscience.org/pubs/hj&sigelman_jpsp2001.pdf.

5 perceptions of higher status and respect: Larissa Z. Tiedens, "Anger and Advancement Versus Sadness and Subjugation: The Effect of Negative Emotion Expressions on Social Status Conferral," *Journal of Personality and Social Psychology* 80, no. 1 (January 2001): 86–94, http://web.mit.edu/curhan/www/docs/Articles/15341_Readings/Affect/Tiedens.pdf.

5 feeling powerless to make change: Jennifer S. Lemer and Dacher Keltner, "Fear, Anger, and Risk," *Journal of Personality and Social Psychology* 81, no. 1 (July 2001): 146–59, doi:10.1023/A:1023531530272.

5 were highly original: Carsten K. W. De Dreu, Bernard A. Nijstad, and Matthijs Baas, "Behavioral Activation Links to Creativity Because of Increased Cognitive Flexibility," *Social Psychological and Personality Science* 2, no. 1 (January 2011): 72–80, https://doi.org/10.1177/1948550610381789.

5 Sad people are also more generous: Deborah A. Small and Jennifer S. Lerner, "Emotional Policy: Personal Sadness and Anger Shape Judgments About a Welfare Case," *Political Psychology* 29, no. 2 (2008): 149–68, http://scholar.harvard.edu/files/jenniferlerner/files/small_lerner_2008.pdf.

5 Sad people expect and are satisfied with less: Jennifer S. Lerner, Ye Li, and Elke U. Weber, "The Financial Costs of Sadness," *Psychological Science* 24, no. 1 (January 2013): 72–79, https://doi.org/10.1177/0956797612450302.

6 both verbal and physical—less and less openly: Jennifer Coates and Pia Pichler, *Language and Gender: A Reader* (Malden, MA: Blackwell, 2011).

6 be angry, but not for girls: Agneta H. Fischer, ed., *Gender and Emotion: Social Psychological Perspectives* (Cambridge: Cambridge University Press, 2000).

7 acceptable for boys but not for girls: D. E. Hagood et al., "Joke's on You! Preschool Boys' Preference for Aggressive Humor" (lecture, Annual Meeting of the Western Psychological Association, San Francisco, July 2012).

7 more often than boys are: Rachel Simmons, *Odd Girl Out: The Hidden Culture of Aggression in Girls* (London: Piatkus, 2012).

7 even in private, after a disappointment: Leslie Brody, *Gender, Emotion, and the Family* (Cambridge, MA: Harvard University Press, 1999).

7 and less assertive or dominant: J. A. Hall and A. G. Halberstadt, "Smiling and Gazing," in *The Psychology of Gender: Advances Through Meta-Analysis*, ed. Janet Shibley Hyde and Marcia C. Linn (Baltimore: John Hopkins University Press, 1986).

8 unhappy with circumstances of inequality: Frantz Fanon, *Black Skin, White Masks*, trans. Richard Philcox (New York: Grove Press, 2008).

9 times more often as protagonists: Of an estimated five thousand books published in 2012, only 3.3 percent featured African Americans; 2.1 percent featured Asian Americans or Pacific Islanders; 1.5 percent featured Latinos; and only 0.6 percent featured Native Americans. In addition, 100 percent of animated stories include male characters, compared with only 33 percent female. Joan Katrina Mann-Boykin, "What the Children Are Reading: A Content Analysis of Minority Male Characters in Preschool Children's Libraries" (thesis, University of Denver, 2016), https://digitalcommons.du.edu/etd/?utm_source=digitalcommons .du.edu%2Fetd%2F1208&utm_medium=PDF&utm_campaign=PDFCoverPages.

9 more often white than not: For detailed studies, see those created by the Geena Davis Institute on Gender in Media; Media, Diversity, and Social Change Initiative; Media Action Network for Asian Americans; Reclaiming Identity: Dismantling Arab Stereotypes; Common Sense Media; National Association for Media Literacy Education; National Hispanic Media Coalition; and Racebending.com.

9 executive positions onscreen and off: Stacy L. Smith, Marc Choueiti, and Katherine Pieper, *Inclusion or Invisibility? Comprehensive Annenberg Report on Diversity in Entertainment* (Los Angeles: Media, Diversity, & Social Change Initiative, Annenberg School for Communication and Journalism, University of Southern California, 2016), http://annenberg.usc.edu/sites/default/files/2017/04/07/MDSCI_ CARD_Report_FINAL_Exec_Summary.pdf.

9 globally is equally skewed: Stacy L. Smith, Marc Choueiti, and Katherine Pieper, *Gender Bias Without Borders: An Investigation of Female Characters in Popular Films Across 11 Countries* (Los Angeles: Media, Diversity, & Social Change Initiative, Annenberg School for Communication & Journalism, University of Southern California, 2014), https://seejane.org/wp-content/uploads/gender-bias-without-borders-full-report.pdf.

9 played a lesbian or bisexual character: Stacy L. Smith et al., *Inequality in 900 Popular Films: Examining Portrayals of Gender, Race, Ethnicity, and LGBT Status from 2007 to 2014* (Los Angeles: Media, Diversity, & Social Change Initiative, Annenberg School for Communication & Journalism, University of Southern California, 2015), https://annenberg.usc.edu/sites/default/files/Dr_Stacy_L_Smith-Inequality_ in_900_Popular_Films.pdf; see further research conducted by the Geena Davis Institute, available at: https://seejane.org/research-informs-empowers; Jeff Guo, "Researchers Have Found a Major Problem with *The Little Mermaid* and Other Disney Movies," *Washington Post*, January 25, 2016, www.washingtonpost.com/ news/wonk/wp/2016/01/25/researchers-have-discovered-a-major-problem-with-the -little-mermaid-and-other-disney-movies/?utm_term=.96cf765e49d6.

As bad as a 70–30 visual split sounds, it is actually a far better ratio than the one related to hearing a woman speak in a movie. Between 2007 and 2012, the percentage of women speakers in the top hundred Hollywood films *declined*. Disney "girl power" princess movies, among the most popular children's films in the world, are even worse. As Jeff Guo explained in 2016, older movies such as *Snow White and the Seven Dwarfs* (1937) might seem retrograde, but they actually featured women speaking. "The plot of *The Little Mermaid*," one of the first modern-generation films in Disney's megalithic princess franchise, he wrote, "involves Ariel literally losing her voice—but in the five Disney princess movies that followed, the women speak even less. On average in those films, men have three times as many lines as women." Older women in Disney films appear, almost uniformly, as unattractive, untrustworthy, and dangerous.

9 bias is also "rife in textbooks": Aaron Benavot and Catherine Jere, "Gender Bias Is Rife in Textbooks," World Education blog, March 8, 2016, https://gemreport unesco.wordpress.com/2016/03/08/gender-bias-is-rife-in-textbooks.

10 that becomes evident in self-esteem: Nicole Martins and Kristen Harrison, "Racial and Gender Differences in the Relationship Between Children's Television Use and Self-Esteem," *Communication Research* 39, no. 3 (2011): 338–57, www .researchgate.net/publication/254084555_Racial_and_Gender_Differences_in_ the_Relationship_Between_Children's_Television_Use_and_Self-Esteem_A_ Longitudinal_Panel_Study; Smith, Choueiti, and Pieper, *Inclusion or Invisibility?*

11 with creativity, humor, and anger: Sesali Bowen, "Bitches Be Like . . . : Memes as Black Girl Counter and Disidentification Tools" (thesis, Georgia State University, 2016), https://scholarworks.gsu.edu/wsi_theses/56.

11 conveying fragility, weakness, and helplessness: Katrina Woznicki, "Parents Encourage Thin Daughters and Substantial Sons at Age Three," *MedPage Today*, December 15, 2005, www.medpagetoday.com/Pediatrics/EatingDisorders/2339.

11 and in need of "protection": Elizabeth Saewyc, "Global Perspective on Gender Roles and Identity," *Journal of Adolescent Health* 61, no. 4 (October 2017): S1–S2, http://www.jahonline.org/article/S1054-139X(17)30356-7/fulltext.

11 tacitly treat girls as more fragile and less capable: Elizabeth E. O'Neal, Jodie M. Plumert, and Carole Peterson, "Parent-Child Injury Prevention Conversations Following a Trip to the Emergency Department," *Journal of Pediatric Psychology* 41, no. 2 (March 2015): 256–64, https://academic.oup.com/jpepsy/article/41/2/256/2579803.

12 but a picture of a Barbie doll: Zach Miners, "The First Woman CEO to Appear in a Google Images Search Is . . . CEO Barbie," *PC World*, April 9, 2015, www .pcworld.com/article/2908592/the-first-woman-ceo-to-appear-in-a-google-images -search-is-ceo-barbie.html.

12 portrayed as existing in a sea of men: The following are ways to describe the phenomenon of depictions in the media of one woman, separate from others, operating within fraternities: (1) Liz Wallace and Alison Bechdel's test for the presence of women in film (Are there more than two women? Do they speak to each other about anything other than a man?); (2) Katha Pollitt's Smurfette Principle (one woman, in a sea of men), which describes the skewed ratios of one sexualized woman in a cast of men; and (3) Ariel Levy's "loophole women"—the exceptional corporate women who make it into boardrooms. The Maki Mori test, which gauges the representation of women who are not white, highlights the relative under-representation of women of color.

12 cultivate camaraderie with other women: Woznicki, "Parents Encourage Thin Daughters and Substantial Sons."

13 "is probably better described as misogyny": Julia Serano, "Bending Over Backwards: An Introduction to the Issue of Trans Woman-Inclusion," in *On the*

Outside Looking In (self-published, 2005), www.juliaserano.com/outside.html. A revised version appears in Julia Serano, *Whipping Girl: A Transsexual Woman on Sexism and the Scapegoating of Femininity* (Berkeley, CA: Seal Press, 2016).

14 the peace and cultivate relationships: Judith Worell, *Encyclopedia of Women and Gender: Sex Similarities and Differences and the Impact of Society on Gender* (San Diego: Academic, 2001).

15 48 percent of girls think girls and women are: Lin Bian, Sarah-Jane Leslie, and Andrei Cimpian, "Gender Stereotypes About Intellectual Ability Emerge Early and Influence Children's Interests," *Science* 355, no. 6323 (January 2017): 389–91, http://science.sciencemag.org/content/355/6323/389.

15 particularly white girls, who do: Richard Weissbourd and the Making Caring Common Team, *Leaning Out: Teen Girls and Leadership Biases* (Cambridge, MA: Harvard Graduate School of Education, 2015), https://mcc.gse.harvard.edu/files/gse-mcc/files/leanout-report.pdf.

16 "In this world, silence can mean invisibility and danger": Simmons, *Odd Girl Out.*

16 status, likeability, and relationships at risk: Simmons, *Odd Girl Out.*

16 and "having too much attitude": Victoria D. Gillon, "The Killing of an 'Angry Black Woman': Sandra Bland and the Politics of Respectability" (student paper, Augustana College, 2016), https://digitalcommons.augustana.edu/cgi/viewcontent.cgi?referer=https://www.google.co.uk/&httpsredir=1&article=1008&context=mabry award; Kelly Brown Douglas, "Sandra Bland and Other 'Angry Black Women,'" *Huffington Post*, July 20, 2015, www.huffingtonpost.com/kelly-brown-douglas/sandra -bland-and-other-angry-black-women_b_7821876.html.

16 less in need of nurturing or protection: Adria Y. Goldman et al., eds., *Black Women and Popular Culture: The Conversation Continues* (Lanham, MD: Lexington Books, 2014).

17 rate of their peers: Adaku Onyeka-Crawford, Kayla Patrick, and Neena Chaudhry, *Let Her Learn: Stopping School Pushout for Girls of Color* (Washington, DC: National Women's Law Center, 2017), https://nwlc.org/resources/stopping-school -pushout-for-girls-of-color.

17 "paint us as hot-blooded and explosive": Edén E. Torres, *Chicana Without Apology: The New Chicana Cultural Studies* (New York: Routledge, 2003).

18 "they were not allowed to be angry": Lela Lee, "About," Angry Little Girls, https:// angrylittlegirls.com/pages/about.

18 "missing white woman syndrome": C. M. Liebler, "Me(di)a Culpa?: The 'Missing White Woman Syndrome' and Media Self-Critique," *Communication, Culture & Critique* 3, no. 4 (December 2010): 549–65, doi:10.1111/j.1753-9137.2010.01085.x.

19 associated mainly with girls and women: Melissa Dittman, "Anger Across the Gender Divide: Researchers Strive to Understand How Men and Women Experience and Express Anger," *Monitor on Psychology* 34, no. 3 (March 2003): 52, www .apa.org/monitor/mar03/angeracross.aspx. A survey of more than 1,200 people, ranging in age from eighteen to ninety, conducted by Raymond DiGiuseppe, chair of the Psychology Department at St. John's University in New York, found that men scored higher for both physical and passive aggression than women did.

19 to regulate group behavior: Joyce F. Benenson, "The Development of Human

Female Competition: Allies and Adversaries," *Philosophical Transactions of the Royal Society B: Biological Sciences* 368, no. 1631 (December 2013): https://doi .org/10.1098/rstb.2013.0079.

19 conditioned to put others at ease: Norbert Mundorf, James Weaver, and Dolf Zillmann, "Effects of Gender Roles and Self Perceptions on Affective Reactions to Horror Films," *Sex Roles* 20, nos. 11–12 (June 1989): 655–73, https://doi .org/10.1007/BF00288078.

19 also increasingly physically aggressive: James Garbarino, *See Jane Hit: Why Girls Are Growing More Violent and What We Can Do About It* (New York: Penguin Books, 2007); Deborah Prothrow-Stith and Howard R. Spivak, *Sugar and Spice and No Longer Nice: How We Can Stop Girls' Violence* (San Francisco: Jossey-Bass, 2005).

20 associated with men and masculinity: For an excellent discussion of gender, social norms, and testosterone, read Cordelia Fine, *Testosterone Rex: Myths of Sex, Science, and Society* (New York: W. W. Norton, 2017).

20 how social norms affect hormones: Sari M. van Anders, Jeffrey Steiger, and Katherine L. Goldey, "Effects of Gendered Behavior on Testosterone in Women and Men," *Proceedings of the National Academy of Sciences of the United States of America* 112, no. 45 (November 2015): 13805–10, https://doi:10.1073/pnas.1509591112.

21 steep declines in testosterone: Lee T. Gettler et al., "Longitudinal Evidence That Fatherhood Decreases Testosterone in Human Males," *Proceedings of the National Academy of Sciences of the United States of America* 108, no. 39 (September 2011): 16194–99, https://doi.org/10.1073/pnas.1105403108.

21 associates labelled "wielding power": Menelaos L. Batrinos, "Testosterone and Aggressive Behavior in Man," *International Journal of Endocrinology and Metabolism* 10, no. 3 (2011): 563–68, https://doi.org/10.5812/ijem.3661.

21 "the quality of her relationship[s]": Lisa Damour, *Untangled: Guiding Teenage Girls Through Seven Stages to Adulthood* (New York: Ballantine Books, 2017).

22 varying degrees, as a significant factor: Lyn Mikel Brown, *Raising Their Voices: The Politics of Girls' Anger* (Cambridge, MA: Harvard University Press, 1999).

23 affect later trajectories of behavior: Erin B. Godfrey, Carlos E. Santos, and Esther Burson, "For Better or Worse? System-Justifying Beliefs in Sixth-Grade Predict Trajectories of Self-Esteem and Behavior Across Early Adolescence," *Child Development* (2017): http://onlinelibrary.wiley.com/doi/10.1111/cdev.12854/full.

24 communalism and not individualism: Jerald G. Bachman et al., "Adolescent Self-Esteem: Differences by Race/Ethnicity, Gender, and Age," *Self and Identity* 10, no. 4 (2011): 445–73, www.ncbi.nlm.nih.gov/pmc/articles/PMC3263756.

24 have the smallest gender gap: Ibid.

24 have higher self-esteem than boys do: Researchers note that although these differences are consistent and significant, self-esteem seems to align more closely with a student's GPA and plans to go to college than with gender and ethnicity.

24 compared with 66 percent of black women: Lonnae O'Neal Parker, "Black Women Heavier and Happier with Their Bodies Than White Women, Poll Finds," *Washington Post*, February 27, 2012, www.washingtonpost.com/lifestyle /style/black-women-heavier-and-happier-with-their-bodies-than-white-women -poll-finds/2012/02/22/gIQAPmcHeR_story.html?utm_term=.5b972a871190.

24 be subservient to the powers that be: Maxine Baca Zinn et al., *Gender Through the Prism of Difference*, 5th ed. (New York: Oxford University Press, 2015).

24 multiple, overlapping social entitlements: Thomas M. Carmony and Raymond DiGiuseppe, "Cognitive Induction of Anger and Depression: The Role of Power, Attribution, and Gender," *Journal of Rational-Emotive and Cognitive-Behavior Therapy* 21, no. 2 (June 2003): 105–18, https://doi.org/10.1023/A:1025099315118.

CHAPTER 2: WOMEN ≠ TOASTERS

28 that number is 33 percent: Kaitlin Lounsbury, Kimberly J. Mitchell, and David Finkelhor, "The True Prevalence of 'Sexting,'" Crimes Against Children Research Center, University of New Hampshire, April 2011, www.unh.edu/ccrc/pdf/Sexting Fact Sheet 4_29_11.pdf.

28 usually of girls, without consent: Nicola Döring, "Consensual Sexting Among Adolescents: Risk Prevention Through Abstinence Education or Safer Sexting?" *Cyberpsychology* 8, no. 1, (2014): article 9, https://dx.doi.org/10.5817/CP2014-1-9.

28 "what is expected of them": Leora Tanenbaum, *I Am Not a Slut: Slut-Shaming in the Age of the Internet* (New York: HarperCollins, 2015).

29 The issue of dignity didn't come up at all: For further reading on this topic, see Martha Nussbaum, *Anger and Forgiveness: Resentment, Generosity, Justice* (New York: Oxford University Press, 2016).

31 invading your imagination: Rachel Dickerson, "America Objectified: An Analysis of the Self-Objectification of Women in America and Some Detrimental Effects of Media Images," *Elements* (2014): 39–44, www.csustan.edu/sites/default/files/honors/documents/journals/elements/Dickerson.pdf.

31 forms frequently eroticizes violence: Susan Bordo and Leslie Haywood, *Unbearable Weight: Feminism, Western Culture, and the Body* (Berkeley: University of California Press, 2004).

31 sexualizing ways in order to be liked: Samantha M. Goodin et al., "'Putting on' Sexiness: A Content Analysis of the Presence of Sexualizing Characteristics in Girls' Clothing," *Sex Roles* 65, nos. 1–2 (July 2011): 1–12, https://doi.org/10.1007/S11199-011-9966-8.

31 they see in the media: Stephanie R. Damiano et al., "Dietary Restraint of 5-Year-Old Girls: Associations with Internalization of the Thin Ideal and Maternal, Media, and Peer Influences," *International Journal of Eating Disorders* 48, no. 8 (December 2015): 1166–69, https://doi.org/10.1002/eat.22432.

31 think they are too fat: *Children, Teens, Media, and Body Image: A Common Sense Research Brief* (San Francisco: Common Sense Media, January 21, 2015), www.commonsensemedia.org/children-teens-body-image-media-infographic.

31 throwing out snacks and school lunches: Deborah L. Cox, Karin H. Bruckner, and Sally D. Stabb, *The Anger Advantage: The Surprising Benefits of Anger and How It Can Change a Woman's Life* (New York: Broadway Books, 2003).

32 asked about their feelings: Margaret L. McGladrey, "Lolita Is in the Eye of the Beholder: Amplifying Preadolescent Girls' Voices in Conversations About Sexualization, Objectification, and Performativity," *Feminist Formations* 27, no. 2 (Summer 2015): 165–90, https://doi.org/10.1353/ff.2015.0012.

34 in-person sexual objectification: Laurel B. Watson et al., "Understanding the Relationships Among White and African American Women's Sexual Objectification Experiences, Physical Safety Anxiety, and Psychological Distress," *Sex Roles* 72, nos. 3–4 (February 2015): 91–104, https:// doi.org/10.1007/s11199-014-0444-y.s.

34 as do Latinas: Kimberly A. Burdette, "Self-Objectification and Self-Surveillance in African American and Latina Girls: Links to Body Dissatisfaction and Self-Worth" (master's thesis, Loyola University Chicago, 2014), http://ecommons.luc .edu/cgi/viewcontent.cgi?article=3231&context=luc_theses.

34 masked, for example, in dress codes: Marissa Higgins, "LGBT Students Are Not Safe at School," *The Atlantic*, October 18, 2016, www.theatlantic.com/education/ archive/2016/10/school-is-still-not-safe-for-lgbt-students/504368.

34 turn us into objects: Judith Rodin, Lisa R. Silberstein, and Ruth H. Striegel-Moore, "Women and Weight: A Normative Discontent," in *Nebraska Symposium on Motivation*, vol. 32, ed. T. B. Sonderegger (Lincoln, NE: University of Nebraska Press, 1984): 267–307; Jamie L. Goldenberg, "Immortal Objects: The Objectification of Women as Terror Management," chap. 4 in *Nebraska Symposium on Motivation*, vol. 60, ed. Sarah J. Gervais (New York: Springer, 2013): 73–95.

35 64 percent of boys: Ana Sofia Elias, Rosalind Gill, and Christina Scharff, *Aesthetic Labour: Rethinking Beauty Politics in Neoliberalism* (London: Palgrave Macmillan, 2017).

35 as "normative discontent": Rodin et al., "Women and Weight."

35 men best as whole: Sarah J. Gervais et al., "Seeing Women as Objects: The Sexual Body Part Recognition Bias," *European Journal of Social Psychology* 42, no. 6 (2012): 743–53, doi:10.1002/ejsp.1890.

35 a "shocking finding": "Normally when you examine social cognition, people's aim is to figure out what the other person is thinking and intending. And we see in these data really no evidence of that. So the deactivation of medial prefrontal cortex to these pictures is really kind of shocking." Susan Fiske, "Women as Sex Objects," *Scientific American* podcast, February 17, 2009.

35 his measures of hostile sexism: Elizabeth Landau, "Men See Bikini-Clad Women as Objects, Psychologists Say," CNN, April 19, 2009, www.cnn.com/2009/HEALTH /02/19/women.bikinis.objects.

36 mental state, almost impossible: Emma Rooney, "The Effects of Sexual Objectification on Women's Mental Health," *Applied Psychology OPUS* (Spring 2016), http://steinhardt.nyu.edu/appsych/opus/issues/2016/spring/rooney.

Girls and women in the United States are aware of the debunked idea that girls aren't good at math but boys are. (Globally, girls, on average, score only 2 percent lower than boys. However, girls in Japan outperform boys in the United States.) Looking at images of a woman in a bikini prior to taking a test, for example, lowers girls' math test scores, whereas looking at an image of women in sweaters doesn't. The same exercise has no effect on men. Just checking off a box marked "female" before taking a math test has been shown to reduce a girl's math score by 20 percent, on average. Not only is the ability to concentrate and perform compromised by concerns about stereotypes, but what amounts to the need to parallel process (simultaneously maintaining two or more separate areas of thought) inhibits motivation and what is commonly referred to as "flow," a creative mental state in which a person is entirely un-self-conscious and focused.

36 heart rate or muscle contractions: Vivien Ainley and Manos Tsakiris, "Body Conscious? Interoceptive Awareness, Measured by Heartbeat Perception, Is Negatively Correlated with Self-Objectification," *PLOS ONE* 8, no. 2 (February 2013): e55568, https://doi.org/10.1371/journal.pone.0055568.

36 to respond with anger: Bonnie Moradi and Yu-Ping Huang, "Objectification Theory and Psychology of Women: A Decade of Advances and Future Directions," *Psychology of Women Quarterly* 32, no. 4 (December 2008): 377–98, https://doi.org/10.1111/j.1471-6402.2008.00452.x.

36 emotions in girls and women: Tomi-Ann Roberts and Jennifer Y. Gettman, "Mere Exposure: Gender Differences in the Negative Effects of Priming a State of Self-Objectification," *Sex Roles* 51, nos. 1–2 (July 2004): 17–27, https://link.springer.com/article/10.1023/B:SERS.0000032306.20462.22.

36 less able, effective, and competent: Leora Pinhas et al., "The Effects of the Ideal of Female Beauty on Mood and Body Satisfaction," *International Journal of Eating Disorders* 25, no. 2 (March 1999): 223–26, www.ncbi.nlm.nih.gov/pubmed/10065400.

36 likely to assert themselves: Haroon Siddique, "Poor Body Image Makes Girls Less Assertive and Risks Health, Study Finds," *Guardian*, October 5, 2017, www.theguardian.com/uk-news/2017/oct/05/poor-body-image-makes-girls-less-assertive-and-risks-health-study-finds.

37 central aspect of depression: Dana Crowley Jack, *Silencing the Self: Women and Depression* (Cambridge, MA: Harvard University Press, 1991).

37 children is roughly equal: Jill M. Cyranowski et al., "Adolescent Onset of the Gender Difference in Lifetime Rates of Major Depression: A Theoretical Model," *Archives of General Psychiatry* 57, no. 1 (January 2000): 21–27, doi:10.1001/archpsyc.57.1.21.

37 with anxiety-related disorders: R. C. Kessler et al., "Lifetime Prevalence and Age-of-Onset Distributions of DSM-IV Disorders in the National Comorbidity Survey Replication (NCS-R)," *Archives of General Psychiatry* 62, no. 6 (June 2005): 593–602, doi:10.1001/archpsyc.62.6.593; "Prevalence of Any Anxiety Disorder Among Children," National Institutes of Mental Health, April 28, 2017, www.nimh.nih.gov/health/statistics/prevalence/any-anxiety-disorder-among-children.shtml.

37 women around the globe: M. Macht, "Characteristics of Eating in Anger, Fear, Sadness and Joy," *Appetite* 33, no. 1 (August 1999): 129–39, https://doi.org/10.1006/appe.1999.0236; Anne E. Becker, "Television, Disordered Eating, and Young Women in Fiji: Negotiating Body Image and Identity During Rapid Social Change," *Culture, Medicine and Psychiatry* 28, no. 4 (December 2004): 533–59, www.asu.edu/lib/tutorials/empirical/narrative.pdf.

One study found that girls in Belize began to experience disordered eating as a direct result of their exposure to Western media. In western Fiji, girls' body image ideas began to shift negatively with consumption of similar content.

37 disorders is 9 to 1: "the female-to-male ratio of clinical eating disorders is about 9:1, and the ratio of subclinical levels is about 3:1." H. Sweeting et al., "Prevalence of Eating Disorders in Males: A Review of Rates Reported in Academic Research and UK Mass Media," *International Journal of Men's Health* 14, no. 2

(2015): doi:10.3149/jmh.1402.86; Niva Piran and Holly C. Cormier, "The Social Construction of Women and Disordered Eating Patterns," *Journal of Counseling Psychology* 52, no. 4 (October 2005): 549–58, doi:10.1037/0022-0167.52.4.549.

37 number is also increasing: Canadian Pediatric Society, "Position Statement: Dieting in Adolescence," *Paediatrics Child Health* 9, no. 7 (September 2004): 487–91, https://www.ncbi.nlm.nih.gov/pmc/articles/PMC2720870/pdf/pch09487.pdf.

37 was "bad for my health": "Almost Half of Female Dieters Use Laxatives to Lose Weight," *Huffington Post* UK, October 2, 2013, www.huffingtonpost.co.uk/2013/10/02/weight-loss-half-female-dieters-use-laxatives_n_4028159.html; Joyce T. McFaddyn, *Your Daughter's Bedroom: Insights for Raising Confident Women* (New York: Macmillan, 2011).

37 a stress response to discrimination: Denee T. Mwendwa et al., "Coping with Perceived Racism: A Significant Factor in the Development of Obesity in African American Women?" *Journal of the National Medical Association* 103, no. 7 (July 2011): 602–8, www.ncbi.nlm.nih.gov/pmc/articles/PMC5003024.

37 anger and body surveillance: Lisa S. Wechsler et al., "Mutuality, Self-Silencing, and Disordered Eating in College Women," *Journal of College Student Psychotherapy* 21, no. 1 (2006): 51–76, http://psychology.unt.edu/riggspg/riggspg3/Wechsler,%20Riggs%20et%20al.pdf.

38 increased chances of depression: Megan E. Haines et al., "Predictors and Effects of Self-Objectification in Lesbians," *Psychology of Women Quarterly* 32, no. 2 (June 2008), 113–224, http://onlinelibrary.wiley.com/doi/10.1111/j.1471-6402.2008.00422.x/full.

38 or eating disorders: Marcie C. Wiseman and Bonnie Moradi, "Body Image and Eating Disorder Symptoms in Sexual Minority Men: A Test and Extension of Objectification Theory," *Journal of Counseling Psychology* 57, no. 2 (April 2010): 154–66, https://dx.doi.org/10.1037/a0018937.

38 people reporting self-harm: Patricia A. Adler and Peter Adler, *The Tender Cut: Inside the Hidden World of Self-Injury* (New York: New York University Press, 2011).

38 deliberately than boys are: Kate Kelland, "One in 12 Teenagers Self-Harm, Study Finds," Reuters, November 16, 2011, www.reuters.com/article/us-self-harm-idUSTRE7AG02520111117.

38 teenage girls had cut herself: Denis Campbell, "NHS Figures Show 'Shocking' Rise in Self-Harm Among Young," *Guardian* UK, October 23, 2016, www.theguardian.com/society/2016/oct/23/nhs-figures-show-shocking-rise-self-harm-young-people.

38 clear relation to anger: Kim L. Lehnert, James C. Overholser, and Anthony Spirito, "Internalized and Externalized Anger in Adolescent Suicide Attempters," *Journal of Adolescent Research* 9, no. 1 (January 1994): 105–19, http://journals.sagepub.com/doi/abs/10.1177/074355489491008

39 "a silent temper tantrum": Len Sperry et al., eds., *Psychopathology and Psychotherapy: DSM-5 Diagnosis, Case Conceptualization, and Treatment*, 3rd edition (New York, Routledge, 2014).

39 the rate that men do: Harvey A. Whiteford et al., "Global Burden of Disease Attributable to Mental and Substance Use Disorders: Findings from the Global Burden of Disease Study 2010," *Lancet* 382 , no. 9904 (November 2013): 1575–86, doi:10.1016/S0140-6736(13)61611-6; Christopher J. L. Murray et al., "The State of

US Health, 1990–2010: Burden of Diseases, Injuries, and Risk Factors," *Journal of the American Medical Association* 310, no. 6 (August 2013): 591–606, https://jamanetwork.com/journals/jama/fullarticle/1710486.

39 22 percent of men: "Anxiety Disorders Are More Common in Women," *Scientific American*, January 29, 2018. Data drawn from: Ronald C. Kessler et al., "Lifetime Prevalence and Age-of-Onset Distributions of DSM-IV Disorders in the National Comorbidity Survey Replication." R. C. Kessler et al., "Prevalence, Severity, and Comorbidity of 12-Month DSM-IV Disorders in the National Comorbidity Survey Replication," *Archives of General Psychiatry* 62, no. 6 (June 2005): 617–27, https://doi.org/10.1001/archpsyc.62.6.617; Philip S. Wang et al., "Twelve-Month Use of Mental Health Services in the United States: Results from the National Comorbidity Survey Replication," *Archives of General Psychiatry* 62, no. 6 (June 2005): 629–40, https://doi.org/10.1001/archpsyc.62.6.629.

39 mental distress much higher: Walter O. Bockting, Gail Knudson, and Joshua M. Goldberg, "Counseling and Mental Health Care for Transgender Adults and Loved Ones," *International Journal of Transgenderism* 9, nos. 3–4 (2006): 35–82, https://doi.org/10.1300/J485v09n03_03.

40 generating more anger: Ernest Becker, *The Denial of Death* (London: Souvenir Press, 1997).

40 "essentially deserving to exist": Mark R. Zaslav, "Shame-Related States of Mind in Psychotherapy," *Journal of Psychotherapy Practice and Research* 7, no. 2 (Spring 1998): 154–66, www.ncbi.nlm.nih.gov/pmc/articles/PMC3330497.

41 functions—even pregnancy: Tomi-Ann Roberts, "Female Trouble: The Menstrual Self-Evaluation Scale and Women's Self-Objectification," *Psychology of Women Quarterly* 28, no. 1 (March 2004): 22–26, doi:10.1111/j.1471-6402.2004.00119.x.

41 difficult for many women: Joan C. Chrisler, *From Menarche to Menopause: The Female Body in Feminist Therapy* (Philadelphia: Haworth Press, 2004).

41 known as Resting Bitch Face: "Treating 'Resting Angry Face' with Plastic Surgery," NBC4 Washington, video, 2:32, January 29, 2018, www.nbcwashington.com/news/health/Treating-_Resting-Angry-Face_-With-Plastic-Surgery_Washington-DC-304358501.html.

41 nice to look at: Maud Lavin, *Push Comes to Shove: New Images of Aggressive Women* (Cambridge, MA: MIT Press, 2010).

42 women to discipline themselves: Esther D. Rothblum and Sondra Solovay, eds., *The Fat Studies Reader* (New York: New York University Press, 2009).

42 is a form of obedience: Sandra Lee Bartky, "Foucault, Femininity and the Modernization of Patriarchal Power," in *Writing on the Body: Female Embodiment and Feminist Theory*, eds. Katie Conboy, Nadia Medina, and Sarah Stanbury (New York: Columbia University Press, 1997), 129–54.

42 often themselves critiqued: David Benatar, *Cutting to the Core: Exploring the Ethics of Contested Surgeries* (Lanham, MD: Rowman & Littlefield, 2006).

43 "really achieving power": Lizette Borreli, "Do Beauty Standards Fuel Income Inequality? Study Finds Women Who Wear Makeup Earn More Money," *Medical Daily*, June 28, 2016, www.medicaldaily.com/beauty-standards-income-inequality-390837.

43 of anger and power: Rebecca Busanich and Kerry R. McGannon, "Deconstruct-

ing Disordered Eating: A Feminist Psychological Approach to the Body, Food, and Exercise Relationship in Female Athletes," *Quest* 62, no. 4 (2010): 385–405, https://doi.org/10.1080/00336297.2010.10483656.

44 symbols of influence and status: Amber L. Horan, "Picture This! Objectification Versus Empowerment in Women's Photos on Social Media" (undergraduate thesis, Bridgewater State University, 2016), http://vc.bridgew.edu/honors_proj/155.

45 report using pornography: Shira Tarrant, *The Pornography Industry: What Everyone Needs to Know* (New York: Oxford University Press, 2016).

45 "degrading depiction of women": Lucia C. Lykke and Philip N. Cohen, "The Widening Gender Gap in Opposition to Pornography, 1975–2012," *Social Currents* 2, no. 4 (December 2015): 307–23, www.terpconnect.umd.edu/~pnc/SC2015.pdf; Tom Jacobs, "Study: Porn Viewing Impacts Attitudes on Women in Workplace," *Pacific Standard*, September 16, 2013, www.psmag.com/books-and-culture/porn -viewing-impacts-attitudes-women-workplace-66280.

46 Poet Adrienne Rich: Adrienne Rich, *On Lies, Secrets, and Silence: Selected Prose, 1966–1978* (New York: W. W. Norton, 1995).

46 body and sexual dissatisfaction: Tracy L. Tylka and Ashley M. Kroon Van Diest, "You Looking at Her 'Hot' Body May Not Be 'Cool' for Me: Integrating Male Partners' Pornography Use into Objectification Theory for Women," *Psychology of Women Quarterly* 39, no. 1 (2015): 67–84, http://u.osu.edu/tracyltylka/files/2015/02/Psychology-of-Women-Quarterly-2015-Tylka-67-84-1l8c512.pdf.

46 report feeling anger about porn: Liana Fattore and Miriam Melis, "Editorial: Exploring Gender and Sex Differences in Behavioral Dyscontrol: From Drug Addiction to Impulse Control Disorders," in *Exploring Gender and Sex Differences in Behavioral Dyscontrol: From Drug Addiction to Impulse Control Disorders*, eds. Liana Fattore and Miriam Melis (Lausanne, Switzerland: Frontiers Media, 2016), file:///C:/Users/Phil/Documents/Documents/Basher%20Bookworks/Freelance/SS%20-%20 Tangled%20Tree%20(The%20Tree%20of%20Life,%20DNA,%20etc.)/Exploring_ Gender_and_Sex_Differences_in_Behavioral_Dyscontrol%20(1).PDF.

46 are openly acting as aggressors: Eileen L. Zurbriggen, "Objectification, Self-Objectification, and Societal Change," *Journal of Social and Political Psychology* 1, no. 1 (2013): 188–215, https://jspp.psychopen.eu/article/view/94/pdf.

CHAPTER 3: ANGRY BODIES

50 physical and mental health: Gillian Bendelow and Simon Williams, "Pain and the Mind-Body Dualism: A Sociological Approach," *Body & Society* 1, no. 2 (June 1995): 83–103, http://journals.sagepub.com/doi/abs/10.1177/1357034x95001002004.

50 think about women's anger: Roger B. Fillingim et al., "Sex, Gender, and Pain: A Review of Recent Clinical and Experimental Findings," *Journal of Pain: Official Journal of the American Pain Society* 10, no. 5 (May 2009): 447–85, https://doi .org/10.1016/j.jpain.2008.12.001.

50 talk about their pain: Anke Samulowitz et al., "'Brave Men' and 'Emotional Women': A Theory-Guided Literature Review on Gender Bias in Health Care and Gendered Norms Towards Patients with Chronic Pain," *Pain Research and Management* (2018): 6358624, https://doi.org/10.1155/2018/6358624.

50 biological sex-based differences: Fillingim et al., "Sex, Gender, and Pain."

51 women are more tolerant of pain: O. A. Alabas et al., "Gender Role Affects Experimental Pain Responses: A Systematic Review with Meta-Analysis," *European Journal of Pain* 16, no. 9 (October 2012): 1211–23, https://doi.org/10.1002/j.1532-2149.2012.00121.x.

51 emotional contributor to pain: Ephrem Fernandez and Dennis C. Turk, "The Scope and Significance of Anger in the Experience of Chronic Pain," *Pain* 61, no. 2 (May 1995): 165–75, https://doi.org/10.1016/0304-3959(95)00192-U.

51 the vast majority are women: Judy Foreman, *A Nation in Pain: Healing Our Nation's Biggest Health Problem* (New York: Oxford University Press, 2015).

52 role of anger in persistent pain: Fernandez and Turk, "The Scope and Significance of Anger in the Experience of Chronic Pain," 165–75.

52 people feel and express anger: Ernest H. Johnson and Clifford L. Broman, "The Relationship of Anger Expression to Health Problems Among Black Americans in a National Survey," *Journal of Behavioral Medicine* 10, no. 2 (April 1987): 103–16, https://link.springer.com/article/10.1007/BF00846419.

53 die from heart-related disease: Fernandez and Turk, "The Scope and Significance of Anger in the Experience of Chronic Pain"; Karina W. Davidson and Elizabeth Mostofsky, "Anger Expression and Risk of Coronary Heart Disease: Evidence from the Nova Scotia Health Survey," *American Heart Journal* 159, no. 2 (February 2010): 199–206, 10.1016/j.ahj.2009.11.007; Elizabeth Mostofsky, Elizabeth Anne Penner, and Murray A. Mittleman, "Outbursts of Anger as a Trigger of Acute Cardiovascular Events: A Systematic Review and Meta-Analysis," *European Heart Journal* 35, no. 21 (June 2014): 1404–10, https://doi.org/10.1093/eurheartj/ehu033.

53 elevated blood pressure, or hypertension: Kevin T. Larkin and Claudia Zayfert, "Anger Expression and Essential Hypertension," *Journal of Psychosomatic Research* 56, no. 1 (January 2004): 113–18, https://doi.org/10.1016/S0022-3999(03)00066-7.

53 defense in fending off disease: A. Romero-Martínez et al., "High Immunoglobulin A Levels Mediate the Association Between High Anger Expression and Low Somatic Symptoms in Intimate Partner Violence Perpetrators," *Journal of Interpersonal Violence* 31, no. 4 (February 2014): 732–42, https://doi.org/10.1177/0886260514556107.

53 develop the common cold: Philip D. Evans and Nick Edgerton, "Life-Events and Mood as Predictors of the Common Cold," *British Journal of Medical Psychology* 64, no. 1 (March 1991): 35–44, https://doi.org/10.1111/j.2044-8341.1991.tb01640.x.

54 than men are: DeLisa Fairweather, Sylvia Frisancho-Kiss, and Noel R. Rose, "Sex Differences in Autoimmune Disease from a Pathological Perspective," *American Journal of Pathology* 173, no. 3 (September 2008): 600–9, https://doi.org/10.2353/ajpath.2008.071008.

54 disease multiple sclerosis: Laurie Edwards, "The Gender Gap in Pain," *New York Times*, March 16, 2013, www.nytimes.com/2013/03/17/opinion/sunday/women-and-the-treatment-of-pain.html; Muhammad B. Yunus, "Gender Differences in Fibromyalgia and Other Related Syndromes," *Journal of Gender Specific Medicine* (March/April 2002), https://www.ncbi.nlm.nih.gov/pubmed/11974674.

54 "extreme suppression of anger": Ahmedin Jemal et al., "Factors That Contributed to Black-White Disparities in Survival Among Nonelderly Women with Breast

Cancer Between 2004 and 2013," *Journal of Clinical Oncology* 36, no. 1 (January 2018): 14–24, https://doi.org/10.1200/JCO.2017.73.7932; S. Greer and Tina Morris, "Psychological Attributes of Women Who Develop Breast Cancer: A Controlled Study," *Journal of Psychosomatic Research* 19, no. 2 (April 1975): 147–53, https://doi.org/10.1016/0022-3999(75)90062-8.

54 suppressing their negative emotions: Benjamin P. Chapman et al., "Emotion Suppression and Mortality Risk over a 12-Year Follow-Up," *Journal of Psychosomatic Research* 75, no. 4 (October 2013): 381–85, 10.1016/j.jpsychores.2013.07.014.

54 their anger to themselves: Claire C. Conley, Brenden T. Bishop, and Barbara L. Andersen, "Emotions and Emotion Regulation in Breast Cancer Survivorship," *Healthcare* 4, no. 3 (August 2016): E56, https://doi.org/10.3390/healthcare 4030056; Barry D. Bultz and Linda E. Carlson, "Emotional Distress: The Sixth Vital Sign in Cancer Care," *Journal of Clinical Oncology* 23, no. 26 (September 2005): 6440–41, https://doi.org/10.1200/JCO.2005.02.3259; M. Pinquart and P. R. Duberstein, "Depression and Cancer Mortality: A Meta-Analysis," *Psychological Medicine* 40, no. 11 (November 2010): 1797–810, https://doi.org/10.1017/S0033291709992285.

55 racialized and classed: Carol Graham, "The High Costs of Being Poor in America: Stress, Pain, and Worry," Social Mobility Memos blog, Brookings Institution, February 19, 2015, www.brookings.edu/blog/social-mobility-memos/2015/02/19/the-high-costs-of-being-poor-in-america-stress-pain-and-worry.

55 middle-aged non-Hispanic whites: Anne Case and Angus Deaton, "Rising Morbidity and Mortality in Midlife Among White Non-Hispanic Americans in the 21st Century," *Proceedings of the National Academy of Sciences* 112, no. 49 (2015): 15078-83, https://www.ncbi.nlm.nih.gov/pubmed/26575631.

55 "with rage directed inwards": Michael Lewis, *Shame: The Exposed Self* (New York: Free Press, 1995).

55 David R. Williams has created: David R. Williams and S. A. Mohammed, "Racism and Health I: Pathways and Scientific Evidence," *American Behavioral Scientist* 57, no. 8 (2013): 1152–7, https://doi.org/10.1177/0002764213487340.

56 prescribed opioid analgesics: Yasamin Sharifzadeh et al., "Pain Catastrophizing Moderates Relationships Between Pain Intensity and Opioid Prescription," *Anesthesiology* 127, no. 1 (July 2017): 136–46, https://doi.org/10.1097/ALN.0000000000001656.

56 higher risk of substance abuse: Janine A. Clayton, Claudette E. Brooks, and Susan G. Kornstein, *Women of Color Health Data Book*, 4th ed. (Washington, DC: National Institutes of Health Office of Research on Women's Health, 2014), https://orwh.od.nih.gov/resources/pdf/WoC-Databook-FINAL.pdf.

56 is inexplicably reversed: Mihaela Fadgyas Stănculete, Cristina Pojoga, and Dan Lucian Dumitraşcu, "Experience of Anger in Patients with Irritable Bowel Syndrome in Romania," *Clujul Medical* 87, no. 2 (2014): 98–101, www.ncbi.nlm.nih.gov/pmc/articles/PMC4462420.

57 "socially acceptable forms of distress": Deborah Cox, Sally Stabb, and Karin Bruckner, *Women's Anger: Clinical and Developmental Perspectives* (Abingdon, VA: Routledge, 1999).

57 taking women's pain seriously: Maya Dusenbery, *Doing Harm: The Truth About How Bad Medicine and Lazy Science Leave Women Dismissed, Misdiagnosed, and Sick* (New York: HarperOne, 2018).

57 more quickly and frequently: Peter Dodek et al., "More Men Than Women Are Admitted to 9 Intensive Care Units in British Columbia," *Journal of Critical Care* 24, no. 4 (December 2009): 630el–630e8, https://doi.org/10.1016/j.jcrc.2009.02.010.

57 the exact same symptoms: Deborah Dillon McDonald and R. Gary Bridge, "Gender Stereotyping and Nursing Care," *Research in Nursing & Health* 14, no. 5 (October 1991): 373–78, www.ncbi.nlm.nih.gov/pubmed/1891623.

57 they get doctors' appointments: Josefina Robertson, "Waiting Time at the Emergency Department from a Gender Equality Perspective" (thesis, University of Gothenburg, Sweden, 2014), https://gupea.ub.gu.se/bitstream/2077/39196/1/gupea_2077_39196_1.pdf.

57 those in low-income areas: Ibid.

57 and 14 percent longer, respectively: Joanne Silberner, "Study: Longer Wait Times for Emergency Rooms," NPR, January 15, 2008, www.npr.org/templates/story/story.php?storyId=18106275.

58 of their pain and symptoms: I. Kirschberger et al., "Sex Differences in Patient-Reported Symptoms Associated with Myocardial Infarction (from the Population-Based MONICA/KORA Myocardial Infarction Registry)," *Yearbook of Cardiology* (2012), DOI: 10.1016/j.amjcard.2011.01.040.

58 due to arthritis have surgery: Dennis Thompson, "Women and Chronic Pain," *Everyday Health*, July 22, 2013, www.everydayhealth.com/pain-management/women-and-chronic-pain.aspx.

58 like these are seen globally: Robertson, "Waiting Time at the Emergency Department from a Gender Equality Perspective."

58 these gynecological procedures: Shankar Bedantam, "Remembering Anarcha, Lucy, and Betsey: The Mothers of Modern Gynecology," *Hidden Brain*, February 16, 2016.

58 blood clots in her lungs: Breanna Edwards, "Family Charges Calif. High School Cheerleader Died After Hospital Dismissed Her Chest Pain Twice," *The Root*, July 19, 2017, www.theroot.com/calif-high-school-cheerleader-dies-after-hospital-dism-1797047892.

58 that clots more quickly: Kelly M. Hoffman et al., "Racial Bias in Pain Assessment," *Proceedings of the National Academy of Sciences of the United States of America* 113, no. 6 (April 2016): 4296–301, https://doi.org/10.1073/pnas.1516047113.

59 resulting from sloppy care: Jochen Profit et al., "Racial/Ethnic Disparity in NICU Quality of Care Delivery," *Pediatrics* 140, no. 3 (September 2017): e20170918, https://doi.org/10.1542/peds.2017-0918.

59 unhealthy and risky stoicism: J. H. Lichtman et al., "Symptom Recognition and Healthcare Experiences of Young Women with Acute Myocardial Infarction," *Circulation: Cardiovascular Quality and Outcomes* 8, no. S2 (March 2015): S31–S38, https://doi.org/10.1161/CIRCOUTCOMES.114.001612.

59 with their normal lives: Pallavi Latthe, Rita Champaneria, and Khalid Khan, "Clinical Evidence Handbook: Dysmenorrhea," *American Family Physician* 85, no. 4 (February 2012): www.aafp.org/afp/2012/0215/p386.html.

59 abdominal pain that men do: E. H. Chen et al., "Gender Disparity in Anal-
gesic Treatment of Emergency Department Patients with Acute Abdominal
Pain," *Academic Emergency Medicine* 15, no. 5 (May 2008): 414–18, https://doi
.org/10.1111/j.1553-2712.2008.00100.x; "75% of Aussie Women Who Have Suffered from Period Pain Say It Has Affected Their Ability to Work," YouGov Survey, August–September 2017, https://au.yougov.com/news/2017/10/12/period-pain
-suffer/.

60 before the disease was identified: Olivia Blair, "Endometriosis: The Common
Condition Which Usually Takes Women 10 Doctors Visits Before Being Diagnosed," *Independent* (UK), May 8, 2017, www.independent.co.uk/life-style/
health-and-families/endometriosis-common-condition-women-health-10-doctors
-visits-before-diagnosed-treatment-periods-a7723796.html.

60 undiagnosed cervical cancer: Radhika Sanghani, " 'It's Just Lady Pains': Are Doctors Not Taking Women's Agony Seriously Enough?" *Telegraph* (UK), October 22,
2015, www.telegraph.co.uk/women/womens-life/11948057/lady-pains-are-doctors
-not-taking-womens-pain-seriously-enough.html.

60 the "beautiful is healthy" problem: Diane L. Lachapelle et al., "Attractiveness,
Diagnostic Ambiguity, and Disability Cues Impact Perceptions of Women
with Pain," *Rehabilitation Psychology* 59, no. 2 (May 2014): 162–70, https://doi
.org/10.1037/a0035894.

60 "less objective information available": Ibid.

60 "have so many problems": "Women in Pain Survey Results," National Pain Report, September 9, 2014, http://nationalpainreport.com/women-in-pain-survey
-results-8824686.html.

61 when a woman's does: Paolo Riva et al., "Gender Effects in Pain Detection:
Speed and Accuracy in Decoding Female and Male Pain Expressions," *European
Journal of Pain* 15, no. 9 (October 2011): 985.e1–985.e11, https://doi.org/10.1016/j
.ejpain.2011.02.006.

61 "and, therefore, 'not real' ": Diane E. Hoffmann and Anita J. Tarzian, "The Girl
Who Cried Pain: A Bias Against Women in the Treatment of Pain," *Journal of
Law, Medicine & Ethics* 29 (2001): 13–27, https://doi.org/10.2139/ssrn.383803.

61 women were given sedatives: Judy Foreman, "Why Women Are Living in the
Discomfort Zone," *Wall Street Journal*, January 31, 2014, www.wsj.com/articles/SB
10001424052702304691904579349212319995486.

61 anger are treated more quickly: Marcus Heneen, "User Insights Promote Gender
Equality in the ER," *Veryday*, January 29, 2018, http://veryday.com/case/genuslabbet.

62 pregnancy, despite *having no uterus*: Randee Dawn, " 'The Worst Pain a Woman
Can Go Through': ER Docs Misdiagnosed My Twisted Ovary," *Today*, June 28,
2017, www.today.com/health/anne-wheaton-er-doctors-misdiagnosed-my-twisted
-ovary-t113173.

62 Similarly, in a collection: Sonya Huber, *Pain Woman Takes Your Keys: And Other
Essays from a Nervous System* (Lincoln, NE: University of Nebraska Press, 2017).

63 their medical care providers: Ephrem Fernandez, "The Relationship Between
Anger and Pain," *Current Pain and Headache Reports* 9, no. 2 (March 2005): 101–5,
https://doi.org/10.1007/s11916-005-0046-z

63 significant improvements in pain relief: In 2008, chronic pain patients in an anger-expression experiment were asked to write letters about their anger. Those in the control group were asked to write about their goals. The letters were rated for levels of expressed anger and the degree to which the patients' writing was "meaning-making"—providing insight into why they felt angry. During a period of nine weeks, the people who wrote anger letters showed increased pain control, less depression, and even reductions in pain severity. The researchers noted that the degree of anger expressed and the meaning that was made in the expression accounted for significant improvements in the lives of the chronic pain sufferers. Jennifer E. Graham et al., "Effects of Written Anger Expression in Chronic Pain Patients: Making Meaning from Pain," *Journal of Behavioral Medicine* 31, no. 3 (June 2008): 201–12, https://link.springer.com/article/10.1007/s10865-008-9149-4.

63 keeping her "anger in": Pyoung Sook Lee, "Correlational Study Among Anger, Perceived Stress and Mental Health Status in Middle Aged Women," *Journal of Korean Academy of Nursing* 33, no. 6 (October 2003): 856–64, https://doi.org/10.4040/jkan.2003.33.6.856.

63 intensity of pain: Whitney Scott et al., "Anger Differentially Mediates the Relationship Between Perceived Injustice and Chronic Pain Outcomes," *Pain* 154, no. 9 (September 2013): 1691–98, http://sullivan-painresearch.mcgill.ca/pdf/abstracts/2013/Pain_154_1691-1698.pdf.

63 anger and depression: Ann-Mari Estlander et al., "Pain Intensity Influences the Relationship Between Anger Management Style and Depression," *Pain* 140, no. 2 (November 2008): 387–92, https://pdfs.semanticscholar.org/b349/23b80dd8e93ce51844e639712b910a2e157d.pdf.

64 improve pain regulation: Francis J. Keefe et al., "Psychological Aspects of Persistent Pain: Current State of the Science," *Journal of Pain* 5, no. 4 (May 2004): 195–211, https://doi.org/10.1016/j.jpain.2004.02.576.

64 masked by pain and anger: Scott et al., "Anger Differentially Mediates the Relationship Between Perceived Injustice and Chronic Pain Outcomes."

64 "'never raised her voice.'": Charles M. Blow, "Opinion: Rosa Parks, Revisited," *New York Times*, February 1, 2013, www.nytimes.com/2013/02/02/opinion/blow-rosa-parks-revisited.html.

64 "I was, was tired of giving in": Peter Dreier, "Rosa Parks: Angry, Not Tired," *Huffington Post* blog, February 3, 2013, www.huffingtonpost.com/peter-dreier/rosa-parks-civil-rights_b_2608964.html.

CHAPTER 4: THE CARING MANDATE

66 levels of daily stress that men do: Olivia Remes et al., "A Systematic Review of Reviews on the Prevalence of Anxiety Disorders in Adult Populations," *Brain and Behavior* 6, no. 7 (July 2016): e00497, https://doi.org/10.1002/brb3.497.

66 higher levels of vicarious stress: Sandra P. Thomas, "Distressing Aspects of Women's Roles, Vicarious Stress, and Health Consequences," *Issues in Mental Health Nursing* 18, no. 6 (November/December 1997): 539–57, https://doi.org/10.3109/01612849709010339.

66 impact of life events intensely: Physiological Society, "Stress of Major Life Events

Impacts Women More Than Men, Shows Poll of 2,000 People," *ScienceDaily*, March 15, 2017, www.sciencedaily.com/releases/2017/03/170315094541.htm.

66 otherwise worn out every day: US Centers for Disease Control, "QuickStats: Percentage of Adults Who Often Felt Very Tired or Exhausted in the Past 3 Months, by Sex and Age Group—National Health Interview Survey, United States, 2010–2011," *Morbidity and Mortality Weekly Report* 62, no. 14 (April 2013): 275, www.cdc.gov/mmwr/pdf/wk/mm6214.pdf.

67 "against their feeling any other way": Ada Calhoun, "The New Midlife Crisis: Why (and How) It's Hitting Gen X Women," Oprah.com, January 29, 2018, www.oprah.com/sp/new-midlife-crisis.html.

67 Women make up: Statistics in this paragraph can be found in US Department of Labor, *Women in the Labor Force in 2010*, January 2011, https://www.dol.gov/wb/factsheets/qf-laborforce-10.htm; Sarah Jane Glynn, "Breadwinning Mothers Are Increasingly the Norm," Center for American Progress, December 19, 2016, https://www.americanprogress.org/issues/women/reports/2016/12/19/295203/breadwinning-mothers-are-increasingly-the-u-s-norm/; Philip Cohen, "Family Diversity Is the New Normal for America's Children," Council on Contemporary Families, September 4, 2014, https://contemporaryfamilies.org/the-new-normal/.

67 male breadwinner (22 percent): Jason Deparle and Sabrina Tavernise, "For Women Under 30, Most Births Occur Outside Marriage," *New York Times*, February 17, 2012, www.nytimes.com/2012/02/18/us/for-women-under-30-most-births-occur-outside-marriage.html.

67 with cohabitating but unmarried partners: Cohen, "Family Diversity Is the New Normal for America's Children."

67 compared with 67 percent of men: US Department of Labor, Bureau of Labor Statistics, "American Time Use Survey Summary," June 27, 2017, www.bls.gov/news.release/atus.nr0.htm.

67 as married fathers do: Council on Contemporary Families, "Mother's Day Social Science—Housework, Gender & Parenting," May 7, 2015, https://contemporaryfamilies.org/housework-symposium-press-release.

68 while women's has shrunk: *Leisure Time in the UK: 2015* (Newport, UK: Office for National Statistics, October 24, 2017), www.ons.gov.uk/economy/nationalaccounts/satelliteaccounts/articles/leisuretimeintheuk.

68 this shift stalled in the 1990s: Evrim Altintas and Oriel Sullivan, "Fifty Years of Change Updated: Cross-National Gender Convergence in Housework," *Demographic Research* 35 (August 2016): 455–70, www.demographic-research.org/volumes/vol35/16. The authors of this article address the problem of US data in the 1980s and 1990s.

68 child-related task: discipline: American Sociological Association, "Sex and Gender More Important Than Income in Determining Views on Division of Chores," *ScienceDaily*, April 7, 2018, www.sciencedaily.com/releases/2016/08/160821093100.htm.

68 compared with 65 percent of men: US Department of Labor, Bureau of Labor Statistics, "American Time Use Survey Summary."

69 maintenance and yard work: N. Qualin and L. Doan, "Making Money, Doing Gender, or Being Essentialist?: Partner Characteristics and Americans' Attitudes Toward Housework," American Sociological Association, 2016.

69 restrictions, in thirty minutes: Alan B. Krueger, "Are We Having More Fun Yet? Categorizing and Evaluating Changes in Time Allocation," *Brookings Papers on Economic Activity*, no. 2 (Fall 2007): 193–217, www.brookings.edu/wpcontent/uploads/2007/09/2007b_bpea_krueger.pdf.

69 a higher stress quotient: Daniel S. Hamermesh and Jungmin Lee, "Stressed Out on Four Continents: Time Crunch or Yuppie Kvetch?" *Review of Economics and Statistics* 89, no. 2 (May 2007): 374–83, www.mitpressjournals.org/doi/abs/10.1162/rest.89.2.374.

69 three times every hour: Gary Novak and Martha B. Peleaz, *Child and Adolescent Development: A Behavioral Systems Approach* (Thousand Oaks, CA: Sage, 2004).

70 stress-hormone level skyrocketing: Sarah Damaske, "CCF Research Brief: Really? Work Lowers People's Stress Levels," Council on Contemporary Families, May 22, 2014, https://contemporaryfamilies.org/work-lowers-stress-levels.

70 income earning, and care: Brigid Schulte, *Overwhelmed: Work, Love and Play When No One Has the Time* (London: Picador, 2015).

71 their domestic contributions: Melissa Dahl, "Why Men Think They're Doing More Chores Than They Actually Are," *The Cut*, November 13, 2015, http://nymag.com/scienceofus/2015/11/why-men-think-theyre-doing-more-chores.html.

71 do the work themselves: Joe Mellor, "Men Messing Up Household Chores Is No Accident," *London Economic*, November 6, 2014, www.thelondoneconomic.com/lifestyle/men-messing-up-household-chores-is-no-accident/06/11.

71 more per day per year: Beatrix Campbell, *End of Equality* (Kolkata, India: Seagull Books, 2014).

71 white fathers and then Hispanic fathers: Jo Jones and William D. Mosher, "Fathers' Involvement with Their Children: United States, 2006–2010," *National Health Statistics Reports* 71 (December 2013): 1–22, https://www.cdc.gov/nchs/data/nhsr/nhsr071.pdf.

71 things by themselves: Safiya A. Jardine and Arlene Dallalfar, "Sex and Gender Roles: Examining Gender Dynamics in the Context of African American Families," *Journal of Pedagogy, Pluralism and Practice* 4, no. 4 (Spring 2012): 17–26, www.lesley.edu/journal-pedagogy-pluralism-practice/safiya-jardine-arlene-dallalfar/sex-gender-roles.

72 enhance their relationships: Ellie Lisitsa, "The 12 Year Study," Gottman Relationship blog, Gottman Institute, December 14, 2012, www.gottman.com/blog/the-12-year-study.

72 in their own marriages: Kevin Matos, "Modern Families: Same & Different Sex Couples Negotiating at Home," Families and Work Institute, 2015, https://docs.google.com/viewer?url=http%3A%2F%2Fwww.familiesandwork.org%2Fdownloads%2Fmodern-families.pdf.

72 frustration, aggression, and rage: Robert Jay Green, "Same-Sex Couples May Have More Egalitarian Relationships," interview by Lourdes Garcia-Navarro, *All Things Considered*, December 29, 2014, www.npr.org/2014/12/29/373835114/same-sex-couples-may-have-more-egalitarian-relationships.

72 women, specifically daughters: Maryam Navaie-Waliser et al., "When the Caregiver Needs Care: The Plight of Vulnerable Caregivers," *American Journal of Public Health* 92, no. 2: (March 2002): 409–13, www.ncbi.nlm.nih.gov/pmc/articles/PMC1447090.

72 "such as sisters or a parent's spouse": "Daughters Provide as Much Elderly Parent Care as They Can, Sons Do as Little as Possible," *ScienceDaily*, August 19, 2014, www.sciencedaily.com/releases/2014/08/140819082912.htm; Angelina Grigoryeva, "Own Gender, Sibling's Gender, Parent's Gender: The Division of Elderly Parent Care Among Adult Children," *American Sociological Review* 82, no. 1 (2017): 116–46, doi:10.1177/0003122416686521.

72 lion's share of parental elder care: Yi Zeng et al., "Older Parents Enjoy Better Filial Piety and Care from Daughters Than Sons in China," *American Journal of Medical Research* 3, no. 1 (2016): 244–72, https://doi.org/10.22381/AJMR3120169.

72 week on unpaid care work: *Underpaid & Overloaded: Women in Low-Wage Jobs* (Washington, DC: National Women's Law Center, 2014), www.nwlc.org/sites/default/files/pdfs/final_nwlc_lowwagereport2014.pdf.

73 women say they do: Taryn Hillin, "Not Feeling It: Why So Many Women Are Faking Orgasms," *Splinter*, November 25, 2014, https://splinternews.com/not-feeling-it-why-so-many-women-are-faking-orgasms-1793844262.

73 than heterosexual men: David A. Frederick et al., "Differences in Orgasm Frequency Among Gay, Lesbian, Bisexual, and Heterosexual Men and Women in a U.S. National Sample," *Archives of Sexual Behavior* 47, no. 1 (January 2018): 273–88, https://doi.org/10.1007/s10508-017-0939-z.

73 in the first place: Gayle Brewer and Colin A. Hendrie, "Evidence to Suggest That Copulatory Vocalizations in Women Are Not a Reflexive Consequence of Orgasm," *Archives of Sexual Behavior* 40, no. 3 (June 2011): 559–64, https://doi.org/10.1007/s10508-010-9632-1.

74 "with their teeth tightly clenched": Lili Loofbourow, "The Female Price of Male Pleasure," *The Week*, January 25, 2018, http://theweek.com/articles/749978/female-price-male-pleasure.

74 "the man who assaulted me": Emma Lindsay, "Men Dump Their Anger into Women," *Medium*, November 30, 2016, https://medium.com/@emmalindsay/men-dump-their-anger-into-women-d5b641fa37bc.

75 general maintenance work: *Harnessing the Power of Data for Girls: Taking Stock and Looking Ahead to 2030* (New York: UNICEF, October 2016), www.unicef.org/gender/files/Harnessing-the-Power-of-Data-for-Girls-Brochure-2016-1-1.pdf.

75 fewer chores than girls do: Lisa Wade, "Children, Chores, and the Gender Pay Gap at Home," Sociological Images blog, March 16, 2015, https://thesocietypages.org/socimages/2015/03/16/children-chores-and-the-gender-pay-gap-at-home.

75 13 percent more than girls: Olga Khazan, "Even in Babysitting, Men Make More Than Women," *The Atlantic*, March 14, 2014, www.theatlantic.com/business/archive/2014/03/even-in-babysitting-men-make-more-than-women/284426.

75 compensated and more profitable: Institute for Social Research, University of Michigan, "Time, Money and Who Does the Laundry," *Research Update* 4 (January 2007): 1–2, http://ns.umich.edu/podcast/img/ISR_Update1-07.pdf; Lisa Power, "A Household Flaw Allows Boys to Pocket More for Doing Household Chores," *Daily Telegraph*, July 15, 2013, www.dailytelegraph.com.au/business/a-household-flaw-allows-boys-to-pocket-more-for-doing-household-chores/story-fni0cp8j-122667981315.

75 done by teenagers: Yasemin Besen-Cassino, *The Cost of Being a Girl: Working Teens and the Origins of the Gender Wage Gap*, 1st ed. (Philadelphia, PA: Temple University Press, 2017).

76 thought they were being watched: Sharon Lamb, Lyn Mikel Brown, and Mark Tappan, *Packaging Boyhood: Saving Our Sons from Superheroes, Slackers, and Other Media Stereotypes* (New York: St. Martin's Press, 2009). Isabelle D. Cherney and Kamala London, "Gender-Linked Differences in the Toys, Television Shows, and Outdoor Activities of 5-13 Year Old Children," *Sex Roles*, 54, no 9–19 (2006).

77 not the other way around: Joanna Moorhead, "Are the Men of the African Aka Tribe the Best Fathers in the World?" *Guardian* (US), June 15, 2005, www.the guardian.com/society/2005/jun/15/childrensservices.familyandrelationships.

77 peak of 23 percent: Stephanie Hallett, "Changing Your Last Name: Survey Reveals How Americans Feel About Women, Men Changing Their Names," *Huffington Post*, April 14, 2013, www.huffingtonpost.com/2013/04/14/changing -your-last-name_n_3073125.html.

78 believe it should be enforced legally: Laura Hamilton, Claudia Geist, and Brian Powell, "Marital Name Change as a Window into Gender Attitudes," *Gender & Society* 25, no. 2 (April 2011): 145–75, http://gas.sagepub.com/content/25/2/145.full.pdf+html.

78 give up their birth names: Robin Hilmantel, "How Men *Really* Feel When You Keep Your Last Name," *Women's Health*, August 8, 2013, https://www.womens healthmag.com/relationships/a19903379/how-men-really-feel-when-you-keep-your -last-name/.

78 "to their domestic situation": Ben Zimmer, "Ms.," *New York Times*, October 23, 2009, https://www.nytimes.com/2009/10/25/magazine/25FOB-onlanguage-t.html.

78 prefix *Dr.* as male: Carla Challis, "Computer Says No! Gym's Sexist System Locks Female Doctor Out of Women's Changing Room," *BT*, March 15, 2015, http:// home.bt.com/lifestyle/computer-says-no-gyms-sexist-system-locks-female-doctor -out-of-womens-changing-room-11363969434794.

78 outside of the home: Melissa A. Barnett, "Economic Disadvantage in Complex Family Systems: Expansion of Family Stress Models," *Clinical Child and Family Psychology Review* 11, no. 3 (September 2008): 145–61, https://doi.org/10.1007/s10567 -008-0034-z; Elizabeth Mendes, Lydia Saad, and Kylie McGeenwy, "Stay-at-Home Moms Report More Depression, Sadness, Anger," Gallup, May 18, 2012, www.gallup .com/poll/154685/stay-home-moms-report-depression-sadness-anger.aspx.

79 "self-focused reactions": Agneta H. Fischer, ed., *Gender and Emotion: Social Psychological Perspectives* (Cambridge: Cambridge University Press, 2000).

79 who initiated separations: Michael J. Rosenfeld, "Who Wants the Breakup? Gender and Breakup in Heterosexual Couples," in *Social Networks and the Life Course: Integrating the Development of Human Lives and Social Relational Networks*, eds. Duane F. Alwin, Diane Helen Felmlee, and Derek A. Kreager (Basel, Switzerland: Springer International Publishing, 2018).

79 "moment of subordination for women": Lisa Wade, "Women Are Less Happy Than Men in Marriage, but Society Pretends It Isn't True," *Business Insider*, January 8, 2017, www.businessinsider.com/society-should-stop-pretending-marriage -makes-women-so-happy-2017-1.

79 to want to remarry: Bella DePaulo, "Once Married, Twice Shy: Remarriage Rates Are Plummeting," Single at Heart blog, October 3, 2015, http://blogs.psychcentral.com/single-at-heart/2015/10/once-married-twice-shy-remarriage-rates-are-plummeting.

80 authority over their wives: Lois M. Collins, "Men Are Helping More Around the House and Favor More Gender Equality, New Research Shows," *Deseret News*, April 3, 2018.

80 neotraditionalist views of gender: Joanna R. Pepin and David A. Cotter, "Trending Towards Traditionalism? Changes in Youths' Gender Ideology" (briefing paper, Council on Contemporary Families, March 31, 2017), https://thesocietypages.org/ccf/2017/04/06/trending-towards-traditionalism-changes-in-youths-gender-ideology.

80 plummets to 8 percent: Claire Cain Miller, "Millennial Men Aren't the Dads They Thought They'd Be," *New York Times*, July 30, 2015, www.nytimes.com/2015/07/31/upshot/millennial-men-find-work-and-family-hard-to-balance.html.

80 take care of children: David S. Pedulla and Sarah Thébaud, "Can We Finish the Revolution? Gender, Work-Family Ideals, and Institutional Constraint," *American Sociological Review* 80, no. 1 (February 2015): 116–39, http://asr.sagepub.com/content/80/1/116.abstract.

81 masculinity backlash: Olga Khazan, "Emasculated Men Refuse to Do Chores—Except Cooking," *The Atlantic*, October 24, 2016, https://www.theatlantic.com/health/archive/2016/10/the-only-chore-men-will-do-is-cook/505067/.

81 into conventional roles: Joanna R. Pepin and David A. Cotter, "Reactions to Other Contributors" (briefing paper, Council on Contemporary Families by Department of Sociology, March 31, 2017), https://contemporaryfamilies.org/9-pepin-cotter-reactions.

81 other young adults: Emily W. Kane, "Racial and Ethnic Variations in Gender-Related Attitudes," *Annual Review of Sociology* 26 (August 2000): 419–39, https://doi.org/10.1146/annurev.soc.26.1.419.

81 their mothers did: David Cotter, Joan M. Hermsen, and Reeve Vanneman, "The End of the Gender Revolution? Gender Role Attitudes from 1977 to 2008," *American Journal of Sociology* 117, no. 1 (July 2011): 259–89, https://doi.org/10.1086/658853.

81 constrained by gender stereotypes: William A. Galston, "Data Point to a New Wave of Female Political Activism That Could Shift the Course of US Politics," Brookings Institution, January 10, 2018, www.brookings.edu/blog/fixgov/2018/01/10/a-new-wave-of-female-political-activism.

81 group in the United States: *Stress in America: The State of Our Nation* (Washington, DC: American Psychological Association, November 2017), www.apa.org/news/press/releases/stress/2017/state-nation.pdf.

82 teacher and nurse: US Department of Labor, Bureau of Labor Statistics, "Occupational Outlook Handbook," January 30, 2018, https://www.dol.gov/wb/stats/most_common_occupations_for_women.htm; Annalyn Kurtz, "Why Secretary Is Still the Top Job for Women," CNN, January 30, 2013, http://money.cnn.com/2013/01/31/news/economy/secretary-women-jobs/index.html.

82 and teachers were "she": Jack Morse, "Google Translate Might Have a Gender Problem," *Mashable*, November 30, 2017, https://mashable.com/2017/11/30/google-translate-sexism/#D2.dTXMEEsq9.

83 suppression are related: Melanie M. Keller et al., "Teachers' Emotional Experiences and Exhaustion as Predictors of Emotional Labor in the Classroom: An Experience Sampling Study," *Frontiers in Psychology* 5 (December 2014): 1442, https://doi.org/10.3389/fpsyg.2014.01442.

83 excessive work demands: Jenny Grant Rankin, "The Teacher Burnout Epidemic," *Psychology Today*, April 5, 2018, https://www.psychologytoday.com/us/blog/much-more-common-core/201611/the-teacher-burnout-epidemic-part-1-2.

83 and unexpressed anger: Won Hee Lee and Chun Ja Kim, "The Relationship Between Depression, Perceived Stress, Fatigue and Anger in Clinical Nurses," *Journal of Korean Academy of Nursing* 36, no. 6 (October 2006): 925–32, https://doi.org/10.4040/jkan.2006.36.6.925.

84 coined the term *emotional labor*: *Emotional labor* is work done that requires feelings as part of what is being compensated. Flight attendants, nurses, teachers and people in service industries are paid to show specific behaviors to customers and clients. Arlie Russell Hochschild, *The Managed Heart: The Commercialization of Human Feeling*, 3rd ed. (Berkeley, CA: University of California Press, 2012).

84 expectations are dashed: Deborah L. Kidder, "The Influence of Gender on the Performance of Organizational Citizenship Behaviors," *Journal of Management* 28, no. 5 (October 2002): 629–48, https://doi.org/10.1177/014920630202800504.

84 "is an angry woman": Victoria L. Brescoll and Eric Luis Uhlmann, "Can an Angry Woman Get Ahead? Status Conferral, Gender, and Expression of Emotion in the Workplace," *Psychological Science* 19, no. 3 (March 2008): 268–75, https://doi.org/10.1111/j.1467-9280.2008.02079.x.

84 "another 217 years": Liz Posner, "Why Is the US Lagging Behind Other Countries in Closing the Gender Pay Gap?" *Salon*, February 6, 2018, www.salon.com/2018/02/06/why-is-the-us-lagging-behind-other-countries-in-closing-the-gender-pay-gap_partner.

84 remaining chronically undervalued: Sarah Jane Glynn, *Explaining the Gender Wage Gap* (Center for American Progress, May 19, 2014), https://www.americanprogress.org/issues/economy/reports/2014/05/19/90039/explaining-the-gender-wage-gap/; Heather Boushey, "Is 'Comparable Worth' Worth It? The Potential Effects of Pay Equity Policies in New York," *Regional Labor Review* (Fall 2000): 29–38, www.hofstra.edu/pdf/CLD_RLR_f00_compworth.pdf.

85 salaries go up: Ruth Mantell, "Women Earn Less Than Men Even in Woman-Dominated Jobs," Capitol Report blog, April 7, 2014, http://blogs.marketwatch.com/capitolreport/2014/04/07/women-earn-less-than-men-even-in-woman-dominated-jobs.

85 are female dominated: Emily Liner, "A Dollar Short: What's Holding Women Back from Equal Pay?" *Third Way*, March 18, 2016, www.thirdway.org/report/a-dollar-short-whats-holding-women-back-from-equal-pay.

85 student loan debt: Melissa Wylie, "Debt-Ridden Millennials Drive Gig Economy," *Bizwomen*, February 8, 2018, www.bizjournals.com/bizwomen/news/latest-news/2018/02/debt-ridden-millennials-drive-gig-economy.html?page=all; Madeline Farber, "Women Hold $833 Billion of America's $1.3 Trillion Student Debt," *Fortune*, May 24, 2017, http://fortune.com/2017/05/24/women-student-loan-debt-study.

A consistent, measurable gender wage gap exists within every demographic group: black women make 94 percent of what black men do; Hispanic women, 91 percent of what Hispanic men do; Asian women, 83 percent of what Asian men do; and white women, 81 percent of what white men do. The gap is narrower for black and Hispanic women because race-based gaps are high and men also experience pay discrimination. Across demographic categories, the differences are more stark: a Hispanic woman makes 59 percent of what a white man makes; an African American woman, 68 percent; a white woman, 81 percent; and an Asian woman, 88 percent. A big factor in these differences is educational opportunity: black and Hispanic women are less likely to be able to pursue higher education, and when they do, in the United States, they incur massive student loan debt. Two-thirds of outstanding student loans are held by women.

85 *worst levels* of access: Heejung Chung, "New Research: Women Aren't Paid Less Because They Have More Flexible Jobs," *Slate*, January 30, 2018, https://slate.com /human-interest/2018/01/the-gender-wage-gap-is-not-about-women-getting-more -flexibility-they-get-less.html?via=recirc_recent.

85 "among ordinary managers": Dana Wilkie, "Managers Distrust Women Who Ask for Flextime More Than Men," Society for Human Resource Management, May 19, 2017, www.shrm.org/ResourcesAndTools/hr-topics/behavioral-competencies/ global-and-cultural-effectiveness/Pages/Managers-Distrust-Women-Flextime.aspx.

86 parents and children: Lawrence F. Katz and Alan Krueger, "The Rise and Nature of Alternative Work Arrangements in the United States, 1995–2015," Princeton University and National Bureau of Economic Research, March 29, 2016, https:// krueger.princeton.edu/sites/default/files/akrueger/files/katz_krueger_cws_-_ march_29_20165.pdf.

86 Few developed nations: In some European countries, for example, women are entitled to between one and three years paid leave. Christopher Ingraham, "The World's Richest Countries Guarantee Mothers More Than a Year of Paid Maternity Leave. The U.S. Guarantees Them Nothing," *Washington Post*, February 5, 2018, https://www.washingtonpost.com/news/wonk/wp/2018/02/05/the-worlds -richest-countries-guarantee-mothers-more-than-a-year-of-paid-maternity-leave -the-u-s-guarantees-them-nothing/?utm_term=.603724989423.

86 "more money conscious": Grace Wyler, "Wisconsin Republican: Women Are Paid Less Because 'Money Is More Important for Men,'" *Business Insider*, April 9, 2012, www.businessinsider.com/wisconsin-republican-says-women-are-paid-less -because-money-is-more-important-for-men-2012-4.

86 would be impossible: Gloria Steinem, *Moving Beyond Words: Age, Rage, Sex, Power, Money, Muscles: Breaking the Boundaries of Gender* (London: Bloomsbury, 1995).

87 women's daily stress: Kelli B. Grant, "More Millennials Are Giving Back to the 'Bank of Mom and Dad,'" CNBC, August 24, 2016, www.cnbc.com/2016/08/24/ turnabout-more-millennials-helping-mom-and-dad.html.

87 saving for retirement: "NAB Consumer Behavior Survey: Q1 2017," NAB Business Research and Insights, May 24, 2017, https://business.nab.com.au/nab-consumer -behavior-survey-q1-2017-24567.

88 to less life satisfaction: Carolyn C. Cannuscio et al., "Reverberations of Family Illness: A Longitudinal Assessment of Informal Caregiving and Mental Health Status in the Nurses' Health Study," *American Journal of Public Health* 92, no. 8 (August 2002): 1305–11, www.ncbi.nlm.nih.gov/pubmed/12144989.

88 shoulder similar responsibilities: *The MetLife Study of Caregiving Costs to Working Caregivers: Double Jeopardy for Baby Boomers Caring for Their Parents* (Westport, CT: MetLife Mature Market Institute, June 2011), www.caregiving.org/wp-content/uploads/2011/06/mmi-caregiving-costs-working-caregivers.pdf.

88 two times more likely: Cannuscio et al., "Reverberations of Family Illness."

88 were virtually eliminated: Jonathan Platt et al., "Unequal Depression for Equal Work? How the Wage Gap Explains Gendered Disparities in Mood Disorders," *Social Science & Medicine* 149 (January 2016): 1–8, https://doi.org/10.1016/j.socscimed.2015.11.056.

88 Mothers who worked part-time: Susan Roxburgh, "Parenting Strains, Distress, and Family Paid Labor," *Journal of Family Issues* 26, no. 8 (November 2005): 1062–81, http://journals.sagepub.com/doi/abs/10.1177/0192513X05277813.

88 deprivation by 46 percent: American Academy of Neurology, "Living with Children May Mean Less Sleep for Women, but Not for Men," *ScienceDaily*, February 26, 2017, www.sciencedaily.com/releases/2017/02/170226212745.htm.

88 to stress and depression: Shirley A. Thomas and A. Antonio González-Prendes, "Powerlessness, Anger, and Stress in African American Women: Implications for Physical and Emotional Health," *Health Care for Women International* 30, nos. 1–2 (2009): 93–113, https://doi.org/10.1080/07399330802523709.

89 in their eighth decade: "Household Survey Shows More Men Than Women Meet Physical Activity Guidelines," NHS Digital, December 13, 2017, https://digital.nhs.uk/article/8359/Household-survey-shows-more-men-than-women-meet-physical-activity-guidelines.

89 homes when they did: Shirley Yee, *Black Women Abolitionists: A Study in Activism, 1828–1860* (Knoxville, TN: University of Tennessee Press, 1992); Gladys Martinez, Kimberly Daniels, and Anjani Chandra, "Fertility of Men and Women Aged 15–44 Years in the United States: National Survey of Family Growth, 2006–2010," *National Health Statistics Reports* 51 (April 2012): 1–28, www.cdc.gov/nchs/data/nhsr/nhsr051.pdf.

90 sex, or giving birth: Aaron Rupar, "Paul Ryan Says American Women Need to Have More Babies," *ThinkProgress*, December 14, 2017, https://thinkprogress.org/paul-ryan-says-american-women-need-to-have-more-babies-dc45cb1afec2.

90 work as low-status pastimes: Cecilia L. Ridgeway, *Framed by Gender: How Gender Inequality Persists in the Modern World* (New York: Oxford University Press, 2011).

CHAPTER 5: MOTHER RAGE

92 more than thirty thousand times: Soraya Chemaly, "That Male Birth Control Story? Women Are Laughing Because We're So Fed Up," *Huffington Post*, November 2, 2016, www.huffingtonpost.com/entry/women-arent-laughing-at-that-male-birth-control-story_us_5818f13fe4b0922c570bd335.

92 at University College London: David Robson, "Why Do We Laugh Inappropri-

ately?" BBC Future, March 23, 2015, www.bbc.com/future/story/20150320-why -do-we-laugh-inappropriately.

92 consuming it is to obtain: Kevin G., "Men Don't Know Anything About Birth Control," BirthControl.com, March 31, 2017, www.birthcontrol.com/men-dont -know-anything-birth-control.

92 difference in their lives: Laurel Raymond, "52 Percent of Men Say They Haven't Benefited from Women Having Affordable Birth Control," ThinkProgress, March 22, 2017, https://thinkprogress.org/congress-is-more-regressive-on-womens-rights -than-most-voters-poll-finds-88efc93d7e59.

92 about unplanned pregnancies: Kelly Mickle, "What Guys Really Know About Birth Control: A Cosmopolitan Survey," Cosmopolitan, October 9, 2017, www .cosmopolitan.com/sex-love/news/a56423/what-guys-really-know-about-birth -control-cosmopolitan-survey.

93 display it in a lockbox: "Inching Towards Progress: ASEC's 2015 Pharmacy Access Study," American Society of Emergency Contraception, December 2015, http://amer icansocietyforec.org/uploads/3/4/5/6/34568220/asec_2015_ec_access_report_1.pdf.

94 denser matrix of obstacles: C. McLeod, "Harm or Mere Inconvenience? Denying Women Emergency Contraception," Hypatia 25, no. 1 (2010): 11–30, doi:10.1111/ j.1527-2001.2009.01082.x.

96 one with less agency: Jonah Lehrer, "The Psychology of Nakedness," Wired, June 3, 2017, www.wired.com/2011/11/the-psychology-of-nakedness.

96 less and speaking less: Nathan A. Heflick and Jamie L. Goldenberg, "Seeing Eye to Body: The Literal Objectification of Women," Current Directions in Psychological Science 23, no. 3 (June 2014): 159–63, http://journals.sagepub.com/doi/ full/10.1177/0963721414531599.

97 "Drama of Life Before Birth": In the 1950s, Nilsson had started experimenting with new techniques for creating scientific images. The 1965 fetal-development issue of Life sold more than eight million copies in less than five days, and, later that year, his photos were included in a book titled A Child Is Born. Nilsson's "in utero" photos, however, were not all taken in utero. Some were of fetuses that had been "surgically removed for a variety of medical reasons" in Sweden, a country with more liberal abortion laws. He could use aborted embryos at varying stages of development, artificially posing them with props and equipment. For example, Nilsson moved a fetus's thumb into its mouth, so that it appeared to be sucking its thumb.

97 in the cultural imagination: Rosalind P. Petchesky, "Fetal Images: The Power of Visual Culture in the Politics of Reproduction," in Reproductive Technologies: Gender, Motherhood and Medicine, ed. Michelle Stanworth (Cambridge, UK: Polity Press, 1987).

99 and 19.8 percent after: "Maternal Mental Health: Fact Sheet," World Health Organization, November 2016, http://www.who.int/mental_health/maternal-child/ maternal_mental_health/en/.

99 of Asian and European descent: Kristina W. Whitworth et al., "Accessing Disadvantaged Pregnant Women in Houston, Texas, and Characterizing Biomarkers of Metal Exposure: A Feasibility Study," International Journal of Environmental Research and Public Health 14, no. 5 (May 2017): 474, https://doi.org/10.3390/ijerph14050474;

Jamila Taylor and Christy M. Gamble, "Suffering in Silence: Mood Disorders Among Pregnant and Postpartum Women of Color," Center for American Progress, November 17, 2017, www.americanprogress.org/issues/women/reports/2017/11/17/443051/suffering-in-silence.

Between 28 and 44 percent of African American women suffer from postpartum depressive symptoms, compared with roughly 31 percent of their white peers. They are also less likely to be treated for their distress despite a willingness to seek treatment.

99 with persistent pelvic pain: Cynthia A. Mannion et al., "The Influence of Back Pain and Urinary Incontinence on Daily Tasks of Mothers at 12 Months Postpartum," PLOS ONE 10, no. 6 (2015): https://doi.org/10.1371/journal.pone.0129615.

99 months after giving birth: E. A. McDonald et al., "Dyspareunia and Childbirth: A Prospective Cohort Study," BJOG 122, no. 5 (April 2015): 672–79, https://doi.org/10.1111/1471-0528.13263; "Postnatal Depression May Be Preventable," Live Science, August 18, 2010. https://www.livescience.com/34847-postnatal-depression-can-be-prevented-study-shows.html.

Persistent post-childbirth pain has been linked with higher risks of postpartum depression in women.

99 intense pain during sex: Chelsea Ritschel, "The 'Husband Stitch' During Episiotomy Repair Is a Disturbing Reality for Many New Mothers," Independent (UK), January 29, 2018, www.independent.co.uk/life-style/husband-stitch-episiotomy-misogyny-motherhood-pregnancy-surgery-stitch-sexism-childbirth-a8184346.html.

100 85 percent of women: Martinez et al., "Fertility of Men and Women Aged 15–44 Years in the United States: National Survey of Family Growth, 2006–2010," National Health Statistics Reports 51 (April 2012): 1–28, www.cdc.gov/nchs/data/nhsr/nhsr051.pdf.

100 on deep prejudices: Shelley J. Correll, Stephen Benard, and In Paik, "Getting a Job: Is There a Motherhood Penalty?" American Journal of Sociology 112, no. 5 (March 2007): 1297–338, https://doi.org/10.1086/511799.

101 earnings increase 6 percent: Michelle J. Budig, "The Fatherhood Bonus and the Motherhood Penalty: Parenthood and the Gender Gap in Pay," Third Way, September 2, 2014, www.thirdway.org/report/the-fatherhood-bonus-and-the-motherhood-penalty-parenthood-and-the-gender-gap-in-pay.

101 more likely to divorce: "Divorce Can Mean a Trip Down the Economic Ladder for Women," NBC News, March 7, 2015, www.nbcnews.com/feature/in-plain-sight/divorce-can-mean-trip-down-economic-ladder-women-n311101.

101 A 2014 survey: Press Association, "40% of Managers Avoid Hiring Younger Women to Get Around Maternity Leave," The Guardian, August 11, 2014, https://www.theguardian.com/money/2014/aug/12/managers-avoid-hiring-younger-women-maternity-leave.

102 labor, and neonatal care: Alicia Adamczyk, "Senate Health Care Bill: How It Impacts Women," Time, June 23, 2017, http://time.com/money/4829295/senate-health-care-bill-bcra-coverage-women.

102 50 percent of these expenses: The Cost of Having a Baby in the United States:

Truven Health Analytics Marketscan Study (Ann Arbor, MI: Truven Health Analytics, January 2013), http://transform.childbirthconnection.org/wp-content/uploads/2013/01/Cost-of-Having-a-Baby1.pdf; Martha Cook Carter et al., "2020 Vision for a High-Quality, High-Value Maternity Care System," *Women's Health Issues* 20, no. 1, supp. (January/February 2010): S7–S17, https://doi.org/10.1016/j.whi.2009.11.006.

102 decisions a woman can make: Ann Crittenden, *The Price of Motherhood: Why the Most Important Job in the World Is Still the Least Valued*, 10th Anniversary ed. (London: Picador, 2010).

102 pregnancy-related complication: Anna Maria Barryjester, "Maternal Health By the Numbers: 20 from '20/20,'" *ABC News*, December 17, 2011, http://abcnews.go.com/Health/maternal-health-numbers/story?id=15172525.

102 sub-Saharan Africa and South Asia: "Maternal Mortality: Fact Sheet," World Health Organization, November 2016, http://www.who.int/news-room/fact-sheets/detail/maternal-mortality.

103 than a white woman is: Nina Martin and Renee Montagne, "Nothing Protects Black Women from Dying in Pregnancy and Childbirth," *ProPublica*, December 7, 2017, www.propublica.org/article/nothing-protects-black-women-from-dying-in-pregnancy-and-childbirth.

103 watching YouTube videos: Selena Simmons-Duffin, "Providence Hospital Closed Its Maternity Ward; Many Women Still Don't Know," WAMU, November 1, 2017, https://wamu.org/story/17/11/01/providence-hospital-closed-maternity-ward-many-women-still-dont-know.

103 identifiable cultural background: Eugene R. Declercq et al., *Listening to Mothers III: Pregnancy and Birth—Report of the Third National U.S. Survey of Women's Childbearing Experiences* (New York: Childbirth Connection, May 2013), http://transform.childbirthconnection.org/wp-content/uploads/2013/06/LTM-III_Pregnancy-and-Birth.pdf.

103 face the highest risks: Nina Martin and Renee Montaigne, "The Last Person You'd Expect to Die in Childbirth," *ProPublica* and National Public Radio, May 12, 2017, www.propublica.org/article/die-in-childbirth-maternal-death-rate-health-care-system.

104 expressly prohibit the practice: Sarah Y. Thomas and Jennifer L. Lanterman, "A National Analysis of Shackling Laws and Policies as They Relate to Pregnant Incarcerated Women," *Feminist Criminology*, November 3, 2017, https://doi.org/10.1177/1557085117737617.

104 "'when I have a beautiful baby?'": Serena Williams, "What My Life-Threatening Experience Taught Me About Giving Birth," CNN, February 20, 2018, www.cnn.com/2018/02/20/opinions/protect-mother-pregnancy-williams-opinion/index.html.

104 "A woman can bleed to death": Korin Miller, "Christy Turlington Could Have Bled to Death After Giving Birth—What Moms-to-Be Need to Know," *Self*, April 18, 2016, https://www.self.com/story/christy-turlington-could-have-bled-to-death-after-giving-birth-what-moms-to-be-need-to-know.

105 "of respect for women": Meghan A. Bohren et al., "The Mistreatment of Women During Childbirth in Health Facilities Globally: A Mixed-Methods Systematic

Review," *PLOS Medicine* 12, no. 6 (June 2015): e1001847, https://doi.org/10.1371/journal.pmed.1001847.

107 going through childbirth: Julia Kaye et al., "Health Care Denied: Patients and Physicians Speak Out About Catholic Hospitals and the Threat to Women's Health and Lives," American Civil Liberties Union and *MergerWatch*, May 2016, https://www.aclu.org/report/report-health-care-denied.

107 deeply hostile to women: *Ethical and Religious Directives for Catholic Health Care Services*, 5th ed. (Washington, DC: US Conference of Catholic Bishops, November 17, 2009), www.usccb.org/issues-and-action/human-life-and-dignity/health-care/upload/Ethical-Religious-Directives-Catholic-Health-Care-Services-fifth-edition-2009.pdf.

107 McBride was excommunicated: Nicholas Kristof, "Sister Margaret's Choice," *New York Times*, May 26, 2010, www.nytimes.com/2010/05/27/opinion/27kristof.html; "Nun Excommunicated for Allowing Abortion," *All Things Considered*, May 19, 2010, https://www.npr.org/templates/story/story.php?storyId=126985072.

108 her death by septicemia: Kitty Holland, "Woman 'Denied a Termination' Dies in Hospital," *Irish Times*, November 14, 2012, https://www.irishtimes.com/news/woman-denied-a-termination-dies-in-hospital-1.551412.

108 "invites" a baby in: Jordan Smith, "Oklahoma Lawmakers Want Men to Approve All Abortions," *The Intercept*, February 13, 2017, https://theintercept.com/2017/02/13/oklahoma-lawmakers-want-men-to-approve-all-abortions.

108 He was convinced: David G. Savage, "Trump Official Sought to Block Abortion for a 17-Year-Old Rape Victim," *Los Angeles Times*, December 21, 2017, http://www.latimes.com/politics/la-na-pol-abortion-trump-migrant-20171221-story.html.

109 progesterone against her will: Carter Sherman, "Undocumented Teen Wanting an Abortion Had Been Raped," *Vice News*, December 21, 2017, https://news.vice.com/en_us/article/bjynwv/undocumented-teen-wanting-an-abortion-had-been-raped; Carter Sherman, "Exclusive: Trump Official Discussed 'Reversing' Abortion for Undocumented Teen," *Vice News*, January 31, 2018, https://news.vice.com/en_us/article/yw5a5g/exclusive-trump-officials-discussed-reversing-abortion-for-undocumented-teen.

109 "thought they could": Robin Marty (@robinmarty), Twitter post, January 31, 2018, 11:27 a.m., https://twitter.com/robinmarty/status/958783713122271233.

109 "even thought about": Licentiathe8th, "Rachel Maddow—Anti-Abortion Ohio Legislator Never Thought About Women," YouTube, September 7, 2012, www.youtube.com/watch?v=xBKieGz5QiMt.

109 and cows on his farm: Lauren Barbato, "At 11th Hour, Georgia Passes 'Women as Livestock' Bill," Ms. Magazine Blog, April 1, 2012, http://msmagazine.com/blog/2012/03/31/at-11th-hour-georgia-passes-women-as-livestock-bill; Adam Peck, "Georgia Republican Compares Women to Cows and Pigs," *ThinkProgress*, March 12, 2012, https://thinkprogress.org/georgia-republican-compares-women-to-cows-pigs-and-chickens-283a4a182964/.

109 "shut that whole thing down": Chris Gentilviso, "Todd Akin on Abortion: 'Legitimate Rape' Victims Have 'Ways to Try to Shut That Whole Thing Down,'" *Huffington Post*, August 19, 2012, www.huffingtonpost.com/2012/08/19/todd-akin-abortion-legitimate-rape_n_1807381.html.

110 vaginas aren't actually connected: Katie McDonough, "Lawmaker Who Thinks the Stomach and Vagina Are Connected: Question Was About 'Safety of the Woman,'" *Salon*, February 24, 2015, www.salon.com/2015/02/24/lawmaker_who_ thinks_the_stomach_and_vagina_are_connected_question_was_about_safety_ of_the_woman.

110 "rights with social justice": Loretta Ross and Rickie Solinger, *Reproductive Justice: An Introduction* (Berkeley, CA: University of California Press, 2017).

110 "healthy, and supportive environments": Dorothy Roberts, "Reproductive Justice, Not Just Rights," *Dissent*, Fall 2015, www.dissentmagazine.org/article/reproductive -justice-not-just-rights.

111 selfish baby killers: "Induced Abortion in the United States Fact Sheet," Gutt-macher Institute, January 2018, https://www.guttmacher.org/fact-sheet/induced -abortion-united-states.

111 didn't regret their decision: Corinne H. Rocca et al., "Decision Rightness and Emo-tional Responses to Abortion in the United States: A Longitudinal Study," *PLOS ONE* 10, no. 7 (2015): e0128832, https://doi.org/10.1371/journal.pone.0128832.

112 guilt, sadness, or anger: In 2015 a group of activists launched #ShoutYourAbortion, a social media campaign to destigmatize abortion by encouraging women to share their abortion experiences without "sadness, shame, or regret." Within weeks, tens of thousands of women around the world had used the hashtag to publish their own accounts. Vauhini Vara, "Can #ShoutYourAbortion Turn Hashtag Activism into a Movement?" *New Yorker*, November 10, 2015, www.newyorker.com/news/ news-desk/can-shoutyourabortion-turn-hashtag-activism-into-a-movement.

112 grief that persist for decades: David A. Grimes, "Abortion Denied: Consequences for Mother and Child," *Huffington Post*, April 2, 2015, www.huffingtonpost.com/ david-a-grimes/abortion-denied-consequences-for-mother-and-child_b_6926988 .html.

112 a pregnancy is respected: Diana Greene Foster et al., "Socioeconomic Outcomes of Women Who Receive and Women Who Are Denied Wanted Abortions in the United States," *American Journal of Public Health* 108, no. 3 (March 2018): 407–13, https://doi.org/10.2105/AJPH.2017.304247.

112 neglect and poor parenting: *Unwanted Pregnancy: Forced Continuation of Preg-nancy and Effects on Mental Health: Position Paper* (Colombia: Global Doctors for Choice Network, December 2011), http://globaldoctorsforchoice.org/wp-content/ uploads/Unwanted-Pregnancy-Forced-Continuation-of-Pregnancy-and-Effects -on-Mental-Health-v2.pdf.

112 bullying other children: Hans Villarica, "Study of the Day: Mother-Toddler Blow-ups Create Angry Little Bullies," *The Atlantic*, October 26, 2011, www.theatlantic .com/health/archive/2011/10/study-of-the-day-mother-toddler-blowups-create -angry-little-bullies/247171.

112 women themselves do: Rachel Thompson, "Doctor No: The Women in Their 20s Being Refused Sterilisations," *Mashable*, May 25, 2016, http://mashable .com/2016/05/25/female-sterilisation-uk.

112 ugly eugenics history: Bill Chappell, "California's Prison Sterilizations Report-edly Echo Eugenics Era," *National Public Radio*, July 9, 2013, https://www.npr

.org/sections/thetwo-way/2013/07/09/200444613/californias-prison-sterilizations
-reportedly-echoes-eugenics-era.

113 children than ever before: Olivia Petter, "Childless Women Are on the Rise," *The Independent*, August 8, 2017, https://www.independent.co.uk/life-style/childless -women-on-rise-more-than-ever-before-fertility-crisis-menopause-career-study -reveals-a7882496.html.

113 "of oppression and subordination": Orna Donath, "Regretting Motherhood: A Sociopolitical Analysis," *Signs* 40, no. 2 (Winter 2015): 343–67, www.academia .edu/9820246/Regretting_Motherhood_A_Sociopolitical_Analysis.

113 anger, compared to American women: In this fascinating 1988 cross-cultural study, more than 60 percent of American women respondents said that they pre- ferred to hide their anger compared to none of their German woman peers. Shula Sommers and Corinne Kosmitzki, "Emotion and Social Context: An American– German Comparison," *British Journal of Social Psychology* 27, no. 1 (March 1988): https://doi.org/10.1111/j.2044-8309.1988.tb00803.x.

114 "regretters" as child abusers: Jedidajah Otte, "Love and Regret: Mothers Who Wish They'd Never Had Children," *The Guardian* (US), May 9, 2016, www .theguardian.com/lifeandstyle/2016/may/09/love-regret-mothers-wish-never-had -children-motherhood.

114 costs of this work can be immense: Barbara Ehrenreich and Arlie Russell Hochs- child, *Global Woman: Nannies, Maids, and Sex Workers in the New Economy* (New York: Holt Paperbacks, 2004).

115 social silence around loss: Arthur L. Greil, Kathleen Slauson-Blevins, and Julia McQuillan, "The Experience of Infertility: A Review of Recent Literature," *Soci- ology of Health & Illness* 32, no. 1 (January 2010): 140–62, https://doi.org/10.1111/ j.1467-9566.2009.01213.x.

115 higher rates of depression: John A. Barry et al., "Testosterone and Mood Dys- function in Women with Polycystic Ovarian Syndrome Compared to Subfertile Controls," *Journal of Psychosomatic Obstetrics and Gynaecology* 21, no. 2 (June 2011): 104–11, https://doi.org/10.3109/0167482X.2011.568129.

115 stress that women feel: S. Fassino et al., "Anxiety, Depression and Anger Sup- pression in Infertile Couples: A Controlled Study," *Human Reproduction* 17, no. 11 (November 1, 2002): 2986–94, https://doi.org/10.1093/humrep/17.11.2986.

117 "birth but have no baby": Jen Gunter, "When a Grieving Mother Talks, Listen," *New York Times*, December 21, 2017, www.nytimes.com/2017/12/21/style/perinatal -death-stillbirth-childbirth.html.

117 mood and anxiety disorders: Kate Kripke, "13 Things You Should Know About Grief After Miscarriage or Baby Loss," *Postpartum Progress*, February 19, 2014, http://www.postpartumprogress.com/13-things-you-should-know-about-grief-after -miscarriage-or-baby-loss.

CHAPTER 6: SMILE, BABY

123 alters the course of their day: "The Prevalence of Street Harassment Statis- tics," Stop Street Harassment, http://www.stopstreetharassment.org/resources/ statistics/statistics-academic-studies/; Holly Kearl, *Unsafe and Harassed in Public*

Spaces: A National Street Harassment Report (Reston, VA: Stop Street Harassment, Spring 2014), www.stopstreetharassment.org/wp-content/uploads/2012/08/National-Street-Harassment-Report-November-29-20151.pdf.

124 advocacy group Hollaback!: "Cornell International Survey on Street Harassment," Hollaback!, May 2015, www.ihollaback.org/cornell-international-survey-on-street-harassment.

124 women using wheelchairs. Mandy Van Deven, "Takin," *Bitch Media*, May 2, 2011, https://www.bitchmedia.org/post/takin%E2%80%99-it-to-the-streets-so-take-it-already; Wendy Lu, "I'm Disabled and I Get Sexually Harassed—Here's Why That Matters," *Teen Vogue*, November 1, 2017, https://www.teenvogue.com/story/disability-and-sexual-harassment.

124 "safe not more fully human": "Disabled Women & Sexual Objectification (or Lack Thereof)," Crippled Scholar blog, September 2016, https://crippledscholar.com/tag/street-harassment/.

125 ninety-five thousand LGBTQ people: "Half of LGBT Members in the EU Avoid Public Places Because of Harassment," Stop Street Harassment, May 17, 2013, www.stopstreetharassment.org/2013/05/eustudy.

125 rates have been documented: Holly Kearl, *Stop Global Street Harassment: Growing Activism Around the World* (Westport, CT: Praeger, 2015).

125 "home in the morning": Heather R. Hlavka, "Normalizing Sexual Violence Young Women Account for Harassment and Abuse," *Gender and Society* 28, no. 3 (June 2014): 337–58, https://doi.org/10.1177/0891243214526468.

125 she rebuffed him: Hawley G. Fogg-Davis, "Theorizing Black Lesbians Within Black Feminism: A Critique of Same-Race Street Harassment," *Politics & Gender* 2, no. 1 (March 2006): 57–76, https://doi.org/10.1017/S1743923X06060028; Ronald Smothers, "Man Charged with Bias Crime for Girl's Killing in Newark," *New York Times*, November 25, 2003, https://www.nytimes.com/2003/11/25/nyregion/man-charged-with-bias-crime-for-girl-s-killing-in-newark.html; Delia Paunescu, "Transgender Woman's Death May Have Happened After Come-on Gone Wrong," *New York Daily Intelligencer*, August 24, 2013, http://nymag.com/daily/intelligencer/2013/08/islan-nettles-assaulted-after-come-on-gone-wrong.html.

125 "correctively" raped and killed: Clare Carter, "The Brutality of 'Corrective Rape,'" *New York Times*, July 25, 2013, www.nytimes.com/interactive/2013/07/26/opinion/26corrective-rape.html.

127 results were much stronger: Haley Miles-McLean et al., "'Stop Looking at Me!' Interpersonal Sexual Objectification as a Source of Insidious Trauma," *Psychology of Women Quarterly* 39, no. 3 (September 2014): 287–304, https://doi.org/10.1177/0361684314561018.

128 when she rebuffed him: "Adrian Mendez Kidnapped a 14-Year-Old Girl, Left Her for Dead," *Ocala Post*, December 7, 2016, www.ocalapost.com/adrian-mendez-kidnapped-14-year-old-girl.

129 "your pain is not a priority": Shanita Hubbard, "Russell Simmons, R. Kelly, and Why Black Women Can't Say #MeToo," *New York Times*, December 15, 2017, https://mobile.nytimes.com/2017/12/15/opinion/russell-simmons-black-women-metoo.html?smid=tw-share&_r=0&referer=https://t.co/AphKOJ2A3J?amp=1.

129 death on the sidewalk: Damon Young, "Her Name Was Janese Talton-Jackson and She Was Killed Because She Said No," *The Root*, January 25, 2016, www.theroot .com/her-name-was-janese-talton-jackson-and-she-was-killed-b-1790854021.

129 women real estate agents: "Florida on Alert After Man Harasses Agents," *Realtor Mag*, January 25, 2016, http://realtormag.realtor.org/daily-news/2016/01/25/florida -alert-after-man-harasses-agents.

130 people as ridiculous: Laura Tarzia et al., "Sexual Violence Associated with Poor Mental Health in Women Attending Australian General Practices," *Australian and New Zealand Journal of Public Health* 41, no. 5 (October 2017): 518–23, https:// doi.org/10.1111/1753-6405.12685.

130 they might *additionally* be raped: Laurel B. Watson et al., "Understanding the Relationships Among White and African American Women's Sexual Objecti-fication Experiences, Physical Safety Anxiety, and Psychological Distress," *Sex Roles* 72, no. 3–4 (2015): 91–104, doi:10.1007/s11199-014-0444-y.

132 marital rape is not illegal: "The Global Rape Epidemic: How Laws Around the World Are Failing to Protect Girls and Women," Equality Now, March 2017, https://www.equalitynow.org/campaigns/rape-laws-report.

132 one in seventy-seven: "Domestic Violence Cases," Bureau of Justice Statistics, March 17, 2018, https://www.bjs.gov/index.cfm?ty=tp&tid=235.

133 know their assailants: "Perpetrators of Sexual Violence: Statistics," Rape, Abuse & Incest National Network, accessed January 30, 2018, https://www.rainn.org/ statistics/perpetrators-sexual-violence.

133 suffering the highest rates: Christopher Krebs et al., *Campus Climate Survey Vali-dation Study: Final Technical Report* (Washington, DC: Bureau of Justice Statistics, January 2016), www.bjs.gov/content/pub/pdf/ccsvsftr.pdf.

133 outside of their own ethnic group: Timothy Williams, "For Native American Women, Scourge of Rape, Rare Justice," *New York Times*, May 22, 2012, www.ny times.com/2012/05/23/us/native-americans-struggle-with-high-rate-of-rape.html ?pagewanted=all.

133 before they turn eighteen: "Domestic Violence in Communities of Color," Women of Color Network, June 2016, www.doj.state.or.us/victims/pdf/women_of_color_ network_facts_sexual_violence_2006.pdf.

133 "the juvenile justice system": Malika Saada Saar et al., *The Sexual Abuse to Prison Pipeline: The Girls' Story* (Washington, DC: Georgetown Law Center on Poverty and Inequality, 2015), https://rights4girls.org/wp-content/uploads/ r4g/2015/02/2015_COP_sexual-abuse_layout_web-1.pdf.

133 than are all women in the United States: Jill Filipovic, "Is the US the Only Coun-try Where More Men Are Raped Than Women?" *The Guardian* (US), February 21, 2012, www.theguardian.com/commentisfree/cifamerica/2012/feb/21/us-more -men-raped-than-women; Christopher Glazek, "Raise the Crime Rate," *N+1*, no. 13 (Winter 2012): https://nplusonemag.com/issue-13/politics/raise-the-crime-rate/.

134 are ever prosecuted and imprisoned: Shauna Prewitt, "Raped, Pregnant and Ordeal Not Over," CNN, August 23, 2012, http://edition.cnn.com/2012/08/22/opinion/ prewitt-rapist-visitation-rights.

134 children born of their raping: Tribune Media Wire, "Michigan Man Accused of

Raping 12-Year-Old Girl Granted Joint Custody of Their Child, Victim's Attorney Says," KTLA, October 9, 2017, http://ktla.com/2017/10/09/man-accused-of-raping -12-year-old-girl-given-joint-custody-of-their-child-attorney-says.

134 relative citizenship rights: Estelle B. Freedman, *Redefining Rape: Sexual Violence in the Era of Suffrage and Segregation* (Cambridge, MA: Harvard University Press, 2013).

134 rape nor tolerant of it: Peggy Sanday, *Fraternity Gang Rape: Sex, Brotherhood, and Privilege on Campus* (New York: New York University Press, 1990).

136 Jyoti Singh Pandey was tortured: Ellen Barry, "In Rare Move, Death Sentence in Delhi Gang Rape Case Is Upheld," *New York Times*, May 5, 2017, https://www .nytimes.com/2017/05/05/world/asia/death-sentence-delhi-gang-rape.html.

136 it drove through Rio de Janeiro: "Rio de Janeiro Bus Rape: Shock over Latest Brazil Attack," BBC News, May 5, 2013, www.bbc.com/news/world-latin-america -22421512.

136 during a 10 a.m. commute: Dan Morse, " 'Don't Do This to Me': Woman Testifies She Was Raped at Knifepoint on Moving Metro Train," *Washington Post*, January 12, 2018, https://www.washingtonpost.com/local/public-safety/dont-do-this-to -me-woman-testifies-she-was-raped-at-knifepoint-on-moving-metro-train/2018 /01/12/3121a774-f724-11e7-b34a-b85626af34ef_story.html?utm_term=.90c25b 9d7e4b.

136 abuse on public transportation: Jill Langlois, "Perspective: An Epidemic of Sexual Assault on São Paulo Public Transit," A Beautiful Perspective blog, September 6, 2017, http://abeautifulperspective.com/2017/08/31/perspective-epidemic-sexual -assault-sao-paulo-public-transit.

137 this writing, he remains in jail: Sandra Laville, "John Worboys Back in Wakefield Prison as Victims Fight His Release," *The Guardian* (UK), February 4, 2018, www .theguardian.com/uk-news/2018/feb/04/john-worboys-wakefield-prison-london.

138 marijuana, "penetrated her vagina": Julia Dahl, "Lawsuit: Cops Subjected Woman to 11-Minute Body Cavity Search During Traffic Stop," CBS News, August 18, 2017, www.cbsnews.com/news/lawsuit-cops-subjected-woman-to-11-minute-body -cavity-search-during-traffic-stop; Tom Dart, "Dashcam Video Shows Police Sexually Assaulted Texas Woman, Lawyer Says," *The Guardian*, August 16, 2017, https://www.theguardian.com/us-news/2017/aug/16/charnesia-corley-houston -texas-police-dashcam-video.

138 stop to use clean gloves: Kevin Krause, "Irving Women Sue State Troopers in Federal Court, Alleging Roadside Body Cavity Searches," *Dallas News*, December 2012, https://www.dallasnews.com/news/irving/2012/12/18/irving-women-sue -state-troopers-in-federal-court-alleging-roadside-body-cavity-searches.

139 identified vulnerable targets: Jessica Lussenhop, "Daniel Holtzclaw Trial: Standing with 'Imperfect' Accusers," BBC News, November 13, 2015, www.bbc.com/ news/magazine-34791191.

139 facilities across the country: Claire Martin, "Detroit Businesswomen Team Up to Get Rape Kits Tested," *New York Times*, November 7, 2015, www.nytimes .com/2015/11/08/business/detroit-businesswomen-team-up-to-get-rape-kits-tested .html.

139 intimidate women into silence: Michael Safi, "Indian Women Still Unprotected Five Years After Gang-Rape That Rocked Nation," *The Guardian* (US), November 8, 2017, www.theguardian.com/world/2017/nov/08/indian-women-still-unprotected -five-years-after-gang-rape-that-rocked-nation.

139 four times the national average: "Police Family Violence Fact Sheet," National Center for Women and Policing, accessed January 30, 2018, http://womenandpolicing .com/violencefs.asp.

140 physical assaults annually: "Violence Prevention," Centers for Disease Control and Prevention, accessed January 30, 2018, www.cdc.gov/ViolencePrevention/ index.html; M.C. Black et al., *The National Intimate Partner and Sexual Violence Survey (NISVS): 2010 Summary Report.* (Atlanta, GA: National Center for Injury Prevention and Control, Centers for Disease Control and Prevention, 2010), https://www.cdc.gov/violenceprevention/pdf/nisvs_executive_summary-a.pdf.

140 accidents, and muggings combined: Philip W. Cook, *Abused Men: The Hidden Side of Domestic Violence*, 2nd ed. (Westport, CT: Praeger, 2009), "Appendix."

140 just under three (2.5) women a day: "Disarming Domestic Abusers," Coalition to Stop Gun Violence, accessed January 30, 2018, https://www.csgv.org/issues/ disarming-domestic-violence.

140 murdered by intimate partners: Olga Khazan, "Nearly Half of All Murdered Women Are Killed by Romantic Partners," *The Atlantic*, July 20, 2017, www.theatlantic.com /health/archive/2017/07/homicides-women/534306.

140 another developed country: "Guns and Domestic Violence Fact Sheet," Everytown for Gun Safety, https://everytownresearch.org/guns-domestic-violence/; Katie Sanders, "Americans Are 20 Times as Likely to Die from Gun Violence," *Politifact*, January 17, 2014, http://www.politifact.com/punditfact/statements/2014/ jan/17/lisa-bloom/americans-are-20-times-likely-die-gun-violence-cit/.

140 have experienced violence: André B. Rosay, *Violence Against American Indian and Alaska Native Women and Men: 2010 Findings from the National Intimate Partner and Sexual Violence Survey* (Washington, DC: National Institute of Justice, May 2016), www.ncjrs.gov/pdffiles1/nij/249736.pdf.

140 spouse, or domestic partner: Claudia García-Moreno et al., *Global and Regional Estimates of Violence Against Women: Prevalence and Health Effects of Intimate Partner Violence and Nonpartner Sexual Violence* (Geneva: World Health Organization Department of Reproductive Health and Research, 2013), http://apps.who.int/iris/ bitstream/10665/85239/1/9789241564625_eng.pdf; "Domestic Violence Affects over 100,000 Women in Germany," *DW*, November 22, 2016, www.dw.com/en /domestic-violence-affects-over-100000-women-in-germany/a-36482282.

In 2015, according to the first statistics ever released about intimate partner crimes in Germany, 82 percent of the 127,457 people murdered, raped, sexually assaulted, stalked, or otherwise targeted with threats and violence by people they were involved with were women. More than 65,000 suffered injuries, and 11,400 were critically hurt. In India, 22 women are killed each day in dowry-related murders, which doesn't include those related to bride burning, suspicious suicides, alleged accidental deaths, and "honor" killings. In South Africa, a woman is killed every six hours by an intimate partner. In Brazil, a woman is assaulted every fifteen seconds.

140 domestic violence conviction: *Washington's Offender Accountability Act: Department of Corrections' Static Risk Instrument* (Olympia, WA: Washington State Institute for Public Policy, March 2007), www.wsipp.wa.gov/ReportFile/977/ Wsipp_Washingtons-Offender-Accountability-Act-Department-of-Corrections -Static-Risk-Instrument_Full-Report-Updated-October-2008.pdf; Laura L. Hayes, "Can We Have Compassion for the Angry?" *Slate*, June 18, 2016, http://www .slate.com/articles/health_and_science/medical_examiner/2016/06/the_biggest_ predictor_of_future_violence_is_past_violence_but_mindfulness.html.

140 histories of domestic violence: Pamela Shifman and Salamishah Tillet, "To Stop Violence, Start at Home," *New York Times*, February 3, 2015, https://www .nytimes.com/2015/02/03/opinion/to-stop-violence-start-at-home.html; Melissa Jeltsen, "We're Missing the Big Picture on Mass Shootings," *Huffington Post*, January 11, 2017, www.huffingtonpost.com/entry/mass-shootings-domestic-violence -women_55d3806ce4b07addcb44542a; Soraya Chemaly, "America's Mass Shooting Problem Is a Domestic Violence Problem," *Village Voice*, November 8, 2017, www.villagevoice.com/2017/11/08/americas-mass-shooting-problem-is-a-domestic -violence-problem.

140 chosen to end their marriages: Melissa Jeltsen, "What the 2 Deadliest Mass Shootings This Year Have in Common," *Huffington Post*, September 13, 2017, www.huffing- tonpost.com/entry/plano-texas-mass-shooting_us_59b7e02ce4b09be416581d2b.s -mass-shooting_us_59b7e02ce4b09be416581d2b.

141 female genital mutilation: "Female Genital Mutilation," World Health Organiza- tion, accessed January 30, 2018, www.who.int/mediacentre/factsheets/fs241/en.

142 "women recorded abroad": Martin Selsoe Sorensen, "Kim Wall Was Stabbed Af- ter Boarding Submarine, Danish Prosecutor Says," *New York Times*, December 22, 2017, https://nytimes.com/2017/10/04/world/europe/kim-wall-peter-madsen -submarine.html.

142 "particularly dangerous nature": "Kim Wall Death: Danish Inventor Madsen Admits Dismembering Journalist," BBC News, October 30, 2017, www.bbc.com/ news/world-europe-41804590.

143 the course of ten years: Jerry Markon, Kimberly Kindy, and Manuel Roig-Franzia, "Ariel Castro, Under Arrest in Cleveland Kidnapping, Had Contradictory Sides," *Washington Post*, May 8, 2013, www.washingtonpost.com/politics/ariel-castro-under -arrest-in-cleveland-kidnapping-had-contradictory-sides/2013/05/08/ecdf6d22-b802 -11e2-92f3-f291801936b8_story.html?utm_term=.2017b962655e.

143 according to some sources: Candace Goforth Desantis et al., "Ariel Castro Is Lone Brother to Be Charged in Kidnapping, Rape of Three Women in His Cleveland Hell House," *Daily News*, May 9, 2013, http://www.nydailynews.com/news/crime/ castro-brothers-spend-night-jail-article-1.1338131.

143 his "house of horrors": "Anthony Sowell's Home of Horror," CBS News, April 4, 2016, www.cbsnews.com/pictures/anthony-sowells-home-of-horror; "'The Cleve- land Strangler': The Story of a Brutal Serial Killer and His Forgotten Victims,"

Vice News, November 3, 2015, https://www.vice.com/en_us/article/5gjkq8/cleveland -strangler-part-100.

143 smelled like rotting bodies: John Kuntz, "Anthony Sowell Home 'Smelled Like a Dead Body' for Years; How Did Cops Miss Victims?" *Plain Dealer*, November 3, 2009, https://www.cbsnews.com/news/anthony-sowell-home-smelled-like-a-dead -body-for-years-how-did-cops-miss-victims/.

144 masks the reality: Steve Crabtree and Faith Nsubuga, "In U.S., 37% Do Not Feel Safe Walking at Night Near Home," Gallup, November 24, 2014, http://news .gallup.com/poll/179558/not-feel-safe-walking-night-near-home.aspx.

144 violence on the ground: Evan Soltas and Seth Stephens-Davidowitz, "The Rise of Hate Speech," *New York Times*, December 12, 2015, www.nytimes.com/2015/12/13/ opinion/sunday/the-rise-of-hate-search.html.

145 and a woman, is significant: A year and a half after the London analysis was issued, a group of Muslim teenagers in Virginia was accosted by a man in a car. The teens ran into their mosque for refuge. After one of the girls, seventeen-year-old Nabra Hassanen, didn't make it back, the police began a search. Hassanen's picture, shared in the media, showed an alert young woman looking directly into the camera, her smiling eyes framed by a halo of colorful Snapchat flowers. Within hours, her body, bludgeoned with a bat by a twenty-two-year-old man later arrested by the police, was found. The police cited road rage as the cause and declined to consider what happened a hate crime. It was later reported that she had also been raped. She was killed two weeks after a man in an Illinois restaurant was filmed screaming, "Fucking goddamn, camel-jacking, motherfucking cunts!" at another group of Muslim girls, and a month after two men were stabbed and killed on a train in Portland, Oregon, while protecting two women, one wearing a hijab, from a man on an anti-Islamic rant. Stephanie Ramirez, "Man Faces Capital Rape, Murder Charges in Death of Muslim Teen Nabra Hassanen," *USA Today*, October 17, 2017, www.usatoday.com/story/news/nation-now/2017/10/17/ murder-rape-charge-muslim-teen-death/771064001.

145 "the brutal trifecta": Mona Eltahawy, "Don't Tell Me Nabra Hassanen's Murder Wasn't a Hate Crime," *The Cut*, June 19, 2017, www.thecut.com/2017/06/nabra -hassanen-murder-hate-crime-mona-eltahawy.html.

145 "A simple double standard is at work here": Catherine MacKinnon, *Are Women Human?: And Other International Dialogues* (New York: Belknap Press, 2007).

146 In 2000, UCLA professor: Nancy K. Dess, "Tend and Befriend," *Psychology Today*, September 1, 2000, https://www.psychologytoday.com/us/articles/200009/tend -and-befriend.

147 are inherent in women: Daniel J. Canary and Tara M. Emmers-Sommer, *Sex and Gender Differences in Personal Relationships* (New York: Guilford Press, 1998).

147 is a path to survival: Esther Inglis-Arkell, "Why Do We Smile and Laugh When We're Terrified?" *io9*, October 7, 2013, https://io9.gizmodo.com/why-do-we-smile -and-laugh-when-were-terrified-1441046376.

147 be a "good" woman: Rachel Kimerling, Paige Ouimette, and Jessica Wolfe, *Gender and PTSD* (New York: Gilford Press, 2002).

147 more egalitarian unions: Janice M. Thompson, Valerie E. Whiffen, and Jennifer A. Aube, "Does Self-Silencing Link Relationships and Depressive Symptoms?" *Journal of Social and Personal Relationships* 18, no. 4 (August 2001): 503–16, http://journals.sagepub.com/doi/pdf/10.1177/0265407501184004.

148 "problem with your anger": Lundy Bancroft, *Why Does He Do That? Inside the Minds of Angry and Controlling Men* (New York: Berkeley Books, 2003).

148 engage in emotional abuse: It is estimated that 68 percent of women in situations of intimate violence are almost strangled to death by their partners at least once. Of these women, 70 percent think they will die. A woman who is killed by a man she knows has, on average, been strangled seven times prior to her death. Only thirty-eight US states have laws that recognize suffocation and strangulation as attempts to kill a person.

148 be abusers or abused: "10 Startling Statistics About Children of Domestic Violence," Childhood Domestic Violence Association, February 21, 2016, https://cdv.org/2014/02/10-startling-domestic-violence-statistics-for-children.

148 domestic violence for victims: "Depression," *Psychology Today*, accessed January 30, 2018, https://www.psychologytoday.com/basics/depression.

149 women's equity and equality: Kweilin Ellingrud et al., *The Power of Parity: Advancing Women's Equality in the United States* (New York: McKinsey Global Institute, April 2016), www.mckinsey.com/~/media/McKinsey/Global%20Themes/Employment%20and%20Growth/The%20power%20of%20parity%20Advancing%20womens%20equality%20in%20the%20United%20States/MGI-Power-of-Parity-in-US-Full-report-April-2016.ashx.

149 Among those with children: US Department of Health and Human Services, "Domestic Violence and Homelessness: Statistics" (2016), https://www.acf.hhs.gov/fysb/resource/dv-homelessness-stats-2016.

149 legal help, and transportation: *Domestic Violence Counts: 11th Annual Census Report*, (National Network to End Domestic Violence, 2017), https://nnedv.org/latest_update/11th-annual-census/.

150 to twenty years in prison: "Florida Woman Sentenced to 20 Years in Controversial Warning Shot Case," CNN, May 11, 2012, http://edition.cnn.com/2012/05/11/justice/florida-stand-ground-sentencing.

150 from a violent partner: Alex Campbell, "Battered, Bereaved, and Behind Bars," *BuzzFeed*, October 2, 2014, www.buzzfeed.com/alexcampbell/how-the-law-turns-battered-women-into-criminals?utm_term=.uvzKQpyn4#.avW1yBljM.

150 returned home in early 2018: Mariame Kaba and Colby Lenz, "Bresha Meadows Returns Home After Collective Organizing Efforts," *Teen Vogue*, April 4, 2018, www.teenvogue.com/story/bresha-meadows-returns-home-after-collective-organizing-efforts; Whitney Kimball and Bresha Meadows, "Teen Domestic Abuse Victim Prosecuted for Her Father's Death, Will Be Freed on Sunday," *Jezebel*, February 3, 2018, https://jezebel.com/bresha-meadows-teen-domestic-abuse-victim-prosecuted-f-1822693959.

150 men who kill women: Megan Hamilton, "Sentences Are Lighter for Men Who Murder Female Partners: Study," *Digital Journal*, November 23, 2015, http://www

.digitaljournal.com/news/crime/sentences-are-lighter-for-men-who-murder-female
-partners-study/article/450197; "Survivors of Abuse and Incarceration," Correctional
Association of New York, accessed January 30, 2018, www.correctionalassociation
.org/issue/domestic-violence; Anita Wadhwani, "Teen Killer's Story Inspires Push to
Change Tennessee Law," *The Tennessean*, July 5, 2016, www.tennessean.com/story/
news/crime/2016/06/30/ruling-offers-hope-teens-sentenced-life-but-not-tennessee/
86247118.

CHAPTER 7: THE DRIP, DRIP, DRIP

154 cleaning staff and administrators: Joan C. Williams, Katherine W. Phillips, and
Erika V. Hall, *Double Jeopardy? Gender Bias Against Women of Color in Science*
(San Francisco: WorkLifeLaw, UC Hastings College of the Law, 2014), www
.uchastings.edu/news/articles/2015/01/double-jeopardy-report.pdf.

154 as helpers to the men: Heather Sarsons, "Gender Differences in Recognition for
Group Work" (working paper, Harvard University, Cambridge, MA, November
4, 2017), https://scholar.harvard.edu/files/sarsons/files/full_v6.pdf.

155 and research to male peers: Parul Sehgal, "Fighting Erasure," *New York Times*,
February 2, 2007, https://www.nytimes.com/2016/02/07/magazine/the-painful
-consequences-of-erasure.html.

155 reference other men's work: Silvia Knobloch-Westerwick and Carroll J. Glynn,
"The Matilda Effect—Role Congruity Effects on Scholarly Communication,"
Communication Research 40, no. 1 (February 2013): 3–26, http://journals.sagepub
.com/doi/full/10.1177/0093650211418339.

155 job market forum: Alice H. Wu, "Gender Stereotyping in Academia: Evidence
from Economics Job Market Rumors Forum" (thesis, Princeton University Center
for Health and Well-Being, available at Social Science Research Network, December 2017), https://dx.doi.org/10.2139/ssrn.3051462.

155 hands and wait their turn: David Sadker, Myra Sadker, and Karen R. Zittleman,
*Still Failing at Fairness: How Gender Bias Cheats Girls and Boys in School and What
We Can Do About It* (New York: Scribner, 2009).

156 nine to ten times more: A. Jule, *Gender, Participation and Silence in the Language
Classroom: Sh-shushing the Girls* (London: Palgrave Macmillan, 2003).

156 "of significance over girls": Keela Keeping, "Shushing the Girls: Study Shows Boys
Encouraged to Speak While Girls Silenced in the Classroom," Trinity Western
University, July 20, 2015, www8.twu.ca/about/news/general/2004/shushing-the
-girls-study-shows-boys-encouraged-to-.html.

156 of subject matter: Sadker, Sadker, and Zittleman, *Still Failing at Fairness*.

156 in law school classes: Dev A. Patel, "In HLS Classes, Women Fall Behind," *Harvard Crimson*, May 8, 2013, www.thecrimson.com/article/2013/5/8/law-school
-gender-classroom.

156 patterns also reflect: Peter Kunsmann, "Gender, Status and Power in Discourse
Behavior of Men and Women," *Linguistik Online* 5, no. 1 (2000): www.linguistik
-online.de/1_00/KUNSMANN.HTM.

156 but gender trumps status: Deborah Tannen, *Gender and Conversational Interaction*
(New York: Oxford University Press, 1993).

156 unless they are women: D. R. Rhoades et al., "Speaking and Interruptions During Primary Care Office Visits," *Family Medicine* 33, no. 7 (July/August 2001): 528–32, www.stfm.org/Portals/49/Documents/FMPDF/FamilyMedicineVol33Issue 7Rhoades528.pdf.

157 one of the benefits: Sarah Kaplan, "'A Towering Legacy of Goodness': Ben Barres's Fight for Diversity in Science," *Washington Post*, December 28, 2017, https://www .washingtonpost.com/news/speaking-of-science/wp/2017/12/28/a-towering-legacy -of-goodness-ben-barress-fight-for-diversity-in-science/?noredirect=on&utm_ term=.62801a99d66f.

157 as often as women's: Shea Bennett, "On Twitter, Men Are Retweeted Far More Than Women (And You're Probably Sexist, Too)," *Adweek*, July 31, 2012, http:// www.adweek.com/digital/twee-q-sexist-witter/?red=at.

157 "10 Words Every Girl Should Learn": Soraya Chemaly, "10 Simple Words Every Girl Should Learn," *Role Reboot*, May 5, 2014, www.rolereboot.org/culture-and -politics/details/2014-05-10-simple-words-every-girl-learn.

158 conversation in the same direction: Xiaoquan Zhao and Walter Gantz, "Disruptive and Cooperative Interruptions in Prime-Time Television Fiction: The Role of Gender, Status, and Topic," *Journal of Communication* 53, no. 2 (June 2003): 347–62, www.interruptions.net/literature/Zhao-JCommunication03.pdf.

159 94 percent of people: *UN Women Sourcebook on Women, Peace and Security* (UN Women, 2012), p. 6, citing *Women's Participation in Peace Negotiations: Connections Between Presence and Influence* (UN Women, 2012), p. 2, http://www.un women.org/en/what-we-do/peace-and-security/facts-and-figures#notes.

159 overrepresentation of *women*: Lauren Bacon, "How Likely Is an All-Male Speakers List, Statistically Speaking? A Mathematician Weighs In," Lauren Bacon's Curiosity Labs blog, October 21, 2015, www.laurenbacon.com/how-likely-is-an-all -male-speakers-list-statistically.

159 boiling wasn't "spontaneous": Tod Perry, "Twitter User Mansplains Physics to a Female Astronaut," *Good*, November 8, 2017, www.good.is/articles/dude-manspains -in-space.

160 did he show any credentials: Derek Hawkins, "Flight Attendant to Black Female Doctor: 'We're Looking for Actual Physicians,'" *Washington Post*, October 14, 2016, www.washingtonpost.com/news/morning-mix/wp/2016/10/14/blatant -discrimination-black-female-doctor-says-flight-crew-questioned-her-credentials -during-medical-emergency/?utm_term=.cbb8d1646193; Tamika Cross, "I'm sure many . . . ," Facebook, October 9, 2016, https://www.facebook.com/tamika.cross.52/ posts/658443077654049?pnref=story.

160 sexist peer review of her work: Leon Jessen, "Why Did I Start the #AddMaleAuthorGate Tag?" Thoughts on Bioinformatics blog, May 1, 2015, https://leonjessen .wordpress.com/2015/05/01/why-did-i-start-the-addmaleauthorgate.

160 "better health and stamina": Cat Ferguson, "Women Scientists Share Their Awful Stories of Sexism in Publishing," *BuzzFeed*, May 2, 2015, www.buzzfeed.com/ catferguson/women-scientists-share-their-stories-of-sexism-in-publishing?utm_ term=.ymkR9aq40#.nmMeQkA5W.

161 nineteen times that of the women: Deborah Bach, "Male Biology Students Con-

sistently Underestimate Female Peers, Study Finds," *UW News*, February 11, 2016, www.washington.edu/news/2016/02/11/male-biology-students-consistently-underestimate-female-peers-study-finds.

161 mention if this made her angry: Maggie Fox, "Not Smart Enough? Men Overestimate Intelligence in Science Class Even When Grades Show Different, Men Overestimated Their Class Ranking," NBC News, April 4, 2018, https://www.nbcnews.com/news/amp/ncna862801?__twitter_impression=true.

162 mouth masks, called "Liberation Wrappers,": Rega Jha, "A Japanese Burger Chain Made Face Masks So Women Can Eat Burgers Elegantly," *BuzzFeed*, November 4, 2014, www.buzzfeed.com/regajha/a-japanese-burger-chain-made-face-masks-so-women-can-eat-bur?utm_term=.ggoYnGzd7#.oeXDqYg8n.

162 "moral decline of modern society": Agence France-Presse, "Turkish Deputy Prime Minister Says Women Should Not Laugh Out Loud," *The Guardian* (US), July 29, 2014, www.theguardian.com/world/2014/jul/29/turkish-minister-women-laugh-loud-bulent-arinc.

162 "this is an important debate": Amanda Terkel, "Legislator Calls Out Her 'White Male' Colleagues for Skipping Speeches By Women of Color," *Huffington Post*, April 4, 2017, https://www.huffingtonpost.com/entry/melissa-hortman-white-male_us_58e3aed1e4b0d0b7e164c7cb.

163 "a screeching ex-wife": Anna Dimond, "Limbaugh on Hillary Clinton: 'She Sounds Like a Screeching Ex-Wife . . . Men Will Know What I Mean By This,'" Media Matters for America, October 10, 2007, www.mediamatters.org/research/2006/03/07/limbaugh-on-hillary-clinton-she-sounds-like-a-s/135031.

163 punched a woman in the face: "Johnny Rotten Settles Suit Alleging He Punched a Woman in the Face," *LA Weekly*, February 3, 2010, http://www.laweekly.com/music/johnny-rotten-settles-suit-alleging-he-punched-a-woman-in-the-face-2406723; Lars Brandle, "Johnny Rotten Outburst on Australian TV Brings an Apology," *Billboard*, April 12, 2013, https://www.billboard.com/articles/news/1557299/johnnys-rotten-outburst-on-australian-tv-brings-an-apology.

163 "man is talking, do not interrupt": Brandle, "Johnny's Rotten Outburst on Australian TV Brings an Apology."

163 supremacy was a national issue: Lindsey Ellefson, "Panelist to Symone Sanders in Fiery Debate: 'Shut Up,'" CNN, August 14, 2017, www.cnn.com/2017/08/14/us/cuccinelli-sanders-new-day-cnntv/index.html.

164 less credible by a jury: Andrew E. Taslitz, *Rape and the Culture of the Courtroom* (New York: New York University Press, 1999).

164 prosecutor is a woman: Christian B. May, "Anger in the Courtroom: The Effects of Attorney Gender and Emotion on Juror Perceptions" (thesis, Georgia Southern University, 2014), http://digitalcommons.georgiasouthern.edu/cgi/viewcontent.cgi?article=1055&context=honors-theses.

164 likely to find her guilty: Meredith Bennett-Smith, "Male Jurors More Likely to Find Fat Women Guilty, Study Says," *Huffington Post*, January 14, 2013, www.huffingtonpost.com/2013/01/14/male-jurors-assume-fat-women-guilty-study-weight-discrimination_n_2464728.html?utm_source=everydayfeminism.com&utm_medium=referral&utm_campaign=pubexchange_article.

164 as they do one another: Tonja Jacobi and Dylan Schweers, "Justice, Interrupted: The Effect of Gender, Ideology and Seniority at Supreme Court Oral Arguments," *Virginia Law Review* 103, no. 7 (November 2017): 1379–496, www.virginialawreview .org/sites/virginialawreview.org/files/JacobiSchweers_Online.pdf.

164 his 2017 nomination hearings: Tonja Jacobi and Dylan Schweers, "Female Supreme Court Justices Are Interrupted More by Male Justices and Advocates," *Harvard Business Review*, April 11, 2017, https://hbr.org/2017/04/female-supreme -court-justices-are-interrupted-more-by-male-justices-and-advocates.

165 more than they do men: Katy Steinmetz, "Study: Why We Think Women Are More Trustworthy Than Men," *Time*, December 13, 2010, http://healthland.time .com/2010/12/13/study-why-we-think-women-are-more-trustworthy-than-men.

165 doubting effects are magnified: Tess M. S. Neal, "Women as Expert Witnesses: A Review of the Literature," *Behavioral Sciences & the Law* 32, no. 2 (March/April 2014): 164–79, https://doi.org/10.1002/bsl.2113.

165 that male newscasters don't: Kristin J. Anderson, *Modern Misogyny: Anti-Feminism in a Post-Feminist Era* (Oxford: Oxford University Press, 2015).

166 "total of two manuscript requests": Catherine Nichols, "Homme de Plume: What I Learned Sending My Novel Out Under a Male Name," *Jezebel*, August 4, 2015, https://jezebel.com/homme-de-plume-what-i-learned-sending-my-novel-out-und -1720637627.

166 writing about women's books: Jane C. Hu, "The Overwhelming Gender Bias in *New York Times* Book Reviews," *Pacific Standard Magazine*, August 28, 2017, https://psmag.com/social-justice/gender-bias-in-book-reviews.

166 "of view of a woman or girl": Alison Flood, "Books About Women Less Likely to Win Prizes, Study Finds," *The Guardian*, June 1, 2015, https://www.theguard ian.com/books/2015/jun/01/books-about-women-less-likely-to-win-prizes-study -finds.

167 virtual one, could only help: Valentina Zarya, "Venture Capital's Funding Gender Gap Is Actually Getting Worse," *Fortune*, March 13, 2017, http://fortune .com/2017/03/13/female-founders-venture-capital.

167 christened Keith Mann: John Paul Titlow, "These Women Entrepreneurs Created a Fake Male Cofounder to Dodge Startup Sexism," *Fast Company*, September 19, 2017, www.fastcompany.com/40456604/these-women-entrepreneurs-created -a-fake-male-cofounder-to-dodge-startup-sexism.

167 and, as a result, lower commissions: "The Vicious Cycle of the Gender Pay Gap," Knowledge@Wharton, June 6, 2012, http://knowledge.wharton.upenn.edu/article/ the-vicious-cycle-of-the-gender-pay-gap.

167 lab manager opening: Corinne A. Moss-Racusin et al., "Science Faculty's Subtle Gender Biases Favor Male Students," *Proceedings of the National Academy of Sciences* (September 2012): 201211286, doi:10.1073/pnas.1211286109.

167 also associated with troublemaking: Macrina Cooper-White, "When 'Deshawn' and 'Greg' Act Out in Class, Guess Who Gets Branded a Troublemaker," *Huffington Post*, April 17, 2015, www.huffingtonpost.com/2015/04/17/black-students -troublemakers_n_7078634.html.

167 "Be a little more patient": Kieran Snyder, "The Abrasiveness Trap: High-Achieving

Men and Women Are Described Differently in Reviews," *Fortune*, August 26, 2014, http://fortune.com/2014/08/26/performance-review-gender-bias.

168 hostile and benevolent: Peter Glick and Susan T. Fiske, "The Ambivalent Sexism Inventory: Differentiating Hostile and Benevolent Sexism," *Journal of Personality and Social Psychology* 70, no. 3 (1996): 491–512, http://citeseerx.ist.psu.edu/viewdoc/download;jsessionid=2C351E87A024847BB699D6CAA71E3631?doi=10.1.1.470.9865&rep=rep1&type=pdf.

168 care for their children: Manuela Barreto and Naomi Ellemers, "The Burden of Benevolent Sexism: How It Contributes to the Maintenance of Gender Inequalities," *European Journal of Social Psychology* 35, no. 5 (October 2005): 633–42, https://doi.org/10.1002/ejsp.270.

168 women than men who don't: Dana Dovey, "Not All Sexism Is Created Equal: Social Cues Predict Men's Benevolent or Hostile Attitudes Toward Women," *Medical Daily*, March 11, 2015, www.medicaldaily.com/not-all-sexism-created-equal-social-cues-predict-mens-benevolent-or-hostile-attitudes-325278.

169 life satisfaction, but there are costs: Kathleen Connelly and Martin Heesacker, "Why Is Benevolent Sexism Appealing?" *Psychology of Women Quarterly* 36, no. 4 (December 2012): 432–43, http://journals.sagepub.com/doi/abs/10.1177/0361684312456369.

169 the need for protection: Andrea L. Miller and Eugene Borgida, "The Separate Spheres Model of Gendered Inequality," *PLOS ONE* 11, no. 1 (2016): e0147315, https://doi.org/10.1371/journal.pone.0147315.

169 self-objectification, and self-surveillance: Rachel M. Calogero and John T. Jost, "Self-Subjugation Among Women: Exposure to Sexist Ideology, Self-Objectification, and the Protective Function of the Need to Avoid Closure," *Journal of Personality and Social Psychology* 100, no. 2 (February 2011): 211–28, https://doi.org/10.1037/a0021864.

170 cognitive processing is disrupted: Benoit Dardenne, Muriel Dumont, and Thierry Bollier, "Insidious Dangers of Benevolent Sexism: Consequences for Women's Performance," *Journal of Personality and Social Psychology* 93, no. 5 (November 2007): 64–79, https://doi.org/10.1037/0022-3514.93.5.764.

170 promotion and leadership: Sreedhari D. Desai, Dolly Chugh, and Arthur Brief, "The Organizational Implications of a Traditional Marriage: Can a Domestic Traditionalist By Night Be an Organizational Egalitarian By Day?" (research paper 2013-99, University of North Carolina, Kenan-Flagler Business School, available at Social Science Research Network, March 2012), https://papers.ssrn.com/sol3/papers.cfm?abstract_id=2018259%20%20##.

170 typically owns a mere: Mariko Lin Chang, *Shortchanged: Why Women Have Less Wealth and What Can Be Done About It* (New York: Oxford University Press, 2010).

171 from joint to individual taxes: Janet G. Stotsky, "How Tax Systems Treat Men and Women Differently," *Finance & Development* 34, no. 1 (March 1997): 30–33, www.imf.org/external/pubs/ft/fandd/1997/03/pdf/stotsky.pdf.

171 50 percent of our reported GDP: John C. Havens, "The GDP Is Sexist," *Quartz*, January 9, 2018, https://qz.com/1174944/the-gdp-is-sexist.

172 holiday-green duct tape: "Photographer Defends 'Horrifying' Awkward Family Photo," News.com.au, December 17, 2015, www.news.com.au/lifestyle/relationships/

family-friends/photographer-criticised-over-image-where-females-have-their-mouths -taped-up/news-story/f98fcb5376ba15ea7dff36c49d18a7d4.

173 more than white women: Chris Matthews, "Here's Why Women Pay More for Mort-gages Than Men," *Fortune*, September 8, 2016, http://fortune.com/2016/09/08/study -finds-women-are-charged-higher-rates-for-mortgages; Gillian B. White, "Why Blacks and Hispanics Have Such Expensive Mortgages," *The Atlantic*, February 25, 2016, www.theatlantic.com/business/archive/2016/02/blacks-hispanics-mortgages/471024.

173 also mystified them: Adam S. Miner, Arnold Milstein, and Stephen Schueller, "Smartphone-Based Conversational Agents and Responses to Questions About Mental Health, Interpersonal Violence, and Physical Health," JAMA *Internal Medicine* 176, no. 5 (May 2016): 619–25, https://jamanetwork.com/journals/jama internalmedicine/fullarticle/2500043.

174 a sixth-grade girl: Madeline Messer, "I'm a 12-year-old Girl. Why Don't the Char-acters in My Apps Look Like Me?" *Washington Post*, March 4, 2015, https://www .washingtonpost.com/posteverything/wp/2015/03/04/im-a-12-year-old-girl-why -dont-the-characters-in-my-apps-look-like-me/?utm_term=.b441046c7728.

174 "luxury items," and tax women accordingly: Sarah Larimer, "The 'Tampon Tax,' Explained," *Washington Post*, January 8, 2016, www.washingtonpost.com/news/ wonk/wp/2016/01/08/the-tampon-tax-explained/?utm_term=.aeb1320c2abf.

174 in notions of self-defense: Caroline Forell and Donna Matthews, *A Law of Her Own: The Reasonable Woman as a Measure of Man* (New York: NYU Press, 2000).

174 "women couldn't stop writing": Clare Foran, "How to Design a City for Women," *CityLab*, October 21, 2016, www.citylab.com/transportation/2013/09/how-design -city-women/6739.

175 offices around apartment buildings: Ibid.

175 bathrooms and social organizations: Soraya Chemaly, "The Everyday Sexism of Women Waiting in Public Toilet Lines," *Time*, January 5, 2015, http://time.com /3653871/womens-bathroom-lines-sexist-potty-parity/.

176 campaign for the "Right to Pee": "I leave home at seven and I have to wait until I get back home—sometimes it's nine hours, sometimes 12. My stomach hurts when I hold it, but what can I do? Men can go anywhere, but where can a woman go?" asked Sarita, a cook interviewed about the campaign in 2014. Chhavi Sachdev, "Women in India Agitate for Their Right to Pee," Public Radio International, November 25, 2015, https://www.pri.org/stories/2014-11-25/women-india-agitate -their-right-pee.

176 women legislators until 2011: Nancy McKeon, "Women in the House Get a Rest-room," *Washington Post*, July 28, 2011, https://www.washingtonpost.com/lifestyle /style/women-in-the-house-get-a-restroom/2011/07/28/gIQAFgdwfI_story.html? utm_term=.bf2f94211931.

177 "It makes you very sensitive": Robin Morgan, *Sisterhood Is Powerful* (New York: Vintage Books, 1970).

177 one and two "impactful" sexist: Janet K. Swim et al., "Everyday Sexism: Evi-dence for Its Incidence, Nature, and Psychological Impact from Three Daily Di-ary Studies," *Journal of Social Issues* 57, no. 1 (Spring 2001): 31–53, https://doi .org/10.1111/0022-4537.00200.

177 or racist experiences a week: Elizabeth Brondolo et al., "Coping with Racism: A Selective Review of the Literature and a Theoretical and Methodological Critique," *Journal of Behavioral Medicine* 32, no. 1 (February 2009): 64–88, https://doi.org/10.1007/s10865-008-9193-0.

177 in measures of self-silencing: Nina Hansen and Kai Sassenberg, "Exploring the Self-Directed Anger of the Stigmatized," *Group Processes & Intergroup Relations* 14, no. 6 (November 2011): 807–18, http://journals.sagepub.com/doi/pdf/10.1177/1368430210392933.

177 post-traumatic stress disorder: Susan H. Berg, "Everyday Sexism and Posttraumatic Stress Disorder in Women: A Correlation Study," *Violence Against Women* 12, no. 10 (October 2006): 970–88, http://journals.sagepub.com/doi/10.1177/1077801206293082.

177 discrimination and poor health: Douglas Jacobs, "We're Sick of Racism, Literally," *New York Times*, November 11, 2017, https://nytimes.com/2017/11/11/opinion/sunday/sick-of-racism-literally.html.

177 life-altering and -threatening outcomes: Lisa Molix, "Sex Differences in Cardiovascular Health: Does Sexism Influence Women's Health?" *American Journal of the Medical Sciences* 348, no. 2 (August 2014): 153–55, https://doi.org/10.1097/MAJ.0000000000000300.

177 about is routinely ignored: Rodney Clark et al., "Racism as a Stressor for African Americans: A Biopsychosocial Model," *American Psychologist* 54, no. 10 (October 1999): 805–16, www.isr.umich.edu/williams/All%20Publications/DRW%20pubs%201999/racism%20as%20a%20stressor%20for%20african%20americans.pdf; Bell Hooks, *Killing Rage: Ending Racism* (New York: Henry Holt, 1995).

178 directly to stress and fatigue: Andrea S. Kramer and Alton B. Harris, "Why Women Feel More Stress at Work," *Harvard Business Review*, August 4, 2016, https://hbr.org/2016/08/why-women-feel-more-stress-at-work.

178 rather than externalized action: Kristen Bellstrom, "Depressed? Anxious? Blame the Gender Pay Gap," *Fortune*, January 7, 2016, http://fortune.com/2016/01/07/depression-anxiety-pay-gap.

178 all contributed to the gap: Janet K. Swim and Lauri L. Hyers, "Excuse Me—What Did You Just Say?!: Women's Public and Private Responses to Sexist Remarks," *Journal of Experimental Social Psychology* 35, no. 1 (January 1999): 68–88, https://doi.org/10.1006/jesp.1998.1370.

178 consciousness yields positive effects: Cheryl R. Kaiser and Carol T. Miller, "Stop Complaining! The Social Costs of Making Attributions to Discrimination," *Personality and Social Psychology Bulletin* 27, no. 2 (February 2001): 254–63, http://journals.sagepub.com/doi/abs/10.1177/0146167201272010.

179 to have self-directed anger: Dawn M. Szymanski et al., "Internalized Misogyny as a Moderator of the Link Between Sexist Events and Women's Psychological Distress," *Sex Roles* 61, nos. 1–2 (July 2009): 101–9, https://doi.org/10.1007/s11199-009-9611-y.

179 satisfaction than those who don't: Janet K. Swim et al., "Self-Silencing to Sexism," *Journal of Social Issues* 66, no. 3 (September 2010): 493–503, https://doi.org/10.1111/j.1540-4560.2010.01658.x; Lauri L. Hyers, "Resisting Prejudice Ev-

ery Day: Exploring Women's Assertive Responses to Anti-Black Racism, Anti-Semitism, Heterosexism, and Sexism," *Sex Roles* 56, nos. 1–2 (January 2007): 1–12, https://doi.org/10.1111/j.1540-4560.2010.01658.x.

179 about power and its imbalances: Robin W. Simon and Kathryn Lively, "Sex, Anger and Depression," *Social Forces* 88, no. 4 (June 2010): 1543–68, http://users.wfu.edu/simonr/pdfs/Simon_Lively%20Social%20Forces%202010.pdf.

179 unpredictable expressions of anger: Christa Reiser, *Reflections on Anger: Women and Men in a Changing Society* (Westport, CT: Praeger, 2001).

179 "self-esteem and appraised value": Charlotte Krause Prozan, *Feminist Psychoanalytic Psychotherapy* (Northvale, NJ: Jason Aronson, 1992).

180 were better players and "winning": Caitlin Dewey, "Men Who Harass Women Online Are Quite Literally Losers, New Study Finds," *Washington Post*, July 20, 2015, www.washingtonpost.com/news/the-intersect/wp/2015/07/20/men-who-harass-women-online-are-quite-literally-losers-new-study-finds/?utm_term=.f92088aff2d8.

180 "I didn't stand up": Lucy Waterlow, "'Rape and Death Threats Are Common': Women Gamers Reveal the Vile Online Abuse They Receive *Every Day* from Men Who Say They Should 'Get Back in the Kitchen,'" *Daily Mail* (UK), February 26, 2016, www.dailymail.co.uk/femail/article-3454588/Women-gamers-reveal-vile-online-abuse-receive-DAY-men-say-kitchen.html.

181 black women, the sexism and racism: Moya Bailey, "Contesting Misogynoir: Black Women's Digital Resistance in American Culture," Northwestern University, February 28, 2018, https://web.northeastern.edu/nulab/contesting-misogynoir-black-womens-digital-resistance-in-american-culture-with-moya-bailey.

CHAPTER 8: THERE ARE NO WORDS

187 generations, experienced: epistemic injustice: Miranda Flicker, *Epistemic Injustice: Power and the Ethics of Knowing* (New York: Oxford University Press, 2007).

188 John, Robert, or William: Justin Wolfers, "Fewer Women Run Big Companies Than Men Named John," *New York Times*, March 2, 2015, www.nytimes.com/2015/03/03/upshot/fewer-women-run-big-companies-than-men-named-john.html?_r=0.

188 88 percent of whom are white: Christy C. Bulkeley, "A Pioneering Generation Marked the Path for Women Journalists," *Nieman Reports* 56, no. 1 (Spring 2002): 60–62, http://niemanreports.org/articles/a-pioneering-generation-marked-the-path-for-women-journalists.

188 17 percent of top management: Maria Edström et al., "The Media Is a Male Business," Nordic Information Center for Media and Communication Research (Nordicom), February 26, 2018, http://nordicom.gu.se/en/latest/news/media-male-business.

188 tech, mirror these numbers: In the film industry, men make up 75 percent of all producers, 80 percent of all editors, 86 percent of all writers, and 95 percent of all directors. Only 3.6 percent of the directors and 13.5 percent of the writers of the top-grossing films of 2015 were women. From 2007 through 2015, in the top grossing 800 films analyzed, more than two-thirds of all speaking characters

were male. A 2017 study found that racial and ethnic minorities are not only underrepresented in every filmmaking and entertainment arena but also have been losing ground in some. "Hollywood Equality: All Talk, Little Action," USC Annenberg School for Journalism and Communication, March 23, 2017, https://annenberg.usc.edu/news/faculty-research/hollywood-equality-all-talk -little-action.

188 marketing advantages, and prominence: Shanley Kane, "Who Is Verified on Twitter, and Why Does It Matter?" *Model View Culture*, August 18, 2016, https://modelviewculture.com/news/who-is-verified-on-twitter-and-why-does-it-matter.

189 written about, and analyzed: *The Status of Women in the U.S. Media 2017* (New York: Women's Media Center, 2017), www.womensmediacenter.com/reports/the -status-of-women-in-u.s.-media-2017.

189 perceive a fifty-fifty gender balance: Colleen DeBaise, "Making Hollywood Less Sexist, One Crowd Scene at a Time," *Story Exchange*, March 5, 2015, https://thestoryexchange.org/making-hollywood-sexist-crowd-scene-time.

189 listeners think they dominate: Anne Cutler and Donia R. Scott, "Speaker Sex and Perceived Apportionment of Talk," *Applied Psycholinguistics* 11, no. 3 (September 1990): 253–72, https://doi.org/10.1017/S0142716400008882.

189 the more biased his views: Mark D. Alicke and Edward Largo, "The Role of Self in the False Consensus Effect," *Journal of Experimental Social Psychology* 31, no. 1 (January 1995): 28–47, https://doi.org/10.1006/jesp.1995.1002; Leandre R. Fabrigar and Jon A. Krosnick, "Attitude Importance and the False Consensus Effect," *Personality and Social Psychology Bulletin* 21, no. 5 (May 1995): 468–79, http://journals.sagepub.com/doi/abs/10.1177/0146167295215005; Lee Ross, David Greene, and Pamela House, "The 'False Consensus Effect': An Egocentric Bias in Social Perception and Attribution Processes," *Journal of Experimental Social Psychology* 13, no. 3 (May 1977): 279–301, www.kafaak.com/wp-content/uploads/2014/06/Ross-et-al-The-false-consensus-effect-an-egocentric-bias-in-social-perception-and -attribution-processes.pdf.

190 powerful movie producer Harvey Weinstein: Isaac Chotiner, "Jodi Kantor on How She Broke the Harvey Weinstein Story," *Slate*, October 11, 2017, www.slate .com/articles/news_and_politics/interrogation/2017/10/ein_kantor_on_how_she_ broke_the_harvey_weinstein_story.html.

190 "crush" her and her career: Ronan Farrow, "From Aggressive Overtures to Sexual Assault: Harvey Weinstein's Accusers Tell Their Stories," *New Yorker*, October 23, 2017, https://www.newyorker.com/news/news-desk/from-aggressive-overtures -to-sexual-assault-harvey-weinsteins-accusers-tell-their-stories.

191 "rape room" located in a hot NYC restaurant: Lisa Ryan, "Hip New York Restaurant Reportedly Had a 'Rape Room,'" *The Cut*, December 12, 2017, www.thecut .com/2017/12/mario-batali-spotted-pig-rape-room.html.

191 recipe for pizza dough cinnamon rolls: Emily Stewart, "Mario Batali's Sexual Misconduct Apology Came with a Cinnamon Roll Recipe," *Vox*, December 16, 2017, www.vox.com/2017/12/16/16784544/mario-batali-cinnamon-roll-apology.

191 by actor Terry Crews: Adam B. Vary, "Actor Anthony Rapp: Kevin Spacey Made a Sexual Advance Toward Me When I Was 14," *BuzzFeed*, October 30, 2017,

www.buzzfeed.com/adambvary/anthony-rapp-kevin-spacey-made-sexual-advance
-when-i-was-14?utm_term=.uiQNq5OXK#.reROXNjPm.

191 surrogates, also stepped down: Jessica Taylor, "Rep. Trent Franks to Resign from
Congress After Discussing Surrogacy with Staffers," NPR, December 7, 2017,
www.npr.org/2017/12/07/569291354/rep-trent-franks-to-resign-from-congress-after
-asking-staffers-about-surrogacy.

191 sexist commentary, and assault: Angelique Chrisafis, " 'We Can No Longer Stay
Silent': Fury Erupts over Sexism in French Politics," *The Guardian* (US), May
13, 2016, www.theguardian.com/world/2016/may/13/we-can-no-longer-stay-silent
-fury-erupts-over-sexism-in-french-politics.

191 "wives' " event instead of the main G20 session: Rowena Mason, "Harriet Harman Says Sexist Habits Still Rife in Parliament," *The Guardian* (US), January
31, 2017, www.theguardian.com/politics/2017/jan/31/harriet-harman-sexist-habits
-parliament-women-mps.

191 he disagreed with her: James Tapsfield, "Tory Grandee Sir Nicholas Soames
Apologises After Making *Barking* Noises at Female SNP MP in the House of
Commons," *Daily Mail* (UK), January 30, 2017, www.dailymail.co.uk/news/article
-4173134/Tory-grandee-sorry-BARKING-female-SNP-MP.html.

191 "that rush of humiliation and anger": Doha Madani, "Congresswoman Invites
#MeToo Creator Tarana Burke to State of the Union," *Huffington Post*, January
11, 2018, www.huffingtonpost.com/entry/jackie-speier-tarana-burke-metoo-state
-of-the-union_us_5a57e7d9e4b0720dc4c594af.

192 more than twenty: Eliza Relmen, "The 22 Women Who Have Accused Trump
of Sexual Misconduct," *Business Insider*, December 21, 2017, http://www.business
insider.com/women-accused-trump-sexual-misconduct-list-2017-12; Sarah Fitz-
patrick and Tracy Connor, "Stormy Daniels Offers to Pay Back $130,000 for
Freedom to Speak About Trump," NBC News, March 12, 2018, https://www
.nbcnews.com/news/us-news/stormy-daniels-offers-pay-back-130g-freedom-talk
-trump-n855746.

192 "Do you think she's fuckable?": Claudia Rosenbaum, "Harvey Weinstein Recast
Lead Role Because She Wasn't 'Fuckable,' Director Says," *BuzzFeed*, October 17,
2017, https://www.buzzfeed.com/claudiarosenbaum/harvey-weinstein-lead-role
-recast?utm_term=.iuJqJrgxa#.hgbNzvng8.

193 including by other women: Debra Birnbaum, "Lena Dunham Apologizes for
Defending 'Girls' Writer Accused of Sexual Assault," *Variety*, November 18,
2017, http://variety.com/2017/tv/news/lena-dunham-apology-girls-writer-murray
-miller-1202618404/.

193 primarily, "for White Women": Bethonie Butler, "Gabrielle Union on #MeToo:
'The Floodgates Have Opened for White Women,' " *Washington Post*, December
8, 2017, www.washingtonpost.com/news/arts-and-entertainment/wp/2017/12/08/
gabrielle-union-on-metoo-the-floodgates-have-opened-for-white-women/?utm_
term=.c4f13b0c7c0c.

193 inevitably, became public: Moira Donegan, "I Started the Media Men List—
My Name Is Moira Donegan," *The Cut*, January 10, 2018, https://www.thecut
.com/2018/01/moira-donegan-i-started-the-media-men-list.html.

193 literary editor, Leon Wieseltier: Adrienne LaFrance, "The 'Harvey Effect' Takes Down Leon Wieseltier's Magazine," *The Atlantic*, October 24, 2017, www.the atlantic.com/entertainment/archive/2017/10/the-harvey-effect-reaches-leon -wieseltier/543897.

193 by at least three women: Brian Stelter and Tom Kludt, "Matt Lauer Fired from NBC News After Complaint About Inappropriate Sexual Behavior," CNN Money, November 29, 2017, http://money.cnn.com/2017/11/29/media/matt-lauer/ index.html.

194 about Trump's actions: Matt Wilstein, "When Mark Halperin Dismissed Sexual Assault Allegations Against Trump," *Daily Beast*, October 26, 2017, www.the dailybeast.com/when-mark-halperin-dismissed-sexual-assault-allegations-against -trump.

194 ramifications of his harassment were: Rebecca Carroll, "My Experience at *Charlie Rose* Went Beyond Sexism," *Esquire*, December 4, 2017, www.esquire.com/enter tainment/tv/a13978884/charlie-rose-sexual-harassment-accuser-story.

195 "becomes a form of protection": Sarah Jeong, "When Whisper Networks Let Us Down," *The Verge*, February 21, 2018, www.theverge.com/2018/2/21/17035552/ sexual-assault-harassment-whisper-network-reporting-failure-marquis-boire.

195 encourage the practice), is not a solution: Katelyn Beaty, "A Christian Case Against the Pence Rule," *New York Times*, November 15, 2017, https://www.nytimes .com/2017/11/15/opinion/pence-rule-christian-graham.html.

196 knowledge *produced by resistant anger*: Alison Bailey, "On Anger, Silence and Epistemic Injustice," *Philosophy* (forthcoming 2018).

198 "myself to whisper . . . me too": Tarana Burke, "The Inception," *Just Be Inc.*, March 12, 2018, http://justbeinc.wixsite.com/justbeinc/the-me-too-movement-cmml.

199 "most part, and by the press": Ellen Pao, "Has Anything Really Changed for Women in Tech?" *New York Times*, September 16, 2017, www.nytimes .com/2017/09/16/opinion/sunday/ellen-pao-sexism-tech.html.

199 kissing, and questions about sex: University of California, "Living for Tips: Why Waitresses Put Up with Sexual Harassment," *Slate*, February 5, 2015, www.slate .com/articles/news_and_politics/uc2/2015/05/why_waitresses_put_up_with_ sexual_harassment.html; *Hands Off Pants On: Sexual Harassment in Chicago's Hospitality Industry* (Chicago: Unite Here Local 1, July 2016), www.handsoffpants on.org/wp-content/uploads/HandsOffReportWeb.pdf.

200 had been sexually harassed: Kathryn B. H. Clancy et al., "Survey of Academic Field Experiences (SAFE): Trainees Report Harassment and Assault," *PLOS ONE* 9, no. 7 (July 2014): e102172, https://doi.org/10.1371/journal.pone.0102172.

200 jobs because of harassment: Bryce Covert, "Sexual Harassment Will Change Your Career Forever," *The Cut*, October 24, 2017, www.thecut.com/2017/10/sexual -harassment-affects-women-career.html.

200 the workplace go unreported: Chai R. Feldblum and Victoria A. Lipnic, *Select Task Force on the Study of Harassment in the Workplace* (Washington, DC: US Equal Employment Opportunity Commission, June 2016), www.eeoc.gov/eeoc/ task_force/harassment/upload/report.pdf.

200 that number at 75 percent: Tara Golshan, "Study Finds 75 Percent of Work-

place Harassment Victims Experienced Retaliation When They Spoke Up," *Vox*, October 15, 2017, www.vox.com/identities/2017/10/15/16438750/weinstein-sexual -harassment-facts.

200 responded and how: Louise F. Fitzgerald, Suzanne Swan, and Karla Fischer, "Why Didn't She Just Report Him? The Psychological and Legal Implications of Women's Responses to Sexual Harassment," *Journal of Social Issues* 51, no. 1 (Spring 1995): 117–38, https://doi.org/10.1111/j.1540-4560.1995.tb01312.x.

200 and leverage in the workplace: Rich Yeselson, "The Decline of Labor, the Increase in Inequality," *Talking Points Memo*, accessed February 23, 2018, http://talking pointsmemo.com/features/marchtoinequality/onedeclineoflabor.

200 engages in activism: "Times Up," Times Up Now, February 23, 2018, www.times upnow.com.

200 more broadly hostile and toxic: Alice H. Wu, "Gender Stereotyping in Academia: Evidence from Economics Job Market Rumors Forum" (thesis, University of California, Berkeley, August 2017), available at www.dropbox.com/s/v6q7gfcbv9feef5/ Wu_EJMR_paper.pdf?dl=0; Valerie Aurora and Leigh Honeywell, "The Al Capone Theory of Sexual Harassment," Valerie Aurora blog, July 18, 2017, https:// blog.valerieaurora.org/2017/07/18/the-al-capone-theory-of-sexual-harassment; Rick Rojas, "Columbia Professor Files Sexual Harassment Suit Against University," *New York Times*, March 23, 2016, www.nytimes.com/2016/03/24/nyregion/ columbia-professor-files-sexual-harassment-suit-against-university.html.

During the past forty years, as women began to reach parity in other social sciences, men moved out of those fields and into economics, which grew hostile and resistant to women. What does this look like? In the case of Carmen Reinhart, one of the most eminent economists living, it looks like having a junior economist listed before her on research papers, despite her seniority and despite the practice's violating rules of alphabetization. That is a "small" and "harmless" complaint, until you realize that Reinhart is the only woman recognized as one of the top fifty economists of the era, and one of only four in the top one hundred. It becomes less easy to dismiss as trivial when it is clear that the vast majority of the people making decisions about whom to mentor, hire, publish with, and give tenure to talk about their female peers this way.

201 "temporarily powerful—and very, very dangerous": Caitin Flanagan, "The Humiliation of Aziz Ansari," *The Atlantic*, January 14, 2018, www.theatlantic.com/ entertainment/archive/2018/01/the-humiliation-of-aziz-ansari/550541.

201 into an anxious frenzy: Katie Way, "I Went on a Date with Aziz Ansari. It Turned into the Worst Night of My Life," *Babe*, January 13, 2018, https://babe .net/2018/01/13/aziz-ansari-28355.

203 each other—is a bankrupt one: Rachael O'Byrne, Susan Hansen, and Mark Rapley, "If a Girl Doesn't Say 'No' . . . : Young Men, Rape, and Claims of 'Insufficient Knowledge,'" *Journal of Community & Applied Social Psychology* 18, no. 3 (May/ June 2008): 168–93, https://doi.org/10.1002/casp.922.

203 "have left us with so little to lose": Ijeoma Oluo, "Does This Year Make Me Look Angry?" *Elle*, January 11, 2018, www.elle.com/culture/career-politics/a15063942/ ijeoma-oluo-women-and-rage-2018.

204 His belief that I lied: Kyle Swenson, "Abuse Survivor Confronts Gymnastics Doctor: 'I Have Been Coming for You for a Long Time,'" *Washington Post*, January 17, 2018, https://www.washingtonpost.com/news/morning-mix/wp/2018/01/17/ive-been-coming-for-you-for-a-long-time-abuse-survivor-confronts-gymnastics-doctor/?utm_term=.ceab15bf9aed.

205 "Hell hath no fury": Des Bieler, "Here Are the Larry Nasser Comments That Drew Gasps in the Courtroom," *Washington Post*, January 24, 2018, https://www.washingtonpost.com/news/early-lead/wp/2018/01/24/here-are-the-larry-nassar-comments-that-drew-gasps-in-the-courtroom/?noredirect=on&utm_term=.746acae4e633.

205 "How much is a young woman worth?": "Larry Nassar Victim: 'How Much Is a Little Girl Worth?'" BBC News, January 24, 2018, video, 3:41, www.bbc.com/news/av/world-us-canada-42810609/larry-nassar-victim-how-much-is-a-little-girl-worth.

205 All three judges were women: Kimberly Curtis, "Three Female Judges Just Made History by Convicting a Commander for Rapes Committed by His Troops," *UN Dispatch*, March 21, 2016, www.undispatch.com/three-female-judges-just-made-history-by-convicting-a-commander-for-rapes-committed-by-his-troops.

206 "insult to me and all women": Katie J. M. Baker, "Here Is the Powerful Letter the Stanford Victim Read Aloud to Her Attacker," *BuzzFeed*, June 3, 2016, www.buzzfeed.com/katiejmbaker/heres-the-powerful-letter-the-stanford-victim-read-to-her-ra?utm_term=.pgqd0AMl6#.divoMj29D.

207 government actors, and former intimates: Max Fisher, "Intimate Video Emerges, Again, of Reporter Investigating Azerbaijan President's Family," *Washington Post*, August 7, 2013, www.washingtonpost.com/news/worldviews/wp/2013/08/07/intimate-video-emerges-again-of-reporter-investigating-azerbaijan-presidents-family/?utm_term=.81d3c618123a.

207 more than seventy million: Becky Gardiner et al., "The Dark Side of *Guardian* Comments," *The Guardian*, April 12, 2016, https://www.theguardian.com/technology/2016/apr/12/the-dark-side-of-guardian-comments.

207 68 percent of the media company's bylines: "How Women Make the Front Page in Britain: Get the Full Data," *The Guardian*, https://www.theguardian.com/news/datablog/2012/oct/15/women-newspapers-front-pages.

208 plastic bag down her throat: Justin Jouvenal, "Before Death of Student, an Altercation with Her Roommate," *Washington Post*, May 7, 2015, https://www.washingtonpost.com/local/crime/before-death-of-student-an-altercation-with-her-roommate/2015/05/07/276ea926-f4f1-11e4-b2f3-af5479e6bbdd_story.html?noredirect=on&utm_term=.353e2ec5b7b0.

209 "rampant in the game industry": Mark Serrels, "What Anita Sarkeesian Couldn't Say at the Sydney Opera House," *Kotaku*, March 10, 2015, video, 4:37, www.kotaku.com.au/2015/03/what-anita-sarkeesian-couldnt-say-at-the-sydney-opera-house.

210 gender-neutral public forum for men: Maeve Duggan, "Men, Women Experience and View Online Harassment Differently," Pew Research Center, July 14, 2017,

www.pewresearch.org/fact-tank/2017/07/14/men-women-experience-and-view-online-harassment-differently.

210 because they fear threats and violence: Alana Barton and Hannah Storm, *Violence and Harassment Against Women in the News Media: A Global Picture* (Washington, DC: International Women's Media Foundation; London: International News Safety Institute, March 10, 2014), https://www.iwmf.org/wp-content/uploads/2014/03/Violence-and-Harassment-against-Women-in-the-News-Media.pdf.

211 24 percent of state legislatures: "Women in the U.S. Congress 2018," Center for American Women and Politics, accessed February 23, 2018, www.cawp.rutgers.edu/women-us-congress-2018.

211 women's representation to 104th: Soo Oh and Sarah Kliff, "The US Is Ranked 104th in Women's Representation in Government," *Vox*, March 8, 2017, www.vox.com/identities/2017/3/8/14854116/women-representation.

211 posts, both record highs: Richard Keen and Richard Cracknell, "Women in Parliament and Government" (briefing paper SN01250, House of Commons Library, February 12, 2018), http://researchbriefings.parliament.uk/Research Briefing/Summary/SN01250.

211 "flouting the rules" of parliament: Marina Koren, "Anger in New Zealand's Parliament," *The Atlantic*, November 11, 2015, www.theatlantic.com/international/archive/2015/11/new-zealand-parliament-sexual-assault/415371.

211 and toxic shock syndrome: Jimmy Jenkins, "'Pads and Tampons and the Problems with Periods': All-Male Committee Hears Arizona Bill on Feminine Hygiene Products in Prison," KJZZ, February 5, 2018, https://kjzz.org/content/602963/%E2%80%98pads-and-tampons-and-problems-periods-all-male-committee-hears-arizona-bill-feminine.

212 provide period supplies in schools: Miranda Larbi, "Why Hundreds of Teens Marched on Westminster for Free Periods," *Metro*, December 21, 2017, http://metro.co.uk/2017/12/21/hundreds-teens-marched-westminster-free-periods-7176619.

212 her more than forty times: Sam Reichman and Jessica Winter, "Watch: Every Single Time a Republican Interrupted the President of Planned Parenthood," *Slate*, September 29, 2015, www.slate.com/blogs/xx_factor/2015/09/29/house_committee_hearing_on_planned_parenthood_every_single_time_a_republican.html?wpsrc=sh_all_dt_tw_ru.

212 not being polite enough: Katie Rogers, "Kamala Harris Is (Again) Interrupted While Pressing a Senate Witness," *New York Times*, June 13, 2017, www.nytimes.com/2017/06/13/us/politics/kamala-harris-interrupted-jeff-sessions.html?_r=0.

213 internet went wild with glee: Christine Emba, "'Reclaiming My Time' Is Bigger Than Maxine Waters," *Washington Post*, August 1, 2017, https://www.washingtonpost.com/blogs/post-partisan/wp/2017/08/01/reclaiming-my-time-is-bigger-than-maxine-waters/?utm_term=.860bf9d0361a.

213 "the workplace and beyond": Tamara Lush, "For Many Women, Watching Trump Interrupt Clinton 51 Times Was Unnerving but Familiar," PBS, September 27, 2016, www.pbs.org/newshour/politics/for-many-women-watching-trump-interrupt-clinton-51-times-was-unnerving-but-familiar.

213 "credibility as a legislator": Gayle Goldin, "Why Speaking Out Against Sexual Harassment Backfires for Women in Office," *Glamour*, November 20, 2017, www .glamour.com/story/rhode-island-senator-gayle-goldin-why-speaking-out-against -sexual-harassment-backfires-for-women-in-office.

214 "over and over and over again": Azmina Dhrodia, "Unsocial Media: Tracking Twitter Abuse Against Women MPs," *Medium*, September 4, 2017, https://medium .com/@AmnestyInsights/unsocial-media-tracking-twitter-abuse-against-women -mps-fc28aeca498a.

214 United Kingdom targeted Abbott: Ibid.

214 public freedom of expression: Lizzy Davies, "Laura Boldrini: The Italian Politician Rising Above the Rape Threats," *The Guardian*, February 9, 2014, https:// www.theguardian.com/politics/2014/feb/09/laura-boldrini-italian-politician-rape -threats.

214 "understands" what it felt like: Elisabetta Povoledo, "Slurs Against Italy's First Black National Official Spur Debate on Racism," *New York Times*, June 22, 2013, www.nytimes.com/2013/06/23/world/europe/slurs-against-italys-first-black-national -official-spur-debate-on-racism.html.

214 assigned a police escort: Erica C. Barnett, "What Happens When Female Politicians Try to Stand Up to Sports Fans," *The Atlantic*, May 21, 2016, www.the atlantic.com/politics/archive/2016/05/seattle-sonics-arena-harassment/483743.

215 the McCain-Palin ticket: Nathan A. Heflick and Jamie L. Goldenberg, "Objectifying Sarah Palin: Evidence That Objectification Causes Women to Be Perceived as Less Competent and Less Fully Human," *Journal of Experimental Social Psychology* 45 (2009): 598–601.

215 positions of leadership and authority: Lizzy Davies, "Julia Gillard Speech Prompts Dictionary to Change 'Misogyny' Definition," *The Guardian* (US), October 17, 2012, www.theguardian.com/world/2012/oct/17/julia-gillard-australia-misogyny -dictionary.

216 on multiple levels, is expanding: "Digging into Data on the Gender Digital Divide," World Wide Web Foundation, October 31, 2016, https://webfoundation .org/2016/10/digging-into-data-on-the-gender-digital-divide.

216 "about rape culture on a Friday, dude": Andrea Grimes, "To the Men Who Are Not Responsible for My Problem," *Medium*, November 10, 2017, https://medium .com/@andreagrimes/to-the-men-who-are-not-responsible-for-my-problem-e6dfb 5b0eeb4.

217 "You do dwell on that": @Gildedspine, #YesAllWomen One Year Later," *The Toast*, May 5, 2015, http://the-toast.net/2015/05/26/yesallwomen-one-year-later/.

CHAPTER 9: THE POLITICS OF DENIAL

222 centered on a hatred of women: Molly Dragiewicz and Ruth M. Mann, "Special Edition: Fighting Feminism—Organised Opposition to Women's Rights: Guest Editors' Introduction," *International Journal for Crime, Justice and Social Democracy* 5, no. 2 (2016), 1–5, https://www.crimejusticejournal.com/article/ view/313/255.

222 communities of men: Talia Lavin, "Someone Please Tell the *Times* That Incels Are Terrorists," *Village Voice*, May 3, 2018, https://www.villagevoice.com/2018/05/03/the-harpy-someone-please-tell-the-times-that-incels-are-terrorists/.

224 his sister was "smokin' hot": Darrell Etherington and Josh Constine, "Rap Genius Drops Co-Founder Following Elliot Rodger Manifesto Annotations," *TechCrunch*, May 26, 2014, https://techcrunch.com/2014/05/26/rap-genius-co-founder-resigns-following-elliot-rodger-manifesto-annotations.

224 is natural and immutable: Kim Parker, Juliana Menasce Horowitz, and Renee Stepler, "On Gender Differences, No Consensus on Nature vs. Nurture," Pew Research Center's Social & Demographic Trends Project, December 5, 2017, www.pewsocialtrends.org/2017/12/05/on-gender-differences-no-consensus-on-nature-vs-nurture.

225 equitable than in the past: Alexis Krivkovich et al., *Women in the Workplace 2017* (New York: McKinsey & Company, 2017), www.mckinsey.com/global-themes/gender-equality/women-in-the-workplace-2017.

225 able, skilled, and competent: Ian M. Handley et al., "Quality of Evidence Revealing Subtle Gender Biases in Science Is in the Eye of the Beholder," *Proceedings of the National Academy of Sciences of the United States of America* 112, no. 43 (October 2015): 13201–6, www.pnas.org/content/112/43/13201.full.pdf.

225 rejecting them as unimportant: Laurel Raymond, "Even with Hard Evidence of Gender Bias in STEM Fields, Men Don't Believe It's Real," *ThinkProgress*, October 19, 2015, https://thinkprogress.org/even-with-hard-evidence-of-gender-bias-in-ste.

225 with 6 percent of men: At the same time, a significant portion of boys and men *do* believe that there is an ideal job for women: making babies and caring for them. According to an earlier Pew study, 35 percent of childless millennial men believe that a woman should be the parent who "take[s] care of the home and children." After the birth of a child, that number jumps to 53 percent. Before having children, 24 percent of millennial men assert that they will take on equal responsibility for child care in their household. But the reality once they become fathers? Only 8 percent.

A 2015 survey of heterosexual American men, in what one newspaper called the "disturbing differences in what men want in their wives and their daughters," revealed that 34 percent wanted a romantic partner who was "independent" compared with the 66 percent who said the same of daughters. Men also favored intelligence in daughters more than in spouses. In other words, they want wives who are more dependent, obedient, and less self-sufficient, but daughters—extensions of themselves in ways that wives aren't—should be smart, ambitious, and independent. Kim Parker and Cary Funk, "Gender Discrimination Comes in Many Forms for Today's Working Women," Pew Research Center, December 14, 2017, www.pewresearch.org/fact-tank/2017/12/14/gender-discrimination-comes-in-many-forms-for-todays-working-women.

226 incidents of sexism or violence: Octavia Calder-Dawe and Nicola Gavey, "Jekyll and Hyde Revisited: Young People's Constructions of Feminism, Feminists and the Practice of 'Reasonable Feminism,'" *Feminism & Psychology* 26, no. 4 (November 2016): 487–507, https://doi.org/10.1177/0959353516660993.

227 harder to be a man today: Michael Kimmel, "Has a Man's World Become a Woman's Nation?" *Shriver Report*, September 11, 2009, http://shriverreport.org/has-a-mans-world-become-a-womans-nation.

227 erectile dysfunction and depression: Jena McGregor, "The Curious Political Effect of Men Losing Their Breadwinner Role," *Washington Post*, April 21, 2017, www.washingtonpost.com/news/on-leadership/wp/2017/04/21/the-curious-political-effect-of-men-losing-their-breadwinners-role.

230 with 49 percent of men: "All the Single Ladies: 61% of Women in the UK Are Happy to Be Single, Compared to 49% of Men," *Mintel*, November 13, 2017, www.mintel.com/press-centre/social-and-lifestyle/all-the-single-ladies-61-of-women-in-the-uk-are-happy-to-be-single-compared-to-49-of-men.

230 not be in relationships: Olivia Rudgard, "Women Prefer Being Single—Because Relationships Are Hard Work, Research Suggests," *The Telegraph* (UK), November 11, 2017, www.telegraph.co.uk/news/2017/11/11/women-prefer-single-relationships-hard-w.

230 smart, ambitious, and independent: Maya Dusenbery, "Men Want Sweet Wives and Independent Daughters," *Pacific Standard*, May 11, 2015, https://psmag.com/social-justice/in-this-economy-we-could-all-use-a-wife.

231 separate-sphere beliefs: Andrea L. Miller and Eugene Borgida, "The Separate Spheres Model of Gendered Inequality," *PLOS ONE* 11, no. 1 (2016): e0147315, https://doi.org/10.1371/journal.pone.0147315; Marianne Bertrand, Emir Kamenica, and Jessica Pan, "Gender Identity and Relative Income Within Households," *Quarterly Journal of Economics* 130, no. 2 (May 2015): 571–614, https://doi.org/10.1093/qje/qjv001.

231 underperform in social sensitivity: Anne M. Koenig and Alice H. Eagly, "Stereotype Threat in Men on a Test of Social Sensitivity," *Sex Roles* 52, nos. 7–8 (April 2005): 489–96, https://doi.org/10.1007/s11199-005-3714-x.

231 "so shall you reap": Eric Bonsang, Vegard Skirbekk, and Ursula M. Staudinger, "As You Sow, So Shall You Reap: Gender-Role Attitudes and Late-Life Cognition," *Psychological Science* 28, no. 9 (September 2017): 1201–13, https://doi.org/10.1177/0956797617708634.

231 blacks and other minorities: Don Gonyea, "Majority of White Americans Say They Believe Whites Face Discrimination," NPR, October 24, 2017, www.npr.org/2017/10/24/559604836/majority-of-white-americans-think-theyre-discriminated-against.

232 "motivated, system-justifying ideology": Miller and Borgida, "The Separate Spheres Model of Gendered Inequality."

232 and their worldview: John T. Jost, Mahzarin R. Banaji, and Brian A. Nosek, "A Decade of System Justification Theory: Accumulated Evidence of Conscious and Unconscious Bolstering of the Status Quo," *Political Psychology* 25, no. 6 (December 2004): 881–919, https://doi.org/10.1111/j.1467-9221.2004.00402.x; Melvin J. Lerner, *The Belief in a Just World: A Fundamental Delusion* (New York: Plenum Press, 1980).

The theory of systems justification was developed by social scientists John T. Jost and Mahzarin R. Banaji in the mid-1990s and was itself influenced by an earlier one, just world theory, first proposed by researcher Melvin Lerner in the mid-1960s.

232 ills that befall them: Jost, Banaji, and Nosek, "A Decade of System Justification Theory."

232 denial is psychologically assuaging: John T. Jost and Orsolya Hunyady, "The Psychology of System Justification and the Palliative Function of Ideology," *European Review of Social Psychology* 13, no. 1 (2003): 111–53, https://doi.org/10 .1080/10463280240000046.

232 "anger related to unfairness": Virginia Eatough, Jonathan A. Smith, and Rachel Shaw, "Women, Anger and Aggression: An Interpretative Phenomenological Analysis," *Journal of Interpersonal Violence* 23, no. 12 (December 2008): 1767–99, https://doi.org/10.1177/0886260508314932.

233 at a clear disadvantage: Jacqueline Yi, "The Role of Benevolent Sexism in Gender Inequality," *Applied Psychology OPUS* (Spring 2015), https://steinhardt.nyu.edu/ appsych/opus/issues/2015/spring/yi.

233 and anxiety-provoking information: Chris G. Sibley, Marc S. Wilson, and John Duckitt, "Antecedents of Men's Hostile and Benevolent Sexism: The Dual Roles of Social Dominance Orientation and Right-Wing Authoritarianism," *Personality and Social Psychology Bulletin* 33, no. 2 (February 2007): 160–72, https://doi .org/10.1177/0146167206294745.

233 "preferred form of social organization": Dan M. Kahan et al., "Culture and Identity-Protective Cognition: Explaining the White Male Effect in Risk Perception," *Journal of Empirical Legal Studies* 4, no. 3 (November 2007): 465–505, https://doi .org/10.1111/j.1740-1461.2007.00097.x.

234 in terms of her own inequality easier: Peter Glick and Susan T. Fiske, "An Ambivalent Alliance: Hostile and Benevolent Sexism as Complementary Justifications for Gender Inequality," *American Psychologist* 56, no. 2 (2001): 109–18, https:// dx.doi.org/10.1037/0003-066X.56.2.109; see also Peter Glick and Susan T. Fiske, "The Ambivalent Sexism Inventory: Differentiating Hostile and Benevolent Sexism," *Journal of Personality and Social Psychology* 70, no. 3 (March 1996): 491–512, http://psycnet.apa.org/buy/1996-03014-006.

234 Denial is rarely based on facts or reasoning: Katherine Stroebe et al., "Is the World a Just Place? Countering the Negative Consequences of Pervasive Discrimination by Affirming the World as Just," *British Journal of Social Psychology* 50, no. 3 (September 2011): 484–500, www.manuelabarreto.com/docs/Stroebe_ Dovidio_Barreto_Ellemers_John_2011.pdf.

234 lower-status ethnic groups do: Anna Olofsson and Saman Rashid, "The White (Male) Effect and Risk Perception: Can Equality Make a Difference?" *Risk Analysis* 31, no. 6 (June 2011): 1016–32, https://doi.org/10.1111/j.1539-6924.2010.01566.x.

234 male perpetration and its prevalence: G. Tendayi Viki and Dominic Abrams, "But She Was Unfaithful: Benevolent Sexism and Reactions to Rape Victims Who Violate Traditional Gender Role Expectations," *Sex Roles* 47, nos. 5–6 (September 2002): 289–93, https://doi.org/10.1023/A:1021342912248.

235 witness or encounter discrimination: Mindi D. Foster and E. Micha Tsarfati, "The Effects of Meritocracy Beliefs on Women's Well-Being After First-Time Gender

Discrimination," *Personality and Social Psychology Bulletin* 31, no. 12 (December 2005): 1730–38, https://doi.org/10.1177/0146167205278709.

236 the angriest people in America: "American Rage: The *Esquire*/NBC News Survey," *Esquire*, January 3, 2016, www.esquire.com/news-politics/a40693/american -rage-nbc-survey.

236 of the same human emotion: Rachael E. Jack, Oliver G. B. Garrod, and Philippe G. Schyns, "Dynamic Facial Expressions of Emotion Transmit an Evolving Hierarchy of Signals over Time," *Current Biology* 24, no. 2 (January 2014): 187–92, https://doi.org/10.1016/j.cub.2013.11.064.

237 "I know where she went": Michael Richardson, "The Disgust of Donald Trump," *Continuum* 31, no. 6 (2017): 747–56, doi:10.1080/10304312.2017.1370077.

237 pump that she was "disgusting": Jeremy Diamond, "Lawyer: Donald Trump Called Me 'Disgusting' for Request to Pump Breast Milk," CNN, July 29, 2015, www.cnn .com/2015/07/29/politics/trump-breast-pump-statement.

237 revulsion toward other women: Joan C. Chrisler, *From Menarche to Menopause: The Female Body in Feminist Therapy* (Philadelphia: Haworth Press, 2004).

238 political anger and punitive agendas: Kate Manne, "Why the Majority of White Women Voted for Trump," *Alternet*, November 13, 2017, https://www.alternet.org/ books/white-women-against-hillary-clinton-logic-misogyny-book.

239 defending the status quo: Kasumi Yoshimura and Curtis D. Hardin, "Cognitive Salience of Subjugation and the Ideological Justification of U.S. Geopolitical Dominance in Japan," *Social Justice Research* 22, nos. 2–3 (September 2009): 298–311, https://doi.org/10.1007/s11211-009-0102-7; Johannes Ullrich and J. Christopher Cohrs, "Terrorism Salience Increases System Justification: Experimental Evidence," *Social Justice Research* 20, no. 2 (June 2007): 117–39, https://doi .org/10.1007/s11211-007-0035-y.

240 toxic border patrol masculinity: Dylann Roof's 2015 mass shooting in the Emanuel African Methodist Episcopal Church in Charleston, South Carolina, provides a tragic example of what white male supremacist ideologies affect by using rape as a justification for male violence. Before the twenty-one-year-old Roof massacred nine black churchgoers, six of them older black women, he explained: "I have to do it. You rape our women, and you are taking over our country. And you have to go."

240 topics people were prioritizing: Reena Flores, "Men and Women Split on Trending Facebook Debate Topics, Trump Tapes," CBS News, October 9, 2016, http://www .cbsnews.com/news/men-and-women-split-on-trending-facebook-debate-topics -trump-tapes.

241 37 percent of their male peers agreed: Melissa Harris Perry, "Women Are Angrier Than Ever Before and They Are Doing Something About It," *Elle*, March 9, 2018, https://www.elle.com/culture/career-politics/a19297903/elle-survey-womens-anger -melissa-harris-perry/.

241 Forty-four percent: "Exit Poll Results from National Election Pool," *Washington Post*, November 29, 2016, https://www.washingtonpost.com/graphics/politics/2016 -election/exit-polls/.

242 into strict and punitive politics: Michael A. Milburn and Sheree D. Conrad, *Raised to Rage: The Politics of Anger and the Roots of Authoritarianism* (Cambridge, MA: MIT Press, 2016).

242 directly to authoritarian beliefs: Gian Sarup, "Gender, Authoritarianism, and Attitudes Toward Feminism," *Social Behavior and Personality* 4, no. 1 (February 1976): 57–64, https://doi.org/10.2224/sbp.1976.4.1.57.

242 political force it was in our politics: Carly Wayne, Nicholas Valentino, and Marzia Oceno, "How Sexism Drives Support for Donald Trump," Monkey Cage blog, October 23, 2016, www.washingtonpost.com/news/monkey-cage/wp/2016/10/23/how-sexism-drives-support-for-donald-trump/?utm_term=.44ac3da84ef1.

242 equality gap in their community: Mark J. Brandt and P. J. Henry, "Gender Inequality and Gender Differences in Authoritarianism," *Personality and Social Psychology Bulletin* 38, no. 10 (October 2012): 1301–15, https://doi.org/10.1177/0146167212449871.

242 usually strictly imposed: David Archard and Colin M. Macleod, *The Moral and Political Status of Children* (Oxford: Oxford University Press, 2005).

242 it is oppressive nonetheless: Bernard E. Whitley and Stefanía Ægisdóttir, "The Gender Belief System, Authoritarianism, Social Dominance Orientation, and Heterosexuals' Attitudes Toward Lesbians and Gay Men," *Sex Roles* 42, nos. 11–12 (June 2000): 947–67, https://doi.org/10.1023/A:1007026016001.

243 authoritarian behaviors in leaders: Milburn and Conrad, *Raised to Rage*.

243 choices, and spanking children: Arlin James Benjamin Jr., "Right-Wing Authoritarianism and Attitudes Toward Torture," *Social Behavior and Personality: An International Journal* 44, no. 6 (July 2016): 881–87, https://doi.org/10.2224/sbp.2016.44.6.881.

244 backlash, and punishment: Miller and Borgida, "The Separate Spheres Model of Gendered Inequality."

244 "Why isn't she even angrier?": Michelle Goldberg, "Why Isn't Hillary Clinton Even Angrier?" *Slate*, September 14, 2017, www.slate.com/articles/news_and_politics/books/2017/09/hillary_clinton_s_what_happened_reviewed.html.

244 "darker, continuous, and hidden side": D. Soyini Madison, "Crazy Patriotism and Angry (Post)Black Women," *Communication and Critical/Cultural Studies* 6, no. 3 (September 2009): 321–26, https://doi.org/10.1080/14791420903063810.

244 "people who write it": Mark Hensch, "Michelle Obama: 'Angry Black Woman' Label Hurt Me," *The Hill*, December 19, 2016, http://thehill.com/homenews/administration/311033-michelle-obama-angry-black-woman-label-hurt-me.

245 saviors for helpless white people: Feminista Jones, "Mammy 2.0: Black Women Won't Save You, So Stop Asking," Feminista Jones blog, August 1, 2017, http://feministajones.com/blog/mammy-2-0-black-women-wont-save-you-so-stop-asking.

245 "engagement than their male peers": William A. Galston, "Data Point to a New Wave of Female Political Activism That Could Shift the Course of US Politics," Brookings Institution, January 10, 2018, www.brookings.edu/blog/fixgov/2018/01/10/a-new-wave-of-female-political-activism.

246 examples of this approach: Hanna Kozlowska, "Mothers Fighting Against Gun Vi-

olence Hope to Repeat the Success of Mothers Against Drunk Driving," *Quartz*, July 26, 2016, https://qz.com/742540/mothers-fighting-against-gun-violence-hope -to-repeat-the-success-of-mothers-against-drunk-driving.

247 "mom can't accomplish much": Jenn Fang, "More Sexism from NYC City Councilman Peter Koo: 'An Angry Mom Can't Accomplish Much,'" Reappropriate blog, September 5, 2017, http://reappropriate.co/2017/09/more-sexism-from-nyc -city-councilman-peter-koo-an-angry-mom-cant-accomplish-much.

247 almost exclusively by women: Ashley Dejean, "These Women Are Leading the Resistance in Texas," *Mother Jones*, September 24, 2017, www.motherjones.com/ politics/2017/09/these-women-are-leading-the-resistance-in-texas.

247 grassroots resistance organizations: Rhonda Colvin, "Resistance Efforts Are Taking Root in Pro-Trump Country—and Women Are Leading the Charge," *Washington Post*, August 14, 2017, www.washingtonpost.com/national/-efforts-are -taking-root-in-pro-trump-country—and-women-are-leading-the-charge/2017/08/ 14/91e69daa-7874-11e7-8f39-eeb7d3a2d304_story.html?utm_term=.447d1f909364.

247 run for office as liberals: Michael Alison Chandler, "In Desire to Turn Red States Blue, DC Women Return to Home Towns to Run for Office," *Washington Post*, July 8, 2017, www.washingtonpost.com/local/social-issues/as-more-women-run -for-office-district-residents-join-the-roster-of-candidates/2017/07/08/005cccf0-5b 3d-11e7-a9f6-7c3296387341_story.html?utm_term=.cebf2c5df790.

248 stranded and detained immigrants: Hanna Kozlowska, "Why Most of the Lawyers You See Battling Trump's Immigration Order Are Women," *Quartz*, February 1, 2017, https://qz.com/900416/most-immigration-lawyers-are-women-and-they-are -helping-stranded-immigrants-and-refugees-at-us-airports/?utm_source=qzfb.

248 counter systemic racism: Jaya Saxena, "The Safety Pin Box Is Making Allies Put Their Words into Action," *Daily Dot*, December 6, 2016, www.dailydot.com/irl/ safety-pin-box.

248 at every turn: L. A. Kauffman, "The Trump Resistance Can Be Best Described in One Adjective: Female," *The Guardian* (US), July 23, 2017, www.theguardian .com/commentisfree/2017/jul/23/trump-resistance-one-adjective-female-womens -march.

248 employed in other sectors: Michael Hansen, "Hidden Factors Contributing to Teacher Strikes in Oklahoma, Kentucky, and Beyond," Brookings Institution, April 6, 2018, https://www.brookings.edu/blog/brown-center-chalkboard/2018/04/06/hidden-factors-contributing-to-teacher-strikes-in-oklahoma-kentucky-and-beyond/.

248 undervaluing and exploitation: "West Virginia Teachers' Strike: Why It's Happening and Why It's Historic," *Fast Company*, March 2, 2018, https://www.fastcompany.com/40538618/west-virginia-teachers-strike-why-its-happening-and-why -its-historic.

249 "you get good at resisting": Jaya Saxena, "Why Women Are Leading the Resistance, Not Men," *Daily Dot*, August 7, 2017, https://www.dailydot.com/irl/women -leading-resistance.

249 "to the politics of the male gaze": Vanessa Friedman, "Buzzed: The Politics of Hair," *New York Times*, April 5, 2018, https://www.nytimes.com/2018/04/05/fashion /buzzed-politics-of-hair-emma-gonzalez-rosemcgowan.html.

252 social and economic justice: Antonio Olivo, "Danica Roem of Virginia to Be First Openly Transgender Person Elected, Seated in a U.S. Statehouse," *Washington Post*, November 8, 2017, www.washingtonpost.com/local/virginia-politics/danica-roem-will-be-vas-first-openly-transgender-elected-official-after-unseating-conservative-robert-g-marshall-in-house-race/2017/11/07/d534bdde-c0af-11e7-959c-fe2b598d8c00_story.html

252 most was being mocked: Beverly Fehr et al., "Anger in Close Relationships: An Interpersonal Script Analysis," *Personality and Social Psychology Bulletin* 25, no. 3 (March 1999): 299–312, https://doi.org/10.1177/0146167299025003003; Agneta Fischer, ed., *Gender and Emotion: Social Psychological Perspectives* (Cambridge: Cambridge University Press, 2000).

253 the men around them are: Jessica M. Salerno and Liana C. Peter-Hagene, "One Angry Woman: Anger Expression Increases Influence for Men, but Decreases Influence for Women, During Group Deliberation," *Law and Human Behavior* 39, no. 6 (December 2015): 581–92, https://doi.org/10.1037/lhb0000147.

253 "the epitome of powerlessness": Sandra P. Thomas, "Women's Anger, Aggression, and Violence," *Health Care for Women International* 26, no. 6 (June/July 2005): 504–22, https://doi.org/10.1080/07399330590962636; Fehr et al., "Anger in Close Relationships."

253 also, disturbingly, teachers: Lyn Mikel Brown, *Raising Their Voices: The Politics of Girls' Anger* (Cambridge, MA: Harvard University Press, 1999).

254 "how a society functions": Valerie M. Hudson et al., *Sex and World Peace* (New York: Columbia University Press, 2014).

254 the more unequal the society: Mark J. Brandt, "Sexism and Gender Inequality Across 57 Societies," *Psychological Science* 22, no. 11 (November 2011): 1413–18, https://doi.org/10.1177/0956797611420445.

255 treated in their own homes: Hudson et al., *Sex and World Peace*.

CHAPTER 10: A RAGE OF YOUR OWN

260 stereotypically associated with men: Deborah Cox, Patricia Van Velsor, and Joseph Hulgus, "Who Me, Angry? Patterns of Anger Diversion in Women," *Health Care for Women International* 25, no. 9 (2004): 872–93.

261 women's expressing anger was "appropriate": A. Antonio González-Prendes, Nancy Praill, and Poco Kernsmith, "Age Differences in Women's Anger Experience and Expression," *International Journal of Psychological Studies* 5, no. 3 (2013): 122–34, https://dx.doi.org/10.5539/ijps.v5n3p122; Nancy Praill, "An Evaluation of Women's Attitudes Towards Anger in Other Women and the Impact of Such on Their Own Anger Expression Style" (thesis, Wayne State University, 2010), https://digitalcommons.wayne.edu/oa_theses/25.

262 regardless of cultural context: Maya Tamir et al., "The Secret to Happiness: Feeling Good or Feeling Right?" *Journal of Experimental Psychology* 146, no. 10 (October 2017): 1448–59, https://dx.doi.org/10.1037/xge0000303.

263 "loaded with information and energy": Audre Lorde, "The Uses of Anger: Women Responding to Racism" (keynote presentation, National Women's Studies Association Conference, Storrs, Connecticut, June 1981).

264 mechanics causing anger or anxiety: Matthew D. Lieberman et al., "Putting Feelings into Words: Affect Labeling Disrupts Amygdala Activity in Response to Affective Stimuli," *Psychological Science* 18, no. 5 (May 2007): 421–28, https://doi .org/10.1111/j.1467-9280.2007.01916.x

265 response to everyday stressors: Lauri L. Hyers, "Resisting Prejudice Every Day: Exploring Women's Assertive Responses to Anti-Black Racism, Anti-Semitism, Heterosexism, and Sexism," *Sex Roles* 56, nos. 1–2 (January 2007): 1–12, https:// doi.org/10.1111/j.1540-4560.2010.01658.x.

265 women are supposed to yield: Cox, Van Velsor, and Hulgus, "Who Me, Angry?"

265 to responses than men do: Lisa A. Mainiero, "Coping with Powerlessness: The Relationship of Gender and Job Dependency to Empowerment-Strategy Usage," *Administrative Science Quarterly* 31, no. 4 (December 1986): 633–53, http://digitalcommons.fairfield.edu/cgi/viewcontent.cgi?article=1049&context= business-facultypubs.

266 There is discomfort in understanding: Megan Boler and Michalinos Zembylas, "Discomforting Truths: The Emotional Terrain of Understanding Difference," ch. 5, in *Pedagogies of Difference: Rethinking Education for Social Change*, ed. Peter Pericles Trifonas (New York: Routledge, 2003), 110–36.

268 emotional expression for everyone: Agneta H. Fischer and Catharine Evers, "The Social Costs and Benefits of Anger as a Function of Gender and Relationship Context," *Sex Roles* 65, nos. 1–2 (July 2011): 23–34, https://doi.org/10.1007/s11199 -011-9956-x.

268 restructuring for liberation: Anjilee Dodge and Myani Gilbert, "His Feminist Facade: The Neoliberal Co-option of the Feminist Movement," *Seattle Journal for Social Justice* 14, no. 2 (Fall 2015): 332–65, https://digitalcommons.law.seattleu .edu/cgi/viewcontent.cgi?article=1813&context=sjsj.

268 what your anger represents: Patricia Van Velsor and Deborah L. Cox, "Anger as a Vehicle in the Treatment of Women Who Are Sexual Abuse Survivors: Reattributing Responsibility and Accessing Personal Power," *Professional Psychology: Research and Practice* 32, no. 6 (December 2001): 618–25, https://dx.doi .org/10.1037/0735-7028.32.6.618.

269 do not deserve to be heard: William H. Grier and Price M. Cobbs, *Black Rage: Two Black Psychiatrists Reveal the Full Dimensions of the Inner Conflicts and the Desperation of Black Life in the United States* (Eugene, OR: Wipf & Stock, 2000).

271 "places to go for help": Carol Kuruvilla, "First Woman to Accuse Nassar Says Church Is One of the 'Worst Places' to Go for Help," *Huffington Post*, February 2, 2018, www.huffingtonpost.com/entry/rachael-denhollander-the-church-isnt -safe-for-sexual-abuse-victims_us_5a73264ce4b06fa61b4e1574?ncid=engmodush pmg00000004.

272 and healthier anger expression: Janet Shibley Hyde and Nicole Else-Quest, *Half the Human Experience: The Psychology of Women*, 8th ed. (Belmont, CA: Wadsworth, Cengage Learning, 2013).

272 more inclined to be leaders: Beth Brooke-Marciniak, "Here's Why Women Who Play Sports Are More Successful," *Fortune*, February 4, 2016, http://fortune .com/2016/02/04/women-sports-successful; Katty Kay and Claire Shipman, "The

Confidence Gap," *The Atlantic*, August 26, 2015, www.theatlantic.com/magazine/archive/2014/05/the-confidence-gap/359815.

273 stopped playing any sports: "Factors Influencing Girls' Participation in Sports," Women's Sports Foundation, September 9, 2016, https://www.womenssportsfoundation.org/support-us/do-you-know-the-factors-influencing-girls-participation-in-sports.

273 take fewer risks: Society for Risk Analysis, "Parents of Newborn Daughters Take Fewer Risks Study Suggests," *ScienceDaily*, June 21, 2017, www.sciencedaily.com/releases/2017/06/170621125447.htm.

274 and neediness than girls do: Taylor Clark, "Nervous Nellies: Girls Don't Start Out More Anxious Than Boys, But They Usually End Up That Way," *Slate*, April 20, 2011, www.slate.com/articles/life/family/2011/04/nervous_nellies.html.

274 cultivate them in girls: Ibid.

274 perceptions are passed on to her: Sule Alan et al., "Transmission of Risk Preferences from Mothers to Daughters," *Journal of Economic Behavior & Organization* 134 (February 2017): 60–77, https://doi.org/10.1016/j.jebo.2016.12.014.

276 but also those around you: Ronda Roberts Callister, Deanna Geddes, and Donald F. Gibson, "When Is Anger Helpful or Hurtful? Status and Role Impact on Anger Expression and Outcomes," *Negotiation and Conflict Management Research* 10 (May 2017): 69–87, https://doi.org/10.1111/ncmr.12090.

276 energy, joy, humor, and resistance: Francesca Guizzo et al., "Objecting to Objectification: Women's Collective Action Against Sexual Objectification on Television," *Sex Roles* 77, nos. 5–6 (September 2017): 352–65, https://doi.org/10.1007/s11199-016-0725-8.

276 representation and understanding: June Crawford et al., "Women Theorising Their Experiences of Anger: A Study Using Memory-Work," *Australian Psychologist* 25, no. 3 (November 1990): 333–50, https://doi.org/10.1080/00050069008260028.

279 woman, a feeler, *is* emotional: Stephanie A. Shields, "Gender and Emotion: What We Think We Know, What We Need to Know, and Why It Matters," *Psychology of Women Quarterly* 37, no. 4 (December 2013): 423–35, https://doi.org/10.1177/0361684313502312.

279 woman does, she's a raging bitch: Lisa Feldman Barrett and Eliza Bliss-Moreau, "She's Emotional. He's Having a Bad Day: Attributional Explanations for Emotion Stereotypes," *Emotion* 9, no. 5 (October 2009): 649–58, https://doi.org/10.1037/a0016821.

279 your rational thoughts: Drew Westen et al., "Neural Bases of Motivated Reasoning: An fMRI Study of Emotional Constraints on Partisan Political Judgment in the 2004 U.S. Presidential Election," *Journal of Cognitive Neuroscience* 18, no. 11 (November 2006): 1947–58, https://doi.org/10.1162/jocn.2006.18.11.1947.

281 women can be a blood sport: Phyllis Chesler, *Woman's Inhumanity to Woman* (Chicago: Chicago Review Press, 2009).

283 to justify higher status: Agneta H. Fischer, ed., *Gender and Emotion: Social Psychological Perspectives* (Cambridge: Cambridge University Press, 2000).

285 "Do what you do": Tom Maxwell, "A History of American Protest Music: When Nina Simone Sang What Everyone Was Thinking," *Longreads*, April 2017,

https://longreads.com/2017/04/20/a-history-of-american-protest-music-when-nina
-simone-sang-what-everyone-was-thinking.

286 up around the country: Penelope Green, "Anger Rooms Are All the Rage. Timidly,
We Gave One a Whack," *New York Times*, August 9, 2017, https://www.nytimes
.com/2017/08/09/style/anger-rooms-the-wrecking-club.html.

286 "intimate with myself and you": Gloria Anzaldúa, "Speaking in Tongues: A Letter to 3rd World Women Writers," May 21, 1980, in *Words in Our Pockets: The
Feminist Writers Guild Handbook*, ed. Rudolph Steiner (San Francisco: Bootlegger,
1980).

286 "Do better": Jacqueline Wernimont, "Angry Bibliography," Jacqueline Wernimont, January 16, 2017, https://jwernimont.com/category/angry-bibliography.

287 "will get you nowhere": Ryan P. Smith, "Civil Rights Icon Dolores Huerta Offers
Advice to a New Generation of Activists," Smithsonian.com, August 25, 2017,
www.smithsonianmag.com/smithsonian-institution/civil-rights-icon-dolores
-huerta-offers-advise-new-generation-activists-180964630.

INDEX